XX20580

D1588760

# Left Behind

# Left Behind

## Lessons from Labour's Heartland

**Peter Kilfoyle**

First published in Great Britain 2000
by Politico's Publishing
8 Artillery Row, London, SW1P 1RZ, England

Tel. 020 7931 0090
Email publishing@politicos.co.uk
Website http://www.politicos.co.uk/publishing

The right of Peter Kilfoyle to be identified as author of this work
has been asserted by him in accordance with the Copyright,
Designs and Patents Act, 1988.

A catalogue record for this book is available from the British
Library.

ISBN 1 90230 166 8

Printed and bound in Great Britain by St Edmundsbury Press.
Cover design by Advantage.
Interior design and production by Duncan Brack.
Typeset in Century Schoolbook.

# Contents

# Main personalities

*Note: references are to Liverpool city councillors, and to Labour Party members, otherwise unless specified.*

| | |
|---|---|
| Josie Aitman | Militant activist, originally in Tuebrook ward; one of the sixteen recommended for expulsion in February 1986, finally expelled March 1988; former wife of Tony. |
| Tony Aitman | Militant activist, originally in Tuebrook ward; one of the sixteen recommended for expulsion in February 1986, and expelled in May; former husband of Josie. |
| David Alton | Liberal councillor, elected 1972, deputy leader of the council 1978; elected MP for Edge Hill in 1979 by-election, held seat (Mossley Hill from 1983) until 1997; created Baron Alton of Liverpool 1997. |
| Lyn Anderson | Council employee in council leader's office; Labour Party member. |
| Paul Astbury | Councillor; one of the sixteen recommended for expulsion in February 1986, but later reprieved; one of the forty-seven councillors surcharged and disqualified in March 1987. |
| Gary Booth | Labour Party Young Socialists activist, though not a Militant; councillor; subsequently Labour Party Merseyside organiser. |
| Bessie Braddock | MP for Liverpool Exchange 1945–70; wife of Jack. |
| Jack Braddock | Leader of Labour group and council 1950–63; husband of Bessie. |
| Tony Byrne | Councillor, Chair of Finance and Strategy; Militant ally, effectively ran the council with Derek Hatton, under John Hamilton; Labour group leader from 1986 until surcharged and disqualified in March 1987. |
| Cyril Carr | Liberal councillor and leader of Liberal group 1962–75; Lord Mayor 1981; President-elect of the (national) Liberal Party but died (1981) before taking office. |

| | |
|---|---|
| Mike Carr | Regional officer of TGWU; MP for Bootle from by-election in May 1990 until death in July 1990. |
| Tommy Carrol | Militant activist in Kensington ward; expelled from Labour Party. |
| Keva Coombes | Solicitor; leader, Merseyside County Council, 1982–86; city councillor, became council leader in 1987 after Harry Rimmer's resignation; replaced as leader in 1990 and suspended from Labour group 1991. |
| Alan Dean | Twice deputy council leader, under Keva Coombes and Harry Rimmer; member, Progressive Left. |
| Joe Devaney | Councillor; one of the forty-seven councillors surcharged and disqualified in March 1987; later re-elected to council, Lord Mayor 1999–2000. |
| Felicity Dowling | Militant councillor; secretary of DLP; one of the sixteen recommended for expulsion in February 1986, expelled October; one of the forty-seven councillors surcharged and disqualified in March 1987. |
| Wally Edwards | Councillor; Labour Party organiser for Liverpool 1970–83. |
| Terry Fields | Militant MP for Liverpool Broadgreen 1983–92; expelled from Labour Party 1991; fought seat in 1992 as 'Socialist Labour'. |
| Ray Gill | Labour Party North West regional organiser 1986–89. |
| Roy Gladden | Councillor; Broad Left but not Militant; one of the forty-seven councillors surcharged and disqualified in March 1987; now GMB official. |
| Joyce Gould | Labour Party Director of Organisation 1985–93; created Baroness Gould of Potternewton 1993. |
| Keith Hackett | Councillor, one of the 'Sainsbury set'; chair of Finance and Policy under Keva Coombes; suspended from Labour group 1991. |
| John Hamilton | Councillor, one of the twenty-one rebels in 1972; council leader 1973–78 and 1978–86; one of the |

|  | forty-seven councillors surcharged and disqualified in March 1987. |
|---|---|
| Terry Harrison | Militant activist, failed Euro candidate for Liverpool, 1979; one of the sixteen recommended for expulsion in February 1986, expelled in June. |
| Derek Hatton | Militant leader and councillor, elected 1979; deputy leader of council 1983–86, under John Hamilton, effectively ran council with Tony Byrne; one of the sixteen recommended for expulsion in February 1986, expelled in June; one of the forty-seven councillors surcharged and disqualified in March 1987. |
| Eric Heffer | MP for Liverpool Walton 1964–91; minister of state, Department of Industry 1974–75; died May 1991. |
| Winnie Hesford | Long-term Labour activist in Liverpool Walton. |
| Jimmy Hollinshead | Militant activist in Anfield; deputy convenor of GMB Branch 5. |
| Lesley Holt | See Lesley Mahmood |
| Tony Hood | Councillor; Militant sympathiser; one of the forty-seven councillors surcharged and disqualified in March 1987. |
| Sean Hughes | MP for Knowsley South 1983–90 (died June 1990). |
| Arthur Irvine | MP for Liverpool Edge Hill 1947–78; Solicitor-General 1967–70. |
| Tony Jennings | Councillor; Militant ally and Broad Left leader; deputy council leader; led break-away 'Liverpool Labour Group of Councillors', 1991. |
| Trevor Jones | Liberal councillor; deputy to Cyril Carr, leader of Liberal group 1976–88, deputy leader of council 1973–76, leader 1976–78; President of the (national) Liberal Party 1973–74; known as 'Jones the Vote'. |
| Jane Kennedy | Former NUPE official; helped found Liverpool Labour Left; MP for Liverpool Broadgreen 1992–97, Liverpool Wavertree 1997–. |

| | |
|---|---|
| Laura Kirton | Long-term Labour activist in Liverpool Walton; supporter of Militant in its early days; agent to Eric Heffer MP. |
| George Knibb | Councillor; former council employee; Broad Left leader, joined 'Liverpool Labour Group of Councillors' in 1991. |
| Richard Knights | Militant full-time organiser; one of the sixteen recommended for expulsion in February 1986, finally expelled December 1990. |
| Bob Lancaster | Councillor; Progressive Left member; one of the forty-seven councillors surcharged and disqualified in March 1987; later regained council seat. |
| Ian Lowes | Convenor, GMB Branch 5; Militant member, but later left; one of the sixteen recommended for expulsion in February 1986, expelled in May. |
| Eddie Loyden | Councillor, leader of the 'twenty-one' rebels in 1972; MP for Liverpool Garston 1974–79 and 1983–97; Militant sympathiser. |
| Lesley Mahmood | Councillor and Militant activist; lost selection for Liverpool Walton parliamentary seat to Peter Kilfoyle; led revolt within Labour group against poll tax implementation, March 1990, and expelled from Labour Party; fought Liverpool Walton by-election in June 1991 as 'Walton Real Labour'. |
| Frank Mills | Councillor; one of the forty-seven councillors surcharged and disqualified in March 1987. |
| Ted Mooney | Councillor; one of the 'twenty-one' rebels in 1972; Militant central committee member. |
| Joe Morgan | Councillor, chair of Housing under Braddock and Sefton; with Sefton over split over Housing Finance Act, 1972; one of the 'scabby/sensible six' in 1984. |
| Tony Mulhearn | Councillor; Militant central committee member; chair of DLP; one of the sixteen recommended for expulsion in February 1986, expelled in May. |

| | |
|---|---|
| Paul Orr | Councillor; twice Lord Mayor; one of the 'scabby/ sensible six' in 1984. |
| Bob Parry | MP for Liverpool Exchange 1970–74, Scotland Exchange 1974–83, Riverside 1983–97; died 2000. |
| Harry Rimmer | Councillor; Progressive Left supporter; deputy leader, Merseyside County Council 1982–86; leader, Liverpool City Council 1987 and 1990–96. |
| Vicky Roberts | Councillor (imposed as candidate at Gillmoss, 1987); chair of Finance and Policy; helped found Liverpool Labour Left. |
| Phil Robinson | Labour Party North West assistant regional organiser. |
| Eddie Roderick | Long-term councillor, ally of Braddock and Sefton; chair of Planning; replaced John Hamilton as Labour leader in short-lived coup, 1978; one of the 'scabby/ sensible six' in 1984, and deselected; reimposed as council candidate, Gillmoss, 1987. |
| Bill Sefton | Labour group leader 1963–73, presided over split over Housing Finance Act, 1972; lost seat 1973, elected to Merseyside County Council 1974, leader 1974–77; became Baron Sefton of Garston, 1978. |
| Sylvia Sharpey-Shafer | Councillor; Militant activist; one of the sixteen recommended for expulsion in February 1986, expelled 1990. |
| Bill Smythe | Councillor; Sefton ally, deselected after 1972 vote on Housing Finance Act; elected as Liberal candidate in 1973, though still a Labour Party member; city council leader 1975–76. |
| Bill Snell | Councillor; organised Eddie Roderick's coup against John Hamilton, 1978; one of the 'scabby/sensible six' in 1984. |
| Ken Stewart | Councillor; Merseyside West MEP 1984–96 (died 1996). |
| Cyril Taylor | Originally Communist Party member, joined Labour and elected as councillor; one of the 'twenty-one' rebels in 1972. |

Cheryl Varley          Militant full-timer; one of the sixteen recommended for expulsion in February 1986, expelled in July; elected to NUS national executive 1989 and subsequently left Militant.

Richard Venton         Militant Merseyside organiser; one of the sixteen recommended for expulsion in February 1986, expelled in June.

Bob Wareing            President, DLP 1974–81; MP for Liverpool West Derby 1983–.

Larry Whitty           Labour Party General Secretary 1985–94; created Baron Whitty of Camberwell, 1996.

Ian Williams           Former railway guard; Labour activist; now a journalist; helped found Liverpool Labour Left.

Cathy Wilson           Militant activist; parliamentary candidate, Isle of Wight, 1983; elected councillor 1990; expelled from Labour Party 1990.

# Labour groupings (chronological order)

| | |
|---|---|
| The twenty-one | Group of Labour rebels who started to meet separately after the Labour group on the city council split on the vote on the Housing Finance Act in August 1972. Led by Eddie Loyden, the twenty-one rejoined the main Labour group in December 1972. |
| The 'scabby' or 'sensible' six | Six councillors (Pat Johnson, Joe Morgan, Peter Murphy, Paul Orr, Eddie Roderick and Bill Snell) who voted against (and, with Liberal and Conservative support, defeated) the Militant-led attempt to set a deficit budget for the council in spring 1984. |
| Liverpool Labour Left | A group of Liverpool Labour activists opposed to Militant who organised meetings and issued publications; its membership included the author, Mike Allen, Jane Kennedy, Vicky Roberts, Paul Thompson and Ian Williams. Formed late 1984; never particularly effective. |
| Broad Left | The name given to the left caucus in the city council Labour group from the early 1980s. The group contained, and was often dominated by, Militant councillors. Sixteen were suspended from the Labour Party in March 1990 for defying party instructions and voting against implementation of the poll tax; after this, the Broad Left moved increasingly into opposition to the main Labour group. |
| The sixteen | The sixteen members of the Liverpool DLP recommended by the Labour NEC majority report in February 1986 for interview with a view to expulsion: Josie Aitman, Tony Aitman, Paul Astbury, Roger Bannister, Carol Darton, Felicity Dowling, Pauline Dunlop, Terry Harrison, Derek Hatton, Richard Knights, Ian Lowes, Tony Mulhearn, Sylvia Sharpey-Shafer, Harry Smith, Cheryl Varley and Richard Venton. |

| | |
|---|---|
| The twelve | What the 'sixteen' became, as charges were dropped against Josie Aitman, Astbury, Dunlop and Sharpey-Shafer. |
| The forty-seven | The forty-seven Labour city councillors who, in March 1987, were surcharged and disqualified from office for their failure to set a legal rate in 1985. (Originally forty-nine, two (Bill Lafferty and Peter Lloyd) died before their appeal reached the Lords.) |
| Progressive Left | The group of anti-Militant councillors organised by Mike Black, Roy Gladden and Bob Lancaster, which began meeting on an informal basis after the 1986 expulsions. Never an effective group. |
| 'Sainsbury set' | Some of the younger members of the Progressive Left – university-educated, mostly from out of town, and mostly based in the south end of Liverpool; so-called for their alleged tastes in food and wine. Main member was Keith Hackett. |
| The twenty-nine | The twenty-nine councillors who were suspended from Labour group membership in 1990 for breaches of its rules; this led to them forming a separate group, which in turn paved the way for their automatic expulsion from the Labour Party. |
| Liverpool Labour Group of Councillors | Formed after the May 1991 local elections by five councillors elected as 'Ward Labour' and twenty of those who had been suspended by the Labour Party. |

# Liverpool City Council composition, 1972–91

| Year | Conservative | Labour | Liberal[i] | Others | Control |
|------|------|------|------|------|------|
| 1972 | 53 | 89 | 15 | 2[ii] | Labour[iii] |
| 1973[iv] | 9 | 42 | 48 | – | – |
| 1974 | 10 | 42 | 47 | – | Liberal |
| 1975 | 14 | 42 | 43 | – | Liberal |
| 1976 | 17 | 42 | 40 | – | Labour |
| 1977 | 17 | 42 | 40 | – | Labour |
| 1978 | 24 | 40 | 35 | – | Liberal[v] |
| 1979 | 23 | 46 | 30 | – | Labour |
| 1980 | 21 | 40 | 38 | – | Liberal |
| 1981 | 21 | 40 | 38 | – | Liberal |
| 1982 | 21 | 42 | 36 | – | Liberal |
| 1983 | 18 | 51 | 30 | – | Labour |
| 1984 | 13 | 58 | 28 | – | Labour |
| 1985 | 13 | 57 | 29 | – | Labour |
| 1986 | 7 | 55 | 37 | – | Labour |
| 1987 | 4 | 51 | 44 | – | Labour |
| 1988 | 2 | 56 | 37 | 4[vi] | Labour |
| 1989 | 2 | 56 | 37 | 4[vi] | Labour |
| 1990 | 2 | 67 | 28 | 2[vii] | Labour |
| 1991 | 2 | 62 | 27 | 7[viii] | Labour |

All figures are for May of each year, and do not account for by-elections that may have adjusted the composition of the council during a particular year.

i   Liberal / Alliance / Liberal Democrats
ii  Two 'Protestant' councillors.
iii Following the elections of this year, there was also one vacancy on the council.
iv  As part of local government reorganisation, elections for the new council took place in 1973. Until 1974, however, the 'new council' shadowed its predecessor.
v   In 1978, and from 1980 to 1982, Labour were the largest party but refused to take office as a minority administration.
vi  Two 'Liberals' and two 'Social Democrats', who refused to join the Liberal Democrats.
vii One 'Liberal' and one 'Social Democrat'.
viii One 'Liberal', one 'Social Democrat', five 'Ward Labour'

# Abbreviations

| | |
|---|---|
| ACAS | Advisory, Conciliation and Arbitration Service |
| AEU | Amalgamated Engineering Union |
| ALP | Australian Labor Party |
| AMA | Association of Metropolitan Authorities |
| ANC | African National Congress |
| BLF | Builders-Labourers' Federation (Australian trade union) |
| CBI | Confederation of British Industry |
| CCT | compulsory competitive tendering |
| CLP | Constituency Labour Party |
| COSATU | Congress of South African Trade Unions |
| CP | Communist Party |
| DLP | District Labour Party |
| DSO | Direct Services Organisation (Liverpool City Council) |
| EETPU | Electrical, Electronic, Telecommunications and Plumbing Union |
| ETU | Electrical Trades Union |
| GLC | Greater London Council |
| GMBATU | General, Municipal, Boilermakers and Allied Trades Union (at times known as, or referred to as GMBWU, GMB and 'the G&M') |
| GMWU | General and Municipal Workers' Union (forerunner of GMBATU) |
| GPMU | Graphical, Paper and Media Union |
| JSSC | Joint Shop Stewards' Committee (of Liverpool City Council trade unions) |
| LCC | Labour Coordinating Committee |
| LPYS | Labour Party Young Socialists (also referred to as 'the YS') |
| LLL | Liverpool Labour Left |
| MDC | Merseyside Development Corporation |
| MSF | Manufacturing, Science and Finance Union |
| NALGO | National and Local Government Officers' Association |
| NATFHE | National Association of Teachers in Further and Higher Education |
| NEC | National Executive Committee (of the Labour Party) |
| NGA | National Graphical Association (also known as NGA '82) |
| NUM | National Union of Mineworkers |

| | |
|---|---|
| NUPE | National Union of Public Employees |
| NUR | National Union of Railwaymen |
| NUS | National Union of Students |
| NUT | National Union of Teachers |
| PASOK | Panhellenic Socialist Movement (of Greece) |
| PLO | Palestine Liberation Organisation |
| PLP | Parliamentary Labour Party |
| POEU | Post Office Engineering Union |
| PPC | prospective parliamentary candidate |
| RSL | Revolutionary Socialist League (the true identity of the Militant Tendency) |
| SDP | Social Democratic Party |
| SOGAT | Society of Graphical and Allied Trades |
| SWP | Socialist Workers' Party |
| TASS | Technical Administrative and Supervisory Section, of the AEU (later to become part of the MSF) |
| TCC | Temporary Coordinating Committee (the body established in 1986 to replace the Liverpool District Labour Party when it was first suspended) |
| TGWU | Transport and General Workers Union (also referred to as 'the T&G') |
| TUC | Trades Union Congress |
| UCATT | Union of Construction, Allied Trades and Technicians |
| UCW | Union of Communication Workers |
| UNISON | the public service union (an amalgam of NALGO, NUPE and the health workers' union COHSE) |
| USDAW | Union of Shop, Distributive and Allied Workers |
| WMCA | Working Men's Conservative Association |
| WRP | Workers' Revolutionary Party |

# Acknowledgements

In charting the developments of the period covered by this book, I have been critically aware of the dangers of hindsight, and have therefore taken extra effort to ensure that many of the key political characters of the time express their own opinions and share their personal recollections through direct quotes in the text. I have drawn heavily on these characters, for many of them were key to the chaos. Some significant individuals, however, are absent. Two of them have already offered their accounts, or at least those of the Militant organisation; a handful expressed distaste for the project; and others have passed on, literally and metaphorically. A few may feel ignored, either from oversight on the author's part or from their own sense of self-importance.

In most cases, interviews were conducted with a set of obvious questions in mind, as well as a series of prompts where the individual being addressed had played a major role or been a key witness to specific events. Occasionally, at the request of an interviewee, a comment has not been attributed. I have always, however, tried to be true to my sources in telling the story of these turbulent years.

I am indebted to Ian Parker, now the Deputy Director of the Social Market Foundation think-tank. His research skills and tenacity (not least with me!) have made this work happen. He has brought calm method to my – at times rather haphazard – application. Thanks also to Iain Dale, of Politico's Publishing, for his faith in the book, and to Duncan Brack, my editor, for his assiduous attention to detail.

*Peter Kilfoyle*
*August 2000*

# Preface

Some tales are worth the telling, and this is one of them. On 11 June 1991, it was announced that the Militant Tendency, under the guise of 'Walton Real Labour', would stand a candidate against the official Labour Party candidate in a parliamentary by-election forced by the death of Eric Heffer. Less than four weeks later, with the official candidate – myself – successfully in place as the new MP for Liverpool Walton, and with my victory reflecting the disarray of Militant and their allies, a period in the history of Liverpool's politics drew to a close. It was a period that stretched back two decades, marking a series of shifts in the political climate of the city reflecting both broader changes within the nature of the global economy and the priorities of politics in Britain.

Like much of the recent politics of Liverpool, Labour's victory in Walton was deliberately imbued with an element of symbolism, partly to dissuade the national media from inventing its own interpretation of events; as with so many other occasions in living memory, the city was then their focal concern. At the end of polling day, 4 July 1991, as the outcome of the by-election became apparent, I declared that the result reflected a new beginning for Labour politics in Liverpool and a new beginning for the city itself. Somewhat ahead of my time, I offered the assembled journalists and party workers the phrase 'New Liverpool'. What follows charts the developments that led up to this rebirth, and the need for it.

Much of this book is the story of the consistent failure of political leadership in one of Britain's great cities over a period of more than twenty years. Liverpool at the end of the 1960s was enjoying a brief Indian summer, as the success of its bands, its comedians and its football clubs masked the serious and long-term decline of its industrial and commercial bases. Its city fathers were, with one or two exceptions, oblivious to these real conditions. The city's Labour MPs were personally weak and politically London-oriented.

Slowly, however, it dawned on a few of Liverpool's councillors that the city was in need of rejuvenation. No one was more committed to this than

# Left Behind: Lessons from Labour's heartland

Bill Sefton, the Labour group leader – successor to the last of the old-style city bosses, Jack Braddock – throughout the late 1960s and early 1970s. Generally regarded, before becoming leader, as a left-wing firebrand in opposition to the establishment, once in charge he recognised the need for compromise inherent in the job. His backing down (as it was perceived on the left) from confrontation with the Heath Government over the Housing Finance Act in 1972, led to a split, the first of many, in the Labour group. It also left Sefton with a much diminished credibility in a political culture dominated by oppositionalist rhetoric, and contributed ultimately to his defeat in the 1973 local elections.

The council Labour group was left not only divided but lacking in ideological coherence. Incapable of providing a political lead, its only driving force was unenlightened self-interest. Into this vacuum moved the partisans of the Revolutionary Socialist League, a Trotskyist grouping far better known as the Militant Tendency, whose primary political objectives were to enter, subvert, overwhelm and finally take over the Labour Party. Militant began their march into the political heart of Liverpool as so-called 'Toytown politics' took hold of city hall in the mid and late 1970s; a peculiar period of no overall control during which Labour and Liberal parties tried to out-manoeuvre each other in a vainglorious attempt to be kings of a crumbling castle. With starkly contrasting agendas translated into spending priorities, a strategic belligerence was spawned that allowed little to occur in the name of long-term development to benefit the city.

By the time Labour regained outright control of Liverpool in 1983, however, Militant's entryist tactics had been so successful that the official leader of the council, John Hamilton, was in effect controlled by his deputy, the rabid Militant Derek Hatton, and fellow-traveller Tony Byrne. The behaviour of Militant in power eventually gave Labour's national leadership the evidence they needed to close down the Liverpool district party apparatus and to purge the worst of the offenders, and in 1987 Margaret Thatcher's government removed the Militants – and many non-Militant councillors – from elected public office as a result of their failure to set a legal rate. The hundreds of thousands of pounds that was subsequently raised to take the disbarred councillors' case to the House of Lords, mainly from Labour Party and trade union resources, might rather more usefully have gone into efforts to remove the Tory government from office.

The following four years saw a variety of Militant attempts at comebacks, through ward and constituency parties, through the reconstituted district party, which was subsequently suspended again, through the city council, which led in time to another split in the Labour group's ranks, and through the anti poll-tax movement. The tale reached a crescendo with Militant's final stab at a return, as redundancies and a prolonged refuse dispute within the council, and the televising of Alan Bleasdale's *GBH* (viewed by most people as a dramatisation of events in Liverpool during the 1980s, despite the author's denials) served as the backdrop to the Walton by-election in 1991.

Behind the façade of 'Walton Real Labour', Militant collected and applied all the support from around the country that it could muster. It was a monumental error. Given a predictable win for Labour at the polls, Militant's brand of political corruption, and many of the entryists, were finally exorcised from the party. But two decades of this political infighting had had terrible effects on the Labour Party and Liverpool. Both were smeared by association with Militant, as unreasonable as blaming two people infected by some new and exotic virulent disease for the illness itself. Of course, it might be said that in each case, the body politic was culpably debilitated enough to host any kind of rogue virus.

This book is a labour of love – of a city, and of a movement pure in aspiration, if not always in application. Objectively, the two decades that the book covers were a twinkling in the eye. Subjectively, however, they were an eternity, and the changes that took place were of a profound nature, vividly illustrating the spectrum of opinion that was – and remains – the Labour Party. It is a story of clashing personalities and warring ideologies, of tragedy, farce, crimes and misdemeanours.

Within Liverpool, the period began with the climb-down of one Labour leader, on the question of legality, and ended with the triumph of his political heir, again, on a matter of obeying the law. In between, careers blossomed and died, and hitherto unsuspected ambitions were revealed. Movers and shakers of the time claimed to understand the direction in which history was progressing with a degree of certainty that at the time was a marvel to behold; but as we travel through this account, we will see how many were embittered by the experiences of events passing them by. Others – more pragmatic, or, to their rivals, more careerist – were to undergo ideological metamorphosis, eventually to arrive safely in the sunny uplands of the modernised Labour Party.

In one sense, the story told in the pages that follow is a morality play, in which 'good politics' triumphs over 'bad politics'. There is, however, a deeper lesson to be drawn, particularly by those who eschew ideology in favour of a technocratic and managerial approach to politics. Such thinking ultimately gives way to a vacuum and, as sure as night follows day, something will fill that gap. This, more than anything else, is the salutary lesson from the Liverpool experience.

*Peter Kilfoyle*
*August 2000*

**To Bernie**

# 1 Rebel, rebel

After the Second World War, Liverpool was a city of nearly 800,000 souls, living largely in dire slum housing. It was also a city in which the working class was split along religious sectarian grounds between the Conservative and Unionist-supporting Protestants and the Labour-supporting Catholics. So marked was the divide that the Liverpool Scotland constituency actually returned an Irish Nationalist Member of Parliament from 1885 to 1929 (seven years beyond Irish partition). Encouraged by the local Tory oligarchs and their political helots, who continued to allow 'Protestant' candidates free passage at local elections in the 'orange' wards of Netherfield, St Domingo and the Dingle, the working class schism was not to be bridged until 1974, with the demise of the last Protestant Party councillor.

It is somewhat ironic that sectarianism in Liverpool began to wane at around the time that more religious tinder was being lit across the Irish Sea. This became clear during the Liverpool Scotland by-election of 1971, prompted by the sitting Labour MP, Walter Aldritt's, decision to resign on becoming regional secretary of the General and Municipal Workers' Union. Despite the presence of Peter Mahon for 'Labour and Anti-Abortion', the non-Catholic official Labour candidate Frank Marsden was easily elected in a contest where the central issues were the economy and industrial relations. Afterwards, his Conservative challenger, Barry Porter, later the MP for Wirral South, declared that the outcome had highlighted the ability of the local electorate 'to forget their differences as Protestants and Catholics and vote instead for people and parties'.[1] Such a statement had an even greater significance as Porter was himself a lifelong supporter of the Orange Order.

Sectarianism, however, had begun to transmute into an altogether more subtle form.

Lacking both the experience of local government and the mix of pragmatism and ideology common in Britain's other great cities, and influenced as it was by the more conspiratorial aspects of Irish politics, Liverpool's Labour Party was deeply affected by Tory-bequeathed boss politics. One local Conservative leader, Archibald Salvidge, had displayed such control that during the 1930s he banned party Central Office from Liverpool, and regularly issued orders to Liverpool's eight Tory MPs on how they should vote in the Commons. Another, Sir Thomas White, was not only boss of the council but also chairman of the Housing Committee, and it came as little surprise when new estates sprang up around the new Bent's Brewery public houses – after all, White was chairman of the brewery. It was even less of a surprise when each of the little parades of shops built in the new estates had a 'Bertie's' grocery shop, for 'Bertie' was Bertie White, son of the illustrious Thomas. When the local elections of 1955 ended a near-continuous run of one hundred years of Conservative rule, and finally saw control of the city fall into Labour hands, many people thought such chicanery would disappear.

This would perhaps have been true if the Labour leader, the legendary Jack Braddock, had not ruled over his fellow group members in the way that he did. Never one to entertain the foolhardy, Braddock was a real 'Boss Hogg' who, with his formidable wife and cohort Bessie, the MP for Liverpool Exchange from 1945 to 1970, oversaw politics in the city with an iron grip, and by methods coated in the language of contracts and contacts, reeking of returnable favours. My own mother was firmly convinced that Bessie decided who got which council houses; if Bessie wanted you to have the house of your dreams, she could and would. It was little wonder that Anthony Howard characterised Liverpool as 'Cook County, UK'.[2]

Until 1964, most of Liverpool's parliamentary seats remained safely in the hands of the Conservatives. At the general election of that year, however, a significant breakthrough occurred when the city returned a majority of Labour MPs, four of whom benefited from some of the largest swings across the nation. For Britain as a whole, the period that followed was one of great disappointment, as Harold Wilson's government failed to deliver the brave new world that he had promised through the 'white heat' of the scientific revolution. This was particularly felt in Liverpool, as the new Prime Minister was the MP for Huyton on the city's outskirts.

Historically, Liverpool has never been a great manufacturing centre. It was, and remains, a great port and a commercial city traditionally reliant upon a few large employers – the docks, the council, Tate & Lyle, British American Tobacco, Dunlop and Plessey. For a long time, it had its own stock exchange, built partly upon the soiled currency of the slave trade. It also had a symbiotic relationship with Manchester and Lancashire, as both customers for, and suppliers of, the goods passing through Liverpool docks. After the Second World War, however, the dock employers failed to inject the capital needed after years of under-investment and the destruction left by the Luftwaffe, despite the urging of union representatives to the Wolfenden Commission, set up to examine the future of Britain's docks. While European ports rebuilt of necessity, the Port of Liverpool awaited the return to the glory days of Empire. These, of course, never came. The great passenger liners gave way to airliners, and containerisation of cargoes overtook the old means of shipping. In 1963, about 25,000 people were employed on Liverpool's docks. Today fewer than a thousand workers shift a bigger tonnage, and make more profits.

The 1960s, however, brought Liverpool a respite from reality. These were the years of the city's Indian summer, where sporting successes for Everton FC and Liverpool FC, and the Beatles-led 'Merseybeat', with its proliferation of pop groups, poets and comedians, made everything seem hunky-dory. The place buzzed with self-confidence, and few could see that Liverpool was in reality dying on its feet. Even the supposedly enlightened shared an optimism with the populace at large that everything would come up rosy in the end. Alas, it was all a mere smokescreen for a city in the wrong place at the wrong time.

The Wilson government did induce large employers, including car manufacturers such as Ford and Standard Triumph, to move into Liverpool and its hinterland, and vast housing estates were built on the outskirts of the city near the factories. However, this was all based on short-term thinking. Nothing was thought through in depth about what these developments would mean to the region, let alone the people who would move into the new estates. There was no attempt to establish any kind of permanence with the new companies' investments. Many of those involved in local politics failed to realise what was happening. Introspective and hidebound by their own limited experiences, politicians who were familiar only with the wards or constituencies that elected them found it difficult to think of the city or region more widely. Ignorance, however, was not the only factor. Long-term objectives were also noticeably absent. When it came down to it, the central objective around which local politicians worked was housing, and a simplistic attitude prevailed of 'What shall we do? I know, let's build a new estate *there*, and we'll get a few factories alongside it.'

Some of the developments taking place would have no lasting benefit to the city. In fact, some of them were nothing short of a confidence trick. A job with a house or flat was used as bait to tempt people out of Liverpool and on to the overspill estates. Yet when firms had soaked up all the available grants, they started to close down or reduce their operations to the role of storage depots. The jobs disappeared and the former employees ended up travelling back into Liverpool to find work. A classic case occurred during the Heath years, when Fisher Bendix announced its intention to close its factory in Kirkby. Having purchased the plant with grants from the previous Wilson government, the company simply set out to strip it down and move the operation to Spain.

On a broader scale, the giant of Europe, the Common Market, was beginning to wake from its slumbers. Following the Treaty of Rome in 1957, much of west and central Europe had been given an impetus to work together. Britain, however, decided to play the awkward card. As the winds of change diluted its colonial interests, attempts were made to strengthen the Atlantic Alliance. The United States, however, was already looking over Britain's shoulder to the colossus that lay beyond, a colossus that was beginning to have a detrimental effect upon Liverpool. As the city rocked to its bands, rolled in the aisles to its comedians and adored its football teams, the American trade upon which the port was so dependent was increasingly switching to Southampton, or directly to the European mainland, and Britain's own export markets were becoming more and more Europe-based.

This was Liverpool at the start of the seventies: ignorant of its plight, devoid of the political nous necessary to cope with its predicament (even if it had been aware of it), geographically misplaced, and living largely in a cultural time warp, as the part-illusory perception of the city as the centre of the swinging sixties proved ever more outdated. The reality was far more prosaic: second-generation, long-term unemployment was growing and job opportunities were becoming fewer as business after business closed down and companies fled a port bedevilled by lack of investment and atrocious industrial relations. The city's population was falling dramatically, not least due to the housing policy of successive councils, and the Scouse diaspora grew as some of its finest talents were forced to look elsewhere to realise their potential. In short, Liverpool faced a gloomy prognosis, to be summed up a decade later by Geoffrey Howe when he advised Michael Heseltine to change the title of a report on the Toxteth riots to 'The Managed Decline of Liverpool'.

The end of the 1960s and the early 1970s was also a time of change for the labour movement in Liverpool. In 1969, following years of protracted debate, the Trades Union Congress and the Labour Party nationally decided to revise their local linkages, opting for a separation of the hitherto jointly organised Trades' Councils and Labour Party bodies. In Liverpool, as in many other places, this move was particularly unpopular with those trade unionists for whom the joint body had become a lever for influencing party activity and policy. In fact, this leverage was a catalyst in the joint body's downfall. In openly criticising or opposing the Wilson government on a whole host of issues and policies, the Liverpool Trades' Council and Labour Party prompted its own demise. Writing in the final report that was presented at a dinner in April 1969 to mark the occasion, the chair, Eddie Loyden, conceded that 'this role ... resulted in the intervention of the National Executive Committee (NEC) of the Labour Party in forcing the splitting of the two bodies'.[3]

With the separation, Simon Fraser, who had been the secretary of the joint body, took responsibility for the running of the Trades' Council. An amiable character from Scotland, Simon's sympathies reflected the perceived priority of the industrial struggle as opposed to party politics. The task of running the newly established Borough Labour Party, meanwhile, fell to Wally Edwards, who up until then had been the party's agent in Wallasey (and previously its agent in Bolton). Having also been active in the Liverpool West Derby constituency during the 1950s, Wally was familiar with the political terrain. Nevertheless, the timing of his appointment could have been better, coinciding as it did with the 1970 general election.

Despite the two organisations' separation, Simon and Wally had already decided between themselves that they would share accommodation, and in that sense they continued to work in partnership. They also shared a clerk/secretary in Pam Thorbinson (who continues to work for the Trades' Council today) before the expanding workload led to the appointment of Maureen Byrne, who now works in the Liverpool Walton constituency office. The first time I met Maureen was just after she had started working at the joint office. It was then in North Hill Street, Toxteth, in a property belonging to the Princes Park ward party. A bit of a pit, the place was quite literally falling apart. It had no heating, gas or lighting downstairs, and was only meant to be a temporary headquarters, but the city party remained there until the ward got into financial difficulties and put the building up for sale. Moves elsewhere, however, were not substantially to improve matters. From Toxteth, the HQ moved to an office in Hatton Garden, in the city's business quarter, until that property was identified for demolition, and then on to an old bank building in Victoria Street, where it stayed until 1983. The upheavals and the shabbiness of these various working conditions perhaps serve as a metaphor for the politics of Liverpool in the 1970s and '80s.

In the early 1970s, the organisation of the Labour Party in Liverpool was more or less rotten. Many wards across the city prevented people from becoming members in order to keep intact the private fiefdoms of particular councillors and MPs. From the age of eight, I had been delivering leaflets in the Dovecot area of the city, with an Irish neighbour called Mick Carey. Through him, I became aware of one of the local councillors, Pat Johnson, a local 'clubman' who sold insurance and who would later appear as one of the 'sensible/scabby six' in the mid-1980s. When in my mid-teens, early in the 1960s, I asked Johnson if I could join the party, his initial reply included words to the effect of: 'No, no, no, you're too young for this. You don't want to be bothered.' When I persisted, he told me that the ward was 'full up' and that there was 'an extended process' for new members wanting to join. Ignorant of the finer procedural details, I accepted his excuses, as well as his advice that I would have to wait until I was older before I could join the party. (I actually joined three years later, as a student at Durham University.)

My youthful experiences indicate how corrupt things were at the time, and how badly organised the party was. They fitted in neatly with Robert Mackenzie's analysis of political parties in Britain, where he highlighted the low conversion rate of votes into membership in a number of north-western constituencies.[4] Liverpool Scotland experienced the lowest transfer of votes into membership in the whole of the north-west – just over 1.2 per cent, with neighbouring Liverpool Kirkdale a close second at 1.8 per cent. In both of these constituencies, and in Liverpool generally, an attitude prevailed of: 'Keep it closed. Keep it tight. Keep new blood out.'

The Liverpool Exchange constituency was a rotten borough of classic proportions that was more or less run by members of one family, the Parrys. Typical of their hold over matters was the decision taken in 1970 to select Bob Parry as the prospective MP. Stan Maddox was at the selection meeting as the Trades' Council observer:

> I had to check the records of the meeting and, reading down the list of those in attendance, it was Parry, Parry, Parry, Parry. If my memory serves me right, there were nine people who were directly related to Bob Parry.

Similarly, John Hamilton, who was also on the short-list for the seat, remembers:

> There was a Parry from all of the ward delegations. When the vote came, there were twenty-four votes for Parry, five for me and none for any of the other candidates. Then the trouble started, because Bob wanted to know who the five were who had ratted on him. This was the way in Exchange – it was all parcelled up.

In fact, it may have been members of Bob's own family who had done the 'ratting'. After all, his brother and fellow councillor Jimmy felt that he ought to have been the MP because he had passed 'the scholarship' to St Francis Xavier College, whereas Bob had only attended Bishop Goss Secondary.

As useful a political representative then as he was on standing down in 1997, Bob Parry did not make his maiden speech in the council until after his parliamentary selection. Yet he carried on being a councillor for two years after becoming an MP. His narrow, parochial focus was exemplified by his preference for travelling back to Liverpool for a meeting at the Town Hall rather than attending work at Westminster. To my knowledge, in his twenty-seven years in the Commons, he never had a desk or a telephone extension, and he only established a constituency presence – in the Transport and General Workers' Union offices in Liverpool – in his last couple of years as an MP. He was not the only one guilty of such contempt for his office, but the manner of his selection, and his subsequent behaviour as a supposed representative of the people, best illustrate the primitive state of Labour in Liverpool at the start of the 1970s.

Aspects of this can be traced back to the party's adolescence in the north of the city where, having struggled to gain the support of the Catholic working class, Labour had become suffused with the Tammany Hall flavour of Irish nationalism. When T. P. O'Connor, the Irish Nationalist MP for Liverpool Scotland, died in 1929, it was no surprise that his (Labour) successor David Logan had previously been associated with the nationalist movement in Ireland. Of greater significance, however, was the influence of the Catholic church. During the Spanish Civil War, for example, one ward party in north Liverpool stood contrary to the rest of Labour in the city (and in the rest of Britain) by expressing support for Franco's right-wing coalition. The local church was in league with a number of large Labour families in the Vauxhall–Scotland area, running what amounted to a Catholic political mafia. At local elections, it was more often than not the case that Catholic

Labour councillors would be elected unopposed. Support for the Conservative Party in the area was extremely weak and the Liberals, at that time, were on an extended sabbatical. Although opposition from the Communist Party did arise after the war, the Communist vote was never enough to break down the hold of the church over politics. Even so, individual priests took it upon themselves to counter what they perceived as a threat to Catholic hegemony. One Communist Party candidate, Cyril Taylor, who later became a long-serving Labour councillor, remembers an occasion at a school which was being used as a polling station where:

> The local priest was parading up and down the playground throughout the polling hours, and inside the school the ballot box had been placed at the foot of a statue of Mary. It was really as good as saying to the faithful: 'If you vote Communist, you're committing a primary [sic] sin.'

At the start of the 1970s, the Catholic church continued to influence the Labour Party in pockets of Liverpool, but neither it nor the influence of Irish nationalism fully account for the course of events that Labour politics in the city was to take. More important was the character of the party's active membership. Unlike other cities in the north of England, Liverpool's Labour Party contained few real thinkers, nor did it have a strong strand of ethical socialism. Such intellectual and ethical influence as existed was concentrated into a handful of wards around and adjacent to the university area of the city. Both the private and public faces of Labour in Liverpool – the borough party and the council Labour group – were on the whole comprised of people whose backgrounds were in the trade union movement, principally the large manual or general unions. As a result, Labour's agenda came straight off the workerist press.

Liverpool's politics reflected the ugliness of a lumpen attitude to life. This came in two forms. On the one hand, there was a local arrogance, a hangover from the self-confidence of the 1960s. On the other, and perhaps more evidently, there was sheer bloody ignorance. Once, at a political education school, organised by the General and Municipal Boilermakers' Union, someone objected to me talking about education because I had passed a scholarship and gone on to grammar school. This had been at a time when the eleven plus served as the only way for working class children to make educational progress. Yet, to this particular character, the idea of even attending a grammar school was a betrayal of the most fundamental type.

Traditionally, Liverpool had not had the vanguardist skilled workforce of other cities that served, amongst other things, to raise the consciousness of the semi- and unskilled sections of the population. As a result, workerist attitudes set a context for a political class in Liverpool that had no real intellectual content and was wholly producer-oriented. Local politics was about protecting people in council jobs, and about looking after narrow interest groups – not in the numerical sense, because, for example, council house tenants were still in the majority, but in the sense that it was not concerned with changing trends. No-one of any significance was looking or planning ahead, and thinking aloud about what was around the corner. Other cities and towns were, seeing their condition for what it was and realising there had to be changes. Every place should have its own futurologist. Liverpool could have done with Alvin Tofler.

The forum where much of the real political activity took place was the Trades' Council. Although Liverpool's unemployment figures were already racing ahead of the national average, the continued existence of a number of large companies meant that there was still a significant trade union presence in the city. Both Plessey and Dunlop had many thousands of unionised employees. The Liverpool Instrument Makers' branch of the Electrical Trades Union (ETU) (of which I was an officer for two years) had nearly five thousand members. The dockworkers still numbered 15,000. In all cases, their respective officials were active on the Trades' Council.

The Trades' Council was the medium for debates on ideology, praxis and the condition of the working class. Many of those who would later become synonymous with Militant cut their teeth in debates there against members of the Communist Party (whose strong presence came mainly through the building and construction workers' union, UCATT), the International Socialists (later the Socialist Workers' Party) and the Socialist Labour League (later the Workers' Revolutionary Party). Individuals such as Bill Hunter, from the Socialist Labour League, enlivened the atmosphere with talk of the downfall of capitalism and how everything was ripe for a climactic event; but he could also be a terrible bore. All of this no doubt appears a world away to those whose politics have been shaped and conditioned by New Labour, but such debates were then a signpost of the times.

Following the failure of Wilson's Labour administration to implement their proposals on industrial disputes, 'In Place of Strife', the arrival of Heath's Conservative government in 1970 saw the introduction of a parcel of measures aimed at curbing industrial unrest. The most contentious part of it was the Industrial Relations Bill, which established a registrar to oversee trade unions and a set of restrictions that, post-Thatcher, would have been viewed with envy but at the time were considered unacceptable. This was an era when trade union leaders such as Hugh Scanlon and Jack Jones – 'the terrible twins', as revisionists have called them – were highly influential, and where the imposition of any new laws or practices could only but infuriate the brethren. Such discontent was magnified in Jones's home town of Liverpool, where demonstrations were rapidly becoming a fixture of the political landscape and the part-real, part-mythical 'militant Scouser' was starting to become a media folk-devil.

I remember speaking on the Industrial Relations Bill to a National Union of Students' national conference at Aston University in 1972; I was a mature student at the time. The atmosphere was electric as I asked my audience to put their money where their mouths were. I referred to the Wolfenden Report on the docks, and how, at the inquiry, it had been the dockers' trade union representatives who had argued for investment and modernisation, whilst the 'fragmented, greedy, rapacious employers' had failed to countenance the necessary changes. I followed this through with observations of how enlightened trade union leadership aspired to work in partnership but the idea was always rejected by the employers. I drew comparisons with Rotterdam, Bremen, Hamburg and Cherbourg, places that had been bombed during the war but had since invested in their ports. Afterwards, I was crowded by a group of middle class students who were so impressed by my awareness of matters that they assumed I was a docker. My knowledge actually stemmed from the fact that I was a delegate to the Trades' Council.

In terms of Liverpool's own politics, a watershed came in the summer of 1972. The previous year, Heath's government had published a white paper, *A Fair Deal for Housing,*[5] that set out plans for a new system of housing finance aimed at 'subsidising people, not bricks and mortar'. Central to the strategy were three aims: 'a decent home for every family at a price within their means'; 'a fairer choice between owning a home and renting one'; and 'fairness between one citizen and another in giving and receiving towards housing cost'.[6] Essentially, the paper proposed that council tenants should pay a rent commensurate with that paid in comparable private-sector housing. This rent would provisionally be set by the local authority, but tenants would then be able to make representations to a Rent Assessment Panel which would be empowered to make any necessary alterations.

Introducing the 1972 Housing Finance Bill in the Commons, Peter Walker, then Secretary of State for the Environment, claimed, with some irony, that what was being proposed amounted to 'one of the most remarkable pieces of practical socialism seen for a long time'.[7] In reality, it was an ideologically laden attempt to introduce market forces into that part of local government finance devoted to council housing. The government wanted to establish the principle of self-financing and thereby facilitate the gradual reduction of subsidies to council tenants. For many of those concerned, the 'fair deal' actually meant a significant rise – approximately £1 a week for the first year and 50p a week in subsequent years until the 'fair' level had been reached. The initial increment alone represented a 20–25 per cent real-terms increase on the average £4–5 weekly rent.[8]

Twenty-eight years down the line, and with the principles of the market evident at all levels of local government, much of what the 'fair deal' proposed appears rather orthodox. But in the economic and political climate of the time, the provisions of the bill and the philosophy that informed it were perceived as threats to a sacred cow. House-building and housing clearances by local authorities had become major characteristics of British society in the post-war period, and the idea of affordable council housing was a central pillar of the welfare state. In the early 1970s, more than 60 per cent of domestic properties in Liverpool belonged to the council, a figure mirrored in many other large conurbations. Consequently, anything and everything connected to the issue assumed great political significance – though with hindsight, the whole issue appears to have been too easily blown up. Many of the poorest tenants would have been able to cover the increase in rent via housing benefit; and the bill also included a number of longer term provisions that would ultimately benefit boroughs such as Liverpool, with its predominance of run-down inner-city properties. In particular, there was a commitment to pay 75 per cent of the deficit on housing clearances and house-building at a time when the cost of such exercises was rapidly increasing.

Nevertheless, the introduction of the bill created opportunities for all kinds of people to throw their weight around. Party and trade union activists alike were still reeling from their failure to defeat Heath on the Industrial Relations Act, a battle that many felt had not been fought with the appropriate degree of vehemence. In addition, as rent increases would be most acutely felt by the employed working classes, they had real and immediate implications for forthcoming wage settlements. Consequently, defeating the bill became the *cause célèbre* of the labour movement. In Liverpool, as in many other places, the Trades' Council helped to organise tenants' associations against the bill, causing the *Guardian* to predict that: 'grassroots opposition within the Labour Party is growing and Labour councils will be under pressure to make a stand'.[9] It was unsurprising, therefore, that Labour groups, either in control of or aiming to control local councils, began to pursue a more vociferous line of defiance.

In the spring of 1972, representatives of a number of local authorities gathered in Sheffield, at the Amalgamated Engineering Union Hall, to discuss the implications of the Housing Finance Bill and the means by which implementation could be contested. Amongst those present was the leader of Liverpool's Labour group, Alderman Bill Sefton. A long-standing member of the group, he had become leader in 1963 and soon developed a reputation as a highly focused politician with much grander concerns than many of his peers. Bob Wareing, today the MP for Liverpool West Derby but then the president and chair of the Liverpool Borough Labour Party, was with Sefton in Sheffield:

> It was a very crowded meeting, and included people from all over the country. There was a lot of argy-bargy and a lot of talk, a lot of rhetoric but no resolutions. Bill passed me a note, upon which he'd written a resolution for uniting to oppose the Act. Then he said to me 'Would you be prepared to speak in support of this, if I put it to the meeting?' I did, and the resolution was passed *nem con*.

A month later, another meeting took place in Sheffield, after a number of Labour groups had backed down. Liverpool, however, was still in the forefront of opposition, setting the pace and encouraging other councils to stand firm in defiance. Again, Bob Wareing was in attendance:

> When myself and Hugh Dalton entered the hall, people asked us where we were from, and we got a tremendous applause. These were ordinary members of the Labour Party and the public who had heard about Bill Sefton's vigorous opposition to the Act.

Significantly, Sefton was not at this second meeting.

The local elections of May 1972 saw the arrival in office of a legion of Labour councillors across Britain, with landslide victories in a number of places bolstering the position of many of the Labour groups articulating defiance of the bill. Finding themselves in control of councils, consideration immediately turned to whether or not they should implement the provisions of the bill once it became law. As *The Economist* observed, prior to the elections: 'It may be quite enough for election purposes to play up the council rent increases ... without actually refusing to implement them when it comes to the point'.[10] In Liverpool, where Labour had fought the local elections with the pledge of non-implementation at the heart of its manifesto, the party regained control of a council that had fallen into Conservative hands five years previously. Yet, despite this clear mandate, reflected in a working majority of nineteen, Bill Sefton found himself in something of a quandary. In the week following the elections, the bill received its final reading in the Commons, increasing the likelihood of it soon becoming an Act, and thereby making the issue of illegality more salient. Having advocated non-implementation so ardently, the Liverpool leader now believed that position to be untenable.

In recalling Sefton's retreat, fellow Labour group members from the time have commented that what struck them most was the way in which he failed to make the change in his thinking apparent. Had he done so, they say, he could have convinced people who would normally have taken his lead that a U-turn had not been made rashly. John Hamilton, a future leader of both the group and the council but then the chair of Education, was one who found this difficult to swallow:

> We had gone all the way down the line and not wavered, having been led by Sefton to do so. To suddenly switch at the last minute would have not been easy on my conscience.

Sefton himself explains his thinking rather differently, questioning the good sense of others and characteristically placing it as only one issue within the broader scheme of things:

> I'm extremely sorry for those who believed the question of the Rent Act [Housing Finance Act] was the most important thing that ever happened in Liverpool, but there were things of a far greater importance from which you couldn't be divorced. I was keen on boosting the city, turning it into a real centre for the region. Of course, you couldn't discuss this in the context of the Rent Act; but I was keen that we shouldn't be side-tracked. The important thing was that the Labour Party should retain control in Liverpool.

It would have been more surprising if the issue of maintaining control of the functions of local government had *not* been central to Sefton's thinking. Any council acting illegally against the provisions of the bill ran a particular risk, the effects of which would perhaps be felt more by the very people it sought to protect. As one newspaper noted, 'The militants should remember that if they refuse to implement the Act, Whitehall will install a Commissioner to administer the housing department. He may have less regard for the tenants than the councillors have.'[11]

Opposing the impact of the bill became even less straightforward after the government decided to make a number of financial concessions. Earlier in the year, following representations from Newcastle that one-sixth of its tenants were already paying 'fair rents', the government was persuaded that not all councils should implement the £1 per week increase. Moreover, in July, on the day before the Labour Party convened a special local government conference in London, a clearer indication was given of the level of increases deemed acceptable. Based on pre-existing rents in the areas specified, these ranged from 19p in Sheffield and 35p in Newcastle to 65p in Birmingham and 75p in Hammersmith. In Liverpool, however, 77 per cent of the city's 98,000 tenants would face a rise in October of either 85p or £1 per week.[12] This difference between what tenants in Liverpool and tenants elsewhere paid to their respective councils was to become a key feature of the city's municipal turmoil. For most of the 1970s and 1980s, the increases in such payments were entirely out of keeping with both the metropolitan district average and the Retail Price Index.[13] This would lead history to repeat itself in Liverpool, and, in tune with Marx's observation, where on the second occasion this brought farce, on the first it gave rise to tragedy.

With the exception of the small Derbyshire district of Clay Cross, where twelve Labour councillors were eventually barred from holding office, accommodations were gradually made by all those Labour groups that had previously adopted a position of defiance.[14] For Liverpool, the climb-down officially happened at a special meeting of the full council on 23 August 1972. As one would expect of an occasion swathed in symbolism and rhetoric, this was a lively affair that at one point saw a Labour councillor, Chris Perry, become the literal object of a tug-of-war. While remonstrating with a policeman, Perry was accused of spitting and was promptly grabbed by his shirt; he was pulled back by his fellow councillors and, after a brief to-ing and fro-ing, had his shirt ripped open. Recalling the court appearance that followed later in the year, at which Perry was fined for a breach of the peace, one of his close friends on the council, Geoff Walsh, noted how afterwards he had his first meeting with a recently established youth worker called Derek Hatton. A coincidence, perhaps, but, as with so much else in Liverpool politics, one that is rich with its own ironies.

A central figure at the special council meeting was the chair of the Housing Committee, Joe Morgan. Then in his second spell as chair, Morgan had originally taken up the position in 1955 following a contest with Bill Smythe, Jack Braddock's protégé and preferred choice. It was one of the few defeats that Braddock ever suffered in the Labour group. A hard taskmaster and misanthrope, Morgan had developed a habit of appearing at the Housing Department in Foster House at 8:30 A.M. to check if the staff arrived on time.

At the special meeting, Morgan proposed that delegated plenary powers should be given to him and his deputy John McPherson to apply the provisions of the Housing Finance Act in a way that would be deemed generous to council tenants. (In doing so, he recommended that an application should be made to the Secretary of State for a minimal rent increase.) Strangely, Morgan also took the opportunity to chastise those in his local tenants' association who had been harassing and intimidating his family. Stan Thorne, later the MP for Preston, then moved an opposing resolution that the council refuse implementation, and called for the support of the Labour movement and tenants' associations to defeat the Act.

With the Liberals requesting a recorded vote, each councillor was asked to state their voting intentions when their name was called by the Town Clerk. Conducted alphabetically by surname, it is possible that some councillors further down the list changed their minds on witnessing the position of others. Of course, no-one would have dared admit this at the time, and it is highly unlikely that they would even do so today. Nevertheless, members of the Labour group and their associates were observing events very carefully; as Bill Snell recalls:

> I was sat at the back of the council chamber, and my agent said: 'You know, Bill, you can vote against this and it will still be carried'; and I said: 'You can't do things like that. You either believe it or you don't.' So I voted for it.

Cyril Taylor, meanwhile, remembers one of the accusations fired at him and others for voting against:

> They said that we had done so safe in the knowledge that we would be defeated.

And so they were. Stan Thorne's amendment for non-implementation was defeated by 80 votes to 43, and the vote was the same in favour of raising rents in line with the Act. (The defeat did Stan no harm in his subsequent selection as a parliamentary candidate.) Nevertheless, it was a bitter pill for the Labour leadership to swallow. With only twenty-seven Labour members taking the Sefton-Morgan line, the support of opposition councillors was needed to carry the day. Perhaps not surprisingly, nineteen Labour councillors absented themselves in one way or another.

The debate on the Housing Finance Act was an early sign of the tradition of setting impossibilist agendas in Liverpool that became so important a decade or so later – though the stance of the forty-three, a clear minority on the council, was more open to accusations of posturing than that taken by their heirs in the 1980s, who were normally in control.

It demonstrated how there were always individuals in the background ready to push others into taking action for which they refused to take responsibility themselves. If the council in Liverpool had voted against implementing the Act, the first in the firing line would have been Bill Sefton, but after the vote he was harangued with cries of 'traitor' and 'sell-out'. More significantly, twenty-one of the forty-three rebels began to meet as a separate group.

Having been present at a rather rowdy Labour group meeting on the Friday before the full council was due to meet, Sefton was well aware that the strength of feeling surrounding the Act could have led to a split. Even so, he was surprised at the number prepared to take that road. For John Hamilton, this was an effective vote of no confidence in Sefton's leadership:

> Sefton knew what he'd done – he'd brought us all that far. Things would have been different if, earlier in the year, we'd been led in a way that gradually veered us away from defiance.

Not that John would give such a lead in the 1980s. Meanwhile, Stan Maddox, who voted for implementation, considers events rather differently:

> We were, to use a contemporary term, on the pragmatic wing. The split was quite deliberate, and much of what occurred was deliberately engineered; partly because of the personalities involved and partly north versus south in the city.

In fact, the split was just another example of what appeared to be a compulsive need for the Labour Party in Liverpool to fissure. It offered an internal enemy with whom one could squabble and fight.

A real hotchpotch of political outlooks and allegiances, the breakaway group consisted of those like Hamilton and Taylor, who were genuinely concerned with the effects the Act would have on tenants in Liverpool, and others whose reasoning was perhaps clouded by the desire for a political punch-up with the Heath government. The latter group's ranks included the rebels' nominal leader Eddie Loyden, the patron saint of lost causes, Militant luminary Ted Mooney, and Alec Doswell, the perennial follower.

That Loyden, who would later serve two spells as the MP for Liverpool Garston, became the rebels' leader came as little surprise. President of the Trades' Council and a lay union official at the docks (he worked on the boats which took out the river pilots to incoming ships), Loyden had developed a reputation for chairing meetings, so much so that his nickname was 'the chairman'. As anyone who has ever been involved in an organisation or body with officers knows, the positions of Secretary and Treasurer usually involve or imply a degree of work, as well as an acceptance of accountability and responsibility. Loyden, however, appeared to avoid such tasks like the plague, preferring instead to chair almost every meeting he ever attended. It was his way of imposing himself on a group, and amounted to nothing short of a power trip.

Mooney, on the other hand, was a different type of political animal. He had written a pamphlet for the Trades' Council attacking 'Fair Deal', thereby giving the more intransigent amongst the rebels their political drive. He only remained on the council for a short time (leaving to attend a teacher training college in Blackburn), but resurfaced in Liverpool at a later date where his long-term involvement on Militant's central committee would become more apparent. As for Doswell, he was a classic example of someone for whom politics contained no grey areas, and for whom arguments revolved around a lexicon of phrases such as: 'You're either with us or against us', 'You're with us because you're one of our class', and 'You're a traitor.'

In addition, there was the somewhat peculiar presence of Paul Orr, whose stance was altogether more anomalous, not least because of his association with the old right of the party, the majority of whom had voted with Sefton. Orr's position on the Act appears even more maverick when considering his role during the mid 1980s as a member of the 'sensible/scabby six'. However, he shared with some of the more obstinate rebels an upbringing in the predominantly Catholic areas of north Liverpool. Within the anthropo-political delineation of the city, Orr, Loyden and others were effectively from the same tribe. In spite of this, they were forever sniping behind one another's backs. You would have to have lived through all such relationships to understand their intricacies, but one person upon whom they had a noticeable effect was Ken Stewart. Physically well built, Ken, later the MEP for Merseyside West, was not the brightest of people and always appeared somewhat in awe of Loyden. In the context of Liverpool politics, the latter was a confident and articulate speaker who could project himself and give the impression of knowledge and experience. It affected those who knew no better, at least until they heard the same speech time and time again. Where Loyden had his one speech, Ken struggled as a speaker; but there was one occasion, soon after the Labour group split, when he came out on top, alleging that Loyden was a hypocrite. This occurred during the so-called 'rent strikes'.

While the breakaway group could do little to reverse the decision that had been taken within the council chamber, many of them helped the various tenants' associations across the city activate rent strikes. Essentially a boycott of the rent increases arising from the implementation of the Act, the strikes were most common in those parts of Liverpool which were dominated by council housing and where the sitting councillors were either members of the twenty-one or of the forty-three who had voted against the Sefton-Morgan line. Activity in other Labour areas, for example in St Mary's ward, was virtually non-existent. Nevertheless, with around 20 per cent of tenants subject to the increases actually participating, the strikes were an organisational success. They also had spin-offs in the adjacent borough of Knowsley, where many council tenants lived in properties belonging to the Liverpool Corporation,[15] and particularly in Kirkby, where the strike was led by Tony Boyle (who later became involved in the Kirkby Unemployed Centre), and where a number of tenants were eventually sent to prison. Of course, not all of the breakaway faction within the Liverpool Labour group were council tenants, and those who were not, such as John Hamilton, often felt uncomfortable about encouraging people to withhold their rent:

> We said: 'If you do go in for a rent strike, put your money in a safe place and keep it there so that when the strike is over you can hand your rent over.' The danger was that if people didn't pay their rent, they would spend it and lose their house.

Such a consideration on Hamilton's part stands in stark contrast to anecdotal evidence that some of his fellow 'rebels', who were living in council housing, paid their rent at a time when they were also sanctioning letters and leaflets that referred to payers as blacklegs. Although Bill Sefton refuses to relate the 'confidences' made to him:

I knew beyond any doubt that some of them were paying their rent.

As it happened, the only one who ended up being prosecuted for non-payment was Ken Stewart. Following his court appearance, he was intrigued to know why fellow council tenant Eddie Loyden had not also been summonsed, only to discover that the latter's rent had been paid. Upset about this, Ken confronted his 'leader' with an accusation of complicity, at which point he was told: 'Oh, the house isn't in my name. It's in Rose's [Loyden's late wife]. Her name's on the rent book and she pays the rent.'

This line of defence, half-echoed by Derek Hatton some years later during a dispute at his son's school, again highlights the hypocrisy of those who, in wanting to lead from behind, push others into impossible situations. In terms of Loyden and Stewart, bitterness did ensue, but the fuzzy logic of Liverpool politics at this time eventually saw Ken, the nascent but unwilling martyr, appointed chair of the council's Housing Committee.

Demonstrations were another way in which attention was drawn to the rent issue. In October 1972, 200 tenants carried a petition to the Town Hall in an atmosphere described at the time as 'positively festive', where 'little girls wore paper bibs and paper hats with slogans, and on the tannoy John and Yoko sang "Power to the People" '.[16] In the same month, 3,000 people, including dockers, building workers and others whose trade unions had called a one-day strike, marched through the city centre in protest against government legislation. I remember this vividly. In the time-honoured way of Liverpool demonstrations, having come down London Road and along Lime Street (where I slipped into the wine lodge for a swift drink to fortify my spirits), we headed towards the Pier Head. On arriving at the waterfront, we were treated to the wit and wisdom of the dockers' leader, Dennis Kelly. Something of a demagogue, he was a fine speaker but he was also very coarse and crude in his observations. As was the norm on these occasions, Loyden stood next to Kelly in a pose reminiscent of Trotsky beside Lenin before Stalin had him airbrushed out.

At the council, attempts were made at mediation between the main Labour group and Loyden's rebel army, most strongly by members of the borough party executive. Wally Edwards, the then Secretary, played a bridging role:

> At the risk of sounding boastful, I think I was well respected by both sides.
> I tried to get them to agree on things, and to some degree I succeeded.

Although his personal view of the Act put him in tune with the 'twenty-one', Wally had to retain a position of impartiality because of the difficulties he faced in financing both his own and his secretary's (Maureen Byrne's) paid appointments in a city party that was lacking a basic membership income. Although funds were raised partly through the running of a tote and partly from trade union affiliation fees, Labour councillors were also vital in raising funds. Keeping both sides happy was, therefore, an essential part of Wally's job.

Bob Wareing, the president of the borough party, also liaised between the two groups, attending the meetings of both sides until the occasion in December 1972 when he was successfully sent by the main group to the breakaway group to try and bring them together. For some in the majority group, such as Eddie Roderick, there was a suspicion of clandestine behaviour surrounding Wareing:

> He used to sit in on our meetings and then tell them what had been said, but he never told us what had been said in their meetings.

Naturally, Wareing disputes the accusation.

> Eddie's wrong about that because I did try to be an honest broker, even though my sympathy was with those who had opposed the Act.

Nevertheless, some municipal subterfuge did take place for, as Roderick conceded, he and others did become aware of much of the rebels' thinking:

> We had one of our own in there who reported back to us privately.

In fairness, it should be pointed out that a claim to inside information was a regular refrain of Eddie's throughout his political life. I had first-hand experience of this as his agent in the 1970 local elections.

At around the time that the two groups began to meet again, the selection process commenced for the following year's local elections. This would have been an awkward enough time for Labour anyway, with the need to patch up the divisions that had bedevilled the group, but it was made even more so by three further factors: the re-election of the entire council, the merging of a number of wards following boundary changes, and the abolition of the aldermanic system. All of this raised a whole range of new challenges. In many of the wards where tenants' associations were active, reselections were primarily determined by the stance that individuals had taken on the rent increases, and in cases where wards had merged, such matters were made more complex by the number of sitting councillors wishing to re-stand. In addition, a handful of the aldermen wished to remain in office and sought an appropriate selection. Their number included the alderman for the Croxteth ward – Bill Sefton.

As with his retreat on the Housing Finance Act, there is an element of contradiction over what actually happened when Sefton attempted to stand for selection for the new council, though this has no doubt been clouded by the mists of political memory. According to one source, Sefton was rejected by his local party in St Mary's ward, and his eventual selection in the then three-way marginal of Anfield was an act of desperation aided by his Co-operative Party membership in a Co-op dominated ward. Sefton, however, remembers events rather differently:

> It was a stupid decision on my part. With the changes in local government, I said to the group: 'Now let's get this straight, as far as I'm concerned, we shouldn't go around peddling for safe seats. If you're asked to stand for a seat, then you stand for it.' … We had suspicions that people were going to turn down wards or not go to selection meetings because they didn't want to be selected. The first one to ask me was Anfield, so I could hardly go against my own belief. But I also had an offer from one of the wards in Toxteth which I would have easily walked.

Whatever the ins and outs of his selection, Sefton faced a number of problems in rallying support in Anfield. Not only was his agent virtually house-bound but polling day coincided with an evening football fixture at Liverpool FC. In keeping with the worst traditions of Liverpool ephemera, the latter served to distract the electorate – and working-class Labour voters in particular – from any concern that they may have had with local politics. Sefton lost the contest and with it his twenty-year seat on the city council. Given the strange priorities of the time, certain elements within the Labour Party celebrated, as his defeat removed one obstacle from their path.

It was not the only one. Sefton's fate was shared by some of those who had voted with him the previous August. Some, such as Ian Levin in Melrose, saw their ward merged with another and found it impossible to get selected elsewhere. Others ended up standing in areas where Labour support was weak and where they were duly defeated. And then there was Bill

Smythe, a councillor for nineteen years in Everton ward, for whom deselection owed something to boundary changes but, in his view at least, much more to the efforts of others:

> I'd been antagonistic towards the Trots, and they'd been far more danger-ous and far more vicious than what the old left in the Labour Party were. Lots of people said 'don't worry'. We had a good membership in Everton and there was a good chance of me getting selected, but I was told that I wouldn't be selected because *they* would take care of it and have me deselected – which I was.

As upset as he was at losing the seat, Smythe looked upon his removal from the council with a degree of optimism, viewing it as a way out of politics that would allow him to go into lecturing. Nevertheless, as will be revealed in the next chapter, Smythe was to regain a seat in the chamber in somewhat bi-zarre circumstances, eventually becoming the leader of the city council.

In the meantime, Bill Sefton took his talents elsewhere. A few months ear-lier, he had been selected to stand for the newly created county council seat of Vauxhall & Sandhills which, considering the religious demography of the area, was a remarkable feat for a self-confessed atheist. Even so, the contest (which took place a month before the municipal elections) was not without its difficulties, partly because of reverberations from the Housing Finance Act, and partly because a tenants' candidate took a substantial portion of the vote. Although Sefton took the seat,[17] and duly became the first leader of the county council, his removal from Liverpool's city politics signalled the end of an era.

As we have seen, for the best part of a century, politics in Liverpool was managed primarily by a number of city 'bosses'. Turn after turn, this was typified by the Conservative leaders Arthur Forwood, Archibald Salvidge, Thomas White and Alfred Shennan, and then Labour's Jack Braddock. Anthony Howard, in his *New Statesman* article, 'Cook County, UK', pub-lished nine months after Braddock's death, observed that history would probably remember the latter as 'the only example of a city boss produced by the Labour movement'.[18] Notwithstanding what was to happen a few years later in Newcastle, under T. Dan Smith, this looked likely to be the case for Liverpool as the leadership of the Labour group and the city council passed into the hands of Bill Sefton.

Before becoming leader, Sefton had gained something of a reputation as the head of a left-wing ginger group, and many of his contemporaries recall how he would wax lyrical about constructive reform via planning and development rather than spend his time engaging in political manipulation. Indeed, Jack Braddock considered him one of the 'young cowboys' who regularly made it difficult for him to ride rough-shod over the Labour group.[19] Although Braddock's tendency to wear a Stetson hat provides a context to this banter, he looked upon Sefton and others with a degree of contempt. Stan Maddox recalls one occasion at the Trades' Council and Labour Party (a forum where support for Braddock was rarely forthcoming) when:

> Jack Braddock called myself, Bill Sefton and a couple of others 'the flat-faced Muscovites from Garston'.

Braddock's strength lay in the north end of the city, while Garston is in the south, again highlighting how loose geographic alliances have long been a part of Labour politics in Liverpool. This remained the case in the debates over the Housing Finance Act, and it is also evident today, albeit in a form qualified by whether or not an individual was born in the city. As they existed in the mid-1960s, these allegiances, compounded by related factors such as the continued presence of Bessie Braddock as a local MP,[20] offer some explanation as to why Sefton's radicalism became diluted when he took over as party leader in Liverpool. As he attempted to realise a future for the city, much of his energy ended up being spent in securing votes or agreements, particularly when he was advancing his more imaginative plans. As a result, Sefton was seen by many of his contemporaries as perpetuating the traditions of the boss. The man himself, however, dismisses the idea that he was the last of Liverpool's true political bosses as 'a load of tripe', and when questioned about his management of the Labour group recalls its response to developments that followed the announcement that Goodison Park had been designated a venue for the 1966 World Cup:

> I remember walking up to the Town Clerk and he said to me: 'We've had a visit from the Minister of Sport, Mr Howells. He's had a meeting with Everton Football Club and they've decided that they want to pull down some houses to build a bigger stand.' My mind was immediately taken aback. I thought: 'They're going to pull a street of houses down – bloody hell, now what am I going to do? Here we are with a national figure from the Labour Government coming up and saying this. Am I going to stand up and oppose it? No! So, what do I do?' I had a choice. I could let it develop in its own way or I could go to the group. I went to the group and

they chucked me out … so, I don't know about me being 'the Boss' and working underhand. I was perfectly happy to go along to the group and try and defend the situation, and I got defeated. Perhaps the reason that people got the idea that I was a boss in the old sense was that I did go to the group too often – although they never listened to what I was saying.

Like Braddock, Sefton acquired his own coterie of people from within the group; in particular, the Belfast-born Brian Crookes, an able and clever politician who helped link people behind Sefton's leadership – normally by putting across alternative and sometimes contradictory angles on particular issues, like a prototype spin doctor. This often resulted in the most unholy of alliances but it also served to bridge some of the more petty divisions that existed. Nonetheless, Crookes made enemies along the way, not the least of whom was Jack Braddock, as one source recalls:

> He used to deliver door-to-door library books on a bike with a trailer at the back. On one occasion I happened to say to Braddock, 'I was just coming around the corner by the cinema into Green Lane and nearly hit Brian Crookes on his stupid bloody bike. How the hell I missed him, I'll never know.' Stony-faced, Jack replied: 'Why did you miss him?'

Sefton and Crookes also became business partners, investing in a petrol station, for which they were to subsequently face an inquiry regarding the planning agreement. It amused me to see Sefton described on election forms as an 'attendant'. I asked him at the time, in all sincerity, whether he was a hospital attendant. He replied that he was a garage attendant, without revealing that he owned the garage. Later, Sefton and Crookes were to be found living close to one another in the same part of North Wales.

One of the ways in which Sefton did differ from Braddock was in the admiration – albeit qualified – that he received, and continues to receive, from those who did not necessarily follow his political line. One of the less obstinate members of the 'twenty-one', Cyril Taylor, opines:

> Bill Sefton was a natural politician with a natural intelligence, who would have been quite a significant person if he had had the opportunities for schooling and education. His interest was much more macro than just parts of Liverpool. I expect he was a lousy ward councillor but he was busy thinking about the macro-economics of the whole area.

Such wider vision on the part of Sefton did not come courtesy of any established professional status. Even when leader of the city council, he contin-

ued to work at his trade as a plumber. Indeed, Cyril Taylor recalls one con-
sultation he had with Sefton, as chair of the Welfare Committee, that took
place in the loft of a house he was working on.

It is important to understand that politics in Liverpool was never the same
after Sefton moved on.[21] It was not that the city was no longer susceptible to
'bossism' – it was, as would later be reaffirmed – but the complex of enmities
that the split over the Housing Finance Act threw up was to make it almost
impossible for another boss figure to emerge. Nobody had control over such
enmities nor the political know-how to override their ramifications.

   None of this, of course, was helped by what was occurring elsewhere in
the city's politics.

# 2 Pavement politics

Unlike Birmingham, Leeds, Manchester and other industrial centres, Liverpool has never, historically, had a strong tradition of urban liberalism, something that has best been explained by the absence of a social basis of 'small and middling size manufacturers plus skilled workers plus a regularly employed factory proletariat'.[22] Support was so lean for the Liberals in post-war Liverpool that they had no-one on the city council until the elections of 1962, when two of their nine candidates were returned. One of these was the local leader, Cyril Carr, who, in successfully defending his Church ward seat, remained the party's only ever-present on the council for the remainder of the decade, during which their number fluctuated between one and three. Beyond the Town Hall, the Liberals were organisationally weak, and their local bodies amounted to the Church ward party, the Wavertree constituency committee and the Liverpool borough party. With the same people sitting on all three, it was not unusual for their business to be sorted in one evening. All of this, however, was to change dramatically between 1969 and 1973, as the municipal *pas-de-deux* that Labour and the Tories had engaged in since the mid-1950s gave the Liberals the opportunity to cut in on an 'excuse me'.

So many different passions and disgruntlements were mixed up in Liverpool politics at this time. The borough council, in the hands of either Labour or the Conservatives, was failing to deliver the most basic and vital of services, particularly street cleaning and refuse collection (matters that would later figure prominently in the downfall of Militant). Many Labour councillors were becoming more and more introspective. Rather than being effective representatives of the people and fulfilling the purposes of local government, they became overly concerned with the divisions within the Labour group and debates within the Trades' Council. The Tories, meanwhile, were tainted by the policies and performance of the Heath government. Most crucially, both parties presided over a redevelopment process in Liverpool which had seen large inner-city communities 'uprooted and transported to outlying housing "bantustans" '.[23]

## Left Behind: Lessons from Labour's heartland

Ultimately, a gap opened up between the local electorate and their notional representatives, into which rode the Liberals with a seemingly fresh agenda of 'pavement politics'. Supporting them was more or less a case of saying to the two established parties, 'a plague on both your houses'. Still, in cultivating this support, the Liberals adopted some campaigning techniques novel to Liverpool at the time, from cars replete with megaphones and background music to stick-on badges and paper hats bearing the party colours and logo. Although he was not the principal person behind all of this, a local Liberal, Trevor Jones, was to receive much of the credit. Partly due to his dynamic and vociferous character, but more because of his ceaseless projection of himself as the key to the party's successes, he became known both locally and nationally as 'Jones the Vote'.

Trevor Jones first came into local politics through involvement in a petition against the proposed inner motorway, and also through his concern with the handling of planning applications for petrol stations (a concern that brought him directly into conflict with Bill Sefton and Brian Crookes). Having had a submission on the latter rejected in the House of Lords, he decided to enter party politics and began to seek election as a Liberal councillor. After unsuccessfully fighting three contests in Childwall ward, Jones took Church in a by-election in 1968, replacing one of the Liberals' existing two councillors. Soon after, he gave his maiden speech on the subject of the inner motorway, receiving a round of applause from the Labour and Conservative benches, whose occupants promptly voted him down. To some people, Jones's politics appeared rather esoteric. What cannot be disputed, however, are the electoral successes that he helped to reap. By 1972, the Liberals' numbers on the council had edged up to a respectable fifteen.

Central to the Liberal strategy was the use of a semi-regular newsletter, ubiquitously known as *Focus*, the 'flexibility' of which allowed it to reach out to electors on ward issues. Typically, *Focus* would include bold headings with variations on the theme of: 'The Liberals have put the pressure on the council and the following things have been done'; whilst underneath would be the equally emphatic: 'We have asked the Labour council about the following but still nothing has been done'. Famously, Harold Wilson spoke of a party with 'a policy for every street corner' but no coherent approach to the larger issues of the day.[24] Bill Sefton, meanwhile, thought the Liberals' narrow concerns were misguided:

> They concentrated on bloody pavements when the unemployed were walking over them!

Nevertheless, as one commentary at the time noted: 'By holding up a magnifying glass to the city's cracked paving stones, and offering "community politics" to mend them, the Liberal Party clearly struck a chord more profound than mere parochialism'.[25] This was more than evident when David Alton somewhat unexpectedly took the Low Hill ward at the 1972 elections. A poor, working-class area of the inner city that Labour had begun to take for granted, Low Hill also had its local pride and Alton, who lived in the area, appealed to this sentiment through promoting a sense of local community. Certainly, I was aware of how much of a 'rotten borough' the wider Edge Hill constituency was. I was agent for Eddie Roderick and Stan Thorne in my local ward of Kensington, next to Alton's ward, at a time when the local Labour Party seemed to consist of myself and two men in late middle age, Walter Gibbs and George Henshaw. Support for Labour was taken for granted, and its residents were expected to accept any rubbish imposed upon them by the politicians.

Before becoming a councillor, Alton had been an energetic and effective campaigner for the Liberals. This was clear at Christ College, the church-endowed college of teacher education where both he and I were students, and which he managed to plaster with Liberal posters at election time. Indeed, Alton's eagerness for publicity for the Liberal causes saw the development of a rapport with the local press that continues to this day. Unsurprisingly, this created much frustration within the Labour group:

> When we used to ask the *Echo* and *Post* why they gave the Liberals so much space, they told us that Alton and others were ringing them up every day with a story.

Allegedly, the Liberals used to drag around the same old mattress, or a dead rat, to different parts of a ward and say to people: 'Look at this rubbish in the entry!' or 'Isn't the council awful? They can't get rid of this.' After clearing it away, they would then go and drop it somewhere else and repeat the process. Each time, they would telephone local journalists to try and get them to write sympathetic copy or print a photograph that would highlight the inefficiency of the Labour council. Whether these accusations are true or not is perhaps irrelevant. What cannot be denied is that they had a receptive audience amongst middle and skilled working classes of Liverpool. Gradually, the Liberals accumulated support from disillusioned Tories, in part delivered by a residual Protestant logic that equated the Liverpool Labour Party with the Vatican, and they also appealed to a fledgling constituency of owner-occupiers, potential owner-occupiers and private-sector tenants, many of whom had been 'brought up' Labour but had since begun to see little in the party to keep them loyal. In 1973 the true extent of Liberal support in Liverpool became apparent. With the whole council up for re-election, forty-eight successful nominal 'Liberals' nearly won a majority of the ninety-nine seats, and with it control of the council. With their cheap confidence tricks, the purveyors of pavement politics had pulled a fast one on a gullible and near-despairing electorate.

Although the reduction of Liverpool's forty wards to thirty-three altered the political composition of a number of areas, mass swings to the Liberals occurred in parts of the city that were associated with one or other of the other parties. All three seats in the Conservative–Labour marginals of Anfield, Clubmoor, Fairfield, Kensington, Picton and Tuebrook went Liberal, as did all three seats in the Conservative purlieus of Aigburth, Childwall and Croxteth. The Liberals also took all three seats in Breckfield & St Domingo, a new ward made up of a Conservative–Labour marginal and one of the city's two Protestant strongholds. Some support in the latter area may have stemmed from an attachment to the Liberals' orange colours, but those who elected them helped to bridge the sectarian divide.

Although they should not be knocked for winning the number and type of seats that they did, it is well known that the Liberals ended up with people on the council who had no idea about political structures, and even less interest in them. Being a councillor was basically just a buzz, for which they were happy to have been given the opportunity. There is a huge difference between harbouring a philosophical position, whether in opposition or in power, and actually running an organisation as large and as complex as a city council. Many of those who were elected as Liberals in 1973 did not understand the distinction. Indeed, anecdotal evidence suggests that the Liberals went around knocking on doors and trawling the streets, asking virtually anyone who sounded vaguely sympathetic and who could string a sentence together to be a Liberal candidate.

One of those who jumped on the Liberal bandwagon was Michael Hefferon. Formerly a merchant seaman, Hefferon used some of his earnings to set up a company called Vandyke Properties, so-called because the first house he bought was in Vandyke Street in Liverpool 8. Having converted this into two flats, he began buying up more old properties and became a classic slum landlord. My wife Bernie and I lived in one of his flats in Edge Hill, and we had mayhem trying to have a fair rent set. It ended up at a rent tribunal where he tried to buy us off, afraid of fair rents being set on all of his flats. Strangely, he was never bothered by the Labour Party posters that we used to put in the front window at election times, and once said to me that whichever party got in, he would 'do business with them' in order to carry on with his 'business'. It was incredible that he ever became a councillor, as his thinking was: 'I can get in there, make a few quid and move on.' Alas he did, in Tuebrook, but within a few months he was found guilty of corruption over planning permission, and later sent to prison. In the subsequent by-election, Dave Mitchell re-took the seat for Labour, holding it until 1978, when Derek Hatton was beaten by the Conservatives.

Some of the Liberals' new breed did take to politics. Mike Storey stood in Liverpool Kirkdale at the October 1974 general election, and is today the party's leader on Liverpool City Council, and, of course, now leader of the council itself. Others, such as Len Tyrer, Frank Doran and Bert Herrity continue to sit in the chamber. But for the most part, the Liberals who swooped into office in 1973 were a politically amorphous bunch who seemed to come and go without leaving much of note. It is very hard to identify what linked them together. They were often, to usurp a more recent term, 'yuppies' – bright, young, but not necessarily high-flying teachers, lawyers and office managers, with a sprinkling of neo-Poujadists. A few of them would perhaps feel at home in 'New Labour' today, but in the context of the early 1970s, their rally to the Liberal cause was a reaction to an increasingly workerist Labour Party.

Following their success, there was an interim period in which the Liberals spent twelve months shadowing the old Labour-led council. This was a time for setting up new systems of governance and appointing the officers to administer them, and although an element of political mischief perhaps could have been expected during the hand-over, none of those interviewed recalled anything of substance. It was time for change, and councillors took their responsibilities for a successful transformation seriously. Unfortunately for Liverpool, this was not to last.

During the 1973 elections, and their year as the shadow administration, the Liberals managed to present themselves as a unified force. Once in office, however, they proved themselves to be as fissiparous and as prone to schism as the Labour Party. As with Labour, this had more to do with personalities than substantive issues, and a series of arguments between the leader, Carr, and his deputy, Jones, accentuated by the Hefferon affair, led to Jones's resignation and move to the back benches. After this, their fellow Liberals became referred to as members of the 'Carr group' and the 'Jones group', and their priority became how well the divisions could be disguised. This would have been difficult enough if the group had been a conventional political party. It was made even more troublesome, however, by the fact that one of the leading 'Liberals' in the chamber was the deselected Labour councillor and former blue-eyed boy of the Braddocks, Bill Smythe.

Smythe, as we have seen, had failed to secure the Labour nomination in Everton, the ward that he had represented for nearly twenty years. With his ambitions set on a career outside municipal politics, he had opted not to stand elsewhere in the city – but then Cyril Carr, who was also his solicitor, approached him:

> He said: 'Can you do me a favour – will you let your name go forward as a Liberal?' Now I told him to get lost but he persisted and said: 'Look Bill, I'm looking for a candidate to stand in Childwall. There's no chance of you winning Childwall. Nobody's going to elect an ex-Labour councillor in Childwall. I only want you as a paper name.' So, after a lot of persuasion, I said: 'Go on, but by God I'll suffer for this.' I took no part in anything – I was still a member of the Labour Party – but I was elected. I got four thousand votes in Childwall!

Strange as it may seem, a Labour Party member standing as a Liberal was elected in a ward that had traditionally voted Conservative. What was even more bizarre was that, for the duration of the 'shadow' year, Smythe continued to sit on the Labour benches, and he did so without too much discomfort. In time, however, things went from the sublime to the ridiculous. Jones resigned as the Liberal group's deputy leader, and his place was taken, on Carr's recommendation, by Smythe. A couple of months later, Carr suffered a series of setbacks to his health, and Smythe – still a member of the Labour Party – became both acting leader of the Liberal group and of the city council.

During this time, Jones (who had since become the Liberal Party's national president) began pushing for Carr to retire from the council, an action that would have forced a contest to elect a new Liberal leader. Carr initially refused, but in November 1975 he suffered a further heart attack and decided to stand down as leader, although he retained his seat on the council. Soon after hearing of this, Smythe was approached by Alfred Stocks, the council's Town Clerk, who informed him that a contest would take place but, with Carr still on the council, it would be for the leadership of the city, not the party:

Stocks said: 'I'll tell you now – I've been told this: there's only fourteen Tories in and they and the Labour Party have both said that, if there's an
election of the leader of the council, they're going to vote for you and not
for Jones. It doesn't matter what the Liberals do.'

Indeed it did not. Half the Liberals did vote against Smythe, but the sum of
the cross-party anti-Jones vote ensured his victory. Even so, the divisions
this caused amongst the Liberals were to have severe repercussions. Early
in 1976, Smythe was again approached by Stocks who, with a couple of the
other officers, drew his attention to the fact that two of the three Childwall
seats had easily been returned to the Conservatives in 1975, and that it was
highly likely that, come the May elections, he would lose his too. Shortly afterwards, Smythe was nominated for the more winnable seat of Broadgreen.
Even so, such marginals were drifting back into the Tory fold and, perhaps
accentuated by his profile as leader of the council, he was narrowly defeated.
Still, Smythe is firm in apportioning the blame for the outcome:

Apart from Rosemary Cooper, I got no help from the Liberals. I got no help
from Rodney Johnston, who was the other councillor in Broadgreen, and
Trevor [Jones] did everything possible to make sure that I got beat.

In losing three seats overall, the Liberals became the second largest party.
Jones's main obstacle to the leadership of the group was removed, yet power
continued to elude him as Labour took control of the city. Furthermore,
Rodney Johnston lost his own seat as well as his place on the county council
at the next two elections. Smythe left municipal politics and, soon after, resigned from the Labour Party – an action he claims to have taken in the
name of academic objectivity, as he finally realised his ambition to become a
lecturer. Within two years, however, he was flirting once more with party
politics, albeit of a quasi-separatist nature, writing to the *Liverpool Echo*
welcoming the emergence of 'a new Liverpool Party with no national dogma
to follow and with only one basic platform, to get Liverpool moving forward
once again'.[26] When he retired from teaching in the early 1990s, Smythe rejoined Labour and within a few years was secretary of his ward party.

Throughout and beyond the Liberals' leadership shenanigans, the boiler of
activities that had brought them into office was kept well and truly stoked.
Some people had been given the impression that the tactics employed in
their *Focus* newsletters would change or calm down once they assumed
control. This was a misapprehension; keen to keep pavement politics as

the basis of their governance, the Liberals recognised that they needed to maintain campaigning momentum. Lacking in both ideology and substance (a charge that would be later levelled at modernisers within the Labour Party), propaganda became all. For Paul Orr:

> Pavement politics? It was gutter politics. After circulating all of these faults that the Labour Party were allegedly taking no notice of, when they took power they began drawing people's attention to: 'Here's what *we've* done.' And what had they done? They'd put up a new gutter or some bloody thing.

The Liberals were mischievous in the extreme. On one occasion during a council election, they distributed a leaflet on housing conditions on a particular estate in the Low Hill & Smithdown ward, informing people of the best ways in which to protest. Yet one of their sitting councillors in the ward, David Alton, was also the chair of the Housing Committee.

Bill Snell recalls his own experience of the Liberal machine:

> My wife was forever complaining that parts of the wall either side of our terraced house were falling down. During the war, a bomb had landed around there, affecting two houses in the middle of a line of streets right through the area. Anyway, after the corporation had re-housed us, the Liberals put an election leaflet out: 'People wait forever but Bill Snell was moved to a lovely house with a garden back and front.' So I went to the Housing Committee and I took Alton on, and he admitted that there'd been no political interference. Give Alton his due because he apologised for the work of those who had sent the leaflet out. But that's how the Liberals worked.

The Liberals behaved more like a glorified tenants' association than a serious political party, and the support that they mustered in the local elections was not repeated in general elections. As one academic noted: 'Merseyside, once the great hope of "New Liberalism", slipped back in October 1974 to become one of the Party's weakest areas ... In Liverpool, despite a local power base, there were lost deposits in six out of eight seats; the average Liberal vote, at 12.7 per cent, was lower than that in any other English or Welsh city.'[27]

In terms of their 'policies', the Liberal administration perpetuated a long tradition in Liverpool of politics revolving around housing issues. Having come to office via the collected debris of the clearance schemes and the Housing Finance Act, they found their niche in the form of the 1974 Housing Act, the essence of which was that 'urban renewal and slum clearance were out, rehabilitation was in. And government money was available to pay for it'.[28] This was manna to the Liberals, who used it to their political advantage. Embarking on a widespread 'build for sale' programme, via the medium of housing associations they ploughed money into areas of the city where their vote was already established or had the potential to be.[29] They neglected the public sector, in which the majority of Liverpool's population continued to live, and continued to increase council rents at the same time as they were running down services in order to subsidise the business rate and secure the *petit-bourgeois* vote. For Bob Wareing, the consequences of this were manifest:

> That grouping did a lot to damage the city. For example, they were building houses for sale in the mid-1970s when there were 29,000 unmet housing needs. They were Thatcherite before Thatcher, if you like. Also, they reduced the rates at a time when inflation, following the oil crisis, was up to 27 per cent. They could only reduce the rates by cutting services, which is what they did. And the budget figures of those Liberal years were used by the Conservative government to determine the Standard Spending Assessment.

In the latter part of the decade, this coalition of Liberal votes and Conservative substance began to take other forms – between 1976 and 1978, in their mutual opposition to Labour's efforts at running a minority administration, and following the 1978 local elections, when the Labour group, despite continuing to have the largest presence, refused to take office out of sheer frustration with its prior experience. Conservative support allowed the Liberals to take control of all of the major committees and, ultimately, the council.

A year later, with Labour in the ascendancy, the Conservatives again combined with the Liberals to prevent Labour taking control of the key Policy and Finance Committee. Elsewhere, there was chaos at the Housing Estate Management sub-committee. Ken Stewart nominated the Tory deputy leader, Reg Flude, as chair but the latter refused. Ken then nominated three further Tories, each of whom in turn refused. So Ken nominated the Liberals' Richard Kemp but he also refused, only to then turn around and nominate Ken himself for the position. Naturally, he refused.

Various Tory councillors were often quoted during the period on how they had no need to be in control of Liverpool as the Liberals were doing their job for them. By the end of the decade, Michael Heseltine was commenting that the Liberals' management of financial affairs in Liverpool was a marker to which all local authorities should aspire.

The real Conservative Party, meanwhile, was experiencing a roller-coaster decade. By 1972, at the half-way point of the Heath government's term in office, Liverpool's Tories had seen their core vote in the city first nibbled then gnawed by the Liberals, their presence on the borough council nearly halved, and overall control move back to Labour. Even then, however, they could not imagine the cataclysmic events that were to befall them between spring 1973 and spring 1974, when the combination of Labour opposition to the Housing Finance Act, Heath's unpopularity and the rolling appeal of the Liberal bandwagon saw them well and truly trounced at all elections. April 1973's polls for the new county chamber saw them take a mere four of the thirty-six available seats. A month later, with the Liverpool electorate voting for an entirely new city council, only nine Conservatives were returned. Then to cap it all, at the general election of February 1974, called by Heath in the mistaken belief that the country thought he knew best, Liverpool Garston was lost to Labour, reducing the number of Tory MPs in the city to one, Anthony Steen, in Wavertree.

Following this series of debacles, the Conservative presence in Liverpool did begin to pick up. A by-election victory in St Michael's ward put their city council representation back into double figures by the time the new council had come out of the shadows. Four subsequent years of electoral success gave them some face in a polity of what was essentially three minority parties. Between 1975 and 1978, successes at municipal elections saw the Tory ranks gradually rise to two dozen. Helped initially by the return of disillusioned 'new Liberals' in wards such as Aigburth, Broadgreen and Croxteth, this mini-revival was consolidated with victories in three-way marginals such as Anfield, Tuebrook and Warbreck. At the county council elections in 1977, twenty-three Conservatives were returned, helping ensure their majority in that chamber.[30]

Labour did lose a number of seats to the Tories during the period, but the latter more usually took seats from the Liberals. Closer scrutiny reveals something more telling about the character of the support that the Tories nurtured. In 1978, for example, almost half the Conservative vote was concentrated in six of the city's thirty-three wards.[31] Away from such pockets, the party was in terminal decline, and 1978 also saw it poll fewer than 1500 votes in twenty of the remaining twenty-seven wards. This amounted to a fifth of its overall vote in the city, and less than a quarter of the total turn-out in these areas. The times were long gone when Conservatives could take or retain seats on the back of a working class Protestant vote that was virulently anti-Labour.

The increase in Conservative numbers between 1975 and 1978 was, therefore, not of very great political moment. Former Tory voters, having become sceptical of Liberal pavement politics, briefly returned to a party with no real chance of retaking the council and which, in many ways, was being 'out-Toried' by the Liberals. At the same time, electoral preferences were heavily distorted by wildly fluctuating turn-outs. As the more affluent parts of the city turned out *en masse*, much of Liverpool's working class stayed at home.[32]

In effect, Conservatives in Liverpool were becoming more like Conservatives in the rest of mainland Britain. Once they had prided themselves on a civic independence that looked out to the world (albeit in a manner that was imperialist rather than internationalist) and down on the children of a lesser God – i.e. Catholics. Now, however, they appeared more concerned with the Protestant work ethic of business efficiency and time management; and with the arrival of the party's new national leader, Margaret Thatcher, they found someone who was a living panacea for their gripes in a Britain under Labour. Thatcher's victory on the national stage, however, coincided with another key political development – the arrival of Militant centre-stage at Liverpool Town Hall.

# 3 A creeping presence

The Militant Tendency – or the Revolutionary Socialist League, to give it its proper title – was one of a number of small Trotskyite groups on the fringes of politics. Each group had its own ideological godfather; in the case of Militant, this was Ted Grant, a South African exile who found soulmates in Liverpool, particularly amongst members of the Liverpool Walton Constituency Labour Party.

In its early days, Militant was meant to be a platform for political education within the wider Labour movement, and attracted support amongst left-wing Liverpudlians like George McCartney, Jimmy and Brian Deane, Pat Wall and Laura Kirton. From a slow start in the late 1950s and '60s, it began to recruit supporters nationwide, through trade unions and labour youth organisations. Whilst its headquarters remained in London, its strongest bases were in Liverpool and Brighton. Its tight discipline and excellent organisation enabled it increasingly to fill a gap in Labour politics in the late 1970s and early '80s, as the Labour Party flirted with self-destruction. At the very least, Militant provided a simple and clear analysis of the political condition, together with soundbite solutions, which struck a chord with the young, the idealistic and the naive.[33]

Members of Militant had been visible on Liverpool City Council since the late 1950s and early 1960s, when Brian Deane and Pat Wall were councillors for County ward. In the early 1970s, the torch was held aloft by Ted Mooney, also in County. Nevertheless, Militant as an organisation never aspired to running the council. Such a distraction did not fit within its main agenda of seeking to educate and pressurise the Labour group from behind the scenes. Militant saw itself as a theoretical influence, arguing for a pure socialist society and keeping the party on the correct path towards that nirvana. A city council was merely a capitalist state in its localised form, and should Militant become embroiled in its operation, it rightly perceived that it would be compromised. Nevertheless, in the wake of the Labour leadership dispute of 1978, which I describe in this chapter, Militant targeted Liverpool as a place in which to advance its entryist strategy, taking the decision to elect an increased number of its supporters on to the council.

The rifts within the Labour group caused by the housing finance debacle of 1972 were still apparent the following May after the full elections of the new council. Those that had formed the rebel faction had long since rejoined the rest of the group, but a combination of the end of the aldermanic system, the machinations of the selection processes, and the failure of less 'left-wing' candidates to win wards captured by the Liberals meant that the overall political character of the group had changed. Nevertheless, in electing a new leader to replace Bill Sefton, existing allegiances, affected partly by personal grievances, were once more reflected in John Hamilton's one-vote defeat of Eddie Loyden.

Loyden had been selected as the party's prospective MP for the then Labour–Tory marginal of Garston, and many who would have otherwise been sympathetic to his leadership may have considered it pointless electing him for the short period before the next general election. Consequently, Hamilton's 'dual credibility' – on the one hand, a member of the 'twenty-one' and on the other, not Loyden – allowed him to gain a spectrum of support that was to persist for some time, as John is keen to point out:

> It wasn't really a split, as both left-wing and right-wing people voted for me. That's how it was in those days. We were very evenly balanced and, in one sense, over those years I had a good passage because the group was a good group. It wasn't difficult to run and with it being evenly balanced, no side pushed the other, and they almost looked upon me as the straight guy in the middle – honest John. Both sides eventually realised that they could trust me.

That Hamilton believes this perhaps says more about the man than the moment. Tensions within the group subsided slightly once the politics of mid-seventies Liverpool changed the nature of the chamber from one of clear working majorities to a numbers game, and a unity of sorts was created around common bemusement with the Liberals' attempts to administer their pavement politics. Significantly, however, nearly half of the Labour group had voted against Hamilton in the leadership contest, and after his election, the opposition and their supporters began to direct their energies elsewhere. Where this became most evident was in the borough party, formally renamed the Liverpool District Labour Party in 1975.

Developments within this body were to prove the key to how Labour politics in early 1980s' Liverpool came to be orchestrated by Militant. For much of the 1970s, however, alliances struggled to capture the position of chair/president as a means to control discussion, reflecting an obsession with dialectics as the key to political power. Having held the position during the turbulence around the Housing Finance Act, Bob Wareing lost out in 1973 before taking hold again the following year by a single vote. Two years later, in 1976, the initial slate had Wareing up against his two vice-chairs, Stan Maddox and known Militant Tony Mulhearn, and Wareing only held on to the post because Mulhearn stood down to ensure the defeat of Maddox, viewed as a classic 'right winger' by Militant. That another challenge was not made by Mulhearn until the early 1980s has been interpreted hyperbolically by Wareing:

> Although it was a longer period of time than the February to October [1917] revolutions in Petrograd, they saw me as a Kerensky figure to Mulhearn's Lenin, overseeing a provisional government that lasted from 1974 to 1981.

At the time, Wareing did not consider himself a Militant proxy, regarding himself as 'dispassionate':

> I would get Tony Mulhearn saying: 'You allow Eddie Roderick and people like him far more time to speak than they should have'. In fact I was just being reasonable.

Bill Snell, however, who held the chair from 1973 to 1974, but who came to the DLP more regularly as a trade union delegate for USDAW, was not impressed by Wareing's style:

> Whenever I put my hand up, he'd ignore me. He'd say 'I'll take two more speakers', and I would say that I'd my hand up, to which he'd reply: 'I decide who's going to speak'. That was his way.

This was typical of the partisan way in which meetings were chaired at all levels. Militant, however, refined this *modus operandi*. Speakers would be decided upon and primed before a given meeting, and with a Militant in the chair and carefully orchestrated speakers, there was little chance of a balanced debate whenever they had the numbers to dictate the conduct of a meeting. Yet this was only a success because of the wholly partisan and anti-democratic way in which party meetings had been traditionally run in

Liverpool. There were, of course, honourable exceptions, but the DLP was not one of them. It could not be, in the eyes of the main antagonists – it was the key to their respective ambitions.

As the DLP became more active, it started to assert itself upon the council Labour group. Some of the more established councillors, however, saw themselves as immune to such authority. Ian Lowes, later to be leader of the Praetorian Guard of the council workforce, GMB Branch 5, recalls how they used an argument similar to MPs who cross the floor of the Commons:

> They were so arrogant because they thought that people had elected them as individuals: 'They voted for me, not because I was a Labour candidate but because I'm "Jim Jones".'

Lowes also recalls how some of the old guard resented both the nature of the changes that were occurring and the new people who were propagating them:

> They'd never been called to account. They'd never been asked to explain why they'd voted for this or done that. A lot of them were older, and if younger people were coming into the party, they would insult them by saying: 'You've only been here five minutes, I've been in the party for thirty-five years and a councillor for twenty-nine. So what right have you got to tell me what to do?'

The Labour group held on to its autonomy for some time. Following the 1976 local elections, Liberal losses to the Tories left Labour with the largest presence on the council for the first time since the reorganisation of local government. Although aware that the opposition parties would combine to make life difficult, the Labour group opted to take minority control, a move that did not go down well at the DLP. Shortly afterwards, a motion from Low Hill & Smithdown ward party expressed 'deep concern' with the decision, observing that the numbers game in the chamber would inevitably lead to the endorsement of Conservative and Liberal policies.[34] In an attempt to temper such criticism, the executive committee unsuccessfully proposed an amendment adding the clause 'unless the group uses the advantages of political power', which Mulhearn, a committee member, was given leave to oppose. The original motion carried, but the decision had no immediate effect upon the Labour group, which in turn voted to carry on as a minority administration.

Seven months later, in March 1977, a further call for the group to stand down from minority rule was put to the DLP by the Wavertree constituency party.[35] Although the executive voted to oppose it, the number asking for leave to speak against the decision not only included Mulhearn again but three new members of the committee, Josie Aitman, Terry Harrison and Derek Hatton (the Wavertree delegate), all of whom were heavily associated with the Militant line. As the Labour group struggled to win votes for its policies in the council chamber, it was becoming more and more apparent that Militant was playing its own numbers game elsewhere in the city.

In fact, 1977 was a key year in Militant's moves to capture both the agenda and the direction of the Liverpool party. In February, support was given to another resolution proposed by Wavertree CLP condemning the national leadership's 'interference' in delaying the appointment of the Militant Andy Bevan as the Labour Party National Youth Officer.[36] More significantly, an executive committee motion (forwarded without 'leave to oppose' by any of those present) was carried at the same meeting deploring the decision of the party's National Executive Committee to set up an investigation into charges of infiltration by 'supporters of the marxist [sic] paper Militant'.[37] In elaborating, the motion emphasised that such an investigation would amount to a 'McCarthyite exercise' and posed 'a threat to the basic democratic traditions of the Labour movement'. To paraphrase the American socio-linguist Noam Chomsky, control over the meaning of language ultimately means control over everything.

As the year went on, debates at both the full DLP and the executive committee became increasingly oriented towards Militant's concerns. By December, with a firemen's strike in full flow on Merseyside, Terry Fields, a local Militant who would later become MP for Liverpool Broadgreen, spoke to the DLP in his capacity as the Regional Secretary of the Fire Brigades Union.[38] Interestingly, and predictably, his words of wisdom and a comradely collection were followed by the election of Mulhearn, Hatton and 'the trade union representatives' to a Firemen's Solidarity Committee.

The increased activity of Militant in Labour Party circles reflected changes in the nature of party meetings. In the early 1970s, city-wide meetings of the party were not overly boisterous affairs, and with the exception of those surrounding the implementation of the Housing Finance Act, they were mostly in keeping with the character of Liverpool politics – often inquorate, always verbose and vitriolic, but never violent. In fact, it was not uncommon for those who opposed each other politically to be seen socialising together immediately afterwards. Alas, by the end of the decade, the divisions at the

DLP had become more entrenched, and the atmosphere had become both petty and nasty, as Wally Edwards explains:

> On one occasion, I can remember looking out from the top table and there was a bloody big gang on one side – sat on the left, of course – and Eddie Roderick and one other on the other side. That was the way it was. Nobody would move over, nobody would make it all nice and central. *They* tended to punch Eddie about, but he wasn't slow to respond as he was a pretty physical lad himself. So there were some punch-ups. Never at the meetings though; it was always afterwards, and prompted by cat-calling: 'You right-wing so and so', that sort of thing.

Bill Snell, another of the 'right-wingers', paints a similar picture:

> There were scuffles, but who's going to hit Paul Orr? I was always with him and I don't think there was ever much likelihood of me getting hit either. Who'd hit Eddie Roderick? The daft thing was that the name Roderick was synonymous with boxing, so people thought he was one of them.

The political life of Eddie Roderick, who bore the brunt of much of the abuse, reads like a script from *Our Friends in the North*. For much of his time on the council, he represented Gillmoss ward, where he had his business interests. Having been a close associate of Braddock when he was leader of the council, Roderick became an ally of Braddock's successor and former rival Sefton, and was chair of the Planning Committee when accusations of backhanders were made regarding planning applications for garages. Others on the committee were prosecuted and sent to prison, but Roderick was eventually cleared. In Gillmoss, his control over the Labour club meant that virtually anything he said in the ward went. Any doubts that people may have had about this soon disappeared when, having voted in favour of the Housing Finance Act, he survived the pre-1973 reselection process in an area with one of the largest council estates in Britain and the city's most active tenants' association. As John Hamilton observes, the tale of how Roderick managed this has taken on a life of its own:

> He was a bit of a thug. You had to be, to get in in Gillmoss. There were all sorts of things said about him in that area: that he was a bit of a tough boy, a bit of a political mafia-like character who engaged in boss politics, and that he had a lot of people to whom he gave credit in his shop from whom he got political support.

That there are elements of both truth and conjecture in this perhaps indicates Roderick's significance to Liverpool's politics; as will become clear, he was still there come the mid 1980s. What Roderick is most remembered for, however, is his role in the spring of 1978, following the local elections, when the municipal equivalent of a *coup d'état* occurred at the Labour group's annual meeting. Dismayed with the apparent failure of John Hamilton to assert his leadership, Bill Snell orchestrated a mixed bag of councillors to vote by twenty-one to sixteen to supplant him with Roderick:

> We'd been working on it for a long time because I'll always believe the saying that 'teachers are giants among children and children amongst men', and Hamilton was. We were dissatisfied with the leadership, let's put it that way. I mean the biggest tragedy that happened to this city was losing Bill Sefton, because he was a leader who everybody would follow. He could argue his corner and he wouldn't back down, and he wouldn't trim things either. Whereas if you said anything to Hamilton, it was 'Oh, all right, we'll go that way', which just got bloody awkward in the end.

For Hamilton, the decision to replace him was 'absolutely stupid', and he is equally scathing of Snell:

> A real bonehead of a fellow. He manipulated it all, and was the Lady Macbeth who put the dagger in Roderick's hand. He had a way about him which you soon recognised. He would go snivelling around and was the sort of person who you realised that you couldn't trust. He came across as very bitter, and appeared to speak with a snarl.

On the day of the group meeting, Snell, having done his homework, did the rounds, gathering the support not only of Roderick's followers but of other, more unlikely, bedfellows:

> I said to Ken Stewart: 'You will still be chair of Housing', and he said 'fair enough' – although he wasn't entirely happy with the decision because the likes of him could go in and twist Hamilton to alter things.

Somewhat surprisingly, Liverpool's political grapevine did not get word back to Hamilton about what was going on, and by the evening, events within the Municipal Annexe and across the road in The Vernon Arms pub – the councillors' local – began to take their course, as Hamilton recalls:

> I couldn't make out why Snell was going around. He came into my office and asked: 'When exactly is the group meeting?' I didn't realise the

significance of it at the time, but come the meeting I noticed that Snell was checking off people coming in. Roderick's side were fully in attendance by 7.30, but our side hadn't been whipped in, and there were one or two of them who had called into the pub and who were finishing their drinks off. Straight away at 7.30, Snell said 'We ought to begin the meeting'. Well, myself and some of my side could see what was happening, and a couple of people rushed over to the pub to get the others in. Of course, there was a snap vote and Roderick won the leadership.

Naturally, this interpretation has been questioned by Snell:

> It was a legitimate vote. The figures prove this. It was a normal annual meeting, and the rules are quite clear on this. All you do is read the minutes of the previous annual meeting, which no-one ever challenges because they are twelve months old, and then you move on to the business. So that's a load of hooey. It's true that I gave a sheet to everyone who came in telling them who to vote for, and we won it that way. Stan Maddox, who was Mr Standing Orders, and who would pull you up if you ever went against standing orders, said 'I don't agree with this, Bill', but then acknowledged that it had all been done properly.

Maddox confirms this, and reveals the actions he took later that evening to keep the group together:

> I took John home with me, and because I was determined to keep building bridges between the two sections, I got on the phone to Bill Snell and Eddie Roderick. I was trying to get them to back off.

In the meantime, accounts began to spread quickly and the DLP's rapid response team – a.k.a. Bob Wareing – was sent to adjudicate:

> I heard the news at the old Wavertree Labour Club on Picton Road, when somebody came in and said 'Have you heard what's happened?' I was astounded. All that weekend, people were ringing me up saying 'You've got to do or say something about this'. I went on Radio City. People were saying 'It's best if you head the protest because you're not a councillor and you haven't got an axe to grind'.

On 11 May 1978, a special meeting of the DLP, which many recall as being packed to the rafters, voted by a huge margin to reinstate Hamilton, who had taken the defeat so badly that he was on leave of absence from the school in Kirkby at which he taught. The following day, a gathering of the

Labour group also saw a vote in Hamilton's favour, as a number of councillors switched their support. (Those attending this supposed 'secret meeting' were greeted by 'residents' of Roderick's ward demonstrating against his appointment.) Nevertheless, Roderick stayed in place because it was up to him as leader to notify the Town Clerk of any change – he later told Michael Crick that he had stayed put in the belief that Militant were behind the pro-Hamilton campaign.[39] By June, however, with the pressure intensifying, Roderick was approached by Wally Edwards, who despite their political differences was a close friend:

> I had a good talk to him about what damage it was doing to the party, and he very quickly withdrew.

Less than three weeks after the coup, John Hamilton was reinstated as leader of the Labour group, unaware that he would soon preside over the most bitter period of politics in Liverpool's history. Given the events that followed, some of those who were instrumental in Hamilton's reinstatement later came to regret their actions. For Stan Maddox:

> John didn't have the strength to impose his decency upon the group. If a group leadership could have been built that would have given him the backbone, it may have prevented Militant coming in. It was a defining moment and I think I was wrong to try and get it reversed. So on reflection I think I may have been wrong.

Likewise, for Bob Wareing:

> I hate to say this, because John Hamilton is a very genuine person and I like him very much, but I can't help thinking some times that if Eddie had stayed leader it might have kept Militant at bay.

Even Hamilton himself observes that the overturning of the coup both paved the way for supporters of Militant and gave them an added incentive to act:

> Their argument was that the DLP should be constituted, should have a say in the leadership because we're not going to have somebody manoeuvring behind the scenes without consulting the party generally. It really opened the field to the Militants, and from then on they not only moved into the DLP but they decided to also move into the group.

At the local elections of 1979, a handful of Militant supporters were elected to sit on the Labour benches. They included Pauline Dunlop in County ward and Julie Lyon Taylor in Arundel, as well as Derek Hatton in Woolton East. Eddie Sabino, a well-known figure in the Liverpool Labour movement, recalls meeting Hatton for the first time at Woolton Labour Club on the night he was elected:

> Derek comes waltzing in, not a hair out of place, absolutely immaculate. I'd been out on the knocker since six o'clock in the morning and I was absolutely drained, a complete and utter shambles. Derek rolls in in a pinstripe three-piece suit, a huge rosette and his hair all coiffured up, and I thought 'Jesus Christ, I don't think I'm going to like Derek'. He seemed to give the wrong image.

Even then, Hatton was an inflated product of his own vivid imagination. In July 1977, he submitted a written application to become a councillor. Firstly, he informed the selection panel that he had been a member of the Labour Party for five years, when in fact he had only joined in the summer of 1974, a fact revealed in his own book.[40] Secondly, he claimed to have been active on the Sheffield Trades' Council from 1974 to 1976. Notwithstanding his own revelations that he spent only six months in Sheffield and went to work in Knowsley in 1975,[41] extensive searching of the records and minutes in Sheffield has failed to flag up his name.[42] Likewise, interviews with key Trades' Council figures from the time have also drawn a blank. Hatton's inattention to personal detail would become increasingly evident at the time of his expulsion from the Labour Party, when he claimed that he had been a member for fifteen years.

In most other political contexts, the presence of such a small number of individuals would amount to little more than an irritating faction or pressure group, but the ineffectiveness of much of the rest of the Labour group exaggerated Militant's strength. More crucially, there was no real or potential city boss, as such, who could resist or contain their excesses. A month before the Roderick coup, Bill Sefton, at Prime Minister Jim Callaghan's request, had made the transition from Merseyside County Council to the House of Lords, and from the local political scene went one of the few people who realised that Militant needed careful but forthright handling:

> They had to be occasionally kicked in the teeth by standing up in the group and saying 'that's bloody nonsense', or by mentioning to some of them 'if you don't shut up, I'm prepared to say so and so' – all that kind of thing. It was personal relations which you just had to handle. Unfortunately, John Hamilton, with his Quaker background, had an undying

belief in real democracy such as asking the group everything, forgetting that the people who really did control the group were determined to have their own way. All of that led to Militant which was a very, very sad story, but I don't know what would have happened if I'd attempted to get back. Well, it would have been resented. So, I just faced up to the fact that in the end there was nothing I could do about it.

By raising its profile within the local party, Militant began to establish a base amongst the Liverpool membership, particularly with the young. For Ian Lowes:

> People came into the Labour Party in that period not because of the Tendency as such – it was going to happen anyway – but the Tendency were able to capitalise on that. The new people who had joined the party would go to meetings and be impressed by what was said by the leading lights in the Tendency.

As the disillusionment of Labour voters in mid-seventies' Liverpool led to a series of abysmal turn-outs for the party at local elections, the nature of the membership was indeed becoming more radical. Some of those who joined came from tenants' associations or single-issue organisations that had established a base in one community or other. Where such individuals became councillors, they had ready-made links with the people they were representing. Even so, and despite his observation of Militant's strategy and tactics, Lowes is wary of the suggestion that there was a blueprint:

> Some say that there was this wonderful plot by the Tendency to go out and get people to join the Labour Party in order to take it over. Well it wasn't like that. People came to independent conclusions. They thought that the Labour Party was the party of working people and that the only way you were going to change it was from the inside.

Similarly, Stan Thorne, the former city councillor who by the late 1970s was MP for Preston, but who was still resident in Liverpool, questions the notion of a master-plan:

> By and large, in the overall campaign in Liverpool, I don't think that there was any behind-the-scenes boss who controlled everything that went on.

For some, it was the indifference of those in official positions that was culpable.

Wally Edwards, the then Secretary of the DLP, has been accused of smoothing Militant's position in Liverpool by acting as the main distributor for its weekly newspaper:

> It used to be sent to the DLP office, and from there it went out. He would never admit it, but Wally was very much with them on a lot of the things they did. He did his share.

Wally denies this, and elaborates upon the particular difficulties he faced:

> I was aware that Militant's activity was increasing and I did my utmost to control it, but the truth about it was that quite a few of them were long and established members of the Labour Party – the likes of Terry Harrison and Tony Mulhearn. These were the ones who, when I was asked about them, I said that they were not Johnny-come-latelies and that they had been active in the party for some years. You can only tell the truth about people as you see it. But there were many others who had been recruited for a purpose.

It was always the case that DLP (and Trades' Council) mailings included mail, where possible, on behalf of 'fraternal' organisations. In this way, Militant circulars about events and rallies were sent on to a wider audience. Sometimes Militant members would help with the stuffing of the envelopes.

In time, it became difficult to stem the tide, and established members of the party started to fade from the scene. For the most part, these individuals were older 'right-wing' councillors who, having long presided over rotten ward parties, found themselves being edged out by the new recruits and their older gurus. Others, however, from the left of the party, such as Cyril Taylor, also found the hassle they were receiving outweighed their desire to remain involved:

> The behaviour and the undisguised ruthlessness of some of the adherents to the Militant line was absolutely objectionable. It was also, perhaps, one of the reasons why I decided to drop off the council.

One of the routine ways in which Militant began to take hold was through keeping meetings going. As 'Mr Standing Orders' Stan Maddox recalls, there were ways and means to combat such tactics but Militant's persistence eventually wore out sections of the membership:

> You had to be quite ruthless about how you operated, but people gave up going to meetings because they couldn't stand it. The Militants were so

petty, and you'd find that you weren't making decisions but going on and on and on.

Generally, Militant took over wards where the party had previously been in the control of a few individuals, something that would usually involve little more than the brisk arrival of half a dozen new members. In places where the elected officers appeared better organised, attempts would be made to invite guests along. Elsewhere, members of Militant had to dig in for a while, operating on the basis of attending and participating but not making apparent their true ambitions until they were confident of support from non-Militant 'comrades'. Although some of the wider membership saw through such façades, most of the people attending ward meetings were oblivious to what was happening.

Others noticed the creeping influence of Militant in the trade union movement, as Wally Edwards, a member of TGWU Branch 522, recalls:

> This developed quite suddenly with the membership of a number of social workers and the like. We used to call it 'the Muppets branch'. It became the ACTTS branch. A few years earlier, you almost had to volunteer for representation on the area and district committees. There was never any competition and consequently they were always looking for people to fill vacancies. With a few years of the Tendency, this stopped being the case and everyone had to battle for their position.

For Militant, holding these posts was important, for it was through the affiliation of such union branches that they increased their numerical presence on the DLP. Both the run-up to the local elections in 1979 and their aftermath smacked of Militant's quest for power, and echoed in particular with the noise of a certain individual. At the annual general meeting of the DLP in March, a motion from Childwall ward party regarding the issue of a wages and price freeze was passed including the following prose – the author will be instantly recognisable to anyone who has heard Cllr Derek Hatton speak in public: 'We declare that cries for a wage freeze by so-called representatives of the Labour movement reflect the demands of the CBI, the Tories and the hysterical bosses' press ...'.[43] At the following month's executive committee, Wavertree CLP submitted six motions, two relating to the continuing dispute surrounding the role of the party's National Youth Officer, an established member of Militant.[44]

Shortly after the elections, an emergency resolution was moved by Hatton and Mulhearn at the DLP, in which the Labour group's minority rule on the council was accepted in principle but with a number of provisos. These included an assurance of 'a clear majority on all committees'; an approach to the task 'with full DLP policy for all the important issues' and a commitment to resign if defeated 'on a major question of policy'; and the establishment of a trade union coordinating committee consisting of delegates from the DLP, the group and local authority trade unions 'to work out plans to fight the now imminent threat of massive cutbacks in public expenditure'.[45] While an amendment from Laura Kirton of Walton tempered the tone of much of the motion, the final clause was carried as read, thus establishing the Joint Shop Stewards' Committee. Within a few years, this body was to have an armlock on any attempt to reform council services.

Another factor in Militant's successes in Liverpool at this time was the character and quality of the city's Labour MPs – 'left', 'right' and, in the case of Bob Parry, it was joked, 'who knows where?' On the left, those such as Eddie Loyden and Eric Heffer have been identified by their opponents as virtual quislings in facilitating Militant's advance. Bill Snell, for example, has commented on Loyden's presence on the fringes of Militant:

> Eddie Roderick once told me of a terrible row that took place within the division [constituency party] when they asked who really belonged to Militant. Loyden denied it and some other feller stood up and said: 'You're a bloody liar, you've worked with me all through it'. Three of them walked out and were banned from the division but Loyden stayed, and lost a lot of credence as a result. He talked them round afterwards when he argued that it was better to have someone in power – the clever bugger.

John Hamilton has noted how Loyden 'double-crossed' people, recalling one incident from a DLP meeting in the late 1970s when Labour were in government nationally, and Loyden was on the Commons committee that examined a housing bill line by line:

> I was giving a report as leader of the council and, from the back of the room, Loyden demanded that we should oppose the bill. I pointed out that it was not easy for us to oppose a Labour government at the time when it had a very slim majority, even if we disagreed with what they were doing. Loyden was shouting that we should have protests and demonstrations, so I turned to him and said: 'You were in the House and voted line by line for this. You never once voted against it. You never even spoke against it. You were on the committee and you carried it

through, and now you're telling me to do what you didn't have the courage to do.'

And then there was Eric Heffer, a self-styled Robert Tressell for a latter generation, though not quite the tradesman that he thought he was – Laura Kirton, his long-term agent, would later relate to me how the shelves he put up in her office fell down two days later. Having twitched about between the Labour and Communist parties for a decade and a half, Eric finally settled on changing the system from within. Elected in Pirrie ward as a councillor in 1960, he soon made his mark with the establishment of the Direct Works Organisation, which sought to secure the employment rights of council workers, ensuring that the producers' interests, no matter how venial, were to supersede those of the rest of the citizenry. Yet Heffer had another side to his character; Bill Snell accuses him of pretentiousness:

> I had to laugh at Eric. He was a real Labour man, solid working class, but he was on the Libraries and Arts Committee, and I remember him standing in front of a painting with his thumb stuck out in front of him going 'You can see the depth'. I said: 'What the bloody hell are you doing? You don't know anything about art', and he said 'Oh, you learn, you know, on this committee about the depth and things like that.'

Four years after his arrival on the council, Heffer was selected, somewhat surprisingly, over Hugh Dalton, to contest the then Conservative seat of Liverpool Walton, and at the 1964 general election he successfully overturned the majority of Tory knight Kenneth Thompson with a massive swing of 16.2 per cent. It was a seat that he would hold until his death.

Ever the internationalist, Heffer had long instigated debates on global affairs, and the trade union branch which he represented in Liverpool would always have a resolution on the agenda regarding the political situation in other countries. He could number amongst his friends Pietro Nenni, the leader of the Italian Socialist Party, and Salvador Allende, the Chilean Marxist whose left reformist government was ousted, and he himself murdered, in a CIA-sponsored coup that brought General Pinochet to power. In affairs closer to home, however, Eric took his eye off the ball, and by the late 1970s had allowed himself to be distracted by the ragged-trousered appeal of Militant, and a personal desire to be the leader of the parliamentary road to socialism. Bill Sefton, who by this time had gone to the Lords, ostensibly as Callaghan's 'Minister for Merseyside', recalls the row he had with Heffer over a dispute surrounding the Mersey Railway Tunnel:

> I wanted it finished before the next election and it wasn't going at all well. I had a meeting with all of the strikers, one of whom was being encouraged by Eric Heffer ... He was in the Central Lobby, throwing himself about, and I went over and said quietly: 'I don't interfere with anything you do down here in the House, so you stop interfering with anything I'm doing in Liverpool'. He brought himself up to this great majestic state and said 'Who do you think you're talking to?', and I said 'I'm talking to Eric Heffer'. Then he said, 'I'm not having you talking to me like that, I'm a parliamentarian'. The whole place went quiet. So I just turned my back and said as loud as I possibly could: 'Oh Christ, he says he's a bloody parliamentarian'.

Amongst the 'right-wingers', Richard Crawshaw, Jimmy Dunn and Eric Ogden, all of whom had beaten Conservative incumbents on becoming MPs in 1964, showed little concern for what was happening locally. Later, they were to join the SDP. But in the struggles of the 1970s, their disinterest amounted to a form of political agnosticism. Still, at least they had the decency to attend to some degree to their respective constituencies' business, something that could certainly not be said about the infamous and ineffectual MP for Liverpool Edge Hill, Arthur Irvine. A hangover from an earlier age, who would say to Bob Wareing, 'call me AJ, dear boy', he is remembered with contempt by Cyril Taylor as 'a bloody great aristocrat who deigned to come and stay in the Adelphi one weekend a month'. My own correspondence to Irvine was always to his Cheyne Walk address in Chelsea; his infrequent replies would begin with a characteristically pompous: 'Dear Kilfoyle'.

Born in Scotland, Irvine had been involved in the legal side of the army as an Advocate General. He stood as a Liberal in Dundee at the 1945 general election, but soon after joined the Labour Party. With Attlee personally keen on getting him in Parliament, Irvine was thrust upon Liverpool in a by-election prompted by the suicide of the sitting MP, Richard Clitherow, in 1947. Although the Conservatives shaved two-thirds off the majority, Irvine took the seat and successfully defended it on nine occasions (twice against a young Michael Howard) before his sudden death in office in December 1978. Under Wilson in the late 1960s, Irvine was made Solicitor-General and, expecting a huge increase in workload, forewarned his local party that this would impose on the time he could spend in the constituency. Yet on the occasions when he did return to Liverpool, he cut a rather bland and patronising figure. In the words of John Hamilton:

> You could write his speeches out before he'd even spoken. He would get

up and start: 'Now my good friends of Edge Hill, we've had a very difficult time. The government has got some very difficult problems to face,
financial problems – but we are doing our best and it's people like you,
the good friends of Edge Hill, that are supporting us and making it all
worth fighting for.'

When Labour lost power in 1970, Irvine failed to restore his local role, and
his relationship with the constituency gradually worsened as he began to
spend more and more time at his London law firm.

The constituency secretary in Edge Hill in the late 1970s was John
Sharpey-Shafer. A lecturer in nuclear physics at Liverpool University, his
professional attitude to the task allowed him to rein in Irvine for a while,
until the latter reacted by cancelling some of his monthly surgeries. That he
was perhaps attending to the needs of his electors whilst at Westminster
was also disproven; John Hamilton has recalled the occasion when Irvine
was asked his feelings towards a particular bill:

> Having replied that he had been in favour of it and had therefore voted ac-
> cordingly, someone commented: 'Well, I've got Hansard and it doesn't
> show you voted for it because you weren't in the House that day'. Poor old
> Irvine was flattened. He just couldn't explain it.

More crucially, Irvine failed to grasp the significance of the inroads being
made by the Liberal Party into the constituency throughout the 1970s. This
was more than evident at one public meeting Bob Wareing attended, where
most of those attending expected Irvine to criticise Liberal promises about
housing repairs. Instead,

> He gave a speech directed against the worst aspects of the Liberal Party
> at the beginning of the century, which just went over the heads of a lot of
> people.

In 1977, following various attempts to oust him, including two deselections
that were overturned because of technical irregularities, Irvine failed to be
short-listed, and would have been without a seat at the following general
election had he not died first. (Members of his family blamed elements
within the Edge Hill Labour Party for bringing on his illness.) In the subsequent by-election, the seat was lost to the Liberal candidate, David Alton on
a 64.9 per cent swing. He ran rings around Labour's Bob Wareing, who had
beaten Frank Field and the Militant Pat Wall to the nomination. Wareing
also stood in Edge Hill at the 1979 general election, which took place six

weeks after the by-election. Although it was not much compensation, he halved Alton's majority.

On the same day, the electorate nationally returned a Conservative government that was to offer no space on its agenda for the entrenched and peculiar problems of Liverpool. Everything held dear in the post-war political consensus was to be challenged by the redoubtable new Prime Minister, Margaret Thatcher, who on arriving at Downing Street began by misquoting St Francis of Assisi. Thatcher was to exhibit a quixotic determination to do battle with many of the orthodoxies of Butskellism, and two of her targets were to have a particular resonance in the unfolding drama in Liverpool – the trade union movement and local government.

The May 1979 election also saw three openly Militant candidates contest parliamentary seats – David White in Croydon Central, Cathy Wilson on the Isle of Wight and Tony Mulhearn at Crosby, north of Liverpool. All three were defeated. The following month, the first elections to the European Parliament saw another prominent Militant, Terry Harrison, fail to take the Liverpool Euro constituency in what should have been an easy victory for Labour but ended up a Tory win.[46] During the second half of 1979, Militant's influence at the Liverpool DLP became increasingly evident. In terms of personnel, new faces on the executive tipped the voting balance in the Trotskyites' favour, and one of the influx, Sylvia Sharpey-Shafer (the Edge Hill constituency delegate and wife of John), took over the key post of Liaison Officer between the DLP and the council Labour group. With regards to the latter, a motion from Low Hill & Smithdown ward, urging the DLP to 'dispense with the timetable of selection meetings and to allow ward branches to select candidates as soon as possible', was referred, ominously, to a 'special executive committee'.[47] On council policy, support for a motion from the Wavertree constituency opposing the freezing of council jobs and any consideration of cuts resulted in the establishment of a DLP 'coordinating committee' with Harrison as chair and Hatton as convenor.[48] On Militant itself, August saw an executive committee resolution (sponsored by Roy Farrar, a Militant supporter in Walton) 'roundly condemning' the action of John Goulding MP in issuing a writ against 'the newspaper *Militant*, and calling upon the NEC to dissuade him from litigation.[49] The motion, which was subsequently carried with an addendum, argued that 'to take legal action against a section of the Labour movement, on the disputing of a report on votes cast for or against a particular policy at an NEC meeting, is, we believe, totally incorrect. Such legal action, we believe, will not only not solve this dispute, but lays open to the capitalist courts and judges precedent to investigate and interfere with basic democratic procedure within our party.' Such sentiments were deeply disingenuous, particularly given what was to happen over the next few years.

# 4 'The fixity of a pensive gaze'

I first went to Australia in 1975. Cyril Carr, the local Liberal leader in Liverpool, had successfully sued me for libel the previous year over an ambiguity in a leaflet that I had produced when acting as Frank Gaier's agent in Arundel at the 1973 county council elections. The offending item referred to 'the Liberal Party leader' – Jeremy Thorpe – and his association with a Rachman-like property company. A local solicitor, Rex Makin, took up the case for Carr, and it taught me the valuable lesson that telling the truth is not all that matters in law; on the contrary, it is the way in which the truth is told that matters most. I was not unduly penalised, but the whole episode was a strain and prompted a desire to get away from it all. In addition, there was the opportunity to go to what I considered a rather exotic place, and make some money in a short period of time. Together, the chance to have a much-needed break and the expectation of new experiences made it all rather attractive.

Originally I and my wife Bernie had planned to go for a year, but it just stretched on, and we ended up staying for a lot longer, doing different things. It was no great dramatic gesture, just young people giving it a go while young enough to enjoy it. We came back to Liverpool in 1978 for family reasons, and I ended up working as the leader of Edge Hill Boys' Club. My time there coincided with the Edge Hill by-election and the general election six weeks later, and I was well placed to help out in both campaigns.

Both Bernie and I had been made very restless by our relatively short period of time in Australia. It made us realise that there are many places and things to see in the world and, after a few months back in Liverpool, we decided to spend some time travelling across America before returning to Australia for a further four years, from early 1980 to February 1984. This was a particularly crucial period, as between those dates I paid no return visit to Liverpool. I had neither the money nor the time, as I was working hard, building a house and trying to get it finished so that we could sell it and return for good. What started out as a six-month building project with another six months to finish actually took about three and a half years. 'Kilfoyle's folly', as it became known to some of my Australian friends, was a real labour of love. Building my own house was something that I had always wanted to do and it gave me a real sense of satisfaction when it was finished.

In Australia, my awareness of developments back in Liverpool came from three sources. Firstly, the constant flow of people from Liverpool, and the rest of the UK, who came out to visit us. Secondly, the regular telephone calls to all sorts of people who kept me informed. And, thirdly, the media. One newspaper article in particular had a lasting effect on me – a piece entitled 'The Museum of Horrifying Example' which appeared in the *International Guardian*. Written in exile from the city by Stanley Reynolds, who for years had worked for the *Liverpool Daily Post*, it first described rush hour in Liverpool – or rather, the lack of it – before moving on to a warts-and-all description of how the city and its people had changed during his absence. A lot of what Reynolds wrote touched a nerve with me, but the flavour of the article was best captured in the brutal words: 'Everyone in Liverpool seems half cut all the time. Then, of course, I remember they were always a little half cut in Liverpool all the time, and me along with them. Suddenly I realised that something has changed in Liverpool – I have come back sober and all my friends look like suicides to me.'[50] This was not the Liverpool that I remembered, and it certainly did not appear to reflect the family and friends I had left behind.

Flaubert once wrote of the period between the security of the pantheistic early Roman Republic and the promise of the Christian empire, when stoic scholars and emperors considered their fate: 'No crying out, no convulsions – nothing but the fixity of a pensive gaze'. So beautifully put, such is the gift given to the exile – the opportunity calmly to consider events in one's homeland. I tried in my humble way to reconsider Liverpool from a very distant Queensland. When I came back in the late seventies, from my first period away, it was a shock to the system. Yet during my second, lengthier, spell away, I found it illuminating to be able to reflect from afar on all sorts of things without any immediate distractions. I began to form a more objective and broader picture of Liverpool.

Nevertheless, on hearing about the Toxteth 'riots', I was taken aback – even more so as we had been living in the area until the time we left for Australia. I felt, however, that, unlike the riots that occurred in Brixton and other parts of Britain, racism was not the central determining factor in Toxteth. Everything I have seen and heard since confirms this view, and it is interesting that little has been made of the serious disturbances that took place in Liverpool the following summer in the almost entirely white areas of Cantril Farm, Everton and Speke.[51] Of course, Toxteth had been the scene of race riots on at least two occasions in the twentieth century, in 1919 and 1948. The disturbances that took place in 1981, however, were a reaction to a pressing political situation, the blame for which must fall partly on the Conservative government, whose policies had induced a recession that was acutely felt on Merseyside, but also on the previous Labour government and the local council in all of its recent political guises. Riots of the sort that occurred in Toxteth do not arise in the space of eighteen months or so, but build up over a long period of time.

Much has been written about Toxteth, and particularly the diverse individuals who make up the local black population and their experiences in Britain. Due to its roles in commerce and trade, Liverpool has long been home to people drawn from further afield than the British Isles and Europe, most notably from the west coast of Africa and the Caribbean. It also boasts the oldest Chinese community in Europe, celebrated only by a plaque outside The Nook pub in Chinatown.

Initially, in ways typical of any group of in-migrants, those who came to Liverpool from Africa and the Caribbean established their own networks and eventually formed a distinct community within the human geography of the city. Yet, where other groups of incomers – Irish Catholics, Irish Protestants, Welsh, and Jewish – fragmented and moved either individually or collectively to other parts of the city-region, Liverpool's blacks continued to remain in or near to the areas where their ancestors had first settled. Some would say they refrained from moving elsewhere, others would perhaps argue that they were informally 'ghettoised'. Whatever, a host of reasons, from the inherent discrimination of institutionalised practices to abject racism, or at least the fear of its consequences, colluded to mark out 'Toxteth', 'Liverpool 8' or 'L8' as a place within a place. It was an area that others from the 'white' parts of Liverpool knew *of* but did not understand, and for them any mention came loaded with preconceptions of those who lived there. With similar attitudes informing local politics, the plight of Liverpool's blacks was marginalised as a municipal concern.

Whilst the Communist Party did contain a number of black members such as Ludwig Hesse and Dorothy Kuya, who later became the secretary of

Merseyside Council for Racial Equality, it was evident to John Hamilton and others representing the area that:

> Many politically active blacks in Liverpool at that time considered them-
> selves almost as lodgers, and thought of Liverpool as a 'white man's city'
> where the disputes between Conservative, Labour and Liberal were
> 'white man's concerns, with which we don't want to interfere'.

Until the reorganisation of local government in 1973, Toxteth had been covered by two wards – Granby and Princes Park – which for the most part returned Labour councillors but at times reflected city-wide trends, as in 1967 and 1968, when Tories were returned. The one constant, however, was that all of the six councillors were always white. At least one, Margaret Simey, found her initial experiences personally enlightening:

> I went under John [Hamilton]'s tuition. John was a very good friend to me
> and well respected in Granby, and he briefed me all through my appren-
> ticeship. He used to insist on my going visiting with him. I was scared stiff
> in these multi-occupied houses with black people – I'd never encountered
> that before.

Such honesty on Margaret's part may come as a surprise to those who know of her and her tireless work for the area, but her observations reflect the fact that while many black people could be relied upon to return Labour votes, their role in party politics was minimal. This is acknowledged by another former councillor for the area, and local GP, Cyril Taylor:

> Relations were perfectly amicable, so I suppose it was quite good. A lot
> were patients, and I was 'the Doctor' to anybody in that area. But I recog-
> nised that we never really succeeded in getting many black people to join
> the Labour Party.

In 1973, Granby and Princes Park wards were merged. Of the six Labour councillors then representing the area, two, Geoff Walsh and John Stevens, retired, three, Taylor, John Hamilton and Alec Doswell, took over as repre-sentatives of the new ward, and Simey herself was elected to the new county council chamber where she would eventually make a political name for her-self as chair of the Police Authority. The initial consequences of the merger, though, were that Labour Party meetings became enlivened, as Margaret Simey recalls:

> When we amalgamated with Princes Park – which was a big strong ward

– Granby was scooped up and the meetings became tremendous every month. Nowadays they can't get a quorum. But Doswell, Hamilton, me and Cyril were quite a team and we worked very closely together, real buddies – it was tremendous fun – and we all reported our activities. Then Sam Semoff volunteered to run a monthly newsletter which he did with such success that all the local shops advertised in it and he actually made a profit. It was wonderful. So we had that going out every month, active councillors and real issues worth discussing. It was real politics.

Despite the support the ward councillors were giving to people in the area, and the respect which they received, the appearances of black faces at ward meetings continued to be a rarity. Moreover, there were those who made it quite apparent that they did not want to work with the Labour Party; they wanted the black community to run its own affairs. John Hamilton recalls a meeting at the Black Community Centre in Stanley House:

Some were saying: 'We don't want an integrated system. We want apart-heid, so long as the blacks have the same rights in their community as the whites, and that there are no dominant white people giving the impression that blacks are inferior.' They were arguing for a system within Britain that would be similar to that in South Africa but based on equal terms. They wanted their own services, their own political parties.

Such thinking was a far cry from the 'lodger' syndrome that had been appar-ent right up to the late 1960s. It heralded the attitudes of at least part of a new generation of Liverpool-born blacks whose political thinking had been shaped as much by black militancy in the US as by the support that they saw Enoch Powell receive from their fellow Britons. Nevertheless, no real political opposition arose to challenge Labour in Granby-Princes Park.

Throughout the 1970s, when a number of Labour-led councils, espe-cially but not exclusively in London, began to attempt what would later be termed 'positive discrimination', Liverpool's political inertia prevented any such practices from entering the local government lexicon. As a result, the relatively high proportion of the local workforce employed by the authority continued to include relatively few black people. Furthermore, a rapidly dwin-dling private sector continued to adopt its own dubious methods of exclusion. Consequently, in a city in which the working class had long been burdened with its own caste structure, those with an L8 postcode became the untouchables of the employment market. All of this was accentuated from 1979 onwards, as the Thatcher government fostered further socioeconomic devastation; and, come the summer of 1981, the ignorance and brutality of some in the local police force was merely the paraffin that set the melting pot alight. Twelve thousand miles away in Queensland, the most racist state in the Australian federation, I could not help but compare the reactionary rule of Joh Bjelke-Petersen and the political agenda of his extreme right-wing coalition with the situation at home and the Conservative government.

It is increasingly difficult, as time goes on, to appreciate the extraordinary extremes of emotion aroused by Margaret Thatcher and her pronouncements and her policies at that time. She made a virtue of her determination not to countenance any compromise in the pursuit of her own political objectives, allowing nothing to stand in her path. With a political vindictiveness that knew no limits, it was no surprise that she was seen in many parts of the country, including Merseyside, as the devil incarnate.

From my vantage point in Australia I looked on with increasing concern as Britain seemed to spiral downwards into an ever-deeper recession. Australians themselves regarded Thatcher as something of an oddity – an attitude which, like that of many people back in Britain, was to change with her stand over the Falkland Islands. My own whole-hearted detestation of her remained, and was in no way diluted by anything that she said or did. Ultimately, she was a thoroughly bad prime minister for the social fabric of the UK. Possibly even worse, though, was her party which, while initially retaining some semblance of decency in the form of people like Ian Gilmour, Ted Heath and Jim Prior, was steadily overrun by a new breed of Conservatives who were venomous towards their political opponents. More often than not this venom was accentuated by hostility and snobbery towards the labour movement and the working class – 'the lower orders' – but amongst the more scathing of the new breed were individuals from less obvious backgrounds.

One such individual was Bernard Ingham, a former Labour councillor from deepest Yorkshire, who, having changed his allegiance in the 1960s, was elevated through the ranks of the civil service to become Thatcher's chief press secretary. (As subsequent events were to show, his promotion was not simply that of a good press officer but also because his politics appeared congruent with those of his political mistress.) Another was Norman Tebbit (a.k.a. the Chingford Skinhead), a former airline pilot from Essex who, as Secretary of State for Employment, oversaw the introduction of numerous curbs on trade union activities and famously told the long-term unemployed of Britain to get on their bikes and look for work. Both of these hard-nosed

Tories also pointedly directed comments at Liverpool. Ingham openly loathed the city and saw its trade unions and working class as the extreme symptom of the British malaise. Tebbit condemned Alan Bleasdale's television drama, *The Boys from the Blackstuff,* which portrayed the ongoing struggles of a number of Liverpudlians in Thatcher's Britain, for single-handedly causing the demise of Liverpool's economy.

Even so, it should not be forgotten that the Tories still had a modicum of support in Liverpool at the time, including two of the city's eight MPs. Their presence at Westminster helped to give succour to Thatcher and her ministers whenever a Liverpool issue raised its head. For a lengthy period in 1982, Anthony Steen regularly asked a set of questions, apparently with the aim of crediting the Conservatives with attempts to 'revive' Liverpool and implying that any remaining problems were indigenous. Then along came Michael Heseltine, who was to create an image of pragmatism in dealing with the problems of inner-city Liverpool, but who still worked within an attitudinal framework that had only shifted marginally in the last two decades.

The Liverpool-based academic Fred Ridley has observed how a near-colonialist approach to the city and its people has been adopted by the London-based establishment: '[Liverpool] is not only a different world, but inhabited by a troublesome people who cost it money and irritate it politically. There is something almost racialist about this view: all people of Liverpool are tarred with the same brush, all are somehow responsible for the crisis and all can be left to stew in their own juice.'[52] Often, as I sat reading the various interpretations of what was occurring back in Liverpool, both the media and their quoted sources appeared to be referring to somewhere beyond the British polity – a place where the government was encountering some little local difficulties, with 'Minister for Merseyside' Heseltine cast willingly as 'our man in Havana' amongst the palm trees of the Liverpool International Garden Festival site.

In some respects, Liverpool was completely alien to them, and at times Liverpool people were presented as the lesser breed without the law. These politically laden caricatures have proved hard to shake off. A few years ago, when I raised concerns about the proposal to build a second prison in the Walton constituency (bearing in mind that it already housed one of the largest prisons in Europe), a Tory minister actually commented that, as there was a disproportionate number of Scousers in British prisons, it would be a good thing to have them together back in Liverpool. With the Ashworth high security institution just up the road in the adjacent constituency, I had the impression that they were hoping to turn Merseyside into some sort of penal colony. Indeed, ahead of his time, Liverpool Tory councillor Tony McVeigh had proposed prison ships on the Mersey in the early 1970s.

Had I not been removed from the context of Liverpool at the start of the 1980s, I might never have been able to understand what was happening in the same way. As it was, my time abroad also allowed me the critical distance to consider the broader political canvas of Britain at the time. This was particularly illuminating in light of what was taking place in the Australian Labor Party, which I saw attempting to 'modernise' itself long before the word was even used in Britain. The ALP was coming to terms with a stark but necessary choice: was it to be a patron saint of lost causes or a political party that wanted to be elected and change things, however piecemeal? In time, it took the latter view and did what was necessary to become electable. It seemed, however, that the British Labour Party was travelling in completely the opposite direction. The Bennites were still in the ascendancy, which some would argue was no bad thing, but alas, as history has since shown, their politics were misguided. They obstinately took the wrong path and, in doing so, offered more rather than less of what the electorate had already rejected.

The distance separating me from the political scene in Britain did not lend enchantment to my view. Between Callaghan and Foot, the Labour Party appeared unable to rethink its position. It seemed incapable of assessing objectively exactly where it stood given the shift to the right that appeared to be taking place in many western countries. No-one would suggest, of course, that Callaghan and his successor, Foot, should do a complete about-face over what they had always stood for. An accommodation of some sort, however, with the new realpolitik would not only have been in the interests of the Labour Party, given its internal tensions, but could also have brought about a more constructive opposition to Thatcher's then faltering government. Everything was to change in the aftermath of the Falklands War; but still, it was a golden opportunity that was missed.

The 'left' was still labouring under the misapprehension that revolution of one sort or another was just around the corner. This, of course, was absurd. It is increasingly the case in sophisticated societies that governments always have the upper hand, and the idea of insurrectionary change emerging from the streets in First-World societies appears increasingly remote. Perhaps at some point in the future, such a revolutionary strategy will become realisable. In the meantime, large-scale change has to come from the inside, and requires both an acceptance by opinion-formers that those proposing the change are fit to govern, and a clear mandate from the people, allowing them to do so.

Support for such a long-term political philosophy can be found within the writings of Antonio Gramsci. A founder and committed member of the Italian Communist Party, who spent much of his short life in Mussolini's prisons, Gramsci, writing in the early decades of the twentieth century, referred to 'wars of movement' and 'wars of position'. The former are those occasions in history when crises cause objective and subjective conditions to coincide and bring about fundamental change. The latter require radicals who are prepared to dig in in order subtly to shift the political and cultural boundaries of nation-states, along with the attitudes and values of people, in order to achieve 'hegemony'. Political parties and other groups without these aims in mind may choose to wear their principles on their coatsleeves, bringing issues and concerns to the fore that might otherwise be marginalised or overlooked – but for the most part, those who associate with such parties are merely posturing.

Of course, posturing is not a pastime exclusive to 'the left' – something that was made evident by the emergence of the Social Democratic Party. Formed by the so-called 'Gang of Four' (Roy Jenkins, David Owen, Bill Rodgers and Shirley Williams), the SDP was initially composed of MPs who had either lost their seats at reselection or were in clear danger of doing so. It never escaped my attention that many of these figures felt they had a divine right to be at Westminster or, in the case of the Gang of Four, to be a leadership to whom everyone would automatically show allegiance. There was a degree of arrogance about these people that has failed to diminish with time.

The rise of the SDP in the early 1980s was a further ingredient in the bubbling cauldron of political change. From afar, the Limehouse Declaration, which marked the SDP's conception in early 1981, did not seem to be as critical an event as it obviously was, a result perhaps of the treatment afforded it in the overseas press. It seemed like yet another of the short-term protests for which the Labour Party is famous, albeit one that saw 'the right' attacking 'the left' for a change. I was concerned, of course, when the SDP later appeared to be going from strength to strength. If they had not joined with the Liberals in their misnamed 'Alliance', they might have done far better in the 1987 election, possibly becoming the second party. This, however, was not to be. As we were to see much later at the Richmond by-election, bickering – both between and within the two parties – was to make their amalgamation inevitable if they were to have any kind of future as the third force in British politics.

In 1982, twenty-six of the twenty-nine MPs sitting for the SDP in the Commons were Labour MPs who had crossed the floor. (The other three included two by-election victors and a lone Conservative, Christopher Brocklebank-Fowler.) They included three Liverpool MPs: Dick Crawshaw, who was also the Deputy Speaker of the House of Commons, Jimmy Dunn and Eric Ogden. In all three cases, their move to the SDP came as no surprise to any observer of their politics and their constituency parties.

Seventeen years earlier, when Harold Wilson's first Labour administration had a majority of four, Crawshaw had voted against a proposal to cut defence spending. Having been a Lieutenant-Colonel in the Army, he was active in the Territorial Army whilst an MP and felt strongly enough on the issue to put it above the survival of the government. It was a pity that Crawshaw did not feel quite as strongly about keeping his word to members of the Toxteth CLP when pressed over his failure to hold surgeries in the constituency. I campaigned for this at meetings in 1971, and one of his lame excuses was that there was a 'lack of appropriate facilities'. So I told him that he could use my home. Sure enough, on the Saturday morning that he put aside for his surgeries, Crawshaw turned up and sat in my living room, spending the time asking me why I was not a hundred and ten per cent supporter of him and his politics. As the morning went on, however, no-one called to the house. I soon realised why. He had not actually bothered to advertise that he was holding the surgeries. The whole incident was typical of how Crawshaw conducted himself.

The other two were no better. Ogden's selection in the early 1960s as prospective MP for West Derby was odd in itself. An NUM candidate who had come straight from the coalface, his elevation was seen by some as a way of bringing income into the non-mining constituency from his sponsors. As John Hamilton, a fellow member of the short-list, recalls:

> [Jack] Braddock said to me afterwards: 'we would have preferred someone else, but we needed the money'.

One of the more notable things about Ogden's selection was that it apparently came with the guarantee of a council house on the corner of Pilch Lane and East Prescot Road. Not only was this a choice position – it looked across to the Greyhound Hotel – but the house itself was a parlour house, a much sought-after style at the time.

There was an element of suspicion about whether Ogden was of the right calibre. Wally Edwards remembers how his wife Sarah, a delegate at the selection meeting, responded when asked what she thought of him:

> She said, 'well, I don't know if he's a Tory but I'll tell you this much, he'll let the Labour Party down'. She was proven right when he joined the SDP.

Dunn, who was the MP for Liverpool Kirkdale, had heavy associations with the church and religious issues, and many people thought of him as a Catholic MP, his party allegiance being deemed secondary. Other than these MPs, no councillors and only a few members of the Liverpool Labour Party jumped ship to the SDP. Of those who did, only Pat Kellett, Dave Mitchell and Roy Stoddart commanded any respect locally.

Not only were the political parties reforming – in the case of the SDP schismatically – but the trade unions were also coming to terms with a very different political scene, not least because of the government-induced recession which caused huge job losses in places like Liverpool. Of course, it would be wrong to attribute all of the changes that were taking place to the government of the day. Liverpool, for example, was in the wrong place at the wrong time, facing west rather than to Europe. Many bastions of trade unionism on Merseyside either closed or were about to close during this period – workplaces such as Dunlop, Tate & Lyle, and Standard Triumph. This had a tremendous effect on the local public-sector trade unions and spurred officials into making demands geared mainly towards ensuring the security of their own members' jobs whatever the cost. Such resistance was to be expected in a local economy that for those worst affected (unskilled and semi-skilled middle-aged males) was short on alternatives. Yet, in adopting the position so politically, local union leaders helped to perpetuate a culture that placed the rights of the producers far above the rights of those to whom they provided services.

This was particularly the case with the large general unions such as the GMB and the TGWU, parts of which had become politicised in a way that many people would not have readily anticipated. One has to bear in mind that there had been a radical shift in emphasis from the Trades' Council to the Labour Party. Whereas in the early 1970s the two had been virtually interchangeable (notwithstanding the national Labour Party's attempts to separate them), there had followed a steady and, viewed from the benefit of hindsight, unalterable shift away from the industrial to the political front. Militant's activities were the most notable symptom of this shift, but the

Communist Party also moved in that direction, albeit into new areas of struggle, around issues of community, race and gender.

The changes that occurred within the GMB were perhaps the biggest surprise, as before the late 1970s, the General and Municipal Workers' Union (which merged with the Boilermakers' Union to form the GMB) was seen as acquiescent and right-wing. In the final year of the Callaghan government, however, the GMWU earned itself a reputation for militancy through a series of local government disputes. The most infamous was the gravediggers' strike in Liverpool which, although overblown and exaggerated (the dispute lasted less than a fortnight and involved only a handful of workers at one cemetery), was to be used in Conservative propaganda for nearly two decades to characterise Labour in office.

The imagery from that dispute and others, such as the refuse collectors' strike, was used as a potent reminder of a feeble Labour government. With the unions having come through a period of unparalleled influence, some talented young people looked there rather than to the Labour Party as the way forward. This was as true on Merseyside as anywhere else. In the TGWU, there was Lenny McCluskey who, whilst I had no personal empathy with him, was politically very bright – at least compared to many of his colleagues – and became one of their youngest full-time officers. In the GMB, there was the organisational and motivational skills of Ian Lowes. In early 1980s' Liverpool, such people were not only establishing strong networks but providing the leadership that full-time officials were not. They were at the forefront of fostering their members' hopes of change, through the application of a strict union line to political matters. It was perhaps a view of change that many people would not have arrived at individually, but it really did not matter to most trade unionists what the politics of that change were – what was important was that change took place. Wonders could be worked if one ideologically strong official like McCluskey found himself amongst weak full-time regional officials, or an astute organiser with a focus, like Lowes, was able to operate in a totally weak structure. There were others, but these two were prime examples of the broader phenomenon.

Out in Australia, I had seen trade unions engaged in their own particular battles. Unionism had a very strong grip in many areas of work, and the Painters and Dockers' Union, the Storemen and Packers' Union, and the Builders-Labourers' Federation, to name but three, were all key players. It could also be argued that they were highly corrupt. 'Big Norm' Gallagher, for example, who led the BLF, managed to do extremely well out of his introduction of 'green bans' in Sydney, acquiring a beach-front house as well as a second home near Melbourne. The guiding principle of the 'green bans' was supposedly the cost to the environment, but permissions were allegedly sought on corrupt grounds, with payments having been made to the BLF and some of its officials, who then used their contacts to ensure that particular building work would proceed. This story, and the way in which other Australian trade unions conducted themselves, did not instil in me a great deal of faith in international trade unionism. The Australian unions seemed to me to display a curious mixture of the political motivation of many trade unionists in Britain and the pure and simple promotion of self-interest which I associated with many major unions in the United States – the 'Johnny Friendly' approach dramatised in *On the Waterfront*. There was also a sprinkling of gangsterism, something that I had never seen before within the trade union movement but that I would one day see again, back home in Liverpool.

Back in Britain, an arrogant Prime Minister was becoming more and more stubborn in the face of the demands being made by local authorities, and more forthright in her attempts to crush those who opposed her. Elsewhere, the Bennites were arguing for the 'democratisation' of the Labour Party and more of the politics which had lost the 1979 general election, whilst their former colleagues now in the SDP were pouring claret on their chips;[53] and the trade unions were becoming more militant (with a small 'm'). It was as if everyone was hurtling down the road at an ever-increasing pace, blissfully unaware of the huge brick wall that they would eventually slam into at the end. This was to be more than evident at the 1983 general election, where any notions that British government and politics would return to the old consensual 'Butskellite' approach were finally shattered. Instead, a stark polarisation set in, where the only apparent choice was wholesale support for or condemnation of Thatcher's government and all it stood for. Yet large elements of the electorate were fickle. In early 1982, Thatcher's popularity had been in the pits. A year on, after her self-proclaimed majesty during the Falklands war (including her personal involvement in the sinking of the Argentinian cruiser, the *Belgrano*, as it sailed away from the British exclusion zone round the islands), she was returned to the Commons with a greatly increased majority.

The Toxteth riots, Heseltine's half-baked attempts at urban regeneration, the re-election of a government with a leader who was so unpopular in

Liverpool that her one trip to the city was shrouded in secrecy (not only was it unannounced, but it began in the early hours of the morning), developments in the Labour movement nationally, and Militant's shift in strategy from the industrial to the political arena – together, all these things made for an explosive mixture and a recipe for chaos. It is debatable, of course, whether the situation that was to arise would have done so regardless of who was running the city. With a different political complexion, there might have been a strategic accommodation of the kind that occurred in Manchester, Sheffield and other Labour-controlled cities. This might have at least tempered the reputation with which the Conservatives and their acolytes in the national media subsequently labelled Liverpool. With Militant, however, only confrontation was on offer, and the city was to become a pariah to some and a whipping boy to others. For many at Westminster and in Whitehall, Liverpool needed to be taught a lesson.

# 5 Adult education

On returning to Liverpool in February 1984, I did not know quite what to expect. In Australia, I had been given various vivid accounts of what was happening. Some came from people flushed with optimism as they created a new life abroad, who wanted to put the past behind them; unconsciously, they possibly painted a bleaker picture of what they had left behind than reality. Others, a minority, were more upbeat about the situation. The media, meanwhile, having set out its stall, continued to offer little more than negative reportage of events in the city, and a uniform pessimism towards prospects of a change for the better.

Arriving home, what struck me first and foremost were the physical improvements in the city. This may seem slightly odd, as Liverpool at this stage was on a downward spiral. But many features of the cityscape – simple things like the roads – appeared much better than they had been before I had left. It may have been the case that these developments had started some years earlier and I had not noticed them, but the impression I had was that certain aspects of life in Liverpool had improved. I saw them optimistically as outward signs of inner grace.

Shortly after my return, I met up with Joe Devaney, with whom I had been at school – I was his prefect at one stage – and for whom I had campaigned in his first unsuccessful attempt to win a council seat. By this time, Joe had become a councillor, for Abercromby ward, and he invited me down for a drink and a game of snooker at St Patrick's club. He asked what I thought of Liverpool after having been away for so long, and I told him of my positive first impressions. He was quite taken aback, and to this day I do not know whether he thought I was winding him up or whether he was genuinely shocked that I should be so laudatory about the city after seeing it through relatively fresh eyes.

The reality, of course, was to prove rather different. There *were* physical improvements, but I soon began to appreciate the enormity of the economic devastation that had taken place and the dangerous political developments that had sprung out of them. Very quickly it became obvious that the local

Labour Party had changed, and that demagogues were running the city council. In the years between 1980 and 1984, the lunatics had taken over the asylum.

As a direct consequence of Liverpool's experiences, there is now a clear time-frame within which local authorities have to set their rates for the forthcoming year. In the early 1980s, this was not the case. The rate was often set as late as possible, with some councils waiting until after the municipal elections. In Liverpool in 1980, a major debate arose within the labour movement on council finances, culminating just before the May elections in a vote for a 50 per cent rate rise. Those who looked at their civic financial responsibilities in a traditional way supported the rise – not for them illegality and confrontation. Those who opposed it predicted that the rise would cost Labour dearly, as the whole council was up for election that year. As it transpired, the party retained the largest presence in the chamber, though losing six seats overall: whilst a couple of gains were picked up in Fazakerley ward, three losses were registered in both Abercromby and Dingle, as well as a further two in Anfield. Many of the individuals who lost their seats had been among those supporting the 50 per cent rise, and their removal served both to weaken the old guard within the Labour group and to act as a further catalyst for the radicalisation of the local party.

With Labour refusing to take the reins again, the Liberals once more found themselves in charge of a hung council. Their own gains at the elections had brought in a number of fresh faces whose enthusiasm for pavement politics resembled that of their elders, seven years earlier. Yet, like their elders, they were also accused of political naivety. One new councillor, Chris Davies – who would later become, for a short while, the MP for Littleborough & Saddleworth, and who is now an MEP – earned the nickname 'fifty-motions Davies' after submitting fifty resolutions to his first full council meeting. Many of these were so out of step with his own party's thinking that the Labour group wickedly supported them, whilst Davies himself was instructed by the Liberal leadership to vote against!

Beyond the political inertia that the slim voting balance on the council was perpetuating, events in Liverpool's municipal sphere reflected those in all other spheres of life in the city, increasingly tinged by antagonism and unrest as the decline of many core industries, rapidly rising mass unemployment way beyond national and regional averages, and growing health and social problems amongst an ageing and ever-dwindling population were accentuated by lacking or inappropriately used investment in new infrastructure. Enter stage right a Conservative government whose philosophy opposed any digging deeper into the public purse, and whose electoral credibility would suffer little or at all from any failure to cure Liverpool's particular ills. The city's ongoing turmoil, with nationally renowned companies folding or leaving the city by the dozen, was much more useful in tarring the Tories' industrial and political rivals. Significantly, in matters of employment, as in much else, the city council was carrying a relatively high burden, and it was here, behind façades of legitimate grievances, that a number of key events occurred which in time heralded a new municipal order.

Considering the area of work in which they were engaged, those who worked as typists for Liverpool City Council at the start of the 1980s received relatively low pay and operated within a virtually non-existent career structure. In the face of a governing Liberal group that depended on Conservative support at the Town Hall, and was therefore in no position to grant favours, the typists' case was a cause ripe for the taking. Nationally, their trade union, NALGO, had negotiated an agreement that established pay scales guaranteeing annual increments. Despite this, and despite also being opposed to local deals in principle, the union's officers in Liverpool attempted to agree further gains over the introduction of new technology. When their initial approaches failed, they called a strike.

The then leader of the Labour group, John Hamilton, who suffered the acute embarrassment of seeing his own personal secretary work throughout the strike, observed broader forces at work:

> It was more about upsetting the Liberals, and it was political. But it wasn't just the Tendency who were pushing for aggravation – much of the trade union movement was. There were a number of agitators in the social services and other pockets in the council. Some of them weren't Militant. Some belonged to the Workers' Revolutionary Party and that sort of thing, which wasn't pro-Militant but had basically the same argument in getting people out on strike.

Initially, the typists' action had the desired effect, in that much of the day-to-day work of the council had to be sent out in hand-written form rather than being typed. Then, however, some officers began to employ the services of outside labour and the dispute widened to include other clerical staff, as Lyn Anderson – known at the time as Lyn Caldow, and both a clerical officer and NALGO official at the council – explains:

> I would prepare my written draft and leave it on a table, and someone in a very senior position would take it out under his coat to be typed by a firm of people in Castle Street. Soon after, I was being asked to send out my hand-written stuff to be typed up. Now the typists were out on a limb. If we started doing that, they were finished, and there were a few of us who felt very strongly, that 'Okay, up until now, people have got around the issue but this is the point for us now to decide whether we let the typists sink or say "no, we're not going to do that",' and we said no. We weren't actually 'on strike' but we were suspended from the payroll.

The typists' dispute, in both its original and expanded forms, gave the opportunity to a number of individuals to thrust themselves up into the public eye. As personnel spokesperson for the Labour group, Derek Hatton was given much scope for verbosity. As Lyn Anderson further recalls, another person who would soon rise to the fore also drew attention to himself during the dispute, although in a somewhat comical manner:

> We were picketing the Town Hall and Tony Byrne stopped to say hello. A big burly police sergeant came towards us and asked Tony to move because he was obstructing the pavement. At that point, a woman with a buggy and a child on foot walked past. So Tony turned around and said to the officer, in a non-aggressive way, 'How can I be when that woman's just got past me?' The sergeant lifted Tony by the collar and threw him in the back of a van. Ken Stewart ran after them, saying 'Officer, officer, you can't arrest him – he's got the opposed business [on the council agenda]'. Tony got this out of his pocket and gave it to Ken who then walked away and left him to be driven off. He then thought better of it and they wouldn't let the council meeting go ahead until the police had released Tony.

Although the typists' dispute ended when a decision taken by ACAS and the North West Provincial Council was accepted by the local NALGO officials, the tone had now been set within the council, radicalising many employees' attitudes.

The second dispute that acted as a catalyst in changing the political hue of Liverpool took place in the field of secondary education provision. For much of the post-war period, the city had had more children than the local authority could handle – a situation that led to the establishment of a plethora of new schools as well as the widespread building of annexes in the grounds of many existing ones. By the late 1970s, however, the demographic shifts affecting both Britain in general (smaller households), and Liverpool in particular (a growing exodus to the surrounding boroughs and beyond), saw a rapid fall in the total number of children in the city. At the same time, marked differences began to appear in the quality of education provided within the public sector, and astute parents began to send their children to the more favoured secondary schools in their catchment area, while a handful of other schools, mainly but not exclusively on the outer estates, were considered, by Liverpool's Liberals at least, to have outlived their utility.

One such school was Croxteth Comprehensive – established in 1966 by the amalgamation of two single-sex secondary schools, and situated on Stonebridge Lane in Gillmoss ward. For over a decade, this had satisfied local parents as an acceptable place for their children's schooling. By the late 1970s, however, it was losing out within its natural catchment to Ellergreen School, on the nearby Norris Green estate, and also to some of the high-status comprehensives a short journey away along Queen's Drive (the major thoroughfare that runs in an arc as an inner ring road through the middle of Liverpool, from Walton in the north to Mossley Hill in the south). Consequently, Croxteth's numbers were dramatically reduced and, in November 1981, the then chair of the Education Committee, Mike Storey, identified the school for closure. It was a move that was met with hostility from the Labour members of the committee, such as John Hamilton, who argued that it was important for communities such as Croxteth to retain a school:

> There were only a few pubs and a few shops. To destroy the school would be to destroy the whole community spirit. Storey took a sudden dive and decided that the school would close. He passed a resolution through the education committee and never even consulted the parents. Of course, that caused them to blow up – there's nothing better to upset parents than not consulting them. They might have been persuaded that the school should be closed, but they were not going to be shotgunned into it.

A detailed and rigorous account of the events that followed is given in Phil Francis Carspecken's *Community Schooling and the Nature of Power: the Battle for Croxteth Comprehensive*.[54] Briefly, what transpired was that a number of parents, teachers and community workers, aided by a handful of outsiders spurred on by the cause, decided to occupy the school with a view to keeping it open. After an initial period of overcoming the obvious difficulties, essentially but not exclusively concerning the recruitment of teaching staff, the continuation of power supplies and the retention of a sufficient number of pupils to make their cause credible, Croxteth – still illegally occupied – was opened as a 'private school', a status it was to hold until a Labour council took it back into local authority control.

Lest anyone be taken in by the notion that 'Croxteth' was purely a struggle between ordinary folk and the authorities, it is the politics of what occurred that makes for more interesting reading. At the start of the occupation, eight months of day-to-day manoeuvring took place, not only between the school's Action Committee and the Liberal council, but also, and perhaps more significantly, amongst those directly involved in the campaign. The less politicised parents of the children who continued to attend the school saw the occupation mainly in terms of convenience – with a low level of car-ownership in the area, few wanted to fork out extra cash to pay for additional bus fares. On the other hand, the 'progressive educationalists' amongst the teaching staff (for the most part members of the Workers' Revolutionary Party, whose very own 'Trotskyite luvvy', Vanessa Redgrave, was invited to perform in Liverpool to raise funds for the school) viewed what was happening in broader terms, particularly regarding methods and styles of teaching. Then, of course, there were those local Labour Party activists who saw the campaign as a means to undermine the Liberal council. Key amongst these were the brothers Knibb – George and Phil (Phil was a community worker in the area) – and the D'Arcys: father Cyril, an involved parent, and daughter Colette, a sixth-former who became head girl during the campaign. It will perhaps come as no surprise to learn that almost all these individuals were mouthpieces for Militant lines, and that at Croxteth they reflected the organisation's interests – but they were more than assisted by the indifference displayed towards the occupation by Gillmoss ward's three Labour councillors, Eddie Roderick, Bill Snell and Peter Murphy. As George Knibb recalls:

> The claim to fame of one of them was that they came over with a bottle of milk and said 'here you are, that'll do for your cup of tea'. That was the only support we got off him.

In truth, the trio, 'right-wingers' schooled in the politics of an earlier era, were out of touch with the direction in which the local party was moving. Roy Gladden, a fellow member of the Labour group and councillor for nearby Clubmoor ward, explains:

> In my first year as a councillor, we had the sit-in at Croxteth. I went with a few other people to give them support, and they were disgusted

that Roderick, Snell and Murphy had refused to come down and give their support. That brought a lot of people into the party and the ground was then there for the Tendency to move into.

In time, Roderick and Snell were removed and replaced by Militant stooges. The D'Arcys and the Knibbs, meanwhile, received their perks. Soon after Labour returned to power in Liverpool, Cyril D'Arcy became Derek Hatton's chauffeur, and his daughter Colette became part of the public relations unit set up within the council. The Knibb brothers benefited similarly, with Phil and George taking up posts within the social services and environmental services directorates respectively (three other members of the Knibb family were also found employment with the council). The disregard of procedures that led to these appointments would eventually become apparent as a symptom of a wider malaise. For George Knibb, however, the important point is that the Croxteth campaign had wider electoral ramifications:

> I believe we should have took and got the credit for Labour taking over control of the city in 1983. We went out from the community and campaigned in other wards on the school issue because it had that much of a profile. I don't hesitate to say that we were very naïve, but we went out there knocking on doors with our Croxteth school badges, and we'd say 'If you vote Labour, they've promised to keep our school open. If you don't ...', and they'd say 'all right'. The turn-out that year was a lot higher. People put it down to different things but the truth of it all is that we picked on certain wards, such as County, which had previously gone Liberal, and turned them over to Labour.

Alongside the typists' dispute and the Croxteth occupation, much of Labour's success in regaining office in 1983 has been attributed to the politicisation of council employees. This phenomenon had typical Liverpudlian dimensions, one of which was 'nomination rights', the process through which the local authority unions were given the right to name candidates when jobs became vacant. This was a very powerful weapon in the unions' armoury in a city with endemic unemployment, and the fact that it was a corrupt practice, leading to a family network of municipal appointments was neither here nor there for the local union leadership; they were certainly unconcerned about those excluded by such practices, particularly members of ethnic minorities. From the union perspective, it was a way to reward friends and relatives and cement industrial alliances. The latter was to be vital in facing fresh challenges to a very cosy arrangement based on unenlightened mutual interest. But this phenomenon was only truly to arrive with the election of a Labour council.

A rising tide of industrial turmoil began to take over Liverpool's city politics in early 1983, and grievances, petty and serious, more often than not turned into strike action. At the same time, some of the more shrewd union officials, fearful of the Liberals' enthusiasm for privatisation schemes, began to realise what could be gained from being openly aligned with the local Labour Party. As Ian Lowes recalls,

> I don't know if it is generally known but the chair of the committee that dealt with refuse collection, David Croft, worked for a private cleansing company ... Trevor Jones wanted to sign a contract with the private firm just before the May elections so that even if he lost, Labour would be lumbered with it because it would have cost millions to get out of it. The campaign that we as trade unionists mounted was unprecedented, and we had hundreds of council workers taking holidays to go around canvassing for Labour.

Local Labour figures travelled around addressing mass meetings of council workers, making all sorts of promises about what they would do once in office. Ken Stewart spoke at a mass meeting of building workers, all of whom were on a temporary scheme that was due to end in May 1983, and urged them to rally a Labour vote with promises of permanent work should the party be returned to office. At the same time, Hatton was doing the rounds, telling council workers that they would get a thirty-five hour week, a minimum wage and more holidays once Labour were in power. As expected, the turn-out among council employees, particularly in the manual sections, showed a marked increase.

Even so, the results of the 1983 local elections in Liverpool surprised many within the city's Labour Party. Having weighed up the wards that they expected to win – where, for example, they had perhaps reaped gains at the previous election – it was assumed that the group would end up with about 46 or 47 seats, setting them up to take over in 1984. As it happened, they increased their presence from 42 to 51, the first time since reorganisation ten years earlier that any party was able to claim a majority in the 99-seat chamber. This result had an immediate and deep-reaching impact on the administration of the council, as Lyn Anderson recalls:

When Labour got into power, they called a halt to everything and said:

'What we want is for all the people around the local authority who know a bit about how things work to come and sit down while we tell you what we're going to do. This is what we've told the electorate we're going to do. These are our policies. You tell us how we deliver them.' People found that very, very difficult. They'd been existing in a hung council where you checked, checked and checked again if you did anything, and all of sudden they were in a situation where it was 'if he says it's going to happen, it's going to happen – they've got the numbers, they can do it, they can drive it through'.

One of the first changes that the new administration brought about was the abolition of the title of Lord Mayor. This caused a great stir but was never actually the great anti-establishment step that people came to see it as. Following local government reorganisation in 1974, the city council was no longer duty bound to elect a Lord Mayor and could, if it so wished, choose a chairman instead – but Toytown politics, the period of no overall control, had kept the issue on the back-burner. The change itself came at the first full meeting of the council following the election, and, naturally, was not without incident. At the start, three-quarters of the Labour group refused to stand for the retiring Lord Mayor, Conservative councillor Stan Airey. Then, when the chairman-elect, Labour councillor Hugh Dalton, moved to take his place, the Liberals began hissing. This was only the start of the fun, as the *Liverpool Echo* noted the following day: 'Last night's meeting saw unprecedented scenes, including the removal of a lady with a blue rinse who was incensed at Labour's actions. Then one unidentified housewife [later identified as 'Elsie', aged forty-six, from Aigburth] stormed the platform, ousted the new chairman from his seat and despite the intervention of security men, grabbed a microphone to bellow at Liberal and Conservative members: "I want a Lord Mayor, you want a Lord Mayor". The rest of her words were drowned in angry shouting from the Labour benches and cheering from their opponents.'[55] At the end of the day, Labour's numbers assured it victory on this issue, as well as on many others that summer.

In trying to understand the changes that had occurred across the political landscape before my return to the city, I wanted to get more of a fix on what had happened within the local Labour Party. So I went along to the Merseyside Trade Union and Unemployed Resource Centre, where the party had moved the previous year, and spoke to Wally Edwards. Although he had not seen me for some years, Wally offered some insight into why the recent changes had taken place. It was all so bizarre to me, and quite difficult to comprehend; I suppose the nearest approximation was that it was like being a football supporter who, having spent some time away from home, had come back to find that, whilst the ground had changed slightly, the team had changed completely and there was nobody about the club that he knew or recognised (save for the ground staff, who in this case were Wally and Maureen Byrne). Moreover, the crowd that were offering their support were acting in a wholly different way to what he had known before. Where they had once been good-humoured, they were embittered, and to be in their company left a nasty taste in the mouth. That was certainly my early impression of the people hanging around the Labour Party office.

Wally was no longer the secretary and had actually been taken into the North West Regional Office to work on the 1984 Euro-election campaign. The gap was filled by Militant Felicity Dowling, on a voluntary basis (there were no funds to replace Wally's paid post). She had immediately organised an office move within the same building, having a doorway constructed between the DLP office and that of Terry Fields MP. It was a Militant take-over in all but name.

It is important to remember that until the late 1970s, it was the Trades' Council rather than the Labour Party that was the centre of political activity in Liverpool. Most people's connections in the party tended to be on a small scale – one to one, or one to two. Consequently, across the city as a whole, the party's organisation was virtually moribund and amounted to a collection of rotten boroughs. During the late 1970s and early 1980s, however, much of this changed, and in the wake of the Roderick coup, which had seen 'the left' in the city council Labour group temporarily lose its hold, the DLP had begun to take on the role of supreme policy-making body. It was also no coincidence that this was the time when Militant started to make inroads on to the executive – they had seen the vacuum and filled it. They recognised the potential of the DLP, both as a political forum and as a lever of power and influence.

This was evident in the wording of a resolution forwarded by the executive committee of the DLP in February 1983, shortly after five members of Militant's editorial board had been removed from the Labour Party:

> This party condemns the decision of the NEC right-wing majority to expel the five members of the Militant editorial board from the Labour Party. We believe that this decision is against the wishes of the vast majority of the rank and file and will do irreparable damage to the party, particularly in

the pre-general election period and more particularly on the eve of an important by-election in Bermondsey. Further, we believe that this heralds the beginning of a widespread witch-hunt and resolve to oppose such a move with all out energy. We note the intention of those expelled to conduct a campaign for reinstatement throughout the Labour movement and declare our full support for such a campaign. We further declare that unlike the NEC we will also concentrate our energies on preparing a high-level campaign to defeat the Tory/Liberal alliance locally and to defeat the Tories at the coming general election. We believe that victory can best be achieved by a Labour Party united on a socialist programme and once again demand that the NEC put the interests of the working people of Britain before their own sectarian interests, by abandoning the witch-hunt, by withdrawing the expulsions, and by using the resources of the party against the Tories rather than the socialists in the party.[56]

By the time I returned to Liverpool in 1984, the DLP executive was more or less controlled by members of Militant. Some individuals were new to me, but I recalled others from my experience on the Trades' Council in the late 1960s. The chair-cum-president, for instance, was Tony Mulhearn. He had long been in the party, although he had never been particularly active. Like many others, his focus had been within the trade union movement, where he was seen as something of a nuisance by many within his own union, the National Graphical Association, and loathed by members of the rival print union SOGAT.

One of Mulhearn's two vice-chairs at the DLP was Terry Harrison. He had once been in the Young Conservatives[57] but, in his own narrow way, had become a committed Trotskyite ideologue, taking many people in with his persuasive capabilities. He was also extremely active behind the scenes – what one would perhaps deem a key mover and shaker. Harrison's forte, however, was youth issues. A firm believer in involving people in politics at an early age, he rabidly attempted to recruit young people into the Young Socialists and, in time, if not immediately, into Militant – so much so, in fact, that he became Youth Officer of Riverside CLP in his mid-forties. This prompted a typically acid-tongued attack from Ian Williams, then a railway guard and member of the Riverside party but now a journalist, who accused Harrison of engaging in 'political paedophilia'. Nevertheless, Harrison could also be fairly shrewd in his calculations – something that was clear in at least one decision he took, when acting in Mulhearn's absence as chair of the DLP executive committee. Paul Orr's selection for the

1984 local government panel had split the executive right down the middle, and it was left to Harrison to cast the deciding vote. To the surprise of everyone present, but perhaps realising the storm that would follow should Orr be rejected, Harrison chose to endorse his candidature.

Following the inroads made by Militant supporters in the late 1970s, they were able by the early 1980s to muster majority support on the DLP executive. This was not the case at the DLP generally, primarily because of the ways in which particular trade unions lined up on votes, but a sea-change in political alignment was under way. Between 1980 and 1984, a marked increase had occurred in the number of lay officials delegated to the DLP by unions whose branches in Liverpool were sympathetic to the Militant line. The TGWU delegation, for example, increased from thirteen to thirty-one, and the number attending from the GMB increased from eighteen to forty-three. With so many of the newer faces only delegates by virtue of the fact that they could be relied upon to vote the right way, Militant became more confident in putting their resolutions through. At the same time, however, the more astute trade unionists, such as Ian Lowes (who was also 'Tendency'), began to make moves on behalf of their members, taking the opportunity to get involved in the party machinery:

> We thought that the best way for us to change things with the council was to get involved. We had a massive recruiting campaign, got branches to affiliate to, and then elect delegates to, the constituencies and the district General Management Committees. It meant that we commanded significant support on the DLP.

This swamping of the DLP by so many one-dimensional activists enabled sections of the local trade union movement, such as Lowes' own GMB Branch 5, to win support for the most self-interested of motions. The following example, successfully proposed in July 1983, is a case in point:

> This branch notes with concern that, despite the fact that Labour is in control of the city council, millions of pounds worth of council work is being carried out by private contractors. We call upon the Labour group to immediately freeze all work to private contractors except that which the council is legally and contractually bound by and to enter into urgent discussions with the local authority trade unions as to how this work can be switched to 'direct labour', thereby creating thousands of city council jobs.

The fact that this would lead to inflated costs to the ratepayer, and the employment of virtual supernumeraries was neither here nor there. It was superficially attractive at a time when unemployment in Liverpool was racing ahead of the national average, and appealed the more to a mindset that refused to entertain any thought of private enterprise.

An overwhelming majority of those who now attended the DLP were considered to be either supporters of Militant, fellow-travellers, or 'of the left' more generally. With such numerical strength, those sections of the local party inclined to propose the more barmy resolutions could be guaranteed support. In September 1981, for example, Garston CLP successfully proposed a motion defending the local Labour Party Young Socialists' branch (Militant's own kindergarten) against attacks by the government, the Liberals and the media in relation to a leaflet distributed during the second day of the Toxteth riots. Part of this defence involved a seven-point plan of action, the seventh of which was the semi-literate 'for a one-day strike to bring down the Tories and not to repeat the failure of previous Labour governments'.[58] Such a suggestion brings to mind Alexei Sayle's remark that those people who are forever calling for general strikes as a way of bringing down British governments 'live in the place where the people from cloud-cuckoo-land go to get away from it all'. Liverpool certainly had its fair share of cuckoos at this time.

One way in which Militant ensured that they controlled the agenda was through the use of model resolutions. The same item would come up for consideration in a host of ward meetings across the city. Having been agreed upon, it would then be considered at meetings of most, if not all, of the constituency parties, where Militant's support was further concentrated. Following agreement there, the resolution would then be heard by the DLP executive, whose bias towards Militant would ensure that the resolution was heard at the full DLP.

Even though the agenda of the DLP was framed in this way, a handful of delegates still attended from 'the right'. For the most part, they were delegated from the Cooperative movement, trade unions such as USDAW and the EETPU, and 'traditional' ward parties such as Dovecot, Gillmoss and Vauxhall. In time, however, faced with outright hostility from many of the new breed, most of these individuals either drifted in and out or dropped away completely. This is apparent when comparing the attendance of all ward delegates for the year 1979–80 to that of 1983–84. Twenty-nine of the thirty-three ward parties in the city registered a delegate to the DLP's 1979 Annual General Meeting, of whom one was replaced during the year and one failed to turn up. Four years later, at the 1983 AGM, thirty-one ward delegates were registered, of whom four were replaced during the year and five never attended. Basically, they became alienated by the conduct and reputation of the DLP. A similar, if less acute, pattern is evident when the corresponding delegate figures for the constituencies are compared. In 1979, forty delegates (five from each of the eight constituency parties) were registered, of whom one was replaced and one did not attend during the year. By 1983, when the city's six constituencies could send seven delegates each, forty of a possible forty-two were registered, two of whom failed to attend.

Some 'right-wingers' did, however, continue to keep up appearances, as Ian Lowes remembers:

> It's the easiest thing in the world when you're in the majority to go along to meetings and everything goes your way. I've had experiences in my own union at national and regional level where I've always been in the minority. So I had respect for people like Eddie Roderick. I didn't agree with him but at least he had the guts to come along and argue his point of view.

Similar changes had taken place at the Town Hall, where some of the host of new members who had joined the party in the late 1970s were now sitting as councillors. When I observed the Labour group, I was shocked to see so many unfamiliar faces. One in particular, however, stood out a mile – Derek Hatton.

As he came relatively late to the party, I had never come across Hatton before going to Australia. Yet, having seen and heard of him on television and in newspapers, and having digested the comments of others who came to visit, I formed a second-hand impression of an egotistical individual taking credit and eschewing blame (this was to be set out in its most extreme form in his autobiography). Meeting him for the first time, I reminded myself: 'this is a phoney, this is a conman' – there was no other way of putting it. I was amazed that so many people were unable to see through him. On meeting up with Joe Devaney for a second time, I expressed these views to him, saying 'Joe, how come this conman seems to be acting as spokesman for the Labour group?' Joe was somewhat equivocal – not that he ever gave the impression of being a supporter of Hatton, but as a councillor he perhaps thought that the smartest thing to do was to be non-committal.

Hatton did not emerge from a tradition of working-class struggle, as his rhetoric suggested; despite his rather transparent attempts to say otherwise,[59] he came from a somewhat *petit-bourgeois* background in the Childwall area of Liverpool. His upbringing was by no means affluent but with his father regularly employed as a fireman, and Hatton himself engaged in church activities, he was far removed from the experiences of most of his supporters. After a brief stint as an office boy and four years in the fire service, Hatton went to Goldsmiths College and then acquired a taste for local politics in London in the early 1970s. In 1972, he returned to Liverpool and two years later joined the Labour Party, thanks partly to Wally Edwards:

> I don't know whether I deserve any credit for this or not, but I must confess that when he did come in, he got stuck into work quite impressively. He is quite a charmer and he certainly took me in for quite a while because in those initial stages, he got involved in any action and was very supportive of the youngsters. In fact, he impressed me so much as an activist that I got him further involved. Although on one occasion, he drove a double-decker bus under a low bridge when he was taking thirty Young Socialists to a rally in Blackpool. The bus belonged to Community Transport, courtesy of Simon Fraser who was now running that and gave us it at a cheap rate, and Hatton knocked the bloody top off. It was very fortunate that no-one was badly hurt. He was devastated, of course, because he had been a fire-engine driver beforehand.

Cyril Taylor bears an even greater cross. He was Hatton's first point of contact, and it was he who attached a covering letter to Hatton's application noting his keenness to get involved:

> With the passing of the Seebohm Act, the Social Services Committee was established, one of the functions of which was the care of the homeless. The facilities for this in Liverpool were in a real Dickensian state, and there was an overflow of people scattered around, coming out of the railway station or off the Irish boats. One of the places where we were having difficulties was with homeless families who were stuck in run-down bed and breakfasts on Lord Nelson Street. In the city centre, there was nowhere very much for the kids to go and food was expensive; however, they were only a few hundred yards away from the Bronte Centre which ran lunch clubs. The backer for these was John Moores Jnr. and I asked him if it would be possible for the facilities to be made available. He said, 'well, we've got a bright, new, young community worker – his name's Derek Hatton and he's a good fellow, he's just come from Goldsmiths College. Why don't you go and see him?' So I did, and he jumped at the idea of helping out. I think it was at the fag end of his period as a devout Christian. I

got to know him that way and I was very astonished to see in his book that he alleged that 'a Liverpool Labour councillor, Dr Cyril Taylor, regarded as a radical figure at the time' – a nice insulting expression – 'had hounded him to join the Labour Party'. Can you imagine hounding Hatton to do anything?

Hatton ran the Bronte Centre for a while, but, as the person in charge, had to leave after an internal inquiry accused him of incompetence and found that £17,000 had inexplicably gone missing.[60] He subsequently took a job in Sheffield, but again returned to Merseyside to take up a position with Knowsley Borough Council. It was at this point that he became increasingly involved in Liverpool politics. In 1977, he applied to become a councillor, and after a defeat in a by-election in Tuebrook the following year, he was elected in 1979 to represent the 'outer estate' ward of Netherley. A year later, during the furore in the council chamber over the 50 per cent rate increases, Hatton made his mark. Before the debate, the Labour group had met and agreed a budget for the following twelve months. In the full council meeting, however, Hatton stood up and moved an entirely different one. Bill Snell, Chief Whip at the time, remembers the occasion well:

> The ideas behind it were marvellous but it would have seen us in the poorhouse. When it was over, I went to Wally [Edwards] because he was secretary of the party and said 'he has got to be disciplined', and Wally said 'it's too near election time to discipline him'. So he got away with it.

At the same time, Hatton had also begun to reveal a darker side to his temperament, as Vicky Roberts recalls:

> I remember going to a DLP meeting at Victoria Street when I actually saw him throw a chair at a friend of mine because he had upset him by proposing something which got carried.

Some people began to question his political integrity. For John Hamilton, Hatton was 'overbearing':

> Wherever it was, he had to be on the front line. Of course, he had no political depth to him at all. Mike Black, who I regularly chatted to, used to say: 'Derek Hatton will end up in the House of Lords as a Tory peer'.

Wally Edwards, meanwhile, remembers his wife Sarah's impressions:

> When I was the agent in West Derby [in the early 1960s], the Treasurer of

the party was a guy called Vincent Burke, who was a bit of a character. He was on the council and was a recognised left-winger. He stood against Bessie [Braddock] for the Exchange seat and it finished up in court because she had called him a Communist. Today, he is a millionaire racehorse owner and the chairman of the Conservative Party in Southport. When my wife, who was an amazing judge of people, first met him, I asked her what she thought and she said: 'Well, if you want me to be straight, Wally, he's a Tory. Mark my words, he's a Tory.' She was proved right on that one. Then came Derek Hatton, who she met very early on. I said 'What do you think of Derek?' She said 'I'll tell you in two words – Vincent Burke'.

So deep runs the man's socialism that soon after his political career came to an end, Hatton began to rather arrogantly advocate the principles of the free market. Following the fall of the Berlin Wall, he found himself on the same train as George Howarth – by then, the MP for Knowsley North – and approached him, saying: 'Hello, George, we should have a chat about "opportunities" with the fall of the Wall'. Howarth asked him what he meant, to which Hatton replied, 'Well, with your political contacts and my business acumen, we could clean up over there'.

On the face of it, it is remarkable that this opportunistic wide-boy was ever given the task of being a Labour councillor, let alone deputy leader of the group, a position to which he was elected in the summer of 1983 following Eddie Loyden's re-election to Parliament. But Hatton had his antecedents. Tony Lane, in his excellent book *Liverpool: Gateway of Empire* (retitled *City of the Sea* for the second edition) sets Hatton with his swagger and style of dress in a long tradition of Liverpool politics, referring to him as an 'arriviste'.[61] In terms of the local 'culture', Hatton was really nothing special at all – just another mouthy chancer with a suntan, some suits and a handful of second-hand soundbites. Indeed, academic Fred Ridley has written of being 'struck by the limited range of simple slogans' Hatton used, 'counters in political debate but no evidence at all of a worked-out theoretical base'.[62] Alas, people in and around the Labour Party fell for Hatton, some out of a desperate hope that he and his ilk might stand up on behalf of Liverpool against the excesses of the Thatcher government, but just as many because they saw something of what they themselves wanted to be. It just goes to show how naive people were, and why so many of them now squeal like stuck pigs when the party adopts a more professional approach in selecting candidates.

One of the more annoying elements to the Hatton factor was the media's obsession with him. Granted, he was televisually presentable and said a lot of outrageous things, but these were either Militant monologues or part of his 'laughing Jack jolly boy' repertoire. A classic example was when he appeared on the television programme *Question Time,* coming out with the usual slogans – 'no cuts in jobs and services' – and over-doing it with his accent. He was basically behaving like a professional Scouser, and would not have looked out of company on a night out with fellow Liverpudlian and 'comedian' Stan Boardman. It is no coincidence that the two now occasionally appear on local radio together.

With Hatton busy shouting off in the name of Militant and his own narrow ends, Tony Byrne was effectively taking over the running of the city. A councillor for Valley ward and, more importantly, the chair of the all-important Finance and Strategy Committee, Byrne was only interested in – indeed, he was monomaniac about – public housing. Ironically though, many of the ideas that he championed were inherited from Ken Stewart, who for all his failings had come up with an embryonic urban regeneration strategy. Having been re-elected to Speke ward in 1983, Ken soon after moved on to become the MEP for Merseyside West, and Byrne took over his council duties. Perhaps in resentment that he had not been given the credit he felt he deserved, Ken once told me how Byrne had allegedly told him that he was unsure as to whether he should join the Liberals or Labour. Either way, Byrne's objective was the same, and on stepping into Ken's shoes, he proceeded to try to put his dreams into effect. His discipline was ruthless, according to one of his fellow councillors, Bob Lancaster:

> Tony Byrne was a man of vision, but with his Jesuit background he saw what was needed and went for it. He didn't care who he cut down. For him, the end justified the means.

Within twelve months Byrne's single-mindedness had led to the creation of a large number of new homes which, along with the construction of a number of sports centres and nurseries around the city, became the centrepiece of the council's 'success'. Yet Byrne was so narrowly focused that he failed to see the most obvious flies in the ointment. Chief amongst these was the way in which the new homes were allocated – on the basis of 'absolute housing need', a method that worked to the detriment of many tenants. Steve

Mumby, a community activist at the time and now himself a Labour council-lor in Liverpool, recalls the outcome:

> They created 'unemployed' housing estates, one of which became known as Smack Valley. A very large number of dealers moved in, creating a nightmare for local people. A lot of these new estates were blighted almost immediately. It wasn't really taking account of where people wanted to live. It was bulldozer politics, something that Liverpool had seen a lot of in the past.

Criticisms were also made of the design of the houses. Unlike the many Parker-Morris style houses that had previously been typical of Liverpool estates, those built under Byrne's oversight were somewhat on the small side, a fault made colourfully clear by Paul Orr:

> They built these stupid little dolls' houses and kidded people saying, 'here's a new house'. It's only when people wanted to move in that they found they couldn't get the furniture from the house that they were leav-ing into them. The bastards built all sorts of houses which nobody wanted to live in. I know because I remember taking my wife to view this house along by the police station on Stanley Road. She went in and I told her 'as I'm very seldom in, you're the one that's going to have to live with what you commit yourself to. What are you going to do with your washing ma-chine? What are you going to do with your spin-dryer? What are you going to do with all of your other domestic appliances when you come into this little place?' The question was resolved for her when Tony Byrne said to me: 'Fuck off you, you're not getting one of these houses at all. You're get-ting nothing.'

The criticism, and the terseness of Byrne's alleged response, cannot be di-vorced from the fact that Orr was a councillor for Vauxhall ward. Here, the Labour Party was effectively the Eldonians Housing Cooperative which, having been granted various funds under the previous Liberal administra-tion, was dead set against the city council's grand strategy (the name 'Eldonians' came from the football team Orr had played for as a youngster). They were purely interested in their own community, the history of which has been well documented, and while what they achieved benefited them greatly, the downside is that much of the money came from other parts of the city that merited equal treatment.

Incredibly, an associate of Militant, Paul Luckock, managed to become a councillor in Vauxhall. One of the staff at the local law centre, the ward party selected him without really knowing his background and he was more or less chosen because of his Irish surname, a badge of honour in the Vauxhall area. On being elected to the council, however, Luckock began to express his support for Byrne's grand strategy rather than the local one of the Eldonians, and he soon became something of a pariah in the area. So much so, in fact, that he was physically prevented from attending ward party meetings.

A few years after the Eldonians Cooperative was established, a power struggle ensued between the founders and the chairman, Tony McGann. With his fingers in various pies, McGann had become a 'boss' in the long tradition of Liverpool politics, although at a very local level; while the Braddocks had two tower blocks named after them, he is celebrated personally in the name of the Eldonians community centre. Indeed, Tony McGann's grip on the Cooperative has remained so tight that a number of those who have been significantly involved in the project have first fallen out with him and then fallen foul of his scorn.

Beyond the more parochial concerns of Vauxhall, it is indisputable that much was achieved on both the house-building and house-refurbishment fronts in Liverpool in the mid 1980s. Away from the plus-points, however, there were two negative issues. The first of these was Byrne's failure to provide an adequate managed maintenance programme. Much of the money that had been allocated to the council to ensure necessary housing repairs was redirected into construction, and whatever the initial quality of the new housing stock, as fast as some places went up, others started to fall apart. As a result, a fairly legitimate policy was cocked up from day one. Over a decade later, the council was still dealing with the backlog.

The second problem derived from how Byrne's housing monomania left other areas of social provision wanting. The social services directorate suffered particularly, not through reducing its budget as such – remember the mantra 'no cuts in jobs and services' – but through the lack of additional funding and staffing at a time when problems within the social services remit were becoming more widespread. Locally, it was often said that this stemmed from Byrne's open dislike for social workers; in his eyes, such people were middle-class do-gooders meddling in the lives of people with whom they could neither empathise nor ultimately help. Instead, like a travelling salesman in turn-of-the-century America, the 'Mad Monk' offered his own all-purpose cure for society's ills: 'Suffering from depression, deprivation or domestic violence? What you need is a two-up, two-down with a garden.' If he could have bottled this potion, he could not have found a better name for it than 'delirium'.

If there was one group of people that Byrne perhaps disliked more than social workers, it was those employed in the voluntary sector. Again, no slashing of budgets occurred, but in his own calculating way, Byrne made it as difficult as possible for individuals and organisations seeking resources or information from the council to understand the decision-making procedure. Vicky Roberts, who at the time acted as an unofficial liaison between the city council and the Council for Voluntary Service, explains the subtle way in which this worked:

> I used to have to process a lot of that information and feed it back to the voluntary sector, to tell them where the pressure points might be for decisions, because decisions would be made and nobody would know that they had. They would be made under 'delegated powers'. They would also use all sorts of arcane sub-committees to route things through. In the end, we developed some relationships with people in the committee section who, whilst they would never tip us off, helped us to find our way through the maze.

Such comments are telling. Remember, this was not some Kafkaesque bureaucracy in which the perpetrators themselves did not understand the logic or results of their actions. This was a city council in which arrogant individuals such as Hatton and Byrne felt both willing and able to ride rough-shod over anything and anyone – their colleagues within the Labour group, the officers of the council, the electorate and, perhaps most significantly, their actual 'leader'.

John Hamilton was, and remains, an intrinsically decent man, a Quaker whom I always suspected of being in awe of his illustrious father. He once told me that it had only ever been his ambition to be chair of the Education Committee, like his father. This self-effacing image, however, was not quite the complete picture. On a number of occasions, John put his name forward as a parliamentary candidate, and he was more than happy to be leader of the Labour group. What he could not do was handle the Militants on the council, or Hatton and Byrne individually, as first Bob Wareing and then Lyn Anderson illustrate:

> I really do regret having to say this because John Hamilton is a wonderful man, but on at least two occasions I said to him 'Look, what are you going

to do about it?' One was when we were on a march and the television people kept interviewing Hatton. When we got to the Town Hall, I said to him in one of the corridors 'Who's the leader of this city council, John?', to which he said 'I am'. So I said, 'Well, he's giving all of the interviews. You want to take a stand.' I've no doubt that if John had taken a stand, he'd have had the support of the majority of the Labour Party.

There were issues around launches of various aspects of policy where it had germinated to a particular point and Tony Byrne would say 'We need to do a press conference', and immediately go to Derek. I actually remember going into the office one day and saying 'Shouldn't John – as leader – be playing a role in all of this?' Tony and Derek looked at one another then looked at me and said 'okay'. So Tony went and saw him but John wasn't prepared to cancel what he was doing, which was either the bench or something that could have easily been rearranged. Tony came back to me and said 'Don't suggest that again'.

Frankly, Hamilton was increasingly humiliated by Hatton, and was later treated with total contempt by Byrne. Anywhere else, he would have had the respect of his peers. But the politics of Liverpool in the 1980s was unlike anywhere else, and Hamilton did not have the wherewithal to take on this wholly ruthless new breed of local politician.

The two principal features of traditional boss politics in Liverpool were, firstly, a controlling figure – for Labour, a Braddock or a Sefton – and, secondly, a degree of pork-barrelling, by which certain 'areas' (or sectional interests) were looked after. In the early 1980s, a troika appeared to have developed, with Byrne looking after finance, Hatton looking after presentation, and Hamilton ostensibly playing the constitutional role. The reality, however, was a *quid pro quo* between Militant and Byrne. The former, in the guises of Hatton, Tony Mulhearn and Terry Harrison, indulged in demagoguery; the latter got on with the urban regeneration strategy.

Behind these figures stood the rest of the Labour group. Some had the ability but not the numbers to challenge the then orthodoxy of the local party, and buried their heads, ostrich-like, in taking the government's cut in Liverpool's rate support grant as justification for what the council was doing. Roy Gladden who, together with others, would later orchestrate a weak challenge to Hatton and Byrne, has made this evident in recalling his role:

It was not just about Labour, Conservative, Liberal, whatever. It was about 'the city'. The feeling was very strong. We were fighting for the city's survival. We were so caught up in the battle that we didn't see what was going on in the world around us. I believed so strongly in what we were doing that I packed my job in and became a full-time councillor.

Tied to a strong sense of collective responsibility, of standing or falling together (even when they thought it might be wrong), Roy and others became bound to the actions of more manipulative minds.

For the most part, those who made up the numbers on the group did little more than that. They were insignificant individuals. Some were happy to remain faceless, while others tried their utmost to be identified as in some way important. Frank Mills in County ward was a case of the latter. A virtual messenger-boy who was led down the garden path by the local leadership of Militant, Frank was never a malicious fellow, but he had little idea about what was going on, and he was considered hopeless as a councillor. He bought lots of new suits, ties and shirts because, in taking his cue from Mulhearn and Hatton in their dapper outfits, he believed that this was the image he should be projecting. More often than not, with many of his fellow group members in jumpers and jeans, poor old Frank looked like a tailor's dummy.

Coveting attention in a different way was Tony Hood, a councillor in Abercromby who, whilst never a Militant, played a very fine game. At the council, he tried to associate himself with the ruling majority group. In his own political backyard, however, he was careful not to lay it on with a trowel, certainly not along Militant lines. Hood saw himself as a left-wing vanguardist, albeit one who was prepared to do deals in order to climb the greasy pole; after all, he made no secret of his parliamentary ambitions.

Another of the Abercromby councillors was Jimmy Routledge, a one-time IRA sympathiser who was more interested in Irish Nationalist politics. When, in 1998, he resigned during his second spell as a councillor, putting the Labour group's administration in jeopardy, I half expected him to say that he wanted to spend more time thinking about the Northern Ireland peace process. Aside from Irish issues, his politics were complex but were in large part determined by perceived insults and disservice. Other councillors were less difficult to fathom, and in many respects constituted little more than voting fodder. Typical of this category were John Humphries in St Mary's ward, Alan Fogg in Kensington and Frank Wiles in Everton. The latter was a somewhat simple-minded bloke who once told me that Bob Parry was good to him because, 'if I do his surgeries, Bob buys me a packet of ciggies'.

Then there was Broadgreen councillor Jimmy Dillon. He seemed bewildered on his good days. I remember one meeting I attended, towards the end of the 1980s, at which a local MEP, Les Huckfield, launched into an attack on a grand conspiracy led by overpaid Labour Party officials. As I listened to him extend this into a grand theory in which he mentioned Felipe Gonzalez, PASOK and Papandreou, and Willy Brandt,[63] I looked over at Jimmy Dillon, who was sat in the front row, and imagined in my own mind's eye a 'think' bubble appearing out of his head, where he was reflecting to himself: 'Panatheniakos, Inter Milan, Barcelona, Borussia Monchengladbach ...' That was about the level of his interest in international affairs.

These were not representative people. In fact, these were people who were not very interested in the wider community, a tradition that has long bedevilled Liverpool politics. Most councillors have had no concept of immersing themselves in the people. For them, politics only involves 'the people' at election time. Ultimately, the significance attached to the idea of being a councillor has encouraged many to put themselves up on pedestals of their own making. For some individuals, election to 'the council' is the acme of their politics, the pinnacle of their ambitions. They don't want to be a councillor for anything or anywhere, they just want to be seen to be 'a councillor'; and it is a sad fact of life that even today many of them are inarticulate and incapable of stringing more than a handful of words together. As for ideas, they lack the ability to think for themselves. I am sure that in a vague way they have entered the council with the belief that they could do some good, but they have no clear view of what the whole thing is about. This phenomenon reached its nadir in the early 1980s, when contrary to what was said at the time, many councillors did not have a clue about administering local government according to a particular political perspective. What they were engaged in was simple, unadulterated tribalism.

It has to be said that the MPs were no different. They were there, every time, on the regular marches that were held in Liverpool during this period, and then up on the Town Hall balcony afterwards behaving like footballers who had just brought home the FA Cup – after all, Bob Parry had once had a trial for Everton. This was the limit of their imagination. It was their only experience and the way in which they thought things were done: 'the council's having a march, I must go on it', 'the T&G's having a march, let's go on it', 'there's a march for the dockers; right, we'll be there'. And, of course, they always had to be seen to be at the front. It was as if they thought the march could not take place without them. It was all about ego and promoting the image of themselves as individual politicians. There was no strategy, no thought, and even less positive effect. This was also true of their activities in Parliament.

Alongside his well-documented connections with the political classes in Serbia, Bob Wareing has had a long history of involvement with exotic forms of politics, particularly in eastern Europe and the Balkans. It was a single Militant vote on the constituency General Management Committee that got him his nomination for Liverpool West Derby in place of Eric Ogden, the sitting MP:

> The deal was that Wareing would get the support of 'the left' in West Derby. It wasn't just the Tendency. I mean, I voted for him and I wasn't Tendency, but they supported him and without their support he wouldn't have got the seat.

Naturally, Bob is keen to refute this:

> No, I don't think that's true. Were there any Militant members on that General Management Committee? Eric Ogden raised it with the NEC but before they reported he moved over to the SDP. Incidentally, I think he would have been reselected if Brian Sedgemore had put in an appearance, because he had been short-listed. He would have taken some of the vote that I got, in fact he would have taken a lot of it, particularly from the Gillmoss ward as they had nominated him. But he would have failed to get the votes from the right and the centre which I got because I think [it is possible to get these votes] when you're known locally and people don't necessarily dislike you because they disagree with your politics.

Having won the nomination, Bob soon after uprooted himself from Liverpool and moved to Croft near Warrington. This was politically dangerous – having been born in the constituency (on the Norris Green estate), and having spent all those years identifying with the place and then becoming its representative, he took a decision to move away. Most people in that position in Liverpool at that time would not have done something that was bound to antagonise so many people. One wonders if, in some strange but reasoned way, Bob's elevation to Parliament was taken by him as a point of departure from the politics of his birthplace.

Between the general elections of 1983 and 1987, there were fifteen adjournment debates in the House of Commons with specific references to

Liverpool; they covered a variety of topics, but for the most part concentrated on education, finance, health, housing, unemployment and urban deprivation.[64] Four of the city's six MPs not only instigated such debates but also 'intervened' (i.e. contributed) or attempted to intervene in many of them. Wareing, however, having participated in the two debates that followed his arrival in Parliament, was thereafter more noticeable by his tendency to absent himself, surfacing once in late 1985 and once in 1987, a few months before the general election.

Eddie Loyden returned to Parliament in 1983, partly as a result of an alleged fix with Militant which put him in the right place at the right time. As he had been the Liverpool Garston MP until losing his seat in 1979, most people assumed that he would seek nomination for the candidature there. The previous year, however, when the wards in the Toxteth constituency nominated their PPC, Loyden appeared on the scene and almost swept the board. Two others also ended up with nominations – Paul Sommerfeld, a Londoner who was Secretary of the Merseyside Race Relations Council, and Tony Mulhearn. Joe Devaney, himself on the ward short-lists for Dingle and Granby, recalls what happened next in the Toxteth selection:

> You had these three on the constituency short-list. Then at the last minute, Loyden withdraws. Suddenly, he gets Garston. I'm not saying a deal was done and I wouldn't want to libel Eddie, but at the time people did say 'well, he's been promised Garston'.

With Sommerfeld considered 'right wing' by many in the Toxteth party, and thus an unsuitable candidate for Liverpool, Mulhearn was instantly cast as the candidate of 'the left' and secured the nomination. He was to be frustrated, however, when the boundary commission reduced the city's constituencies from eight to six, and the Liverpool Toxteth seat disappeared from the electoral map. Garston, of course, did not and Loyden arrived back at the Commons for what would eventually be a fourteen-year spell.

Like many of his contemporaries, Eddie was locked in a time-warp, viewing politics primarily in terms of his tribal loyalties. He appeared to relish debates that specifically concerned Liverpool, instigating many himself and always ready to intervene in others. In doing so, he would wax lyrical, armed with up-to-date statistics and the art of rhetoric. But, as the following example illustrates, his speeches often sounded like a Scouse variation of Monty Python's 'Yorkshire policemen' sketch:

> I was born in Liverpool in 1923, in the heart of the slums of that city.

During my life there I experienced, worked and lived with and went to school in abject poverty and misery ... My first job on leaving school was in a boot warehouse in Scotland Road. I received the princely sum of 6s 6d a week, which went towards the budget of my family. I was one of many thousands of kids in Liverpool who were in the same position. When I went to sea at the age of fourteen and a half, I found an even worse world among the seamen ... I recall the misery of the courts, with twelve people to a court, with one tap and one lavatory.[65]

Much of this particular speech was lost on the minister it was aimed at, the then Parliamentary Under-Secretary of State for the Environment, Angela Rumbold; in replying on behalf of the government, she chose instead to patronise Eddie for having sincere and passionate feelings but ill-defined objectives. Yet she was wrong; Loyden did have well-defined objectives, set within a frame of meaning that spawned his political stances. The problem was that the frame itself had become increasingly outdated.

The parliamentary career of Bob Parry is a case study in itself. Known at Westminster as Gulliver, and in his Liverpool Riverside constituency as the Right Honourable Member for Hong Kong, he brought a new meaning to the phrase 'fellow traveller'. The raw data suggest a man of prolific activity on behalf of his lucky constituents, who in twelve parliaments between 1980 and 1992 made no fewer than 840 contributions with regard to Liverpool. A trawl through Bob's work, however, reveals a number of facts which in time came to give his political enemies plenty of ammunition. Most evident amongst these was Bob's knack for tabling written questions for the same set of information on a regular basis – questions that were asked in the most basic way and which concerned information that could have easily been obtained from the Commons library. Had he done so, he might have been able to use his time more constructively in representing what for a long time was the poorest constituency in England. He actually did spend time in the library, regularly falling asleep in there, as he never had an office in all of his time at Westminster.

Parry was reselected time after time, mainly because his constituency members could never agree on a replacement. That, and the support of the TGWU, ensured that he continued to spend his time way out of his depth. At each election, he was seized with panic as though his seat was a marginal, and, more often than not, he fell ill. There was even one election when his dog, Paddy, took him into the path of a motor vehicle as they left one of his watering holes. Mind you, his absence was an advantage to any election campaign, especially his own. Like others, his arrogance and sense of self-importance increased with his years in Parliament. In my view, Bob made no contribution of any worth whatsoever during his twenty-seven years in the House of Commons. In terms of the image of Liverpool, he was an unmitigated disaster. As Keva Coombes puts it:

> The drunken Bob Parry pissed away Channel 5 coming to Liverpool by getting drunk in the House of Commons; pisses himself in the toilet before he meets the Minister and comes in all wet around the front of his trousers. That's a pretty fair reflection of Bob Parry's contribution to Liverpool.

On those occasions when people within Walton attempt to criticise my role, they do so by stating how much of a constituency MP my predecessor, Eric Heffer, was. They may therefore be surprised to hear that his contribution in Parliament to issues concerning Liverpool waned during the heady days of the 1980s. In the ten parliamentary sessions between October 1980 and June 1990, Heffer made forty-eight contributions with reference to Liverpool – no insignificant figure in itself, until it is revealed that nineteen of these were oral questions and that eight more were interventions in adjournment debates (even there, his contribution between 1983 and 1987 was less than that of Wareing). The remaining twenty-one adds up to an average of two written questions a year on behalf of his deep-suffering proletariat back in Liverpool. What is more intriguing, however, is that seven of the twenty-one written or oral questions he posed between December 1980 and March 1987 were to Thatcher herself. It is well known, of course, that she considered Heffer her favourite Labour politician, but one cannot help thinking that Eric felt that he had a direct line to her.[66]

Having developed a reputation, along with Tony Benn, Dennis Skinner and others, as a darling of the parliamentary left, Heffer was elected in 1975 to the NEC and retained a seat for eleven years. Whilst a member of the NEC, he became increasingly vocal in his opposition towards the party's actions in investigating the Militant organisation or its individual members, and on at least one occasion compared the case for such actions with the Nazi propaganda machine.[67] Yet this was at a time at which Militant were running rife through his own constituency party, something a man so allegedly astute as Heffer could not have failed to notice. In the long run, his attempts to live with this contradiction became increasingly apparent, and, as Gary Booth, and then Bob Lancaster, recall, he ended up privately castigating them:

There were times when I ear-wigged what he had said to other people, that he was never that enamoured with the Tendency.

while publicly remaining equivocal:

It was fun and games. Eric was a nice person, an intelligent person, who was widely travelled and experienced but he was everything to everybody.

His silence, like that of a number of his parliamentary colleagues, cost Liverpool and Labour dearly. Jane Kennedy, then district secretary of NUPE, and now the MP for Liverpool Wavertree, recalls how she viewed Heffer, Loyden and Parry at this time:

They were tired old men. They just toed the line and argued the case on behalf of the Militant council and did it quite blindly.

Liverpool's one other Labour MP in the mid 1980s was the openly Militant Terry Fields. Many people, perhaps, would say favourable things of him, but I considered him neither to be very bright nor a decent sort with whom I could get on. In common with virtually all of Militant's zealots, Fields had a vicious and vindictive streak directed towards his political enemies. In 1988, he was to threaten me in the columns of the *Sunday Times* with breach of his parliamentary privilege. I had charged him with missing important House of Commons votes in favour of attending Young Socialist meetings, where he spoke to recruit for Militant. He produced a letter from the then pairing whip, Ray Powell, saying that his attendance was exemplary. I knew this to be untrue, but I did not understand the trade-off between Powell and Fields (and others) for shadow cabinet votes until I entered Parliament myself.

Fields came to prominence as a local Fire Brigades Union representative during the 1978–79 firemen's strike, after which Militant successfully pushed him forward as the prospective parliamentary candidate for Liverpool Kirkdale. In 1982, however, following boundary changes, the constituency ceased to exist and was divided out into Walton, Riverside and the fledgling Liverpool Broadgreen, itself made up for the most part out of another dissolved seat, Liverpool Wavertree. Derek Hatton, who had already been selected for Wavertree, was in a commanding position to become the candidate in Broadgreen, but following the initiation of a new selection process, mysteriously stepped down, allowing Fields to secure the nomination. Soon after, at the 1983 general election, Fields was thrust down the parliamentary road to socialism and, although a less gifted orator, began to share Loyden's passion for talking about the deprivation of his upbringing.

He more often than not took up well over half of the allocated time in adjournment debates, leaving government representatives little time to respond. Still, one can only wonder what effect the following words had on William Waldegrave, another Parliamentary Under-Secretary of State for the Environment, as Fields told the House:

> I was born in a dock area before the war. My father was a docker, so I feel qualified to speak on some of the matters on which I hope to enlarge ... My father was proud, and characteristic of the spirit of people in Liverpool. We had dignity and got through decades of struggle. I have never known anything other than bad housing, high unemployment and lack of opportunity for Liverpool people.[68]

It is doubtful that Waldegrave would have blinked throughout this, even if Fields had added 'and we used to live in a cardboard box in the middle of the road', prompting a retort from Loyden of 'You were lucky!'

Coincidentally, having appeared on a Labour Party platform with the actor Tony Booth a few weeks before his election, Fields discovered that his Militant colleague, Dave Nellist, initially shared an office with Booth's son-in-law, another new MP, Tony Blair! Very quickly, Nellist changed offices to share with his comrade Fields. Unlike Nellist, Fields was wholly unable to adapt to the needs of the House, and withdrew further and further into himself. His role beyond the Commons was more than apparent to Jane Kennedy, then a member of the party in Broadgreen:

> Terry Fields was a complete waste of space as a constituency MP. He seemed to do surgeries but not personally on a regular basis. He spent most of his time campaigning on picket-lines all over the country. If you had a strike or were raising funds anywhere in Britain, you could be sure that you'd get Terry Fields to join you.

Ultimately, Fields was a Member of Parliament for Militant, serving three purposes – a name to be attached to every one of their idiotic resolutions, a recruiting sergeant for their cause, particularly with youth, and a resource for their political activities. As long as this continued, both Liverpool and the Labour Party would suffer.

These, then, were the leading lights of the Labour establishment in Liverpool, representing the city locally and nationally. Anywhere else, the situation would have given rise to healthy opposition – but when I returned to

Liverpool in 1984, the opposition in the city seemed to be non-existent. The cult of personality within politics is generally distasteful, and is becoming increasingly so, but it can be useful in local government if there is a figure in whom people can identify dynamism and leadership. During this time, the Liberals had no-one. Of their hierarchy, Paul Clark and Richard Kemp had nothing to offer, and Trevor Jones came across as a shrill and weak leader, far from the image he had of himself as a model local statesman. Their group gave the impression of a rudderless ship, drifting with the tides. The Liberal Party always had a problem in Liverpool in terms of the ease with which Labour could paint them as jumped-up Tories. Even accounting for their collusions with the local Conservatives between 1974 and 1983, the Liberals were never really able to carve out a separate identity for themselves. For the Tories, meanwhile, it was one-way traffic out of the Town Hall.

Opposition did arise, however, within the Labour group. Caught numerically between the Famous Five and the Magnificent Seven, and locally between 'the twenty-one' and the soon-to-be-revered 'forty-seven', the 'scabby/sensible six' (depending on your viewpoint) were so labelled because of their opposition to the attempt by their colleagues to set a deficit budget in the spring of 1984. Having built up over several months, this conflict came to a head at a full council meeting in early March when the six, who had informed the *Liverpool Echo*, but not the rest of the Labour group, of their intentions, turned up and voted with the Liberals and Tories. The rationale underlying their actions is explained by one of their number, Bill Snell:

> In the old days, you would be on your committees, you would get your agenda, you'd work out your budgets and they would be submitted. You'd have to fine them down and you'd find the gaps, and you did it to stay within the law. But in the Militant period, you put down what you wanted and they would say 'If that's what we need then that's what we must have'. There was no debate. That's the way it was done.

As well as Snell, the six included Pat Johnson, Joe Morgan, Peter Murphy, Paul Orr and Eddie Roderick, all of whom had long been considered to be part of the 'old guard' within the local party – out of touch with the direction in which it was moving, but at the same time offering nothing in the way of constructive criticism that could steer it elsewhere. This interpretation of their 'opposition' was as true outside the group as it was inside. Peter Devaney, now an officer of Liverpool City Council but then active within the

Liverpool Mossley Hill CLP, remembers how the perception outside the council was that the six had broken the whip:

> Ignoring the fact that Militant were involved, it was generally felt that they should have voted with the group. They were seen within the Labour Party as just a group of people who basically didn't like not getting their own way. To an extent, the characters involved personified that. They were definitely a rogue element.

Bob Lancaster recalls the conversation he had with Eddie Roderick drawing attention to Roderick's experiences twelve years earlier during the housing finance debacle:

> I said 'Eddie, you've got a lot to answer for. Not because you separated yourself when you voted but because you're the ones with the experience, the ones who should stand up and say "Hang on, I don't care what you call me, this is where you're going and this is what's liable to happen".'

With the political numbers on the council finely balanced, the votes of the six led to a clear defeat for Labour's budget proposals, after which the Liberals and Tories both had their plans rejected. At this point, Paul Orr successfully moved an amendment aimed at adjourning the meeting until early April, by which time the council officers would have been able to look more closely at alternatives. Tony Byrne, however, subsequently succeeded in moving an amendment to Orr's proposal (which, in procedural terms, had become the substantive motion to be voted on), calling for the establishment of a committee to run essential services pending the April meeting. Orr's motion with Byrne's amendment was then put to the vote. Alas, it was scuppered when the majority of the Labour group abstained and the Liberals voted it down. With no other proposals being put to the council, the meeting ended acrimoniously.

After their opposition, the six rebels found themselves faced initially merely with the wrath of the DLP, which declared its outrage at their actions in a special meeting of the executive committee the following day. Soon after, however, the six were removed from their posts on various council committees and sub-committees. Then came the intimidation, as first Bill Snell and then Paul Orr recall:

> Me and my wife used to go to Broadway for our groceries and they'd all be standing there howling at me. So one day I stopped and took them on. I said to one who was a lecturer 'This lot I can forgive but not you, you're a

lecturer', and to the rest of them 'As for you lot, you've all got jobs on the parks and gardens thanks to Hatton', to which one kid said 'I haven't, I'm on the bins', and I replied 'It's the same story'. I went through it with them and tore them to pieces and we had a crowd around us. At the end, I said 'Right, you know I come past here every week, so keep it buttoned and I will too because it doesn't do anybody any good. But open your mouth and you'll bloody well get it back.' When I came along the next Saturday, one went to say something but the others told him to shut up.

It came to the point where we had to get brought to and taken out of the council chamber in police vehicles. But when we had meetings in the Annexe of the group, the Militants would be there. They'd be doing all sorts to us – spitting. But immediately you gave one of them a belt – and they got many belts, I can tell you – they'd be 'Did you see him? Did you see what he done? I want witnesses!' But we never shirked going to any Labour group meeting where it was likely to be a question of a Militant involvement. You could never mistake it because you couldn't get into the bloody Annexe. I was absolutely snowed under with hundreds of trade unionists and others, and of course they used to say 'You fucking Tory'. It was terrible.

Orr himself was part of a long tradition of city politics in which rational argument quickly descended to the suggestion that a disagreement could be settled in more physical ways. John Hamilton remembers one occasion at the Town Hall in the late seventies, when Orr was the Lord Mayor and Trevor Jones kept interrupting the proceedings in the council chamber:

Orr turned round and said: 'If you stand up once again, I'll come down there and punch you in the nose'. That was his style. He was the best Lord Mayor the Labour Party ever had in Liverpool, but this was not exactly what a Lord Mayor should say. Jones took him on his word and never interrupted again. I think he was convinced, and rightly so, that Orr would not have thought twice about hitting him.

Yet Hamilton also suspects Orr's motives for voting against the group on the decision to defy central government:

Orr was a very good chair of Personnel and he knew the Whitley Council laws inside out. When the Militants came in he didn't like them. They offended him religiously and ethically as much as politically. He certainly didn't like Derek Hatton and he wasn't afraid to say so. This coloured his political thinking. He would probably have been in agreement with the stance on the rates but he wasn't going to go along with them. After they threw him out of the chairmanship, he was very bitter. He had to accept it and they put other people in. In fact, it was Hatton that took over the chair of Personnel.

Regardless of why Orr opposed the decision to defy the government, he became identified as someone who was able to give Hatton and co. headaches, as Paul himself explains with respect to a meeting he had with Neil Kinnock at Westminster:

> He said: 'All I want you to do is to give me Hatton's head on a platter, and I'll do the rest'. And I said, 'Well, what help are you going to give us to get his fucking head on the platter?'

Following the May elections of 1984, the Gillmoss ward party deselected Eddie Roderick. At the same time, the Labour presence on the council grew to fifty-eight. In part a consequence of rising popular support for the council's stance, this was also aided by disillusionment and apathy amongst non-Labour voters confused by, if not tired of, partisan factions within the SDP/Liberal Alliance, or unwilling to sanction the local face of Margaret Thatcher. With the Alliance and Tory groups at the Town Hall reduced to a total of forty-one, and Orr, Snell and co. reduced to five, the 'leadership' of the Labour group no longer had to worry about the numbers game. Where, in the normal course of events, clear single-party rule could have given rise to more open debate concerning the whys and wherefores of the council's strategy, mid 1980s' Liverpool saw paranoia and dogma prevail. Central to this was the discipline enforced by the caucus system.

Caucusing for support within the Labour group had long been a feature of city politics in Liverpool. In the 1950s and early 1960s, Jack Braddock and his allies formed one caucus, whilst 'the left' and 'Catholic Action' formed two others. The aim in all cases was to muster an initial level of coherent support with a view to directing the overall position of the group. What was different in the 1980s, however, was that the left caucus, by this time known as the 'Broad Left', was itself being caucused. Michael Crick, in his book *Militant*, cites Eddie Roderick's understanding of how this worked from the perception of someone on the outside.[69] Perhaps more enlightening, however, are the following comments from Bob Lancaster and Roy Gladden, both of whom attended Broad Left meetings in the mid 1980s:

You got the impression that you were taking part in a political discussion aimed at achieving a consensus of opinion in order to take that course of action. In reality it wasn't. You'd be going to a Broad Left meeting where you thought you were a secretive group, making decisions to be passed on to somebody else, but those decisions had already been made the previous night.

Amongst the senior councillors – Ken Stewart, Mike Black, Hughie Dalton, Bill Lafferty, Alec Doswell – you felt part of a group. These were people who had the magnetism. They were old Labour stalwarts. We grew up ourselves looking up to these people and we learnt from them. Eventually, it became apparent, though, that there was a caucus operating within the caucus. This was made up of the twelve or so members of the Tendency and their 'runners', whose support guaranteed that the Tendency would always have two or three votes more than anyone else.

Militant's numerical strength within the left caucus increased significantly after the 1984 elections, with at least five of the fifteen new faces in the Labour group sporting Tendency colours. These included Peter Ferguson in Dingle, Billy Harper in Netherley and Tony Rimmer in Gillmoss – and, more significantly, Felicity Dowling in Speke and Tony Mulhearn in St Mary's. Respectively the secretary and the chair of the DLP, Dowling and Mulhearn's arrivals also signalled a tightening of that body's stranglehold over the group.

The process by which this was achieved was simple. Militant would decide their line and then take it to the Broad Left caucus where, whilst numerically in the minority, they were the largest organised faction – which, together with their plausible arguments, generally meant that the Militant line prevailed. Whether through a distorted sense of group loyalty or in pursuit of their own political advantage, the other members of the Broad Left would then consider themselves bound by this line. Peer-group pressure, well-crafted rhetoric, and enlightened self-interest combined to give the caucus a unity of political purpose which could then be applied to the Labour group and, ultimately, the council. Such manoeuvring was by no means straightforward. Within the group, informed opposition acted to contain excesses, and in terms of the council, it was circumscribed by law – as Lyn Anderson recalls of Dowling's attempt to run the DLP from the office in the council:

She couldn't understand why I wouldn't let her. I said 'No, we're not paying for that. Rules are rules and what you're doing should be done up at

Hardman Street. What goes on here is to do with local government', to which she replied 'But it's all to do with the Labour Party'. Again, I pointed out the difference, but then she started calling me 'a cow' and other things.

Labour councillors were, however, open to manipulation via the DLP, particularly if, like Roy Gladden, they were relatively naive about the way in which the local party was organised:

> When I first became a councillor I actually believed that the DLP ruled me. When it passed a resolution, I believed that I had to carry it out unless my conscience said otherwise. That was how I was brought up in politics in Liverpool – the district party was the all-encompassing, democratic organisation that met, that made policy and gave it us to fight the election on. I actually believed that that was the way it should be. I wanted a resolution to go to the ward, to the constituency, to the district and to a policy conference; and if it got through it was because it was a good one. To me the DLP was like a continuing conference. Here was this marvellous organisation which people came along to from every ward and constituency, and from trade unions; and I think in its purist sense it was correct. The problem, of course, came with the kind of organisation that controlled my union, the GMB.

Despite the catalogue of misdemeanours that was eventually unearthed, some local players continue to this day to hold a sepia-tinted view of how Liverpool politics was then organised. Eddie Sabino, for example, is doubtful as to whether or not the DLP ever determined policy in the city:

> My view is that it was always done by the Labour group, and that the DLP was in fact used by the group to bolster support for its policies. Of course, the group and the DLP weren't two separate bodies – they were two separate names but there was actual linking between officers of one group and the officers of the other. You always had this closeness, but no-one could claim in any real sense that the DLP determined the policy and then forced it down the throats of the Labour group.

The proof of the pudding, however, lies in the eating – within Eddie's observation of how the same personalities held office in both bodies, something that ultimately led to a confusion of roles. The councillors were legally elected and therefore liable for council decisions, whilst members of the DLP were not. How, therefore, could the latter dictate the former's role in council?

That was surely power without responsibility, the harlot's role of the DLP. By the time councillors like Joe Devaney recognised the incongruity, it was already too late:

> As the stranglehold on the DLP became more and more obvious, it started telling the council what to do. They started seeing the councillors as delegates of the DLP. I'll always remember two incidents. They recommended to the Labour group AGM who should be chairs of council committees, and they even went as far to say 'and Felicity Dowling will be chair of the schools sub-committee'. Amazingly, the group AGM rubber-stamped it. The other thing was Tony Byrne coming along to the Labour group and saying 'the DLP exec has said this, and therefore it must be right'.

In their determination to keep a hold over the DLP, Militant and their allies played a variety of tricks, the most simple of which was the way in which they would call an emergency executive meeting late one evening for early the following morning. Such cultivated spontaneity was difficult for most people to keep up with and, consequently, it became a means of controlling the agenda and the decisions of the organisation by ensuring that Militant supporters attended meetings effectively denied to others. It was also in direct contradiction of, and thus an abuse of, Labour Party standing orders. Sadly, regional officials, either through culpable ignorance or indolence, or both, failed to impose the strictures of the rule book. At the same time, it was Militant's way of engendering a state of crisis. They wanted to keep people on edge all the time and, by winding them up in a way that any 'enemy' could not hope to replicate, they induced what can best be described as a collective paranoia amongst their members and supporters. It became so bad that, at one DLP meeting, Dowling's secretary's report included a sub-section 'state of emergency', in which she declared: 'In the event of Thatcher sending in troops on to the docks etc., emergency meetings will be called at short notice to decide our reply'.[70]

Militant and its acolytes at the DLP also used the organisational means available to prevent people who had spoken out against them from getting on to the local government panel. At this time, becoming a Labour candidate in local elections tended to involve no more than the nomination of a legitimate individual and a formal interview by the DLP executive, where a handful of fairly innocuous questions would be asked to ascertain their loyalty to the council's strategy. This led to the selection of candidates who, if they were not Tendency, were either sympathetic to 'the line' or could be trusted as mere voting fodder. However, panic set in when someone slipped through the net who could not be considered 'on-message'. The stops would be pulled out in the most concerted way to prevent this happening, even where individuals had outstanding abilities and were very loyal, long-standing members of the party.

A case in point was that of Vicky Roberts. A member of the party in Aigburth, Vicky was known city-wide because of her work in the voluntary sector and had helped the relevant chair at the time to write the DLP's policy on child-care. As a consequence, another ward party, Arundel, asked her to be their candidate at the 1984 local elections. Psephologically, Arundel was then a marginal, but this did not unduly worry Vicky, who had previously stood and lost for Labour back home in North Wales, and she willingly took up the offer. Then she attended her panel interview:

> It was a pretty horrendous experience really. They were all sat around this long table and I was made to walk the length of the room past all of these hostile people. I had to run the gauntlet basically, and then I was sat down next to Tony Mulhearn. I'd been waiting with a lot of other people who were in and out, in and out, in and out. They just went to town with me basically, which I was prepared for and wasn't worried about, but they asked me questions relating to the stance of defiance that the council was taking, on not complying with central government restrictions on capping. At this time, following national discussions, the other Labour-controlled metropolitan authorities were basically taking the view that you don't break the law. So, I was asked specifically, 'If it was the DLP view, if it was the Labour group view, would you agree to setting a rate above the cap?' I gave what I thought was a considered answer, that we obviously had to take into account the views and the positions of other metropolitan authorities. I really didn't think that there was any virtue in going it alone. Well, I was berated by Tony Byrne who considered it anti-democratic that I did not want to go with the democratic will of the DLP.

As she expected, Vicky was rejected for the panel. Yet while it was Byrne who left the most indelible mark upon her, the move to prevent Vicky from standing originated with Hatton, as Ian Lowes, who was also present, recalls:

> It all came about from Derek playing student union politics. It was a personal thing. He didn't like her and just moved 'no panel' before we'd even had a discussion. One of the things that used to stand in the Tendency was that whichever comrade makes the first point, that is the line that you all fall in behind (I was a bit naive then!). Unfortunately, because

Derek got in there first, his was the line and we couldn't be seen to disagree with him, and be seen to be a maverick over policy.

In response to the decision not to select Vicky for the panel, the regional party conducted an appeal and then gave the DLP the opportunity to put her on again by proposing a re-interview. Again, however, her nomination was rejected, after which the regional office finally started to understand what was going on and ordered the DLP to include Vicky on the panel. Ian Lowes, who represented the DLP at her appeal, makes it clear once again that this was not about ability but ideological discrimination:

> I knew quite well that there was no way that she wasn't going to win it. She had given all of the right answers and I knew that she couldn't be knocked back. It was all about not having her and others rocking the boat.

Certain meetings of the DLP were determined aggregate meetings, at which any member of the local party could attend. Instead of the twenty-odd members who made up the executive, or the eighty to ninety delegates on the General Management Committee (the normal DLP), you would have crowds of two to three hundred. They were basically mass meetings of the old style 'show of hands' nature, geared towards affirming the stance being taken by the Labour group. Militant, however, treated such occasions as a call to arms, akin to those given in the years before the Bolshevik revolution. For Eddie Sabino, 'the aggregate' was the means through which Militant could get their propaganda across:

> They'd moved all of their troops in. They were rallies more than anything. I mean, there was nothing to be decided. Decisions had already been taken behind closed doors, but they then got a mass of people there, wound them all up so eventually they ended up in the position where they could say: 'Well, this was given mass support'. It wasn't even a case of them seeking ratification. It was just a case, at the end of the meeting, of a lot of clapping and shouting when in fact most of the people there didn't know where it was leading.

Roy Gladden, however, offers a more forthright interpretation, via a comparison with the British Union of Fascists:

> The Channel 4 drama *Mosley* reminded me of some of the DLP meetings in Liverpool during the time that it was 'backs against the wall'. You'd go into an aggregate meeting and it was 'Hang on, should all of these people be here?'

With such votes determining the direction of Liverpool's battle with the Thatcher government, the buck ultimately stopped with the ruling Labour group. Its nominal leader, John Hamilton, well understood this, but continued to sit tight:

> With all due respect, if you get any group of working men – bricklayers, painters, what have you – coming to a meeting and somebody puts a resolution down for more jobs or more work or more houses built, who's going to say no? If you say 'We haven't got the money for it', they come back with 'Well, get the money'. It was not easy for someone to get up in those meetings and say 'We just can't do it' when you were not dealing with economists, financiers and the like, but ordinary working people who are saying get it done, whatever. The next thing, of course, was how you did it within the rates ... If you are in a climate where everybody wants you to do something and you find that you can't do it, you can either go on with it knowing the consequences or you can resign. This was the sort of situation that I was in.

John never resigned. Refusing to speak out sooner than he did was his greatest error.

In the mid 1970s, when I left Liverpool, I could not have envisaged what was coming. Signs of the changes that occurred were invisible to me; all I saw was a Labour Party trundling on without any meaningful discussion. But when I returned, and looked for those who had been active before I left, I found that many were no longer involved. Geoff Walsh, having left the council in the early 1970s, had given up being an activist, Tony Janes had moved to the south of England, and Peter Weightman, who was still an academic at the university, had dropped out of politics altogether. The only one of my old comrades with whom I did not immediately get in touch was John Sharpey-Shafer. In the early 1970s, I had produced regular leaflets with him (and Weightman) in an effort to get a proper line of communication between the party and its members and the voters. It is difficult to believe now, but keeping people informed, let alone having a dialogue with them, was not a feature of the party then, at least not in Liverpool.

As it turned out, I was glad that I did not immediately seek out John, for when the name Sharpey-Shafer came up, it was in the form of his third wife, Sylvia, who had become one of Militant's strong women in Liverpool. John himself had been through several tragic personal events. Politically, however, he was one of those to whom I would have looked for some insight into what was going on across the city. Like others, he had gone (or, rather, he was 'off limits'); in fact, much of the educated – what Militant would have derogatively cast as 'middle class' – element of the local party had either been driven out or had left of their own volition. 'Too smart for their own good', each had become *persona non grata*. I found this an absolute tragedy.

There were others, of course, who during my absence had made a name for themselves by taking pot-shots at Militant, albeit in a rather uncoordinated way. In the main, these were the people who would later make up a grouping called Liverpool Labour Left. They included Ian Williams, Vicky Roberts, Mike Allen, Jane Saren and Neville Bann, as well as Jane and Malcolm Kennedy. These were very disparate elements, but what they had in common was their status as 'outsiders' – not just in the sense of being from outside Liverpool, although many of them were, but in terms of being outside the very closed and almost incestuous grouping that had come to dominate politics in the city.

Of course, I was immediately seen as an outsider because as far as most of the new order were concerned, I had just appeared out of the blue. Many of them, particularly the recent recruits, had no idea who I was. (This would later help to colour some of their more bizarre theories about my background.) Moreover, they were not interested in the old stagers that I had known. This had advantages, in so far as I had never become involved in the factional politics which had long poisoned Liverpool politics, and which had solidified with particular emphasis on and around Militant. There were also, however, disadvantages, particularly in the very real sense of exclusion for anyone 'new' and not on the 'inside' – the rationale of which centred upon the hard suspicion of 'Where are they coming from?' There was a great deal of wariness about anyone whom the local Labour establishment did not know intimately. Even when they did, they were never really satisfied that you were on their side. The first thing that they wanted to establish was whether you could be designated as an enemy – something which drove many people out of politics altogether. For an already weak party base, this further weakening of the ideological infusion of new members was alarming. Overall, membership numbers did improve, yet the increase was one-dimensional and the intake came mainly from the traditional working class – council employees (for the most part, members of the GMB and the TGWU), people involved in manual occupations and the unemployed. They were loyal to a fault, seeing, in their own narrow way, the labour movement as their great emancipator. Sadly, however, the nature of this loyalty lacked even the slightest cerebral dimension, and it would be fair to say that such people would do anything for the movement – anything, that is, but think.

# 6 Left and right; right and wrong

Far-fetched though their promises and solutions were, it should be acknowledged that Militant recognised a vacuum in Liverpool politics and at least offered something to fill it. Nobody else was trying to do so. More importantly, they engendered an enthusiasm amongst many people who would not have normally been interested in active politics, but who saw in Militant an outlet for a growing disquiet with their social and economic conditions. That said, Militant used a host of clever, if somewhat two-dimensional, arguments to explain this popularity, but in the final analysis, they did little more than appeal to the politics of the lowest common denominator. The policies of the Thatcher governments spawned desperation in many parts of Britain, and desperate people seek desperate solutions.

A widespread belief prevailed in Liverpool that the city was being victimised. This was made apparent by a poll conducted in the middle of 1984, and referred to in Michael Parkinson's book *Liverpool on the Brink*, that revealed a deep 'pro-city, anti-Government sentiment' running through supporters of all political parties (including the Tories!).[71] Nevertheless, as Parkinson notes, this mood of local patriotism was qualified by comments such as 'I can't stand the Militant. But at least someone is standing up to the bitch in London.' This is telling. Beyond the inner circles of the local Labour Party, many people would not have appreciated the wider aims of Militant and its 'transitional programme', yet the very same individuals latched readily on to its war cry, 'no cuts in jobs and services'.

This devious soundbite served two purposes. On the one hand, it became the justification for Liverpool's struggle with central government; on the other, it became the bridge that linked the workerist mentality of many within the city's labour movement to a bastardised version of vanguardist ideas cribbed from Lenin and Trotsky. Recognising this, I began to appreciate fully the importance of the ownership and control of political discourse, and the relevance this has to individuals' political consciousness. Until then,

I had only read about this interpretation of politics, and had yet to encounter an experience where I could apply it first hand. In doing so, I found it both difficult and frustrating to have to argue around such very simplistic premises. I did not want to see cuts in jobs, nor did I want to see cuts in services, but I recognised early on that something would eventually have to give. In fact, despite the myths and rhetoric that continue to colour many memories of mid 1980s' Liverpool, more people were prosecuted for rate arrears under the Militant-influenced council than ever before, services did disappear, and jobs were cut. Slogans and soundbites were one thing; the reality was rather different.

Another feature of Militant's politics in Liverpool was numerical exaggeration. It is understandable, of course, when figures are bumped up as political hyperbole, but Militant and their associates took this practice to previously unscaled heights, chanting their mantras: 'one thousand jobs created'; 'five thousand houses built'. The former claim is difficult to reconcile with the facts; as fast as new posts were created, other jobs – in teaching, for example – were either lost or left unfilled. The house-building total, meanwhile, and its accompanying claim that Liverpool City Council built more houses in the financial years 1983–84 and 1984–85 than all other local authorities in England put together, was pure fallacy. According to the figures that Liverpool itself submitted to the Department of the Environment, 1,979 new dwellings were created between June 1983 and June 1985, whilst the total for the rest of England was 41,189.[72]

Similarly, when calculating the numbers who attended the large demonstrations taking place in the city during this period, Militant would claim a turn-out of fifty or sixty thousand, when the real figure was nearer to twenty thousand (the police, for reasons best known to themselves, tended to underestimate attendance at such gatherings). This practice has remained a feature of Liverpool politics. The 1995–98 dock dispute saw eighty employees made redundant by the private contractor Torside as it went into liquidation, as well as 329 others employed by the Mersey Docks and Harbour Company who refused to cross their picket line – a total of 409 sacked workers in all. But from the very start of the dispute, it became common to refer to the 'five hundred sacked Liverpool dockers'. Such misappropriation and repetition of round numbers to highlight or address a political point plays on the gullibility of those who, having given their initial support, are expected to swallow all that is subsequently fed to them. This practice was at its pinnacle in the mid-eighties, and the distortion of reality was backed up by non-stop propaganda in the form of a steady 'line' (anticipating New Labour) in local media outlets, a barrage of leaflets, and the regular publication *Not the Liverpool Echo*. As Joe Devaney recalls, the latter detailed the council's achievements in the most partisan and polemical way:

> It reminded me of the full-page adverts which the People's Republic of North Korea or the Jamahiriya of Libya would place in the *Guardian* in the late seventies and the early eighties.

Although Militant's membership in Liverpool was relatively small, the significance of its organisation was magnified by a mass of supporters of different gradations. There were those who bought Militant publications but were not 'Tendency' as such; those who thought of themselves as on 'the left', not with Militant but at one on the issues – or rather *the* issue, 'no cuts in jobs and services'; and those who just identified with the solidarity demanded in time of trial – in other words, the usual rag, tag and bobtail set of individuals and groups, with no real coherent shared ideology, but masquerading together behind the banner of the Labour Party. In addition, there were those self-styled intellectuals, originally from beyond the city, who were mesmerised by the deep-rooted workerism of Liverpool and perhaps looked upon events romantically – as they would a painting by Brueghel featuring earthy people engaged in a more wholesome way of life. Much of this was in keeping with the times; it had become ultra-fashionable in the trendier circles of 'the left' to identify with a long history of proletarian struggle. In fact, it was questionable whether many of them had ever struggled in their lives, other than to establish a base from which to launch a political career. Many of the younger ones, of course, never got that far once Militant had squeezed their youthful zest and energy from them.

Militant deemed the young particularly important. From their perspective, idealistic and impressionable young minds were there to be shaped and motivated along Militant lines. All other matters, from the election successes of their candidates to particular political issues, were secondary to the recruitment of fresh members, as Cheryl Varley, a full-time Militant activist at the time, explains:

> Two or three of us would organise a big meeting in the canteen of a college with comrades from South Africa to talk about what was going on in the struggle there. Hundreds of people turned out, they would get massive support and we'd organise a collection of money. There'd be a lot of raising of consciousness and understanding, and we would see

that as a big success. Then somebody from Militant would say 'But how many papers did you sell?' The thinking was that if you don't recruit for the revolutionary party, there is no point in whatever reform you achieve under capitalism, because it will be taken away under capitalism.

Young socialists would be tempted by the organisation's powerful rhetoric, which could be construed by an urgent mind as radical and exciting. Once part of the set-up, however, it would become clear that the contrary was true, and that the politics of Militant were in reality stagnant, amounting to an endless round of paper sales, demonstrations, meetings and recruitment drives. In time, this exhausted body and soul, and many dropped away, not only from Militant but from political activity altogether. In Liverpool, this effectively led to the removal of a whole generation of activists from the Labour Party – individuals who, having been at the peak of their enthusiasm, became disillusioned with political processes and have been left cynical for life. Some younger members did survive; although never actually a member of Militant, Gary Booth – today the Labour Party's Merseyside organiser – recalls their concerted attempts to court him:

> Because of the circles that I mixed in, where everyone supported Militant, it was very difficult to distinguish what was the actual party and what was their core. Anyway, I was invited along to a supposed meeting and when I got there, it was just me and Tony Aitman, and I thought 'Hang on, what's going on here?' He then took his time trying to convince me to sell the paper. This was when I was seventeen, and a young radical. What finished it for me though was the constant stream of people calling at my door inviting me to meetings. There were crazy situations where I was having to pretend that I wasn't in. These people would not leave me alone. They saw me as a potential good recruit because I was working and involved in my trade union.

Gary soon dropped out of the Labour Party, before renewing his membership a few years later, in the early 1980s.

In understanding Militant's political manoeuvring in Liverpool, it is important to recognise the significance of geography. In the areas north of the city centre, despite the mass relocations that followed the demolition and clearances of the 1950s and '60s, a handful of relatively stable communities remained in place – as evidenced by the Vauxhall community's intransigence towards the urban regeneration strategy. The politics of this community was based upon a network of strong family links, something that proved impossible for Militant to infiltrate (despite the nomination and election of one of their fellow-travellers, Paul Luckock, as a councillor). There were many more wards, however, where Militant called the shots.

County ward, which falls within the Liverpool Walton constituency, covers an area that is predominantly made up of classic terraced housing, set around a lengthy high street and two recognisable landmarks – Walton Church and Goodison Park, the home of Everton football club. Yet County is also renowned for being the birthplace of the Militant organisation, the site where Keith Dickinson, Ted Grant, Peter Taaffe and Pat Wall first collectively articulated their rhetoric. And they had plenty of comrades willing to debate the issues from a Trotskyite perspective: George McCartney, Jimmy and Brian Deane (and their formidable mother, Gertie) and the dynamic Laura Kirton all helped to make County, and the wider constituency, a cauldron of left-wing politics. Following a visit to Walton in 1956, the then leader of the Labour Party, Hugh Gaitskell, wrote in his diary, 'All very friendly and jolly, though it is one of the worst constituencies from the point of view of the Trotskyists and the Bevanites. I imagine they kept away.'[73]

By the 1980s, Wall had moved to Bradford, and Dickinson, Grant and Taaffe had long become a feature of Militant's London hierarchy. The task of keeping a grip on the County ward party was thus left to Ted Mooney, who, for reasons upon which I can only speculate, chose in the late 1970s to drop 'Edward' for the more prole-friendly 'Ted' when printing his name at the bottom of leaflets. A former councillor who had played a key role within 'the twenty-one' at the time of the Housing Finance Act, Mooney had become associated with Militant, and was a member of its central committee. His commitment was such that he actively sought to channel funds into Militant's coffers. This had been clear to Gary Booth when, as member in County ward in the late 1970s, he was a delegate to a YS conference at Llandudno:

> Ted Mooney got me a donation of fifty quid via the Labour Club. By the time I arrived at the conference, the Tendency knew that I had this fifty quid and they were constantly coming up to me going 'Come to this, come to that', 'You want to buy this, you want to buy that', and I ended up buying more bloody books, leaflets and pamphlets than I could fill my bags with.

In time, Mooney switched his attention to much bigger fish.

When Liverpool's constituency boundaries were reorganised in 1982, Walton lost Pirrie ward to West Derby CLP, and with it the financial and organisational benefits of Pirrie Labour Club. Recognising the need to fill this void, Laura Kirton, who had superbly overseen the running of the Pirrie club, attempted to offer the County ward headquarters at 39 Hale Road as a replacement. Ted Mooney, however, aspired to use the same premises for Militant's purposes. For him, it was a political resource where new members could be recruited, and the small licensed bar had revenue potential (though the days of such clubs were numbered). More importantly, Mooney saw 39 Hale Road as a financial asset, both as a property and as a reserve. Consequently, a struggle ensued in which Laura had to fight long and hard to keep the building in the hands of the Labour Party and out of the clutches of Mooney and his political godfathers.

As with other places, Militant were also able to infiltrate the party in areas of Liverpool that could be termed 'bedsitter land' – those wards within the city in and out of which people constantly move. These were often wards where it was difficult to organise politically, precisely because of the transient nature of a proportion of the electorate. 'Student' wards such as Arundel and Kensington, for example, continued to slip in and out of Labour Party control for many years.

Although by no means a student area, the same could be said of Anfield, a ward with an abundance of private rented accommodation. Similar to County in terms of the remainder of its housing stock and in that it also contains a football landmark – Liverpool FC – Anfield was part of the Liverpool Kirkdale constituency until the early 1980s, when boundary changes brought it into Walton. Having been resolutely Tory up until 1971, the ward then became electorally erratic. In the main, this favoured Labour and the Liberals but, until 1980 at least, there were also turns back to the Conservatives – probably due to the residual Protestant-Conservative vote (part of Anfield borders the former orange stronghold of St Domingo) managing to elect councillors when the Liberals were out of favour and the Labour vote stayed at home.

For much of the 1980s, however, one aspect of Anfield ward politics was predictable – the allegiance of almost all those who made up the Labour Party's active membership. It was a Militant heartland; if County was the place where the organisation was spawned, then Anfield was where it lived out its adolescence. Central to this development were Jimmy Hollinshead and Felicity Dowling, two highly charged Trotskyites whose presence in the ward was contagious. Hollinshead, to whom I habitually referred as 'Hollowhead', was originally from Chester, and had first become involved in Liverpool politics via the University Labour Society; by 1980 he was the YS member on the DLP executive. A couple of years later, he became a gravedigger (probably the only gravedigger who leant on his shovel reading Russian novels in the original), and through this an officer of the GMB's infamous Branch 5. Dowling was a local schoolteacher, a key functionary within the DLP and, following the 1984 local elections, a councillor and the education spokesperson for the Labour group.

Hollinshead and Dowling lived together on Arkles Lane, near to Liverpool FC's ground, in a large four-storey house which became the nerve centre for Militant within the area. As Gary Booth recalls, even the most innocuous gathering would be turned into a fund-raising event:

> I went to a party at 48 Arkles Lane. That was a night to remember. It wasn't so much a bring-your-own-bottle as a bring-your-own-wallet. You had to pay for everything. And there were no glasses – I ended up drinking out of a mini-saucepan. Fortunately, I didn't have to pay for that. I was only there about an hour. It was heaving and full of all of these Tendency people and their hangers on.

Neighbouring Tuebrook ward was another haven of Militant activity. Like Anfield, this was also part of the Kirkdale division until the boundary changes of the early 1980s, after which it became part of the new Broadgreen constituency. Similar to Anfield in its demographic make-up, Tuebrook more often than not voted Liberal. But the primary feature of politics in the ward was that it housed Militant's Merseyside headquarters, at 2 Lower Breck Road, in premises that had been formerly purchased from the Labour Party. With known Militants Tony and Josie Aitman virtually running the ward, the Tuebrook party regularly held its meetings in the building. Jane Kennedy's experiences of these are etched in her memory:

> At one meeting, there was a motion on the table that the party should disband the Young Socialists, and Malcolm [Kennedy] spoke in favour of it. He argued against Militant and how they were taking over the party. This was resoundingly defeated, and we retired to the pub around the corner. Over the next few months, a degree of mutual hatred built up between the Aitmans and us, and we sort of settled into a pattern. We went into one meeting and the Young Socialists – so they said – had papered the walls of the room with 'Dead Kennedys' posters – a US punk-rock band of the time. It was obviously their way of trying to stop us coming to meetings.

Raised as Plymouth Brethren, Jane and Malcolm would have known intuitively how an exclusive sect operated.

Eventually, Militant stopped the Tuebrook party meeting at 2 Lower Breck Road, by which time the Kennedys had gathered an abundance of information, as Jane further explains:

> Whatever we saw in there, we kept notes of. There were always stacks of newspapers, and on the walls were lists of who the collectors were and how many they would take. We had all of that carefully noted down. We also found a cheque that Tony Mulhearn had signed, drawn on the Militant account that paid for the property.

Winnie Hesford, another local member who had previously attended meetings of the Kirkdale CLP within the building, also recalls the lay-out:

> They had a secret room upstairs, or so we used to say. But there were rooms that other people were not allowed in, even though it was a Labour Club. It was also where they got their messages from London.

Clarification of this is given by one of those who had free movement around the building, Cheryl Varley:

> The back rooms into which non-Militant people were not allowed was where the printing and that went on. There wasn't anything hidden paper-wise but there were at times meetings taking place were people weren't allowed in because you had the hierarchy there. The full-timers were the authority and if they were meeting, a non-full-timer was not allowed in. That was because we would be discussing strategy and policy. But no, there weren't any hidden stocks of anything. One councillor, Jimmy Hackett, who was off his head, used to say to me 'AK47s, AK47s – that's what you've got to get, and get out there training'.

Again, this served to reinforce the air of mystery surrounding Militant, impressing some but alienating others.

The same exclusivity surrounded political activity in the south end of the city at the Woolton Labour Club, where the Garston CLP and two of its ward parties used to meet. While there were no 'no-go' areas as such, at least to my knowledge, it was made very clear that only those who were 'on side' with Hatton, Mulhearn *et al.* were welcome within the building. It was a very dispiriting place in which to attend party meetings and challenge the Militant line.

Other than in these quite specific parts of Liverpool, it is difficult to argue that there were 'hard areas' in which Militant was concentrated. However, there were strong cross-city links that showed up in a variety of ways, particularly with those people who became sporadically active in different places at different times, and in their reasons for doing so. Councillors and leading lights in the DLP would encourage relations, friends or contacts to stand for the council, not because they were any good, but simply because they could depend on them when it came to votes. Phil Knibb (who, with his brother George, had first come to prominence during the Croxteth Comprehensive occupation) had a foot in two inner-city wards and an outer estate, with family in Everton, Breckfield and Gillmoss. Mulhearn, meanwhile, lived out in Childwall Valley, but having been to Holy Cross School, had his connections in the Catholic mafia in the old Liverpool Scotland constituency. Mulhearn's non-Militant cousin, Frank Mills, also had family connections via Les Evans (a former county councillor and aspiring city councillor in Garston), the Knibbs, and Valley ward councillors Harry Smith and Paul Astbury. These links were the key to understanding the invisible grip which Militant and their close allies had over the council and the local Labour Party, and which was maintained after so many of their leading lights were expelled from office. These relationships were just a reinforcement of a very old – not only Liverpool but Irish – way of politics, and they were to cause problems for many years to come.

From time to time, it was suspected that members of Militant were trying to join different wards in order to alter the political balance within a local party. Already members of the party elsewhere, they would turn up in a constituency and tell the officers that they had moved into the area, offering a relevant address. Few people bothered to check up on such details but when they did, they often found the address was merely for 'convenience' and that the individuals concerned were still resident elsewhere. In Militant-controlled Anfield, the ward's leading lights, Hollinshead and Dowling, actively encouraged the tactic, as Winnie Hesford (a member of the Walton CLP executive) recounts:

> There would be a long list of new members – six or seven each time – with the address 48 Arkles Lane. God knows where they came from. They weren't actually living there. It was infiltration, and they tried it in other wards in the Walton division but they couldn't get the foothold that they did there.

One of the brains allegedly behind this tactic was Dave Cotterill, a bigger player than he has perhaps been given credit for. Later on, I was to drive him and Ted Mooney close to apoplexy at meetings of the County ward party. It became a battle of who had the strongest nerves and will. They would glare at me with hatred, appearing to be thinking 'When is he going to give up?' It always intrigued me how Cotterill, then in his thirties, managed to be housed in a pensioner's flat in Heatherlow Towers, from where he ran the World Book Club. Indeed, there were many other interesting questions about accommodation, not least concerning the drug dealer Tommy 'Takka' Comerford. He managed to get a flat in one of the blocks in Netherley, which he used as a drug shop, when he owned a detached house around the corner in the more affluent suburb of Gateacre, literally the other side of the railway line. Many believed he could only have only have obtained such a tenancy through a housing fiddle.

Courtesy of a kind soul, I was later passed a mislaid filofax, which contained the numbers of many members of Militant in Bradford and other parts of the country. I discovered that Militant had long been sending people into Liverpool for 'training', after which they were expected to apply their newly found skills in agitation elsewhere. It would only take one or two of them for mayhem to ensue. They would turn up in another constituency unused to the attritional methods honed in Liverpool, and would stir up everyone who was discontented, either through a grudge against their MP, their councillors or the officers of the constituency, or through generally carrying a chip on their shoulder. Militant supporters were a magnet for such dissent; it was a parody of the biblical quote 'wherever one or two gather in my name …', substituting Trotsky for Christ. A classic example was Terry Harrison's daughter's move from Liverpool to Swansea, after which a stream of complaints about her behaviour in meetings came to my notice. Similarly, Tommy Sheridan, the Glasgow Militant, came to Liverpool before applying the techniques he had learnt to Scotland. And there were certainly many others. Some were transferring in as others were transferring out. It was all part of a broader conspiracy to destabilise the Labour Party.

Over the years, many people have talked of how intimidated they felt at meetings involving Militant and their supporters. In a number of cases, I thought it was because they were not from the city and were unfamiliar with the rough and tumble of the Liverpudlian approach, which appears very aggressive at times but falls well short of being threatening. It eventually became clear, however, that there was something more serious afoot when people who were experienced political operators also began to find the naked hostility of Militant off-putting. Laura Kirton, once considered 'the Godmother of the Tendency', was physically threatened at the DLP, and Ian Williams was told by Hatton in a brief telephone conversation 'You'd better be careful next time I see you. You're a bottle-less, spine-less little bastard, Williams. And I'll get you.'[74]

Then I experienced it personally. It occurred at an allegedly open meeting, staged by Militant and involving a Cambridge economist – their darling and economic apologist in the mid 1980s – when I asked some simple questions about the definition of terms. No-one appeared to be there to do anything other than provide an audience, within which members and supporters of Militant were dotted about very carefully with their pre-arranged questions. I had gone along simply to find out what it was all about, what their thinking was. But the speaker used a term – I cannot now recall what it was – after which I asked, as any sensible person would have done, what he meant by it. Did it mean the same thing as I understood it to mean? For example, if someone used the phrase 'a significant minority of serving police officers are corrupt', does the term 'significant' mean 'a large proportion' or 'those holding important positions'? In any free and open debate you need clarity on such things. How else can you have real communication of ideas? How else should you try to convince other people?

Anyway, a couple of the younger Militants from Riverside CLP became aggressive towards me. It was quite incredible, the slavishness of the way in which they operated. Then one of their full-time youth officers, Peter Tyson, stood up and asked a question which was highly supportive of what the speaker had said, and equally fatuous. Within this, he made an assumption that went along the lines of: 'and it's obvious that a Labour government can't …', and I said 'Why not? It's not obvious to me.' At this point, two blokes sitting near me started saying 'Why don't you keep your mouth shut?' and 'Do you want a smack?', things like this, to which I replied 'Why don't you bugger off?' It was then that I noticed that the number sitting around me had increased to about six. Dealing with one or two of them was one thing, but there would have been no hope for me versus half a dozen.

This behaviour became acute between the end of 1984 and the end of 1986. If there was a high point, however, it was in the summer and autumn of 1985, when a siege mentality set in. It was like Arthur Miller's allegorical study of McCarthyism, *The Crucible*, in which he observes how hysteria builds up to the point that people begin to believe the most twisted propaganda. I saw the same thing happen with Militant. They would wind themselves up to the point at which their perception of reality became the only credible one. Anyone in a position of significance who they thought might veer from this had a close watch kept on them, something that was more than evident to John Hamilton when he spoke at meetings in other towns and cities:

> Somewhere at the back of the room there would be a Militant taking a note of what I was saying and reporting it back to Liverpool. So whereas I might feel free to be a little bit more open, being away from Liverpool, I was always aware that someone would be there keeping an eye on me.

As the crisis in Liverpool deepened, Militant's hold over public perceptions was further strengthened when a 'Special Executive Committee' of the DLP opted to make Terry Harrison 'DLP Press Officer'.[75]

Militant were quite vicious in their verbal attacks on anyone who stood in their way. I recall Mulhearn abusing Jack Cunningham at a DLP aggregate meeting for the sins of his father Andy, a north-east 'boss' who had been convicted in the T. Dan Smith case. I was neither for nor against Jack, but I thought it was terrible to taint someone in this way. What they were saying, by implication – and a not very well disguised implication – was that Jack was 'bent' because he was from 'a bent family'. It was a crude character assassination, which had no place in the labour movement. His actual 'crime', of course, was to take Militant to task.

It was difficult to expect people who led normal lives and were not zealots to go out in their own time on a wet January evening just to be abused by a load of cranks or to listen to the abuse of others. Those who did were either mad or masochistic, or incredibly virtuous. A Red Guard approach was encountered where, as part of your political 're-education', you were verbally blasted for your failings and then shown the error of your ways. This was not so bad at constituency or ward level because people could call on their friends and allies; but there were exceptions where Militant were in complete control, such as Anfield where it really was like entering the lion's den. Here, the dissident Paul Lally was repeatedly intimidated, both verbally and physically, to the point that he was not only terrified at meetings but also in his home. I could sense this whenever I spoke to him. It made me feel awful, but I understood the reasons why he felt threatened. Incidentally, a similar phenomenon was shown at times by the 'old right' in the Liverpool Labour Party with regard to those whom they considered too left-wing.

Where such intimidation was different was at the DLP and in certain areas of the trades union movement. Here, you would have to take on the collective weight of local levels of political and labour organisation. It seems small beer now, but at the time, and considering the way in which members of Militant were well drilled at giving speeches, it took a certain amount of guts to speak out with a contrary view. One usually ended up being either ridiculed or attacked. For the most part, this would be verbal, but it would occasionally spill over into a more physical form. Vicky Roberts recalls one such experience at the DLP:

> A couple of us had our way barred by Tony Aitman as we attempted to leave one meeting. He was basically saying 'Come on then, have a go', you know, that sort of thing – the little greasy individual.

John Whelan, the Regional Secretary of the GMB, was portrayed in a famous cartoon in the *Militant* newspaper as hiding under the table while the convenor of GMB Branch 80, Peter Lennard – then a fellow-traveller of Militant – was looking for him. Lennard was a big intimidating figure who was not very political, and would later leave his union role under a cloud when his branch 'bought' him a car. An aggressive recruiter, he was given an added incentive after it was arranged that a percentage of recruitment money would be directed into a special fund of which he received a share.

Branch 5 of the GMB was something else again. It really was the 'Johnny Friendly' school of trade unionism, and adopted the whole *On the Waterfront* approach towards trade unionism – the bullying antithesis to the protection of the weak which has traditionally epitomised the labour movement. I was actually on good personal terms with Ian Lowes, the chair of the branch, and Steve Vose, the secretary, both of whom were members of Militant. When on holiday, I would send Vose postcards c/o Woolton Labour Club, in order to sow doubts in his comrades' minds about him – it was so easy to stimulate their paranoia. He and Lowes, however, were never in total control of Branch 5. Jimmy 'Hollowhead' was the deputy convenor, and there were many more unsavoury characters lurking in the shadows.

The fear of intimidation certainly pervaded relations within the Labour group. On one occasion, I was in John Hamilton's office when Felicity Dowling came in wanting to rearrange the flowers. After she left, John told me that there was a microphone in the flowers. I never bothered to check, but by that time nothing surprised me. It certainly affected John's role as leader of the council:

> I was being watched all of the time and those press men who came to interview me were sieved through the system, so I didn't get everybody coming to interview me who wanted to or that I would have liked to have seen. In any case, they were checking on what I was saying and they would send people along afterwards to rectify this. So I felt as if I was being observed all of the time. I had be careful about what I was saying and how I was saying it. Sometimes I got people coming in to interview me who were supposedly from the press when in fact they were Militants who were testing me.

Another of John's contentions was that telephone calls were not being put through to him – a suggestion that is vehemently denied by Lyn Anderson, who worked in the adjacent office:

> It's just not true. The ancient switchboard that we had at the council caused many phone calls not to be put through, so we had a mini-switchboard for the area around the leader's and deputy leader's offices. John and Derek both had a direct line and if they weren't in, the calls could be answered at the switchboard (the switchboard number was also available for people to ring). The phones themselves had buttons on to stop the ringing, so instead of the ringing you got a flashing light. More than once in the time that I was there, you could hear John's phone ringing and he wouldn't answer it. You knew it was ringing and that he was in there, and you would end up having to go into his room and say 'John, your phone's ringing!' The light would be flashing while he was working away. He'd inadvertently pressed the button, switching the ringer off because he didn't understand the technology.

True or false, Militant and those willing to work with them created an atmosphere in which anything was plausible. There were certainly video cameras stationed outside the leader's and deputy leader's offices; ostensibly, this was a security measure, but it also allowed those with a monitor, including Hatton, to eavesdrop on conversations in the corridor. This came to light in an infamous article written by David Selbourne: 'On Hatton's desk was an innocent enough TV console, its blue screen showing the corridor outside and a janitor passing. Hamilton then bent over the screen in all his civic majesty, and turned up the sound. You could hear every footfall, every whisper.'[76]

In helping to reveal the extent to which such factors had moved centre stage, Selbourne was rather unscrupulous. Having gone to Hamilton on the grounds that he was a Labour supporter wanting to get a background view, Selbourne foxed John into giving him statements that he would not have given to the press at that time:

> I'd clearly said 'What I say is off the record' but he went and used it. Of course, the rest of the press homed in on me straight away. I was in London at a meeting when the article came out, and when I got back to Lime Street Station, there was a whole posse of press men with cameras wanting to interview me, and I thought 'What the hell's gone on in Liverpool today?' Of course, the Militants were on to me straight away, pressurising me. They sympathised with me, in that Selbourne had put his own slant on it, but they asked if I agreed with the things that I had been quoted on.

As a result of his article on Liverpool, Selbourne was kicked out of the Press Association for breaking an unwritten rule amongst reporters on using 'off the record' material. At the time, he was also a lecturer at Ruskin College, Oxford, and many students refused to be taught by him. This was to leave a lasting mark. Some years later, in November 1990, I met Selbourne in a café, and he raged about the impertinence of these 'working class people', these 'rough shop stewards and trade unionists', who had challenged his wisdom. The arrogance of the man was insufferable and I could not believe that he thought himself beyond questioning by those 'who ought to know their place'. Then again, he is not untypical of a certain type of intellectual.

Once I had the measure of what Militant were about, I tried to provoke them more and more, raising things often for the fun of seeing them go off the deep end. Peter Tyson, who was in my own ward party in Grassendale, was always in political hyperactive mode, fully wound up and ready to let loose. All it required was for me to go into a meeting where he was in attendance, and say 'Did you see the load of crap that was printed in *Militant* last week? They're so crooked, they couldn't lie straight in bed.' Instead of responding in kind, or biting his lip, he would take the bait and start spouting the usual rubbish. It was both amusing and educational to watch. Richard Knights, another of the Militant fanatics, appeared to need a retune every now and then before he could be sent back into the fray. He would over-extend himself, and get into a terrible state. I always thought that he was a decent enough sort and I occasionally felt sorry for him. He was really plugged into Militant, but he might just as well have been in the Hare Krishna or the Children of God – anything as long as it gave his life the purpose and meaning it required. He wanted to be at the sharp end of disputes and demonstrations. Recalling his own time as a county councillor, Bob Wareing remembers how Knights was certainly close enough to the action at one historic moment:

> On the night that the Toxteth riots broke out, Richard Knights rang me at home around about a quarter past midnight to tell me that he had just heard somebody in a police car say that CS gas was going to be used.

Militant were experts at procuring money, ostensibly for comrades in different parts of the world, when it was actually going straight into the coffers of Militant HQ. There was always a question mark over bucket collections made, for example, for striking miners. No proper checks were made on these, and many assumed that Militant was creaming off a percentage. Within the Labour Party, and in Liverpool in particular, ordinary members were very trusting. Suckers for a good cause, they would freely give their money, and time and time again they would be approached to contribute in aid of one good cause or another. Usually it was some obscure activist in a small organisation; they would be projected as heroes and their case hammered home with 'We want donations for the defence of [A. Comrade]'. In the Mossley Hill CLP, for example, claims would often come in on behalf of someone or other in South Africa. Their case would be explained in the most heart-rending way, and before you knew it, the chair, Eddie Sabino, a genuine and generous character who was certainly not Tendency, would say 'move fifty quid'. Strangely though, Eddie disputes his own role when interpreting why this occurred:

> It used to really get up my nose because you could be put in the position where you are refusing to send a fiver or tenner or whatever it was to help this 'needy comrade'. Once the argument had been made in that sort of context, it was pretty difficult to win any minds that were still open.'

Perhaps it serves to demonstrate how Eddie's innate decency prevented him from challenging the leeches.

Quite often there would be a resolution – usually a couple of pages long – attached to such requests for assistance, containing clauses to which the African National Congress, let alone the British Labour Party, were not committed. On one occasion, I challenged a resolution that proposed money for help to buy guns. More regularly, I questioned whether specific causes had anything to do with the ANC, the Congress of South African Trade Unions, or other such recognised organisations. Invariably, they did not. They were merely smokescreens behind which Militant were wringing money from ordinary people.

Terry Fields personally took on the case of a Palestinian called Mahmoud Masarwa, who had been imprisoned in Israel. I contacted Ian Williams about this, as his wife was a Palestinian with an acute knowledge of the PLO, and it turned out that while Masarwa may have had a case in his own right, he had little to do with mainstream Palestinian opinion or the struggle in the Middle East. What he did have was an affiliation to a tiny splinter Trotskyite group with whom Militant were associated (this was later revealed by Peter Taaffe[77]). Individuals such as this, and the organisations to which they belonged, were far removed from the true liberation movements in their own country. The only country where Militant's associates had a real base was Sri Lanka, hardly the place from where the workers of the world would take their cue. Still, it was not surprising that many of the Merseyside Militants who achieved positions of political office had views on all international issues but little to say about areas that fell within their remit. Knowsley Parish Council, in one of Liverpool's neighbouring boroughs, had a policy for 'Nicaragua', 'El Salvador', 'Vietnam' and other such conflicts, but had no opinion on mending a bench in Knowsley Village near the Pipe and Gannex pub, named in honour of the area's former MP, Harold Wilson.

One of the more wounding charges made against members of Militant was that they were social fascists. They resented anyone who read novels or enjoyed attending the theatre; such cultural pastimes could not be accommodated in their way of thinking about inner-city life in Liverpool or in the rest of Britain. Yet for most people, a whole new world was opening up where they were encountering a far wider range of experiences than the purely economic or utilitarian. All this passed Militant by. I understood why; they were stuck in a conceptual time-warp and could not adapt. One indicator of this was their stance on disarmament, which referred to a 'workers' nuclear bomb'! All life's issues, great and trivial alike, were dealt with through a binary logic of yes/no and right/wrong answers. They were so unable to deal with complexities that they closed them out. In the Militant mind-set, lateral considerations diverted them from their linear task.

This was also the case with equal opportunities. Blinkered from the start, the whole question of racism never entered Militant's consciousness. They had neither the framework of meaning nor the breadth of imagination necessary to deal with such concerns. This caused them tremendous problems with Toxteth's self-selected 'Black Caucus' in October 1984 over the appointment of Sam Bond, a Militant activist from London with little experience of anti-racist campaigning, as the city council's Principal Race Relations Officer. John Hamilton explains Militant's attitude:

> 'You don't go along with us, you don't like our ways, you're talking about racism, and we will put in "our" black person.' Now black people in Toxteth were not prepared to have someone imposed upon them. It was the last thing that should have been done. It was like putting in a secret policeman to spy on them.

I was never a big fan of the Black Caucus. They included many decent, committed people with whom anyone would be proud to work, but there was also a small criminal element which had forced its way forward as 'representatives' of the black community. Such individuals preyed on black and white alike, and had neither credibility nor a mandate. The Sam Bond affair was partly about Militant's arrogance over how best to tackle race issues, but an unkind soul might also argue that the Black Caucus's stance had as much to do with crooks within the organisation recognising the opportunist in Hatton, and wanting to keep him (in the form of his Militant colleague Bond) off their patch. This is apparent in the views of at least two of those interviewed:

> There was a group of people within the Caucus for whom it had nothing to do with politics. For them, it was to do with money – the money that came into the community, the money that for decades has gone into that community and has never reached down to the people but has stopped with a layer who have profited. Sam Bond would have had a very large say over where that money went, and he would have been able to make those organisations accountable. He would have been able to say 'Where's the money? Where did it go? What did it get spent on?' There was a lot of corruption in organisations in Toxteth. So on the one hand you had the ideological struggle, but on the other hand you had very violent people with guns whose concern was with the money that was involved.

I didn't have any time for a number of the people who were involved in the Black Caucus – there were a few murderers, smack-dealing pimps and other people who were fairly crooked. There were a lot of very decent people as well but, being frank, I think a lot of it was about turf wars over grass rather than real ideological issues.

Shortly after Bond's appointment, Liverpool saw what the *Liverpool Daily Post* described as 'the worst scenes ever witnessed at a council meeting'.[78] During a fraught hour at the Town Hall, beginning with black community leader Steve French being refused permission to address the full council, security staff and protesters squared up to one another as the latter chanted 'Hatton, racist, Hatton, racist', and a Radio City reporter was assaulted after having had his microphone snapped in two. If that was not bad enough, council employee George Knibb opted to take a swing at a Liberal councillor, Eddie Clein, at the front of the chamber in full view of the local media. Knibb was prevented from making contact with Clein by a council press officer, but then Labour councillor David Lloyd took it upon himself to run at Clein, sending him crashing on to the council benches. It was pandemonium.

Of course, Militant and their allies' intransigence over this issue meant that things stood little chance of improving. Following Bond's arrival in Liverpool to take up the post, members of the Black Caucus occupied the deputy leader's office in protest, holding Hatton 'hostage' and meting out violence to another councillor in the process. This was all witnessed by Lyn Anderson:

> People tried to persuade Denise [Myerson – Hatton's secretary] and I to leave the office. It culminated in us being asked to go into John's office – he had left via another door – as they were in our room and Derek's, trying to come up with some solution before that day's full council meeting. I happened to open the door at a point when one of the Black Caucus floored Tony Hood. One of the protesters, who was white and also happened to be a member of the Labour Party, started crying because she knew I'd seen it. It was totally out of control.

The day after, Sam Bond was dragged from his own office and attacked. There then followed a couple of well-documented cases of party meetings in Granby ward being abandoned on the orders of some of the more unsavoury elements within the area. Even so, while such elements found it difficult to distinguish between Hatton and Militant on the one hand, and the rest of the local party on the other, some members of the Labour group openly voiced criticism of Bond's appointment. Dave Leach, a councillor for Granby, was particularly vocal – so much so, in fact, that Militant conspired to have him omitted from the local government panel even though the Labour Party's constitution stated that a sitting councillor coming up for re-election should automatically be included.

Although much of the blame for what arose during the Sam Bond affair lay with Militant for misjudging the situation, blindness to racial issues was not peculiar to Militant members in Liverpool. I remember having a discussion with some comrades from the docks about apartheid and racism, and they proffered the fallacy that the dockers had always stood by South Africa's blacks. More interested in political practice than stand-alone theory, I highlighted something that had become apparent to me as a youngster when I worked for the fruit importers Bonney's in the South Docks. At the time, there were seven miles of docks in Liverpool and more than 20,000 dockers. But I can only recall one black docker – 'Clicker' Clarke from Page Moss, on the outskirts of the city, who would travel in on one of the 'dockers' specials', as a particular bus service was known. This disparity was particularly noticeable given how much of the South Docks bordered Toxteth. It was part of the tribal patronage, the 'keep it in the family' attitude, that went with so much of Liverpool economic life, where people helped their sons, brothers, nephews and cousins find jobs; in those days, big extended families looked after each other. Everything became like a repeat of medieval guilds, and these traditional white family networks meant that black people rarely obtained the magic 'card' entitling them to work on the docks. These attitudes were still evident in 1989 when Torside (the company at the centre of the 1995–98 dock dispute) was set up. With the collaboration of the workforce, Torside created jobs for the sons of dockers and union officials – the time-honoured practices by which black people continued to be excluded. Trying to change such embedded attitudes remains an urgent challenge, and the romanticisation of the dockers and their kin by people who should know better has only served to make the task more difficult.

As it transpired, Militant's handling of the race issue in Liverpool was a key event in helping people to see the divide between the council's stance against the government and wider concerns with ideology and praxis. Many of those who supported Militant within the Labour Party, or who empathised from the comfort of other Trotskyite groups, had until that stage been reluctant to criticise their game-plan. Now they had something to challenge them with, as Cheryl Varley admits:

> What went on around Sam Bond was wrong. We were genuinely trying to fight to change the world to make it a better place, and we didn't have time to talk to nobody because we were fighting for world revolution.

There was no time for discussion and we became a little bit arrogant, and we weren't listening to people with other perspectives. We just went tear-arseing on with 'this is what we're going to do'.

Considering the rise of feminism, the approach of male members of Militant to the condition of women in society was extremely conservative. In public, they talked about changing social relations between men and women. In private, they had partners who ran the home and looked after the kids. It was often a strict demarcation with reactionary undertones. With both Hatton and Mulhearn, it was understood that they would do their thing whilst their wives guarded the fort. Admittedly, such criticisms could be applied to me – but then again, I was not interested in devoting myself entirely to politics on a voluntary basis. Apart from anything else, I had a life to lead and a full-time job. At the same time, my wife Bernie was teaching, and we were trying to balance the demands of these two jobs with the needs of the family.

There were also peculiar ways in which Liverpool's Militants married and divorced one another, swapping bits of their family as they went. For example, Josie Aitman was not Tony Aitman's first wife; that privilege fell to Julie Mclean, one of their city councillors. Her father, John Mclean, a regular guy, ex-councillor and AEU official, was mortified by the way she turned out politically. When she and Tony Aitman divorced, she married again within the fold and became Julie Lyon-Taylor. Phil Holt, Ray Williams and Richard Venton also married ex-wives of their comrades. I found it all rather strange and cult-like. Then there was Lesley Farrar, who became Lesley Holt, via marriage to Phil, before she found political infamy as Lesley Mahmood (Mr Mahmood was from the Netherlands where, it was said, he worked at a Voorwaerts factory – I assume they met at some Militant summer school). It was all so odd the way that their private and political lives were so entwined. Perhaps it was an accepted norm that marital breakdowns would lead to people taking up with the ex-partners of other members of the organisation.

In short, what we had in Liverpool at this time was a sectarian political group controlling a major city. It had an ideological framework, articulate spokespersons, a well-oiled organisation, high morale and an almost incestuous network of trusted individuals. What remained of the older Liverpool Labour Party was very simply no match for this, on any level. A new, more thoughtful and more energetic internal opposition was needed if the local party was to be reclaimed, and the spread of Militant first halted and then smashed. An attempt to establish this came with the formation of Liverpool Labour Left.

The question of how this body came about and who initially said 'Let's call it "Liverpool Labour Left" ', is difficult to answer, but the wheels were set in motion in late 1984. There had always been ad hoc alliances amongst non-Militants in the local party, but opposition was still rather disparate, as Jane Kennedy makes clear in recalling how she and her then husband Malcolm became involved:

> Ian Williams had started writing hilarious articles for the *New Statesman* – articles which you would read and think 'Christ, there's somebody else in the city who's normal, who thinks like we do, and who is actually laughing at the Trots'. Largely through Ian, we realised that it was okay to laugh at them. We made contact with him, and he said 'Oh there's quite a few of us', and gradually we started coming out of our bunkers.

In the mid 1980s, there were very few people in the Liverpool Labour Party who would stand up and say 'Yes, we're the right wing, we're against you'. Of course, no-one considered themselves 'right wing'; it was a purely pejorative term. I always considered Militant's *modus operandi* extremely right-wing, and they would erupt when charged as such; it was the deepest calumny one could utter against them. Even so, it was an amazing departure for myself and others to identify ourselves as the 'Liverpool Labour Left', and Militant's consternation over this is more than evident in comments in their principal account of the period: 'It was so "left" that it included the witch-hunter Jane Kennedy in its ranks!'; and 'The Liverpool Labour Left only found its support amongst a gaggle of frustrated councillors or would-be councillors, trade union officials who feared that control over their rank and file was slipping out of their hands, and some very middle-class ex-"left wingers".'[79]

Our inaugural meeting, which was held at the trade union centre, was immediately vilified by Militant, and some people felt wary about being seen to be entering the building. The following morning, we held a press conference at the Adelphi Hotel. We sat together at the top table in front of the assembled journalists; we must have looked like the Politburo, but it was very much in keeping with the old Labour way of doing things. Anyone said what they wanted, and it perhaps gave the impression that our strategy lacked cohesion. Nevertheless, the nature of our organisation reflected the times; things were so different in terms of presentation, in terms of having a spokesperson and sticking to a 'line'. When somebody asked whether we were going to stand candidates, I said something trite along the lines of 'No. We're not a party within a party. We just want to reclaim the debate.' Like the others, I was trying hard to think of something clever to say, something that could capture people's eyes or ears in the media – but, to be honest, we had not really armed ourselves with any soundbites.

Although it was not quite revolutionary St Petersburg, these were relatively heady times in Liverpool, and the fast-moving situation in which we were immersed was changing on a daily basis. Even so, the whole venture of Liverpool Labour Left was all very odd. I recall being concerned about our finances, and to this day, I have never found out how we were funded – something that will raise suspicions amongst the more paranoid comrades that we were stooges of MI5 or some other body. Of course, we had collections and fund-raising events, all of which were geared towards the cost of publications. But this was nothing to compare with the money that Militant could raise via their propaganda machine.

A bloke from Sheffield called Alex Carena, who now runs a drugs rehabilitation unit in Liverpool, appeared out of the blue and spent most of our resources on a single leaflet, the contents of which did not accord with the views of anyone else in the organisation. This perhaps illustrates how ramshackle the set-up was. Carena was said to be a 'community youth worker'. Now, there are many regular youth workers – I was one myself, once – but under the broad aegis of 'community' there are all sorts of weird and wonderful people and Carena was one such character. Ian Williams and I were a little Stalinistic in our approach and attempted to block the publication of the leaflet. Unfortunately, many others were more idealistic and wanted to give him a chance. On this occasion, such idealism was to the detriment of our broader aims.

In time, we organised a couple of high-profile meetings, where first Robin Cook and then Bea Campbell came to speak. The meeting with Cook represented an attempt to steer the debate back to the party policies that were consuming members elsewhere in Britain, while that with Campbell was an attempt to broach political issues other than the workerist concerns of Militant or the 'Trot initiative' of the moment. In sum, the motives of Liverpool Labour Left were to make other things happen in the city. One of the perennial problems of Liverpool's politics has been the periodic appearance of a political vacuum. The old maxim that nature abhors a vacuum rings true, but Labour locally has consistently failed to recognise it. Still, by bringing guest speakers into the city, we were attempting to offer something to fill the void. We were also trying to pull people together by providing an alternative focus for those non-Militants who felt that there were certain 'left-wing' stances that ought to be taken. It was a way of overcoming the stark division between being with Militant and being called 'comrade', or being against it and being labelled 'a right-wing, petit-bourgeois, scabby sell-out shit'.

Unlike members of Militant, who were totally immersed in politics twenty-four hours a day, those of us involved in Liverpool Labour Left were all relatively normal people with everyday concerns, and run-of-the-mill activities. We also had our own lives to lead. No-one was obliged to attend anything and everything, and if people could not make it to some event or meeting, it was accepted that they had other things on the go. In the long run, however, while our aims were true, our numbers were low, and a lack of direct influence meant that we could only ever have been a ginger group. This was not such a bad thing in itself, but it would have been preferable if we could have attracted some of the more able councillors such as Tony Hood or Paul Astbury. Alas, they continued to lean in Militant's direction, or at least, give credence to the faith by remaining silent. Whether this was done for personal advantage or because they shared a similar ideological standpoint was difficult to ascertain.

Our relationship with the trade unions tended to be at the level of individual members rather than branches. In a vague sort of way, Liverpool Labour Left was forward-looking enough to consider changing the nature of the party's relationship with the unions. We also had a good relationship with the local branch of the Communist Party. Some saw advantages in the idea of a broad front, but many others, including myself, considered it a political cul-de-sac that had been discredited in the 1930s. There were individuals in the CP with whom I shared many views, but I thought more official ties, even if possible, would give succour to an organisation that was going no-where fast. There was, of course, absolutely no relationship between Liverpool Labour Left and the local Liberals. That was something to which I could never have warmed.

One grouping from within the local Labour Party that we did become involved with was the Labour Coordinating Committee. Their numbers included people such as Paul Thompson (today the editor of *Renewal*), Paul Lally and Mike Allen. The latter was elected from Everton ward on to the DLP executive and was one of the few people on that body who would speak out against Militant. Nevertheless, the LCC was primarily concerned with the national perspective and I had always seen them as a self-appointed 'representative' group. They were never very representative numerically but they were a marvellous stepping-stone for all sorts of student politicians to make their way into the national arena. Without local credibility or a local base, a party member had no chance of being a political player in Liverpool. Granted, many of those in Liverpool Labour Left also lacked such credibility, but at least the organisation attempted to pull people together in a way that made the totality greater than a mere sum of the constituent parts. To be honest, I am not sure how successful we were. What I do know is that the emphasis that we placed on understanding and working within the peculiarities of the Liverpool context led directly to me working for the Labour Party.

# 7 The Cato tendency

The decision in February 1983 to expel five members of *Militant*'s editorial board from the Labour Party – about which a young Tony Blair gave legal advice – was merely a prelude to all-out war upon the Trotskyite group's entryists. As it turned out, the central battleground was to be their power bases within Liverpool: the District Labour Party and the council Labour group. On 1 October 1985, Neil Kinnock addressed the party's annual conference at Bournemouth and made the speech that Jim Callaghan later remarked to me that *he* should have made when he was leader.

The background to the speech developed during the weeks leading up to the conference. In early September, the leadership of Liverpool City Council instructed the city solicitor to prepare formal redundancy notices for the council's 31,000 employees. This tactic, devised to keep the council solvent for the three months until the end of December, and more immediately to apply pressure on the Government for more finance for the city, backfired as the members of the Joint Shop Stewards' Committee, sensing perhaps that the workforce they represented was no longer a sacred cow but a sacrificial lamb, rejected the proposal. A week later, with the threat of financial bankruptcy for Liverpool on the horizon (political bankruptcy had long been apparent), the JSSC voted to ballot their respective members on an all-out indefinite strike, a move that they considered would force the Thatcher government to lend a helping hand. As Jane Kennedy, then District Secretary of NUPE, recalls, this created panic in some quarters of the workforce:

> I used to get home-helps ringing me up in tears, particularly about what was going to happen to their clients. They were not going to stop working. They couldn't leave their clients unattended in case something happened to them, and then they would blame themselves.

Naturally, such people were also worried about their own futures – 'Who will pay us? Are our jobs safe?' Their primary concern, however – for those in their charge – shows where true socialist values were to be found in Liverpool at this time.

## Left Behind: Lessons from Labour's heartland

The balloting of the workforce over indefinite strike action came during the third week of September. Two teaching unions, NATFHE and the NUT, and the electricians' union, EETPU, all rejected the idea of the 'general strike', as did NUPE. For the latter, the decision occurred in somewhat unexpected circumstances, after Jane Kennedy had invited the home-helps to a meeting in the Municipal Buildings:

> On a good day, the room would hold fifty, but seven, eight hundred turned up! In the department that I worked, the officers and home-help organisers knew what I was about, and they encouraged every home-help in the city to go to the meeting. They blocked off Dale Street – the traffic couldn't get through. The police came and gave me a loudhailer, so I could speak to all of the home-helps at once. They were angry. They hadn't had a ballot, and they felt that I hadn't allowed them the chance to vote no. I always regretted that, but I kept saying 'I know you want to vote no, and this show of hands will do it – that is as good. Only if we want you to vote yes would we need the careful preparation that a postal ballot requires.'

As expected, the GMB, the TGWU and the building workers' union, UCATT, all voted in favour of the strike, but when their numbers were totted up, they reflected a minority of the total workforce. The decision, therefore, rested with the one union yet to vote, NALGO. For both political and occupational reasons, its local membership had shown an almost blind loyalty to the council as it moved ever nearer to the political precipice. On this occasion, however, they opened their eyes, took a peek over the edge and then stepped back, withdrawing their support and voting almost three to one against the proposed action.

The significance of this lack of enthusiasm for the strike among those who had previously followed the line cannot be overstated. Even so, it was perhaps overlooked, given the endorsements two days later, by both the JSSC (at which NALGO delegates walked out in protest) and an aggregate DLP meeting, to support the plan to issue the redundancy notices after all. Although Militant and their acolytes were misreading the political runes, once the line was set they would support it unflinchingly. Lateral or independent thinking was not part of their make-up. With the support of the so-called 'representatives' of less than half of the workforce, and of a wholly distorted DLP, the council embarked on a disastrous attempt to bluff both its own workforce and the Thatcher government. On 30 September, Peter Lennard, the chairman of Liverpool GMB local authority convenors, arranged for the redundancy notices to be delivered in a fleet of twenty-seven taxis (until then, the notices had been kept in a lock-up garage in Toxteth). Taking apparent pleasure in seeing the horrified response of innocent teachers, Lennard travelled around in one of the taxis delivering notices to schools, and in one instance, posted them through a hatch when members of his own union barricaded the doors. It was not for nothing that he earned the nickname 'Hatton's poodle'.

One question that has never quite been answered about the whole affair concerns who actually hit upon the 'redundancy' tactic. George Knibb, by this time part of the team organising the council's campaign for more resources from central government, professes his ignorance:

> A ploy was thought up – by I don't know who – to threaten the government to give us the money that we badly needed. That's all that I ever knew about those redundancy notices. I haven't got inside knowledge of anything else.

In their account of the period, Taaffe and Mulhearn point the finger at the then District Auditor of Liverpool, Thomas McMahon, accusing him of being the first to suggest that redundancy notices should be prepared.[80] Whether this is true or not, what they fail to acknowledge is that it was Militant supporters who took up the idea and ran with it, as Ian Lowes, who voiced his own doubts about the tactic, reveals:

> They called a meeting of 'members' to have a vote on the issue. I attended this, and there were all sorts of people who I had never ever seen before in my life with mohican hair-cuts, purple hair, nose-rings and all the rest of it. I don't think they were from this planet. But that was the Tendency's style. If you can't get a majority from within the accepted sphere, then move in other people.

Confirming this to be the case, Cheryl Varley also refers to the divisions it caused:

> The decision on the redundancy notices was taken at a meeting which was made up of Liverpool councillors and executive committee members from the Militant, most of whom were from London … There was a lot of people who thought it was a bad tactic in the first place; and then, when Kinnock used it so effectively, the same people were saying 'Well, I told you so, we shouldn't have done it'. There were then meetings where the people who pushed that tactic through explained why we had to do it and then, funnily enough, a few months later they decided that it had been a

mistake and said so to a meeting. I think it was one of the few U-turns that they made.

Whatever the facts about the decision to send out the redundancy notices, the outcome was that Militant, in sanctioning the tactic, shot itself in both feet. Sensing this, Neil Kinnock seized the moment, taking the rostrum at Bournemouth and giving a speech that was a *coup de théâtre* and a political coming of age rolled into one. The high point came as he uttered the words:

> You start with far-fetched resolutions. They are then pickled into a rigid dogma, a code, and you go through the years sticking to that, out-dated, misplaced, irrelevant to the real needs, and you end in the grotesque chaos of a Labour council – *a Labour council* – hiring taxis to scuttle around the city handing out redundancy notices to its own workers.

The whole occasion was one of those rarely witnessed in a political lifetime. It was to have a dramatic effect, not just in terms of the pressing issue within Liverpool but also in terms of the direction that would then be taken by the party and the broader labour movement. Other than Neil's closest confidants, most people were unaware of his intentions, and the speech took conference by surprise. I was not privileged to be in the hall to hear it firsthand, but a number of those who were told me afterwards that the atmosphere was electric – and it certainly affected those, like myself, who watched it on television. I knew instantly that the content of the speech and the way in which it was delivered would have a profound impact on politics within the city of Liverpool and beyond. The initial heat, however, was felt inside the hall.

Famously, Eric Heffer, long-time member of the NEC and self-styled man of principle, chose to walk off the platform during the speech, adding an element of pantomime to the unfolding drama. Six years later, in his autobiography, Eric commented: 'I will never forgive Neil Kinnock for what he did to my city and my party.'[81] Bob Lancaster, one of the Liverpool councillors then taking on the Government, and a member of Heffer's constituency party, remembers how he and others in Walton later questioned his motives:

> We asked him: 'Why did you walk off, Eric? Why didn't you stay? As it turned out, you actually contributed to the media approach to it.'

As anyone who watched the live television coverage or saw the news reports knows, the other enduring image of this pivotal moment in British politics was Hatton and Mulhearn shouting 'liar' at Neil as he spoke. This was an interesting charge, particularly from Hatton who, nine days before the despatch of the redundancy notices, had written to NALGO's Liverpool Secretary, Peter Cresswell, assuring him that the Labour group would not vote for anything that could be construed to mean job cuts. Oddly, Hatton and Mulhearn opted to remain in the hall, even after Heffer had made his way out. Joe Devaney, who as a fellow municipal delegate from Liverpool was sitting with them, explains why:

> Before Kinnock's speech, Hatton tells me: 'Kieran Devaney of Radio Merseyside has phoned me up with the embargoed speech'. So Hatton knew what was coming. It was still quite shocking because we'd had the backing of the party nationally up until then and we were doing what we were told. Anyway Kinnock stood up and started giving his speech, and Hatton said to me and Mulhearn, 'Come on, let's walk out'. I just said 'Sit down. We're not going to be seen as being undignified here, letting Kinnock get to us.' While I'm talking, Eric Heffer slips past. We're engaged in conversation and we didn't see Eric walk by. Obviously, they'd have followed him and I suppose, reluctantly, I would have had to go with them.'

After Neil had finished his speech, Hatton and the other Liverpool delegates left the hall. Another incident made Bob Wareing note who was really running the show:

> I went through the tunnel that was the exit from the hall. As I came out the other end, there was Hatton with his back to the wall with Peter Taaffe wagging his finger at him and laying the law down. It was very unusual to see Hatton getting told off. I couldn't hear exactly what Taaffe was saying, but it was clear that in the relationship between him and Hatton it was the former who was on top.

That evening, as the buzz from the speech resonated around Bournemouth, one of Liverpool's non-Militant councillors, Roy Gladden, had a chance to speak to Neil face to face:

> My initial response was that I wanted to strangle the bastard. I couldn't understand that this was the man I had supported. I put my arms around him and said 'Do me a favour, Neil. I'm one of the councillors from Liverpool – can you take that fucking knife out of my back that you put in this afternoon?' His aide suddenly rushed in to try and usher him away but Kinnock was okay about it and said 'I'm sorry, but you're all out of control.'

# Left Behind: Lessons from Labour's heartland

Back in Liverpool, the nominal leader of the Labour group, John Hamilton, was having mixed feelings about what had happened:

> I didn't know that Kinnock had become that acquainted with what was going on, and I didn't know that Hatton was having the redundancy notices sent around the city. All of this was news to me, and when Kinnock announced it in his speech, it came as a bit of a bombshell, an absolute bombshell. Of course, I didn't mind him making those statements but then he tarred the whole lot of us. He never discriminated between those who were being carried along with it and the pure Militants.

Harsh as it may seem on those who had begun to question the way in which both the Labour group and the district party were heading, Neil's view of the situation was an informed one. Granted, it was slightly distant; distinguishing between individuals in terms of how deeply they were implicated in a local mire was not for him. He was the leader of a national party wishing to be elected on his and its ability to govern the country as a whole. As long as he and the rest of the party hierarchy were preoccupied with the behaviour of members on the ground, there was little chance of the broader electorate tuning in to Labour's policies. Some people considered Liverpool an easy target – after all, the city and its inhabitants had been readily vilified during the previous few years by sections of the national media – but it is indisputable that the local party was in more need of attention than any other at that time. Neil Kinnock not only did the Labour Party, but the city of Liverpool itself, a favour. I can only gag at what would have happened had the boil been left unlanced.

The day after Neil spoke, there was a debate at conference on the situation in Liverpool. Before this, NALGO distributed a double-sided leaflet, one side of which reproduced a redundancy notice, and the other the letter of denial, written a month earlier by Hatton, saying that there was no intention, nor would there ever be any intention, of issuing a single redundancy notice. The man really was as good as his word. Arrogantly, however, he attempted to make his presence felt during the debate. NUPE General Secretary Rodney Bickerstaffe arranged for the conference chair to take a speaker from his trade union, and volunteered Jane Kennedy:

> In my speech, I talked about how wrong the strategy was, what it was like being a council worker in Liverpool, how we were facing Christmas with uncertainty. I just tried to give a bit of a flavour of what was going on to

conference – that this was not the way to run a city, that it was appalling. NUPE had put some of our political staff in seats behind Derek Hatton and the rest of the Liverpool group, and they found it really funny. Apparently, Hatton was on his feet throughout my speech, screaming 'You're not getting your fucking job back, either, Kennedy'.

In fact, the last laugh, and more, was to be had at Hatton's expense. Shortly after conference, Jane organised a mass meeting in Liverpool of the local membership of NUPE and invited Hatton along to discuss the unfolding situation:

> It was one of the meetings where we had bouncers on the door. It was very strict – NUPE members only. Hatton had all his minders with him. It was like a pantomime. As he came into the hall from the back and down through the crowd, there was a boo here and a boo there. By the time he reached the platform, he was quite rattled. He'd never had that kind of reception before, and joked to me 'It's worse than facing the Black Caucus'. He stood up and stuck to the line. They hated it and booed him. I put the opposite point of view, and got a standing ovation. That's the way it went. It was my homecoming.

In the two months following conference, emotions on the ground in Liverpool intensified, and an increased number of openly brutal incidents took place. Towards the end of October, local NUT leader Jim Ferguson had thirty ten-pence pieces ('thirty pieces of silver') showered over his head by a large group of council employees – most definitely members of the GMB – who had entered the room at the Town Hall where he was lobbying the council leadership. What made the incident even more unsavoury was that Hatton allegedly walked straight over to the visibly shaken Ferguson and remarked 'That is just a small taste of what is to come for you'.[82] More infamous was the case of the Harthill gardeners. These were six highly skilled horticulturalists who had voted against the all-out strike in September, on the grounds that the city's internationally renowned orchid collection needed daily care if it was to be maintained. Their claim was refuted, and the six subsequently sacked, essentially for their alleged lack of 'solidarity'. An appeal was launched and public pressure increased to give the men their jobs back. In a vicious act of retribution, however, Tony Byrne had the orchid collection broken up and the site bulldozed. The six were reinstated soon afterwards, but they were allocated to grass-cutting tasks. One of them came in during his first week to find that his machine had been dismantled. When he complained, he was given a spanner to put it back together again.

In the meantime, Liverpool's financial turmoil was growing. Byrne's solutions to the problems of ever-dwindling resources were not necessarily shared by many of Labour's other councillors. Yet whenever he came up with a proposal, most of the group were too busy making political gestures to look at the fine detail; and, time after time, they proved quite happy to accept Byrne's word. Liverpool Labour Left were not, and we suggested the modest alternative of a 5 per cent rate increase. This would be of minimal cost to the average rate-payer in the city – about £15 for the whole year – whilst those households that were on a full rate rebate (over half of Liverpool's properties) would see their increased bill paid for by the government.

Others beyond the city also came up with solutions. The Stonefrost Commission (headed by Maurice Stonefrost, a former official of the Greater London Council) invested much time and energy in offering Byrne professional advice on how they believed Liverpool's mounting financial problems could be addressed, and ended up publishing a detailed report to this effect. Alas, they were more often than not met with intransigence from a man who was unwilling to compromise his very singular views. I was told of one meeting with the Stonefrost group to which Byrne turned up carrying a packet of fish and chips. Dressed in his usual attire – a pair of off-white trainers, jeans, a tee-shirt and a red zip-up nylon jacket – he treated them contemptuously, with words to the effect of 'Well, you've got fifteen minutes to convince me – you're not going to, but carry on and do your best'. As they talked, Byrne continued to eat his fish and chips out of the packet. In a similar act of disregard, Tony Mulhearn stormed out of a meeting at the headquarters of the Association of Metropolitan Authorities to hold an 'impromptu' rally on the steps of the building with a group of supporters who had, conveniently, just arrived.

The final insult came towards the end of November, when it was revealed that Byrne had spent much of the summer securing a loan of £30 million from Swiss banks. Repayable over a seven-year period, this allowed the council to set a rate and balance its books for the forthcoming year; but in sealing the deal, Byrne had mortgaged the family silver, giving over as security the houses that had been built since 1983. Locally, some saw such measures as being born out of desperation. Others, like Paul Orr, were more suspicious:

They were cooking the fucking books.

If Byrne's Swiss loan brought an end to Liverpool's financial crisis (or rather, delayed it for another twelve months), the announcement of the deal at a DLP aggregate meeting signalled the start of something else. Rational argument had long given way to verbal threats amongst certain elements of the DLP, but these same individuals began to reveal an even darker side to their politics, as Jane Kennedy recalls:

> NUPE and NALGO delegates were held to blame. The meeting was held at the T&G offices, and when we came out afterwards, they had lined the four flights of stairs down from the room. They were kicking and pushing and shoving us. It was all very scary, but I had Malcolm on one side of me and Frank Jones, my convenor, on the other. They picked me up by the elbows and just razzed me down the stairs. I can't remember touching the floor. It was amazing, but very, very frightening.

It also reflected the wider malaise within the DLP that required treatment – and soon!

At a lengthy meeting of the Labour Party NEC at the end of November 1985, a resolution was put forward that the Liverpool party should be suspended pending the outcome of investigations into alleged misconduct. The proposal followed a report from Labour's North West Regional Office, which referred specifically to irregularities at DLP meetings earlier in the month, and was also a response to letters from two major national trade unions detailing Militant's excesses in Liverpool. Although the usual suspects opposed the resolution, arguing that it would lead to a widespread purge, the NEC voted in favour by an overwhelming majority of twenty-one to five. Speaking to the Oxford University Labour Club the following day, one of the five, Eric Heffer, described the decision to suspend the Liverpool party as 'an own goal of monumental proportions'.[83] This was rich coming from someone who had so often stuck the ball in the back of his own net, only to blame others for not having told him which way he was supposed to be kicking.

Although it had always been an option, the NEC's decision to suspend the Liverpool party was a relatively new one that had come about in October, on the Wednesday and Thursday of the Labour Party conference. The evening after Jane Kennedy addressed the floor in the Liverpool debate, she responded to an approach from Tom Sawyer as to whether there was anything that the party should do to help those fighting 'on the side of good' in Liverpool by requesting an urgent meeting with Neil Kinnock:

> It took place under the stage, in a windowless room. Charles Clarke was

there, Tom was there, and some other people, and Neil just swept in and talked. He was on a high. So much had happened during the week, and he just poured it all out for about five minutes. Conscious of the time, I was saying to myself, 'If I don't say something soon, I won't be able to shut him up'. So I said words to the effect of, 'Look, Neil, what you did was absolutely wonderful and it's given everyone in Liverpool a lot of heart and encouragement, but myself and Jane Saren (who had broken her constituency mandate in the vote on Liverpool), have got to go home and face it. It is a daily struggle for us. You can't let it go on as it is.' He said 'Well, what should we do?', and I replied 'Suspend the local party. You've got to disband it and start again from scratch.' He sort of went 'Oh, right'.

There can be little doubt that certain members of the NEC had been waiting for a long time to settle old scores, with Militant as well as with others on the left (something that stemmed from experiences during the Bennite ascendancy). I came to think of these individuals as the Cato Tendency, so committed were they to the destruction of Militant. For some, like Charlie Turnock of the National Union of Railwaymen, it was part of a mission to purge anyone he considered 'leftish'. For others, it was entirely consistent with their long-term recognition of the dangers of entryist Trotskyites. Members of the NEC such as Gwyneth Dunwoody, Betty Boothroyd and John Evans needed no Pauline conversion on the road to Bournemouth. They had always had a clear view – '*delenda est* Militant'.

There were, however, others on the NEC for whom the decision to take on Militant came after a long period of political soul-searching. For these individuals, the party was and should remain a broad church within which differing but compatible viewpoints vied to influence policy and strategy, but for whom the common and ultimate goal was returning a Labour government geared towards improving the lot of the majority of people in Britain. Militant had once been willing participants in this, serving to educate fellow party members in more theoretical concerns and happy to breathe its conscience on to everything from international affairs to domestic unemployment. All of that, however, changed in the late 1970s and early 1980s as Militant, i.e. the Revolutionary Socialist League, metamorphosed into a more distinct grouping, replete with its own structures and organisation.

Once this had become evident, those on the nominally 'soft left' who had previously shared platforms with Militant (Neil Kinnock and Tom Sawyer, to name but two), and those for whom it had been merely another faction at conferences or in their local party, started to make hard choices. Yes, they would be labelled 'right wing' and 'traitors' by Militant and their acolytes. Yes, they would be cast as willing participants in 'a McCarthyite witch-hunt'. Yet, at the same time, they were showing foresight, recognising the direction in which the party was starting to move, and revealing a perceptive understanding of British politics and the long and arduous road that democratic socialists have to follow. Of course, for others on the NEC, the decision to take on Militant sprang from the simple self-interest of careerist politicians.

In November 1985, the NEC established a team of eight of its members to look into the affairs and practices of the Liverpool party; specifically, the organisation and conduct of DLP meetings, the selection of council candidates, the choice of delegates from affiliated bodies and the recruitment of new members. Charlie Turnock was made chair of the team, and was quickly stigmatised by Militant as a Torquemada figure, given his unremitting hostility to 'the left'. Under him were a number of fellow trade unionists, Tony Clarke of the Union of Communication Workers, Eddie Haigh from the TGWU, Neville Hough from the GMB (who was also the chair of the NEC) and Tom Sawyer of NUPE; the MPs Margaret Beckett and Betty Boothroyd; and Audrey Wise. The whole exercise was to be overseen by the party's General Secretary, Larry Whitty:

> In very broad terms, it had been quite difficult to get the NEC to agree to an inquiry. Some of the trade union members were quite perturbed but, to be fair, I don't think any of them realised how dire the situation was. Indeed, for some of the inquiry team, it was a revealing experience.

The inquiry, which would include over sixty hours of hearings, began in early December with a four-day visit to Liverpool, including a meeting between the team and the local party leaders, the manner of which took the latter by surprise. Eddie Loyden, deputy chair of the DLP and MP for Garston, told the *Guardian*, 'We were expecting it possibly to be more fierce. It was not that way at all and was conducted in a very civilised way, and we can only register our satisfaction about the way it was conducted.'[84] The inquiry team, however, were perhaps playing a more careful game, having spent the previous few days hearing evidence from a host of local sources, ranging from the concerns of affiliated trade union branches over the extent to which the DLP was running the council to allegations of physical intimidation, particularly at party meetings, and specifically involving the use of the council's uniformed Static Security Force as 'stewards'. More often than not, their presence accentuated hostility towards anyone questioning 'the line'. Vicky Roberts recalls their 'militia-like' behaviour:

> If you made a fuss and tried to leave, you got barracked. This was quite apart from the general language, which was violent. I mean, I've never been over-sensitive about that but I don't think it's comradely behaviour. It was designed to intimidate people. I only spoke once or twice but when I did, I had to go up to a podium and speak into a microphone. You had them all there looking at you, and it was a matter of looking out to the tiny pockets of sympathy and support that there might have been.

Jane Kennedy paints a similar picture:

> There would be about forty of us, tops, who were not part of the campaign, and who were anti-Militant. We'd all sit there and huddle together for comfort. We were outnumbered twenty to one by these people. And they used to put the Branch 5 security guys near us, to have them try and intimidate us. Trying to speak in that atmosphere was appalling, but we would always be called. If we put our hands up to speak, Mulhearn would always recognise us. We were sort of token traitors.

Perhaps the most well-documented case of members of the Static Security Force acting as stewards to the DLP involved the ejection of Lew Baxter, a freelance journalist who had written articles critical of Hatton. On the latter's orders, Tony Stanton, a forbidding figure from Everton ward, physically removed Baxter from one DLP meeting, despite his legitimate right to be there as a delegate. Such were the prevailing winds at this time. Nevertheless, people who should know better continue to question the validity of claims of intimidation, with Eddie Sabino claiming that certain individuals 'made a meal' of what occurred:

> Some of them had never been intimidated in their lives – I mean hard-nosed bully boys themselves who had never ever been, and wouldn't allow themselves to be, intimidated. But if that happened to be your political stance, well, why not use it? If you're opposed to what went on at these meetings, why not say 'Well, yes, we were all intimidated'? I suppose intimidation in itself will affect different people in different ways, and a lot of the ones who were complaining about it have dished it out as much as they have received it. I've seen some of those who were moaning about it ten, twelve years ago doing exactly the same in the aftermath of all that without the Tendency being there.

Eddie recalls the 'intimidation' that he received on dismissing the inquiry team's assertion that violence and intimidation had taken place at DLP meetings:

> I'm not exaggerating when I say this. I mean, everyone knew where I was coming from, and there was absolutely no problem because I'd had this anti-Militant thing going back to the sixties. But I was attacked to such an extent that at one point Margaret Beckett had to dive in to defend me from Charlie Turnock.

This does not accord with Eddie Loyden's view of 'civilised' proceedings, and may be a reflection of Eddie Sabino's selective memory. Alternatively, there may have been a simple clash of personalities between him and Turnock, given his hostility to 'right-wing' trade union officials. Whatever the case, there was little at the time to suggest that the inquiry team conducted their business with anything less than the normal civilities.

The team completed its investigation into the DLP in the middle of February 1986, with six of them submitting a 'majority report' concluding that a number of malpractices had become characteristic of the organisation.[85] Principal amongst these malpractices were misuse of the agenda and power of the DLP, selective notification of executive meetings, swamping of the DLP by unelected people, false accounting of membership and intimidation and abuse of members. There had been differences of opinion amongst the inquiry team as to the seriousness of each of these charges, and Margaret Beckett and Audrey Wise issued a 'minority report', published alongside the majority report. One of their more memorable points of contention was their acceptance 'that it is a characteristic of Liverpool to be robust, lively and even abusive to an extent which might be unusual or unacceptable elsewhere but that these spirited exchanges are not intended to be basically offensive'.[86] This infuriated many people in Liverpool, including Vicky Roberts:

> That was appalling. Audrey Wise and Margaret Beckett accused us of being soft, and were basically saying 'If you can't stand the heat, get out of the kitchen'. They were sanctioning the way things were done. I don't think they knew how bad it was. Having people talk to you about it and actually experiencing it is quite different. I mean, if they had been in the T&G hall with all of these marauding hordes around them ...

It was a truly outrageous statement to make, described at the time as 'racist' by the Labour Coordinating Committee. Verbal abuse had long added colour to party meetings in Liverpool, but what went on during the 1980s was not typical of what had gone before. Similarly, intimidation and physical abuse were occurring within branches of the GMB, but such behaviour was not characteristic of other trade unions in the city. The common denominator, of course, was Militant, which used such tactics in both the party and the GMB to quash any opposition.

With regard to the action to be taken, although the minority report argued for discipline rather than expulsions, opinions within the 'majority' view ranged from those of Turnock, who wanted to see a wholesale purge of Militant, beginning in Liverpool but extending party-wide, to those of Tom Sawyer, who wanted to limit expulsions to those who had actively plotted to subvert the party's constitution. As Larry Whitty explains,

> The question was: 'How many of these people are Militant?', after which came the question of what to do with them – whether their abuses should lead to their removal from the party or whether they should be disciplined in a less finalised way.

The report recommended that the DLP should be suspended, and that sixteen members should be interviewed with a view to their expulsion. By name, they were Josie Aitman, Tony Aitman, Paul Astbury, Roger Bannister, Carol Darton, Felicity Dowling, Pauline Dunlop, Terry Harrison, Derek Hatton, Richard Knights, Ian Lowes, Tony Mulhearn, Sylvia Sharpey-Shafer, Harry Smith, Cheryl Varley and Richard Venton. By number, this being Liverpool politics, with its 'forty-nine', 'twenty-one' and 'six', they quickly became identified as 'the sixteen'.

Before the inquiry, talk of expulsions had triggered an exchange of views in the national press. Dominic Brady, a councillor for Everton ward and the city's chair of Education, announced that 'on behalf of the other non-Militant members of the Labour group, I will say this to Neil Kinnock: if he continues to consider expulsions of our comrades in the Labour group, he will do so over our dead bodies'.[87] A few days later, Paul Lally and Paul Thompson, members of the Merseyside Labour Coordinating Committee, responded to Brady, criticising both the tone of his comments as well as his wider sentiments, but then adding 'The inquiry is a regrettable necessity. It should not be used as a means of expelling people, but to make much-needed reforms in the way that the District Labour Party works, and to end the many malpractices that have given the local party such a bad name in the city.'[88] This implied a structural determinism that ignored the extent to which Militant permeated Merseyside politics. There was not the luxury of time to await the long-term effects of organisational changes unless the key figures in the cancer of Militant were taken out.

Brady's rhetoric was no more than to be expected from someone who, while intelligent and capable in his role, was considered by many to be a nasty piece of work; but what struck me most about Lally and Thompson was their continuing naivety in the face of personal experience. This stemmed from a rose-tinted view of how the party should operate, one that owed more to an undergraduate interpretation of democracy than the politics of the real world. Expulsions, however distasteful in normal circumstances, had become a necessity born of the abuses and malpractices engaged in by Militant and its key players on Merseyside. Purely for the benefit of their own organisation, they had systematically corrupted the rules and standing orders of the Labour Party, and cynically manipulated funds and members. All of this was entrenched and demanded critical attention.

On 26 February 1986, the NEC met to consider the details and proposals contained within the inquiry team's report. Militant, of course, pulled the stops out and organised a protest of 600 or so supporters on the pavement at Walworth Road. Naturally, their allies on the NEC indulged their egos with some rabble-rousing rhetoric. Other NEC members were forced to run the gauntlet, and at one stage David Blunkett had his path blocked by Hatton and Mulhearn. The meeting, when it finally got under way, lasted seven hours and involved some terse words. Neil Kinnock accused Eric Heffer of lacking the courage to act against the evil of Militant. Eric then told Neil that he would never forgive him and the NEC for their actions against the people of Liverpool and the local Labour Party (a few days later, Alan Watkins wrote in the *Observer* that Heffer's real trouble was that he could not forgive Kinnock for having decisively beaten him for the leadership[89]). Neil then responded with a comment on the idea of the Labour Party as a broad church, remarking that a church without walls is merely an open space for all and sundry to trample over. And so the meeting carried on, in the same vein, until the NEC voted by nineteen to ten to endorse the majority report and to commence proceedings against the sixteen individuals who had been recommended for interview. Amongst those voting against the endorsement were the five who had originally voted for no inquiry, Beckett and Wise, and Michael Meacher.

Early in March, 'the sixteen' became 'the twelve' as charges were dropped against Astbury, Josie Aitman, Dunlop and Sharpey-Shafer on advice from party lawyers that the evidence against them was too thin. The remainder, however, were variously charged with having brought the party into disrepute through breaches of the rules concerning practices and procedures of the DLP or for their membership of Militant. Some, such as Tony Aitman, Harrison, Mulhearn and Venton, were challenged with both. The NEC's first attempt to interview 'the twelve' over their individual charges was a farce from start to finish. For some unknown reason, those who turned up were left in a room with no-one to watch over them, as Cheryl Varley recalls:

> We had a laugh that day, a really good laugh in there. We were having a
> look through the drawers and the files and everything.

Worse still, the room had a window opening out on to the side of the building, through which Hatton and Mulhearn were able to give interviews and pose for photographs whilst the NEC began the hearing.

The hearing itself proved no less farcical. Earlier the same week, the High Court had ruled that the eight members of the inquiry team could not legally preside over evidence that they themselves had gathered, thus reducing the NEC to twenty-one. On the day itself, this number was further reduced when Heffer, Benn and five others staged a walk-out on the premise that the first accused, Felicity Dowling, had been refused a clear written statement of the revised charges against her (in fact, while some of the initial charges had been dropped, there were no new ones as such). At one stage, the hearing hung in the balance as Eric Clarke of the NUM toyed with the idea of staying. Eventually, he decided to walk, reducing the NEC to fourteen, one below its quorum, and thereby putting an end to the proceedings – temporarily, at least.

Outside, on the steps of Walworth Road, Heffer read what amounted to a prepared statement concerning the NEC's 'treatment' of Dowling, and his own view of 'the purge', following which a gathering of seventy or so Militant supporters started up a series of terrace-like chants of 'Liverpool, Liverpool', 'twelve-nil' and 'here we go'. Then, their very own monotoned tribune, Terry Fields, MP for Liverpool Broadgreen, led them in renditions of the 'Internationale' and the 'Red Flag'. In the meantime, those of the twelve accused who had made it to the hearing emerged smugly from the building, having collected expenses from Labour officials. As Larry Whitty freely admits,

We made the mistake of trying to get all of the interviews done on the one day. On reflection, that was bound to backfire.

Acrimony followed. Neil Kinnock described the seven who walked out as 'something less than magnificent', condemned them for 'sabotage' and 'a desertion of duty', and for being 'capricious', 'pathetic', 'infantile' and 'stupid', and disputed as 'misleading' the suggestion that Dowling had not been given a written statement of her charges.[90] David Blunkett, who commented on the day that Heffer and co. had 'put their egos before the interests of the party', later accused them of misleading people over the Dowling situation, before adding: 'Whilst purporting to have the interests of individuals and natural justice at heart, they have refused constantly to accept the duty of the party to take disciplinary action on breach of procedures and practices'.[91] Heffer responded by claiming that he had never shirked his duties as he had often gone to CLPs on behalf of the NEC to inform them of the latter's decisions, before reasserting his interpretation of the party as a broad church: 'I am against expulsions for political reasons and I want to make it clear that I personally will continue to oppose them'.[92] Oppose them he did, but to no avail. The expulsions were eventually to go ahead, and were of huge importance. They not only underlined the party's determination to rid itself of the individuals concerned, but also changed forever the notion that the Labour Party was a harbour for ideological flotsam and jetsam on the political sea. This was to be a vital point in the modernisation process.

Militant and those who defended them argued time after time that the inquiry and the proposed expulsions would damage the party's electoral fortunes. The reverse, however, was the truth. Two weeks later, on 11 April, Labour's Nick Raynsford won the Fulham by-election with a 10.9 per cent swing from the Tories, on a remarkably high turn-out of 70.1 per cent (ironically, in this time of great ferment for the people's party, the SDP/Liberal Alliance candidate was one Roger Liddle, later to rejoin the Labour Party and co-author the oxymoronic *Blair Revolution* with Peter Mandelson). With this sure signal from the electorate, Neil Kinnock and others could only become more committed in their attempts to remove those who continued to attack the party from within, and would persist in marching along the path of change. The times were also changing for Peter Kilfoyle.

One evening in late November 1985, just after the inquiry into the Liverpool party had been announced, I was having a pint with Ian Williams and Mike Allen, both anti-Militant stalwarts, at the Willow Bank pub on Smithdown

Road in the city. Larry Whitty had just been appointed General Secretary, and his assistant and general gofer, Tony Mainwaring, was a friend of Ian's who had told him that they would be looking for a full-time local organiser once the inquiry had made its recommendations. That night, Ian and Mike decided that I was going to have to do the job.

Unlike the pair of them, I had not been compromised enough locally to be precluded from taking on the role, having been away during the crucial period when alliances were being formed and reputations either burnished or tarnished. Militant and their allies seemed to hate Ian with a passion, primarily because of his acid tongue, but also because of his Maoist background. His obvious enmity for Militant ruled him out of the job, and he was also suffering from post-viral syndrome; a couple of years before, he had contracted an exotic disease whilst in India on a TUC scholarship and had never quite recovered. At the time, I assumed his ambitions were in a different direction – perhaps that is why he now works as a correspondent at the United Nations in New York. In Mike's case, whilst he had been one of the few brave dissidents on the DLP executive, he was also keen on pursuing his academic career (he now lectures at Cranfield College). I also suspected, and this was later confirmed by Ian, that I represented a more credible working-class alternative in terms of image, accent and so on. Mike was from Wallasey and Ian from Huyton, but they both saw themselves as a little apart from the style and language of the lumpen elements of the local party. Although neither was so impolite as to actually say that I had this necessary 'Liverpool' dimension, it was apparent that this underpinned their thinking – and so I half-agreed.

I was still, however, far from convinced. As much as anything else, I was already employed managing a large youth and community project in Runcorn. It was a good job and better paid than the Labour Party were to offer. I was happy in what I was doing, as it allowed me to get home at reasonable hours, and I had a decent working relationship with my two deputies with whom I worked a rota. It all added up to a pleasant and relatively simple life. Against this, there were the uncharted waters of resolving Labour Party difficulties.

The party still had to go through the process of advertising the post, but before this happened, I met Tony Mainwaring at Ian's house where we were to brief him on the local situation. I remember the occasion well because they were both vegetarians and when I turned up they were having a conversation about the respective merits of different types of lentils. It was an insight into a part of the party with which I was not *au fait*. Jane Kennedy, whom I did not know particularly well, was also there and, once we began to talk about the sort of person who should be employed as the organiser, Mainwaring said to her: 'Well, what about somebody like Peter? Would you have a problem with him if he was given the task?' Jane said no, and it struck home that there seemed to be a consensus growing that I was the most appropriate candidate – or possibly the only one considered mad enough – to do the job. Soon after, I applied.

To this day, I am still not clear about what Mainwaring and the many others who followed him up on reconnaissance duty were thinking. I found them all rather unimpressive. In they came, one by one, trying to find out what was happening on the ground in order to sound out potential alternative focuses for opposition to the prevailing orthodoxy in Liverpool. Their approach did not seem very systematic. The party never really had a strategic view of what it wanted to achieve in Liverpool, and there was no operational plan as such other than resolving the immediate problem of Militant on Merseyside. Many key figures knew that Militant was a pain, although not everyone was really convinced. Larry Whitty himself was very reluctant to engage in what he would describe as 'witch-hunts', and he was more concerned with targeting the ring leaders:

> A very firm line had been drawn about membership of Militant, but my view was that we should only kick some of them out. There was always this dilemma about whether they were breaking party rules or whether they were actively undermining the party.

Some in the party saw Larry as soft on this kind of thing. Andy Bevan was still the National Youth Officer at Walworth Road; a full-time Militant, he was regarded within Labour Party HQ as their resident spy. He was amiable enough on a person-to-person level but there was no doubting where his sympathies lay. Everybody knew this, but there was a general reluctance to do anything about it, and Bevan would remain at the core as long as the Labour Party continued to be a sclerotic organisation incapable of putting its house in order. It was only when Neil Kinnock and Joyce Gould, Director of Organisation, got the bit between their teeth that effective action was taken. These two individuals, more than anyone, were to be the key to the changes that made Labour electable once more. They demonstrated a political awareness of the damage done by Militant that few others could match, and also displayed personal courage and tenacity. Given that they held such senior positions, their influence cannot be overstated. They recognised the huge responsibility that they had, both to the party, and to those millions of people who looked to Labour to address their concerns. Their conclusions were simple: the Labour Party had to do what was necessary to be elected, and that meant removing the Militant blight from its midst. Neither Neil nor Joyce was found wanting in that challenge.

Of course, there were others who had been biding their time within the party apparatus, trying to get a feel for what was happening more generally with Militant. They included David Hughes, the national agent, originally from Dingle in Liverpool, and George Rogers, who had been the MP for Chorley and was now working in the library at Walworth Road. Rogers had always been on the left of the party, including the PLP, but understood the dangers posed by Militant. Along with Hughes and many others, however, he did not really have a handle on what was happening in Liverpool, where the situation had become far more complex.

The other people apart from myself on the short-list for the Liverpool post included Danny Bermingham and Felicity Dowling, one of those being recommended for expulsion. Bermingham had been all over the place, politically. Having been with Militant and then repudiated them, he then became involved with Liverpool Labour Left, along with his partner Hannah Folan. (Later, as a councillor, he would throw in his lot with Militant's second eleven on Liverpool council when personal interest dictated.) For Dowling, it was all a bit of a lark because she could not lose either way. If she was given the job, that would have been the icing on the cake – a known Militant employed by the Labour Party to ensure that Militant did not engage in abuse of the DLP! Should she fail, it could merely be blamed on 'the NEC's bias towards good and real socialists'. That she was ever put on the short-list reveals something in itself about the mind-set of the party as it emerged from its Bennite phase.

The NEC really had no idea what it wanted. In one sense, it thought that the creation of the post amounted to sending in a bruiser to sort people out. Obviously, a shrinking violet would not have been able to do some of the things necessary for the job, if only because they would have been bowed into submission in a short space of time. At the risk of sounding immodest, it required an awareness of the cultural context, an understanding of the personalities involved and a shrewd appreciation of what you could and could not get away with. It might not have worked if the NEC had put in a younger member of the party from Liverpool, or someone from beyond the city who might have known the rule-book inside out but had no idea of local circumstances.

Still, it was by no means obvious that the job was mine. When I attended Walworth Road for the interview, I did not see the others who had been short-listed. I saw Liz Djilali, who was on Larry Whitty's staff (and who now works for PLP). She gave me a cup of tea and I waited my turn. I had the interview with Larry, Joyce Gould and others whose names I now fail to recall, and then returned to Liverpool. I cannot remember much about the interview other than the fact that I took issue rather stridently with Larry for making a presumption about Liverpool as a place. I was subsequently to discover that Mo Mowlam was considered for the job. To this day, I do not know whether or not she was approached and turned it down. Mo was at the Northern College at the time, and it would have been as hard for her as it was for me to change jobs. Not long after, she was to begin her parliamentary career as MP for Redcar, and so the experience was not a missed opportunity!

My reasons for taking the job were pure and simple. I had a deep regard for the city of Liverpool and a deep regard for the Labour Party. Militant was damaging both, and I considered it a personal challenge that I should be given the opportunity to help rectify this. Following the interview, and before being told formally what decision had been taken, it was indicated to me that I would be offered the post, and so I resigned from my job at Runcorn in anticipation. That was no longer as difficult a choice as I had expected it to be. My line manager was making my work life increasingly difficult and, on that level at least, I saw some relief in the prospect of a new challenge. Even so, there was a brief period of trepidation in which I felt unsure about whether I had done the right thing for my family.

During this interim period, Phil Robinson, then one of the party's three assistant regional organisers, and Wally Edwards, who had previously been the party's agent in Liverpool, came to see me to discuss how they saw things developing. I have long been an admirer of Wally. I know it is a cliché, but he really is one of life's gentlemen. Ever since I have known him, he has been relaxed and easy-going, and without any malice. Sometimes, however, Wally has been too laid back, and for the kind of job that I was taking on, his 'nice guy' approach was the wrong sort of role model – not just because we were not dealing with nice guys (nor girls), but because he would not have been sufficiently proactive. Wally would rather have shrugged his shoulders and said 'Oh well, that's the way of the world, I'll just keep my head down' and carry on in his own sweet way.

Phil Robinson was a different type of person altogether, and I immediately found him rather hostile. Subsequently, I was to find that this was his way; he was poor in his interpersonal and communication skills. Some of the other regional full-timers were no better, and in time it became apparent that they were difficult people with whom to work. Peter Killeen, who is still employed by the party, had a reputation as a wheeler-dealer fixer but lacked any clear agenda that anyone else could understand; few people had any respect for him. Ray Gill was officially the head of the team, a position that was way beyond his capacity, and this eventually led to real problems for him and the party. Robinson, Killeen and Gill really were an odd bunch, and their appointments revealed much about the party's failings in terms of recruitment, training and upskilling. Very often, jobs were filled to keep people out, rather than ensuring that the best possible candidate was appointed.

In fact, the regional office had long been part of the problem. A previous Regional Secretary, Paul Carmody, had effectively ordered Merseyside a 'no-go area' back in the 1970s, exacerbating what were already serious organisational problems. That approach, if that is the appropriate term for it, had demonstrably failed. The regional office was neither capable nor willing to face up to Militant and their acolytes in the sub-region; quite frankly, they seemed to be paralysed with fright at the thought of getting involved. They were very good at sending letters. They were also good at attending the odd meeting, as long as they did not have to say anything. What they were no good at was standing up and being counted.

When I finally began work as the full-time organiser in Liverpool, on April Fool's Day, 1986, a week after the farce of the first attempt to interview 'the twelve', a period of uncertainty followed over the terms of my remit. Rather than just being an adjunct of the regional office, I saw flexibility and the freedom to move as absolutely crucial. Yet it was unclear as to how far this approach would be recognised by the NEC. Because of the absence of a game plan, I was happy to be left to fly by the seat of my pants to sort out 'the problem'. As it turned out, my enterprise was welcomed when it worked, while at other times I was reprimanded for exceeding what were seen to be my terms of reference. Soon after I started, it became apparent that the regional bureaucracy was trying to rein me in. They wanted to get a handle on everything I was doing. This is presumably why Robinson had come to see me with Wally, to smooth things over before I began my task.

I understood their thinking in normal organisational terms, and because of the way in which the whole thing had blown up in the public eye, the regional officers became very irritated by the amount of publicity that began to accrue to me personally. It was not jealousy as such, but they seemed to resent the fact that it was me and not them who became the focus of media attention. I actually came across a memo from Robinson to Gill in which he wrote of me, 'He is appearing in print, on radio and on TV as if he's some form of celebrity'. This came as no surprise. These were people who had long been in office and had done nothing about Militant. They were scared of their own shadows and they were terrified that I was undermining their authority by having a separate line into Larry Whitty or Joyce Gould, or even Neil Kinnock. As it happened, I was to have separate lines all over the place. At the outset, however, my primary concern was with asserting the authority of the NEC upon the party in Liverpool.

Shortly after my appointment, I had a conversation with Ray Gill which led to a widely reported incident regarding a telephone. Gill said that the first thing we should do was stop the suspended DLP from functioning. The office was in the trade union centre; the DLP and Trades' Council were together in one office, while Terry Fields' 'constituency' office was immediately next door, connected to the DLP office by an internal door. Militant effectively ran the corridor, and nobody could go about their business without them either listening in or visually monitoring movements. Gill had previously instructed the officers of the suspended DLP to have the telephone line stopped, but they had refused to take any notice of him, and for some odd reason we could not get BT to turn the phone off. As a result, the DLP was still running up bills when it no longer existed as a body, and as with its other debts, the national party was left to pay. It was necessary, therefore, to show that I meant business, and to make an impact. In moving a table, I had half knocked the telephone off the wall, but I then decided to finish the job and pulled it out completely. I have never been proud of this, and at the time I told the local press the half-truth that it was wholly an accident, that the phone wires had been caught around a table that was being moved.

Contrary to my own wishes, the regional party also took an office in the trade union centre. People outside were saying that the move was 'good politics', and all the usual tosh about keeping in with the unions, but I was of the view that you can never keep in with people who are purely opportunists. This centre had been accommodating to all-comers – basically anyone who would pay the money to help sustain its existence. As such, it was all things to all people. Moreover, I had a very low opinion of the way it was run. At that time, it was to all intents and purposes overseen by Kevin Coyne, whose career moves have long bewildered me. He was on the TGWU national executive for a while but left when he went to work for the MSF as a regional official. His place at the trade union centre was taken by Bob Braddock, the regional chair of the MSF. It was musical chairs in a closed shop.

Our office had the most basic furnishings, scrounged from friendly trade unions. We lacked even a typewriter, and so I acquired the one from the DLP office. There was anger about this but I had to make it repeatedly known that due to the suspension everything within the office now belonged both legally and practically to the national party. As I had effectively become the DLP, it was necessary to re-impose some kind of order within the rules of the party. On a personal level, I took my first tentative steps to try to turn Liverpool's image around, the first stage of which was to kill off as much media interest as was possible. I tried to do all of these things; while I could never gauge how successful I was in total, many individual successes were chalked up.

In both the rehabilitation of Liverpool and the recapture of the Labour Party, the media's role was vital. Obviously, different journalists held different attitudes at different times. It would be very easy to dwell on what we perceived in the city as the anti-Liverpool bias of journalists. There was a great deal of that, but I have always thought it too simplistic to talk of anti-Liverpool or anti-Merseyside sentiment. There were certainly those who were plain lazy, including people inside as well as outside the city. Once Peter Phellps had won the Journalist of the Year award on the back of the Liverpool stories that he had written, there were plenty of people wanting to emulate him and willing to repeat the formula in order to make their name as journalists. There were those who were politically biased and wanted to use the city to score points against the Labour Party nationally. There were those who wanted to believe the most absurd things about Liverpool. There were others who systematically tried to link up local criminality with politics in a sensationalist way, such as John Davison at the *Sunday Times*. I was quite convinced that there were certain political connections with the criminal fraternity in the background but caution was necessary, and I did not want to have Liverpool once again portrayed as 'Cook County, UK'.

There were also those, like Jonathan Foster of the *Independent* and Alan Dunne of the *Guardian,* who seemed to be both mesmerised and tortured by the whole thing. Foster got on reasonably well with some of the local rebels, particularly Byrne, and he also seemed to have a soft spot for Hatton. He was always incredibly pleasant to me – at least to my face – but my conversations with him used to develop into a protracted debate over the rights and wrongs of the situation in terms of the traditional left rather than of the realities of the Labour Party in the broadest sense. Dunne, whilst never keen on Hatton, seemed to be sympathetic to the aims of Mulhearn and Byrne. I always suspected his views were coloured by a resentment towards London, stemming from when the *Guardian* had moved from its base in Manchester and he was left behind to become a 'provincial' reporter. Interestingly, I recall Dunne telling me that at the time of the move he had been offered a job on the foreign desk but he declined the offer because of his fear of flying. I suspect that, to a lesser degree, anti-London resentment also underpinned Foster. It has been rather crudely said that 'he bores for Sheffield'.

It was perfectly reasonable for Dunne and Foster to have their own views, but I use them as illustrations to point up how different the position really was from a purely black and white story. Locally, there were solid defenders of Liverpool, like David Hope of the *Liverpool Daily Post*, Ian Hamilton-Fazey of the *Financial Times*, and Ian Brandis, who ran his own press agency. There was also the freelance Lew Baxter, who more often than not focused on the negative aspects of the Liverpool political scene. He later worked for the Xinhua Press Agency in China, though I doubt whether he gave the ruling party a bad press there.

As a step to normalising things, I made it quite apparent that I was not put off by some of the more intimidatory methods of Militant and their cohorts, making it abundantly clear that by the terms of my appointment, I was only answerable to the NEC. On one occasion, when walking along a corridor in the trade union centre, I was stopped and surrounded by Frank Mills and a crowd of others who had come to tell me that Mulhearn requested my presence. I had been summoned! Irritated by their hostility, I said 'Tell him to ring my office and make an appointment'. They were not expecting this, and Mills replied 'He wants to see you now!', to which I said 'I'm afraid I'm rather busy – I'm just going to see Bill Snell', which I knew would inflame them further, adding once more for effect: 'so if Mulhearn wants to see me, tell him to get on to the office and make an appointment'. They had no idea how to handle this, but their attitude betrayed how such intimidation – through numbers, demeanour and language – was central to Militant's strategy on Merseyside. I had no choice but to face up to them, and to assert the authority of the Labour Party.

# 8  Mind games

Shortly after the suspension of the Liverpool District Labour Party, a 'temporary coordinating committee' was set up by the NEC to try to continue the normal business of the local party. Its first meeting took place on 27 March 1986, the day after the NEC's initial attempt to interview the dozen transgressors; as it turned out, the chaos of events at Walworth Road reverberated straight back to Liverpool. At the start of the meeting, Tony Mulhearn was elected chair of the temporary body and two of his fellow Militants, Ted Mooney and Phil Rowe, became the treasurer and secretary respectively. The proceedings were then bogged down in a long discussion about whether or not the national party should be taken to court over its threat to expel 'the twelve'. Despite all the evidence to the contrary and years of personal experience, many of the non-Militants present at the TCC failed to appreciate that the dozen were not dissident comrades, but members of an organisation antagonistic to the Labour Party. Cheryl Varley makes this apparent in recalling how she and the rest of 'the twelve' were working in Militant's interest:

> We wanted to draw out the process for as long as we could, for the maximum publicity. We would phone in sick saying that we couldn't come, just to keep it going and going.

Of course, the ultimate aim of Varley, Mulhearn and the others was, to quote Trotsky, 'to support the Labour Party as the rope supports the hanging man'.

It was one of Militant's main claims that Labour's NEC was using organisational means to stifle socialist discussion. These, however, were the very same organisational means they used to stop people even from getting themselves into a position where they could debate. They prevented people joining bodies if they thought that they were not the right material – i.e. sympathetic to Militant – and if someone did slip through the net, they were made to feel as unwelcome as possible. Such hostility was blindingly obvious when I attended an inaugural meeting of the Labour Party Young Socialists' liaison committee at Transport House in Liverpool. One of those attending sat literally on his own, whilst the rest were together on the other side of the room. I suspected that the lad who was alone may have been a supporter of some other Trotskyite grouping (Socialist Organiser probably), but he was still ostracised. This was how Militant used the party's organisations, not only to project their ideas and policies, but also to stifle any semblance of an alternative point of view. In doing so, they created an atmosphere that was inimical to open and free debate.

On many occasions, key Militants behaved like children, demeaning what ought to have been serious occasions. At one TCC meeting Hatton decided to play at being 'Jack the lad'. At one point, he suddenly stood up and left the room; being used to sitting in disciplined meetings, I was quite taken aback. A short while later, however, he returned and interrupted the proceedings by announcing the score of an Everton game that was taking place that evening. There he stood, mouthing off about football as we tried to agree a *modus vivendi* between the TCC and the NEC. His superficiality appalled me.

It was a similar situation at the Labour group. Anyone who observed the council at that time would understand exactly what I mean. There was no sense of proper procedure, order or discipline unless Militant wanted it to be right. If their councillors were not wandering about, they were talking across people. These were deliberate tactics to put people off and to show their contempt for the norms of political discussion. It showed me how shallow Militant's claims were that the processes of debate in Liverpool politics were democratic. Having presented their own ideas, they ignored or shouted down anybody who wanted to speak up against them. They thrived on disruption and mayhem; it offended any sense of intellectual propriety and general fair play.

For the 1986 local elections, the TCC appointed Josie Aitman as the campaign coordinator, and I had to work alongside her and a number of other Militant sympathisers. It really was peculiar, and an almost schizophrenic relationship developed. I was helping people whom I knew to be supporters of Militant but who had been endorsed as Labour candidates. Of course, I was committed to changing the nature of the party's base on the council, but at those elections I had to dig in so as to avoid losing any ground to the Liberals. I did all the run of the mill things – running around with leaflets and posters and helping with other organisational matters – and avoided getting embroiled in the politics of the campaign. Militant tried their best to do everything by the book, but the reality was that their objectives were far different to my own and those of the legitimate Labour Party.

On the evening of the count, I was invited by John Hamilton to the media centre that had been set up within the Municipal Building. Hatton saw me in John's office and went off at the deep end, wanting to know what I was doing there. I told him that I was not interested in anything he had to say because I had been invited by 'the leader'. Just before the count, I saw Hatton smoking; he appeared overly nervous, and obviously anticipated a real drubbing by the Liberals. Soon after the results revealed that Labour had done far better than expected, however, he began shouting out his usual soundbites and claiming the credit for the Labour victory.

During my first month as the local organiser, the NEC hauled back on track the process of interviewing 'the twelve'. Notice had been served on Militant with the removal of their editorial board from the party in 1983, Neil Kinnock's 1985 conference speech, the findings of the inquiry into the DLP and my appointment. They had been tumbled, and the Labour Party was, quite rightly, going to remove them under its rules and constitution. There could be no compromise; we were at daggers drawn.

The first of those up for interview was Mulhearn. A nasty piece of work, in my view, he spent much of this period engineering some of the more personally vindictive things said about myself. He had a habit of writing fictitious accounts of the things I was supposedly doing. Even when he had a smidgen of substance, he would misrepresent it in the most stereotypical way, as was shown in a letter to the *Liverpool Echo* in which he wrote, 'The Liverpool Labour Party was well prepared to fight and win elections long before witch-hunters like Mr Kilfoyle and Co. appeared on the scene. I have been a member of the Labour Party for twenty-three years, vice-president of the Liverpool Labour Party since 1975 and president since 1981 and had never heard of Peter Kilfoyle until recently. It is certainly not long-standing party members like myself who are infiltrators – it is those who have recently arrived on the scene demanding adherence to a grey/pink flag and the abandonment of socialist policies.'[93]

This was typical of his attempts to undermine my political credibility and authority on behalf of the NEC. A week later, Eddie Roderick wrote in response to confirm that I had been his agent in the late 1960s, long before Mulhearn had begun to take an active role in the party. In his own account of the proceedings that resulted in his expulsion, Mulhearn and his co-author, Peter Taaffe, write of how he 'brilliantly rebutted' the charges made against him, but that 'the right ... were determined to give the bourgeois his head'.[94]

Even if this rather vain assertion were true, his claimed brilliance did not prevent Mulhearn being expelled and removed from all positions of office. No longer could he lord it over the DLP and its successor; no more would he dominate Liverpool Garston CLP; never again would he lay down the law to the council Labour group. That, at any rate, was the theory.

The day after his expulsion, Mulhearn attended a meeting of the Garston constituency party, at the start of which I rose on a point of order concerning his presence. Despite my repeated insistence, this was refused consideration, and when two Cooperative Society delegates attempted to do likewise, they were shouted down from some quarters as 'arseholes'. Standing orders were then suspended to allow Mulhearn the opportunity to speak on his expulsion. He launched into a diatribe against the NEC and 'front-benchers with law degrees', before claiming that he had been the victim of a kangaroo court. After this, the meeting descended into farce. As I refused to discuss party business while Mulhearn remained in the room, the chair, Jimmy Wilson, in turn refused to let me give my scheduled address. At the very end of the meeting, Steve Vose, the secretary of Garston and a known Militant, said to me 'You should have come to work for us if you needed a job'. I assume he felt that I had taken the job with the Labour Party because I could find no other work! My reasoning was way beyond their comprehension.

The following day, Mulhearn attended a meeting of the council Labour group, an appearance that was sanctioned by John Hamilton, in comments to the press: 'Mr Mulhearn is a member of the Labour group and will remain a member until the group decides otherwise, should it do so. There is nothing to stop the Labour group inviting people to its meetings, even though they are not members of the party.'[95] Notwithstanding the fact that John was considered to be the respectable face of the party in Liverpool, his words speak volumes about the broader complexities within which I was attempting to work. I was actually turfed out of this meeting, after a vote in favour of my debarment (councillors Mike Black and Bill Westbury walked out in protest). What was more frustrating, however, was that I was kept waiting for nearly two hours outside the meeting room, on the understanding that I would at some point be allowed to speak to the group on what Mulhearn's expulsion meant for them. At no point did anyone bother to come and inform me that I had been declined the opportunity to do so.

The Mulhearn saga carried on for some time. In July, I attended Garston's AGM to ensure that he was no longer recognised by his local party. Having run the gauntlet going into the meeting, which involved both verbal and physical abuse (I was kicked and spat upon), what most struck me was the sheer gall of Mulhearn when he slipped in just after the start. I immediately raised it with the chair, pointing out that either Mulhearn went or I did, and if I went, the meeting and the CLP would be declared closed. They asked for a short recess to consider this, which I was happy to allow, and eventually agreed to ask Mulhearn to leave. But, in doing so, they staged a big farewell; I half expected them to present him with a clock for his length of service. Naturally, the media had been summoned and several local journalists were gathered outside the building. Mulhearn considered himself so important that he would risk the well-being of his own constituency party – something to which he gave the impression of being so devoted – for the sake of a few minutes of television and radio coverage.

Six years later, on the night of the 1992 general election, I appeared on a programme at the BBC in Liverpool, after which they had booked a taxi to take me home. The car-hire firm with which they had the contract was the same one where Mulhearn was then employed. Come the early hours of the morning, after the programme had ended, he duly arrived to pick up his fare, and on seeing who it was refused to take me. This did not bother me, of course – there was no way that I was getting into a car with Mulhearn. My dislike of the man persists to this day, and I am sure that he still feels the same antipathy towards me.

The day after Mulhearn was expelled was one of mixed fortunes for Militant. Another of 'the twelve', Harry Smith, treated the NEC to one of his Liverpool-comic style monologues, full of humorous anecdotes and pithy witticisms. Having apparently been charmed by this, the NEC dropped the charges against him, allowing Smith to remain in the party for what turned out to be a few more years. Tony Aitman, however, twenty-two years an entryist, was expelled, as was Ian Lowes:

> I was given the opportunity to make statements about the Tendency but I wasn't prepared to do that, and so the Labour Party kicked me out.

On a personal level, I have always got on very well with Lowes. He actually joined and left Militant before he was expelled from the party, and it was in some ways ironic that he was not expelled from his union, given his many fights with the union machine and its full-time officials. Then again, why should he have been when he had done well by his members, winning them conditions which they otherwise would not have had? Some would argue that Lowes and his members went over the top, but in the narrow sense of judging him by how he looked after the interests of those who elected him, he did extremely well. Full time GMB officials detested him, but they were either incapable or unwilling to take him on. I tried to persuade both his General Secretary, John Edmonds, and his Regional Secretary, John Whelan, to tackle Lowes and his branch. Neither of them were up to the challenge, offering rather lame excuses as to why they could not act.

Three weeks after the first round of interviews came the second bout. Again, charges were dropped against one of those accused, Carol Darton. Disappointing as this was, she had never been a key player and the NEC successfully fried four bigger fish on the same day. They included the youth-obsessed Terry Harrison, Militant's own Janet Street-Porter, the humourless Roger Bannister, a NALGO official, and Richard Venton, Militant's Merseyside organiser, originally from Northern Ireland and someone who typified the archetypal bigot from either side of the sectarian divide. Most crucial of all, however, was the scalp of Derek Hatton.

As I have already made clear, I had taken an instant dislike to Hatton the first time I met him. I thought he was totally shallow, what in the Liverpool argot we call 'a phoney'; his primary motivation was his own narrow self-interest. I never saw anything to make me change that view, so my relationship with him has always been antagonistic. Even to this day I cannot bear him. A few years ago, I caught a train at Runcorn, and as I walked through the carriage I passed Hatton who, on spotting me, said 'All right, Peter?' I ignored him and carried on to the far end of the otherwise empty carriage, sat down, lit a cigarette and thought 'That's all I need'. Then I heard his voice from along the aisle. He was on a mobile phone and I could hear him say, 'And you know what, the ignorant sod won't even speak to me'.

Perhaps the only thing worse than Hatton himself was the esteem with which he was held in some quarters. On one New Year's Eve in the mid 1980s, I went to see a local band playing in the Scotty Club in Liverpool. Technically, they were all unemployed, but they were making good money performing regularly, and for this particular gig they each received about a hundred pounds. Afterwards, I was engaged in conversation with a circle of people including members of the band when one of the latter suddenly launched into a personal attack: 'You – you're a bloody action man for the Labour Party'. When I asked him what he was talking about, he said that I was persecuting 'poor Derek' and 'giving him no peace' (something had been in the papers that week concerning Hatton and me). He continued, 'I've got you all weighed up – the money you're on. You've betrayed your roots. You've moved from a house in Dingle to one in Allerton with a garden.' (This was ironic, as Liverpool's housing policy at the time was that all new council houses were to be built with a garden.) He then started going on about his wife, from whom he was separated and who was also living in the 'posh end' of Liverpool, before saying: 'I've seen you lot, when you take your kids to school – you all wear duffel coats'.

This charge of affluence was rich coming from someone who was able to collect around a hundred pounds for a night's work on top of his dole, while I was only taking home a hundred and ten pounds a week working for the Labour Party. I picked him up on his defence of Hatton, remarking that the latter had more suits than I had had hot dinners, that he was driving a top-of-the-range Volvo paid for by the council while I was in my own battered old Renault, that he had two jobs, giving him an income of around twenty thousand pounds a year, and that his kids had horses. When I had finished, he immediately turned to me and said 'That's typical – there you go again, maligning the man'. I just could not win. It was all part of a twisted class warfare where hatred and bitterness were focused on the lifestyle of anyone outside the Liverpool orthodoxy except for Hatton and his ilk, who were exempted.

It has been well documented that Hatton was expelled from the party *in absentia*. I have always believed him to be guilty of moral cowardice, unable to face up to unpalatable situations. What fascinated me about his actual expulsion was the David Blunkett/Michael Meacher argument at the NEC that Hatton should be debarred from 'office, delegacy and candidature' but not expelled. This showed how some within the legitimate left were still reluctant to grasp the expulsion nettle. They wanted to believe that these were wayward comrades, loyal but misdirected. The reality was a parasitic organisation using Labour as its host body. As such, Hatton and others had to be extirpated, not mollified.

Taaffe and Mulhearn compared the NEC's decision to expel Hatton in his absence with the expulsion of Brendan Behan from the IRA in the 1950s, noting Behan's pithy rebuke that they could also carry out the death sentence they had ordered 'in my absence'.[96] Although such similarities are rather tenuous, the choice of Behan perhaps reveals more about their view of Hatton. Here too was an egotist with an ability to hit the self-destruct button. On receiving the news of his expulsion, Hatton responded as I expected, citing once again the myth of his 'fifteen years in the party', before adding, 'I have a Labour Party card in my pocket and will continue to have that membership card. My ward and constituency who gave me that card have indicated that they will continue to recognise me as a party member and the Labour group will continue to recognise me as deputy leader.'[97]

I knew that he would try to play this game, and when the time came I was ready to frustrate his moves, turning up at various meetings of the group as well as of Hatton's local party. He revealed the nastier side of his temperament; I remember well the Childwall ward meeting when Hatton turned up with a band of his heavies. He had previously been the chair, but his expulsion deprived him of the position; he should not even have been in the room. Nevertheless, when Hatton came in, he immediately went up to the top table where he proceeded to push the newly elected chair, Judy Edwards, out of her seat. As this was going on, Hatton's wife, Shirley, began screaming hysterically at me, while her husband's cronies set about intimidating people. What made the whole incident even more distasteful was that Judy and her husband Paul, who was also present, were until that evening close friends of the Hattons and, indeed, godparents to their eldest child.

Hatton, Harrison, Mulhearn – I had no love towards any of them, and the feeling was mutual. I was trying to put a stop to their political ambitions, not only in terms of running the city council but also their parliamentary hopes. It is worth recalling that, before the boundary review of 1982, the three of them were all lined up as prospective Labour candidates alongside Terry Fields. What a fine body of people they would have been to represent Liverpool. It just goes to show how bad things were at that time in the local party that there was no viable alternative on offer. These individuals were neither good nor smart, but they and their organisation provided something that was simplistic and glib, and appeared to offer some answers to the city's problems.

With the expulsion of Hatton, three cases from the revised list of twelve remained. That of Richard Knights was put on hold (he was eventually expelled in December 1990), but the charges against Cheryl Varley and Felicity Dowling were pursued. These two were among the more shrill of the local Militants. To the outside world, they would present themselves as if butter would not melt in their mouths, but once they were in full flow, the venom was incredible. Listening to Varley was equivalent to assault and battery of the eardrums. As for Felicity (what a misnomer!) Dowling, I recall one meeting in Speke at which I was defending myself against some terrible crime or other. Dowling, a councillor for the ward, was in the front row, mouthing

'You're a fucking liar, you're a fucking liar' at me, over and over again with-out making a sound. As she had her back to everyone else, only the chair and myself were aware of what was going on.

Having been the first to be interviewed at the farcical meeting in March, Dowling's case was to drag on beyond the party conference until late Octo-ber, when the NEC finally voted to expel her. Varley's expulsion, meanwhile, had taken place in July:

> In the end we were members of the Militant but they couldn't prove that. My charges were three articles that I'd written for the *Mersey Militant* and one that I'd written for *Labour Militant*. I went through every article and there was not a word in any of them that was against Labour Party policy. So there was no evidence, really. It was all decided beforehand that I was going to be expelled. It was a foregone conclusion, but I didn't care. I'd only been in there three years.

Varley remains scathing of some of those who were present at her interview:

> I remember getting really angry because they kept asking me a group of questions again and again. I was answering but I was thinking to myself 'Why can't you understand what I'm saying here?', and then it dawned upon me that some of them were stupid. You'd have thought that when you got to the NEC of the Labour Party that you would only find intelli-gent people. I remember one NEC member drinking himself into the state where he was virtually falling off of his chair, another one knitting throughout.

The straightforward expulsion of Varley received additional attention when it became apparent that she had taken a journalist, Quentin McDonald, in with her as her 'friend'. This was a catch-all term that basically covered anyone and everyone. Two months later, McDonald, who worked for *City Limits*, gave a detailed account of the proceedings in a piece in the *New Statesman*. It was never clear whether he was also a Militant, but the tone of his article sug-gested that he and Varley were like-minded. So were many other people at a superficial level, based on Militant's transitional programme, which appealed to a simple analysis of the political situation.

Back in Liverpool, Militant and their acolytes were trying to make it difficult for me to carry out my job. I went to meetings where they would have ban-ners with 'We don't give a XXXX for you, Kilfoyle', 'Go back to Australia' and all that kind of stuff. Many of them thought that I had been brought in from Australia specially, a belief that informed the perceptions of others in the local party, including Bob Lancaster:

> Peter was brought back from Australia to do the job. I said to people in Walton, 'Peter's come to do the Tendency over'. I'd no problem with that. There were some decent comrades in the Tendency and I said to them 'All you're doing is giving Peter ammunition, and he'll do you'.

There was a lot of nonsense spoken about how I had been specially recruited, and I was accused later of having been trained in the Australian intelligence services. Some James Bond I would have made! The way in which people were prone to exaggeration was particularly acute in Liverpool at the time, and I was regularly faced with such comments. It was a load of bull; nothing could have been further from the truth. I was just an ordinary party member doing a job for his party and his city, a personal burden that continues. Interestingly though, just before Christmas 1997, John Spellar MP passed on to me a series of cuttings from the *Sydney Morning Herald* relating to a former member of the Australian SAS who had been involved in a venture to train former military personnel as 'industrial mercenaries'.[98] His name? Peter Kilfoyle. This got me thinking about the lengths and depths that Militant must have gone to in trying to check me out, and led me to wonder if they had a contact somewhere in the Australian system. Those who wish to still question my background may find succour for their notions in *that* Peter Kilfoyle's refusal to be photographed, despite ongoing notoriety in Australian politics.

Perhaps the most verbally vicious of all the individuals I had to deal with was Tony Byrne. As we have seen, he had an understanding with Militant that he could get on with running the council whilst they got on with their political trickery. He always struck me as a bit of an odd character, with slightly schizophrenic attitudes. Occasionally, I would have a little chat with him outside St Anthony of Padua school, where I would be collecting my son and Byrne would be collecting his nephew. However, it was not uncommon to find him berating me and calling me the most vile names at a meeting that same night. Peter Ferguson, another leading councillor, was also a bit like this – pleasant, almost deferential, on a one-to-one basis but full of vitriol when you argued with him at meetings. It was as if the political persona was entirely at odds with the private one.

Whenever they had to mention my name, it became *de rigueur* for Militant and their acolytes to spit it out. In fact my local reference became DFK, which stood for 'dat fucking Kilfoyle'. Many of those who had never met me were shocked to discover that my roots lay in the city. I understood why. Some of them had very rarely travelled outside their own area of Liverpool, and had little knowledge of the party beyond their particular ward or constituency. Added to this, many had only been in the party for a relatively short period, and there were others who were relatively recent incomers to the city, often arriving as students. So it came as no surprise that many of these people were unaware of my background. Occasionally, though, I would go into a meeting and be chatting away, only to discover that I was talking to someone whom I had known years before who would say 'I didn't realise you were the same person. We wondered who this character was.'

A classic example of this occurred with Brian Lawless. A council 'gardener' and a shop steward of GMB Branch 5, Brian was also a delegate from Warbreck ward to the Walton CLP (he was also a keen supporter of the Robert Tressell memorial and museum in the area). One night, as I was going into a meeting, he approached me and said 'You're Peter Kilfoyle who lived in Dovecot, aren't you?', and I said 'And you're Brian Lawless who lived in Dovecot'. We had been at school together and lived around the corner from one another as children. It must have been hard for Brian and people like him to carry around this image of me that had been pumped out – that I was not from Liverpool and had been brought in from abroad, and all of the associated nonsense – and then to meet up with me and realise that they knew differently.

By the time of Labour's 1986 conference in Blackpool, the end of the road was in sight for the eight members of Militant whom the NEC had successfully removed from the party. In accordance with the appeal procedure, each of them had accepted the opportunity to address the floor of conference, prior to a vote being taken on whether or not their expulsions should be sanctioned. My task in all of this was to identify them so that they could gain entry to the building. By then, most people knew their names but other than Hatton and, perhaps, Mulhearn, they would not know who was who. There was strict security, as these were the days when there would invariably be a mass protest rally outside the conference hall, and this occasion was no exception. Rather than have the eight coming in through the main entrance, we had asked them to come in through the VIP entrance. This was strictly a security measure but, naturally, they revelled in this and, true to form, turned up with their massed supporters.

It was ridiculous. We had people from GMB Branch 5 trying to get in with them, obviously with a view to wreaking mayhem once inside. The media were also there, of course, and Hatton was performing for the cameras. I remember him spotting me and shouting from outside, 'Oh, there he is! Just give me a few rounds in the ring with him and I'll sort him out.' This was one of the images that Hatton liked to project – a tough-guy, a boxer, and all the rest of it – but he was all hot air. Once he came in, away from the cameras and the support of his acolytes, his whole demeanour changed. I knew then that he would bottle out and so I said to him, 'You won't appear – you haven't got the guts. You won't get up on that platform because you know you're finished.' And that is precisely what happened. Hatton and the others were taken away to give their individual speeches to conference, at which point they requested more time to explain their individual cases. When the NEC refused, the eight staged a walk-out. They called it 'a protest' but the truth of the matter was that they had lost the vote before they even spoke. Conference voted resoundingly, by over six million to 300,000, to endorse their expulsions.

Even more telling, however, is Cheryl Varley's account of what happened afterwards:

> Ken Smith, Militant's press officer, got us all together and said that we were going to have a press conference. We had a little run-through where I was told to address youth by speaking on youth issues. Ian Lowes was told to address the trade unions. We all had our different little agendas to speak on. And I'll never forget it. As we arrived at the press conference, a taxi came past with Derek and two camera crews in the back, and he was doing his own press conference. Ken Smith could not control him by that stage. Derek had everybody in the press's numbers and contacts.

A year on from the sending out of the redundancy notices and Neil Kinnock's momentous speech, Hatton's decision to conduct a press conference in a taxi was an irony too far. Nevertheless, it signalled that the ego had landed. For Ian Lowes, who had had his own arguments with Hatton over his conduct (including a celebrated 'incident' in the Vernon Arms pub, the councillors' local), this had long been on the cards:

> I had my differences with the Tendency for allowing one of its leading lights to carry on like a playboy. I remember having conversations with Peter Taaffe, Tony Mulhearn and Terry Harrison where I said 'Look, you're going to have to get a grip of him. You've got to get him back on the

straight and narrow because the way he's carrying on is embarrassing.' Genuine people that would have defended Derek before were horrified at his behaviour. It got to the stage where he saw himself as bigger than the Tendency.

From the point of view of Militant, and those like Lowes who had recently left the organisation, Hatton was out of control. Within his own narrow terms, he was grasping the entrepreneurial nettle. A month after his expulsion, and having also lost his job at Knowsley council, Hatton set up a company called Settleside, the primary concern of which was to consult on land deals. Given his particular history, this came as little surprise. With so many contacts still in place, Hatton was looked upon by many within the local business community as a highly useful tool.

As the media's concern with the fine details of the expulsions began to fade, I began to deal with problems in two of Merseyside's other boroughs. In St Helens, the local Labour Party had been suspended for a variety of wrongdoings, and was technically not allowed to meet. One evening, however, I was coming out of a meeting with the officers of the St Helens South CLP at the town's trade union centre when I noticed that the main hallway was packed with familiar faces from the local party. Given the circumstances, I tried to be as nonchalant as possible, but Gerry Caughey, a central figure in the borough's problems, saw me and came over to say hello. He told me that what was taking place was a meeting of the 'North West Ferret Breeders' Association', a tongue-in-cheek cover for the party to meet unofficially. They met a number of times in this guise, but the key people behind it all were soon to get their come-uppance.

In some ways, St Helens' problems were more vicious than those of Liverpool. What was different was the cross-over between a number of non-Militants locally and known Militants in Liverpool. One particular link came through the printing trade, via Brian Green, the deputy leader of St Helens council, and Jimmy Wilson, the Militant chair of the Garston party. They had both worked for the same company, Smurfitts, and had been active in SOGAT. Even an ad hoc liaison between Green and Wilson was problematical. Links, however, were further reinforced by the political machinations of the Merseyside East MEP, Les Huckfield, whose catchment included both St Helens and Garston.

Neighbouring Knowsley, meanwhile, had thrown up a right can of worms. For some time, Robert Kilroy-Silk, the terminally slick MP for

Knowsley North, had been under increasing pressure from his constituency party (something elaborated upon in his book *Hard Left*), and, at the start of August, he walked away into a full-time career in television. As his resignation had been on the cards for some time, a contest was already afoot to claim the inheritance of what was, and still is, one of the safest parliamentary seats in Britain. If there really was one place where you could stick a red rosette on a hat-stand and have it elected, then it was Knowsley North.

Militant's intended candidate was Mulhearn. Notwithstanding the fact that he was in the process of appealing against his expulsion from the party, it was readily apparent that the NEC would not have him. Les Huckfield, the local MEP, also tried desperately for the nomination, and an attempt was made to flag up Lesley Holt as a compromise candidate acceptable to the Militant-influenced constituency party. The selection, however, was part of a wider battle, each stage of which was crucial in preventing Militant from gaining an extra toe-hold. The NEC was determined to have a 'safe' candidate, one not tarred by the recent politics of Merseyside but with strong local connections. George Howarth was ideal. Originally from Knowsley, where he had been in the YS with Sean Hughes, the Knowsley South MP, George had once been a local councillor, but was at this time working in South Wales for Cooperative Development Services. He became the candidate and, despite the refusal of some elements within the CLP to campaign for him, he won the seat comfortably. Problems followed in the wake of the by-election, relating to the people who had taken their bat home, and an inquiry was ordered into the way in which the local party had been run.

From a political point of view, the most telling moments of the Knowsley North by-election happened in and around Neil Kinnock's pre-election address at the Kirkby Centre. Inside, the only real hiccup came when a trendy local vicar, replete with motorcycle leathers, heckled Neil from the floor. Outside, however, it was a different matter. Militant had assembled what can best be described as a howling mob, who as well as threatening party officers thrust a blind man, Jimmy Richardson, to the forefront of a challenge on the door. As someone present on the door, I bore witness that a Militant former chair of the Knowsley North party, Jim McGinley, was agitating the situation in a most disgraceful way. He was responsible for the near hysteria of Richardson, who was led away by police for his own safety. In their account of these events, Taaffe and Mulhearn play the emotive card in recalling how the man 'was dragged across the road outside by at least six policemen'.[99] This from the same Mulhearn who, along with Hatton, had blocked

David Blunkett's path outside the NEC back in March 1986, a fact notice-ably absent from his and Taaffe's book.

One humorous incident that occurred during the campaign was the infa-mous tale of the Labour Party worker who mistook mushy peas for guacamole in a local chip-shop. Many variations of this incident have been told, a number of which pointed to Peter Mandelson as the culprit; *Observer* journalist Andy McSmith, who at the time was the party's Press Officer, re-veals in his book *Faces of Labour* that this was not helped by the fact that Mandelson himself planted the story with a newspaper in his Hartlepool constituency, which then passed it on to the *Independent*. McSmith reveals, however, that the person who actually uttered the words was an American woman named Shelley (a researcher for Jack Straw) who was most unfamil-iar with the culinary nuances of the north of England. This, of course, does not explain why Mandelson felt the need to cast himself in such a way.

In Liverpool, the council Labour group were becoming more and more preoc-cupied with their impending surcharge and suspension from office, and their attempts to find a legal loophole to escape it. Surcharge and suspension were the penalties that would follow the District Auditor's findings that they had set the rate late, at a loss to the city and its ratepayers. This coloured the thinking of many of them towards what I was doing on behalf of the NEC. If they had had more sense, they would have been able to see how fighting the surcharge that had arisen as a result of Byrne's miscalculations was quite distinct from perpetuating a political confrontation with the national party. Larry Whitty had made this clear back in March, when speaking at the Scot-tish Labour Party conference, in an attack on the legal treatment meted out to councillors in Liverpool and Lambeth: 'Whatever differences we may have with comrades in local government, this party utterly condemns the use of draconian legislation and bureaucracy and the use of court powers to remove elected councillors from office'.[100] Soon after, Larry wrote to all CLPs asking for contributions to the Local Government Defence Fund, which would help the councillors in their appeal against surcharge and disqualification.

As with the breakaway group in the early 1970s, many people assumed that 'the forty-seven' who were eventually surcharged and disqualified formed a homogeneous group. The truth, however, is the opposite. Granted, they all went down the same path together and were bound by the belief (correctly held in my view) that the District Auditor had acted vindictively towards them. But on a personal level, some of them were vociferously critical of each other, and politically many were light years apart. Hamilton and Hatton could not have been more different. Nor could John Linden, an articulate solicitor, have had much in common with the monosyllabic Jimmy Dillon.

Much was done on their behalf, not just across Merseyside but all over the country. Meetings were organised and collections were taken. One in particular sticks in my mind. At the 1987 conference in Brighton, I had permission from Larry Whitty to organise a bucket collection at the entrance to the hall. Eric Heffer went through the roof at this, because he wanted to organise it, but Whitty only agreed as long as I, an official, kept an eye on the counting of the money. Heffer and I ended up sitting in a vacant stall at the conference exhibition counting it together. It was very strange, but I had to laugh; I was reminded of the classic scene in the film version of *Tom Thumb* where Peter Sellers and Terry-Thomas are seen trying to add up their spoils but are unable to agree on a total. For all Eric's literacy, he showed an incredible lack of numeracy, and it took us ages to agree on what was collected for 'the forty-seven'.

People were happy to give. They believed that the councillors had been hard done by. The problem was that their sympathy became abused when Militant started to use it as a platform for its own purposes. It became increasingly difficult for people outside the inner circles of the local Labour Party, or indeed the inner circles of the surcharged councillors, to recognise where Militant ended and where 'the forty-seven' began. You could not practically differentiate between the interests of individual councillors, even those like Hatton who had been expelled, and those of the group as a whole. You gave to all of them or you gave to none, but there was always a nagging doubt about how the issue itself was being used to attack the party. As it turned out, Militant abused the good will and good nature of people for their own ends.

All of this was unfolding against a background of many minor newsworthy incidents. Not for the first time, Liverpool's crematorium workers were in dispute over pay and conditions. A Labour councillor, Jimmy Hackett, was suspended by the TGWU over charges of sexual harassment – an issue in itself, but the fact that the bloke was both literally and metaphorically a clown meant it was of no consequence. Then there was the case of the councillors who were found drinking after hours in the Vernon Arms. It was typical of the times, of the class, of the attitudes, of the social lifestyle but it really was, to use an Americanism, small potatoes.

What was important were two separate meetings between the party's General Secretary, Larry Whitty, and the Labour group. The first took place in October 1986 at the trade union centre, where it was thought that Larry would explain his prognosis for the group, and the latter would accept it as a reasonable way forward. Over the summer, a number of things had begun to characterise the group's behaviour. Following their refusal to allow me to speak on Mulhearn's suspension, I was continually debarred, mainly through the actions of a hard core of councillors including Astbury, Brady, Byrne, Hood and Linden. Throughout the same period, however, Mulhearn and Hatton were allowed to address group meetings, the average turn-out at which had slumped to between two and three dozen out of the fifty-plus councillors eligible to attend.

Although repeatedly denied entry, I insisted on presenting myself each time. Paul Astbury once asked me why I kept coming back. I pointed out that it served to remind them that the party would not give up on the situation. Each rejection of my legitimate *ex officio* attendance was another nail in their political coffin. It all came to a head at the August meeting, which Joyce Gould attended. Requesting to speak on a directive that she had sent regarding the participation of Mulhearn and Hatton in group affairs, Joyce was voted down. Two responses followed. Immediately after the vote, John Hamilton led nine other members of the group out of the room. Subsequently, the NEC ruled that the group should be reconstituted. The meeting in October was to be the first attempt.

Before the meeting started, I was stationed at the door with another party member, Mickey Keating, in order to prevent those who had been expelled from gaining access. Unfortunately, when Hatton and Mulhearn arrived they did so with a gang of their supporters, and came charging up to the door in the shape of a rugby scrum, forcing themselves through. Harry Smith started screaming like a stuck pig, claiming that he had been hit on the way in, but even his own people tired of this and told him to shut up. There was no doubt what their tactics were – they wanted to disrupt and cause as much mayhem as possible. They were putting two fingers up to the proper process; their attitude was that it was they, not the NEC, who decided who was in the Labour Party in Liverpool. Once the meeting was under way, Byrne suddenly stood up with his back to myself and Larry, and took over. Larry was absolutely gobsmacked. He had never come across this kind of behaviour before and asked me what he should do. I suggested he put his arm around Byrne's neck and yank him backwards over the table. Larry looked at me blankly. We had lost the meeting, and so, on my recommendation, we retired to my office to lick our wounds.

Six weeks later, a second attempt took place at reconstitution, at the SOGAT building in Walton. We had to recover some authority after the abortive meeting at the trade union centre, and give some support to the more genuine members of the Labour group. Again, I manned the door, with support from SOGAT's Eddie Kirkpatrick (a stalwart in the Liverpool battles), to ensure no-one entered other than those who were entitled to. Outside, meanwhile, some of the arriving councillors were facing the wrath of the crowd that had assembled, as Roy Gladden recalls:

> There had to be about a hundred [GMB] Branch 5 outside the meeting, and as we were going in Bob Lancaster and I took a few smacks. Beforehand, as we parked the car up, Bob had said 'This is what we mean when we talk about character building'.

The attention Gladden received was primarily a result of him having challenged Hatton some months earlier for the deputy leadership of the group. In doing so, Roy was supported by more than a dozen others, who became known as the 'et al' group on account of a letter that had been sent challenging Hatton's position. Roy, Mike Black and Bob Lancaster had signed the letter but, unable to find the rest of their number, they added the words 'et al'. Hatton retained his position, and Gladden's stance brought him all sorts of abuse:

> On one occasion, I'd had to get my brother around to watch my house because I had a call: 'By the way, Gladden, when you go out to the meeting tonight, we'll be around and let's see how your kids' faces look with acid in them'. I blew it then. I went into the group and said to the Tendency, 'You bastards, you come near my kids and I'll kill you'. They said it was nothing to do with them but once you employ thugs, you can't control everything they do.

Many such people were gathered outside the SOGAT meeting, whilst inside a schism had appeared. Twenty-one members of the group had refused to sign a pledge of loyalty to the rules and constitution of the party which had been sent out after the October meeting. I therefore refused them entry. However, the twenty-eight who had signed the pledge were in attendance and discussion ensued about administering the council as a minority group. With Larry Whitty keen to include as many of the group as possible in the proceedings, he insisted on allowing the refuseniks a second chance, thanks mainly to the entreaties of Frank Mills (who knew Larry from the GMB). My advice was overturned. I knew what Mills and those he spoke for were like, but Larry, out of kindness, gave them the benefit of the doubt (as did Bob Lancaster, who in political terms was all over the place). A delegation of those from inside the meeting, including Mills and John Brazier, were given permission to leave the meeting to 'persuade' the renegade group, who had retired to a nearby pub, to sign an undertaking pledging loyalty to the party's rules. This they did, but once they were allowed in they quickly moved a motion for a vote of no confidence in the group leadership, and John Hamilton was replaced by Byrne. Larry Whitty was dumbfounded:

> I made a serious misjudgement, but I think had they formed a minority, the Liberals would have sat on their hands, and we would have had an even bigger crisis on our hands. By the time it came to the vote, I had prepared myself. In the long run, the knock-on effect of that meeting was actually quite benign, but at the time it was a total disaster. There had certainly been no great strategy to get into that situation!

This was to prove another turning point in Liverpool politics. It certainly affected Hamilton, who, having defended 'the Tendency' for so long as good and honest socialists, was soon telling the local press that he considered Militant's tactics 'fascistic'. His emotions were, not for the first time, colouring his outlook. In fact, John had been absolutely beside himself all of the way through this period. Partly because he was an ineffective leader – *de jure* rather than *de facto* – and partly, in terms of the impending surcharge, because he was afraid he was going to lose his home. I had taken the view very early on that I would provide as much support for him as possible, as he was the only leader we had. He had an encyclopaedic knowledge of the workings of the council and was respected in the community, but he was never what could be considered a wartime leader, and this really was a time of war. In another context, he might have been fine but he was hopelessly out of kilter with the task in hand. In some respects, his removal was a blessing in disguise.

Nevertheless, both I and Joyce Gould felt that Byrne needed to be sorted out. This was a man who had a blatant and cynical disregard for the membership rules of the party. He claimed to live at Cllr Dot Mathews's flat in Botanic Road in Smithdown ward, when everybody knew he had a house in Picton ward at Britannia Avenue, where he lived with his daughter Toni (now a city council union official). It was just farcical. Byrne was claiming to have this other address for reasons best known to himself. He could have very easily transferred into Picton but refused to do so. When a team representing the NEC met him at the Town Hall, he not only refused to answer their questions on his membership, claiming that they were not within their terms of reference, but failed to return to the meeting after they allowed him thirty minutes to consider his position. When the team finally gave up waiting and left the building, they were met by security staff who insisted that they were to sign out of the building, 'on Councillor Byrne's instructions'. This was Byrne being deliberately vexatious. It may have seemed a small issue, but the whole matter typified his disdain for the Labour Party.

Shortly after the Byrne coup, Hatton formally resigned his position as deputy leader. He tried to give the impression that he was still in control, but it was inevitable that he would be removed from the various offices he held by virtue of being in the party. It was the same with his role as chair of Personnel, which he vacated in December. Such a post had a legal dimension to it – it was a council appointment rather than a Labour Party one – but Hatton would easily have been undone via due process.

My main priority going into 1987 was to ensure the selection of non-Militants for key positions within the party in Liverpool and also as prospective councillors, particularly in the safe seats. I wanted the people standing for Labour to be legitimate representatives, not devotees of Militant. I was constantly attending selection meetings across the city, sometimes up to four in an evening, making sure that everything was being done by the book. Every nomination, every selection was vital. Militant had no idea where I was going to pop up next, but it took non-stop organisation on my part, because I knew that there was a whole new strain of parasites ready to move in.

The fate of 'the forty-seven' was more or less sealed in January, when their case was rejected by the Courts of Appeal. Their last recourse was to be an appeal to the House of Lords. On 12 March 1987, however, the Law Lords signalled the end of the road. In accordance with the draconian legislation the Conservative government had dug up to use against them, each of the forty-seven surviving councillors from the forty-nine who had voted to delay the setting of a legal rate were surcharged with costs (a total of around £4,000 each), and banned from holding local government office for five years. No further legal manoeuvre could be employed on their behalf against this judgement. However, at a meeting of the group a few nights later, Bob Lancaster called for a further push:

I said 'Hang on, let's not accept this, we've done nothing wrong. Let's challenge it. Let's take it to the European Court. Let's see how strong they are, and if they want to put us in gaol then fine, I'll go to gaol.' I'm no revolutionary – I never have been – but we'd reached that level of commitment that I said 'Let them make heroes out of us'. I was convinced they wouldn't put us in gaol because we would become class heroes to the trade union movement, and it would be utilised to keep the fires going.

This was typical Bob – stubborn, combative, but hopelessly out of step. His colleagues, meanwhile, were nervously looking at the surcharge and costs, recognising that they were jointly and severally liable – that is, they were all in it until every last penny had been paid. It is worth noting, however, that some of them had been quite cute with their finances. Peter Ferguson, for instance, had moved from his pleasant suburban house in Hunts Cross to a larger place in Cressington Park, Grassendale, just before the surcharge came into effect. The latter was apparently set up as a cooperative, thus protecting the asset from the District Auditor. Then there was Hatton who, in establishing himself in business long before the surcharge was confirmed, showed his determination to ensure that he and his family were well catered for. In fact, he indulged a bit too much, and it would not be long before his name was linked to alleged improprieties on a number of land and property deals around the city.

Of course, the surcharge and debarment of the councillors was not strictly the end of the matter, for the cause of 'the forty-seven' was to become an end in itself. The 'forty-seven fund' continued to have an emotional appeal to many kind hearts in the labour movement who sent in their money, much of which would otherwise have been spent on campaigning against the Thatcher government. The fund did help pay off the surcharge and legal fees, but it also became a sluice through which many thousands of pounds were washed; and, although never proven, it was alleged that a not insignificant amount went into Militant's coffers. In time, the fund became a bone of contention within 'the forty-seven', as Roy Gladden explains:

> The fund stopped when we reached what we needed, but as we were paying it off, at four thousand a month, the rest was gaining interest. So the fund was left with more money than was needed. Now you can't send the five pounds and ten pounds back to people. There used to be meetings where we'd talk about who to give it to – people in dispute. The account was finally cleared when we gave money [£40,000] to the Liverpool dockers. Again,

though, it was quite funny because only certain people would be notified of the meetings.

As has been indicated, the *idea* of 'the forty-seven', as opposed to their actions, fitted a particular mentality within Liverpool politics, where a minority battles against all sense and all the odds. Inevitably, they are glorious failures, but their protest is admired as worthy in itself. An unspoken rationale of such struggles is that those involved have been engaged in something special, and, in many respects, sacred. This is evident in Bob Lancaster's feelings about 'the forty-seven':

> I still owe an allegiance to them, individually, whether they were Tendency, what they were, what they have become, what they are perceived as. People say to me 'I've seen you shaking hands with Derek Hatton, why?' We went through a situation in those years that was particular to politics. Not many people have been through a situation like that.

Bob, who has long been back on the council, may therefore be surprised to hear the views of a fellow member of the current Labour group, Steve Mumby:

> On one level, it was wrong for them to be disbarred but I also thought that they'd been complete idiots – they'd been wrong in principle and wrong in practice, and I had very little sympathy for them. Although, in retrospect, I'm not sure whether it was wrong to disbar them. They wreaked a lot of havoc on the city.

After the Law Lords' judgement, the echoing voice of 'the forty-seven' campaign was not merely a drain on resources, it was also a drain on my attempts to alter the terrain of Labour politics in Liverpool. More than anything else, it made the drive towards a regular political style more difficult, particularly with a 'second eleven' of Militants and fellow-travellers waiting to take their places amongst the vacant seats. Chanting the same platitudes as their predecessors, they would delay yet further the normalisation of the city's politics. It was to be a time, therefore, for stoic application.

# 9 Street-fighting years

With the expulsion of 'the forty-seven', the SDP/Liberal Alliance found themselves with a clear majority on what remained of Liverpool's council, and took over the running of the administration for what would turn out to be six weeks. Under the leadership of Sir Trevor Jones, one of the first things they did was to reinstate the title of Lord Mayor, with Jones's wife and fellow-councillor Lady Doreen taking on the role. Indeed, much of what the Alliance managed to achieve in their brief period in office was geared towards reversing decisions taken by the previous council. Not only did they challenge the funding of specific concerns, such as Croxteth Community School, they also attempted to remove a number of individuals from their posts. Targets included Sam Bond, the Knibbs and the D'Arcys, as well as one Beryl Molyneux, an associate of Derek Hatton whose transformation from a lollipop lady to a senior council officer had caused a major rumpus. Molyneux had become involved in politics during a campaign on school reorganisation, after which Felicity Dowling had groomed her as an office-helper for the District Labour Party, specifically tasked with following up membership applications.

As the Alliance pursued their short-term aims, Militant and their associates were fighting hard to get their second eleven into place in time for the May 1987 council elections. I was trying my best to limit this, and managed to remove Richard Knights and Josie Aitman from the list of candidates on the grounds that they had not accepted the ward where they had been selected to stand, without good reason. John Sharpe, one of our party lawyers, and Alan Wilkie, our barrister, were quite convinced that I was going to be wiped out in court. The judge, however, said it was common sense that the party should decide who stood for it, and that, as I was *de facto* the local party on behalf of the NEC, I should apply the rules.

Other members of Militant slipped through the net. Jackie Smith, for example, became one of Labour's two candidates in Anfield. The other was Malcolm Kennedy, whom I imposed upon the ward party, and whose then wife Jane recalls one particular outcome that arose from campaigning alongside Smith and her agent, Jimmy Hollinshead:

They produced a leaflet which attacked Trevor Jones and effectively said that he'd got his knighthood for services to the Conservative Party. This was a libellous statement but they put it out with Malcolm's name on it without consulting him (he was his own agent). We'd gone on holiday – it was a typical Militant trick, really – and we came back to find ourselves faced with a law-suit. We settled it quickly through the courts, admitting liability and coughing up quite a bit of money. Militant were furious with us for doing this, because it meant that they were clearly in breach of the law as well, and so they couldn't fight it. They had wanted to make it another of their causes.

Militant's long-term presence in Anfield and other wards in the Walton constituency was at this time reflected in their overall position at the CLP, where Hollinshead and others continued to ride rough-shod over the rule book. Gary Booth recalls one meeting at the Pirrie Labour Club:

As per usual, Hollinshead was banging at it. What we used to do was put our point of view forward or oppose them on something and if we weren't happy with the way it was going, we tried to move a vote of no confidence in the chair, Roy Farrar. This time, he said 'I'm not taking that', and we said 'Hang on, you can't not take it. You've got to.' Farrar stood up and said: 'Listen, I'm not taking it. I've counted heads, we've got more than you and you'll lose it anyway.' So we all walked out.

I received two letters of complaint in relation to this meeting, one from a delegate of County ward, and another from a group of Breckfield ward delegates. In both cases, it was alleged that Farrar had allowed Hollinshead to ramble on (for thirty-plus minutes, apparently) beyond the seven minutes which he had been allocated to propose a motion. When Farrar refused to acknowledge this, allegedly replying, 'My watch is different from yours', the vote of no confidence was called and events unfolded as Gary recalls. One of the correspondents also noted that those leaving the meeting were told 'Go and join the SDP'.

I also had my differences with Farrar, a POEU delegate and brother of Lesley Holt; to be honest, I found him a bit creepy. At one meeting in Walton, when he was seeking advice on a debate regarding the previous year's AGM, he would only address me through an intermediary, the secretary, John Brazier. Farrar actually said that he did not want to recognise me, either as a human being or as a party officer (similar sentiments had been expressed by Shirley Hatton at the Childwall ward meeting at which her wonderful husband manhandled Judy Edwards). Throughout all this, Eric Heffer was at the end of the table, fuming. All he wanted to do was to make his MP's report and get out.

In addition to Malcolm Kennedy in Anfield, I imposed two local election candidates in Gillmoss ward, the meeting to do so being one of the hairiest I ever attended. It was held at the eleventh hour on a Sunday morning, the day before nominations closed, and mayhem ensued. As the ward officers refused to decide a short-list, I gave them one. The candidates were jeered, hissed and booed during their speeches and while answering the questions that followed. After this, the officers declined to ballot, in an attempt to force their own nominations from outside the short-list. Consequently, I imposed Eddie Roderick and Vicky Roberts. It all ended up with Tony Jennings and Phil Knibb coming into my office, early the following morning, in an attempt to intimidate me. Their language was atrocious and I told them to get out. But they were determined. So much so, in fact, that they met me outside the electoral registration office a couple of hours later, as I submitted the candidates' names, again, to try and persuade me not to put Roderick and Roberts forward.

I also imposed myself in Allerton, primarily because I could find nobody else to do it. There had been a number of potential candidates but they all went to ground (they were literally 'uncontactable') rather than stand in what was seen as a no-hoper of a ward. In a double irony, I came second in the election to Eddie Roderick's son Frank, who was standing for the Alliance (I had previously been his prefect at school), and the following year Labour took the seat comfortably.

Naturally, there was some response to my imposition of candidates, the most notable of which came from Bernie Hogan, the Secretary of GMB Branch 200. One of the refuse workers' convenors, I can only ever recall seeing Hogan in varying states of insobriety, especially at meetings of the DLP. A highly abusive individual, he really was the worst example of old Labour trade unionism – beer without the sandwiches. On this occasion, however, he was notifying me of a motion that his branch had passed the previous night, strongly condemning 'the complicity of certain individuals who aim to select political friends'. The nature of the letter smacked of ignorance in relation to the actual impositions, but the tone indicated another's hand at work.

Many of the other selections were more straightforward, although even these had quite bizarre aspects to them. A case in point was Everton ward. Here, one of the nominees, John Brady, had not been in the party for long and at that time was about seventy years of age. It was quite ridiculous that he should come forward, but the way that he put it was that he was taking the place of his son Dominic, one of the surcharged councillors. Again in Everton, we had Judy Nelson, wife of John Nelson, another surcharged councillor, who literally could not string two words together at her interview (rejected by Everton, she was selected for Smithdown ward, for which she became a councillor). Then there was George Knibb:

> I used to live in Everton. I was born and bred near Scotland Road on Byrom Street. I went to school down there and played football there. I knew everybody – I socialised down there and I still went for a pint on a Friday night with the lads that I went to school with. Once I started getting involved, people asked me to go forward.

True as this may have been, the notion of keeping it in the family, keeping it close, clearly prevailed.

Despite the tension surrounding the selection and nomination of candidates, there was still a sense of pulling together, if only to prove a point to the government after the debarment of 'the forty-seven'. This paid off and, in May, Labour again took control of the city, much to the surprise of the Liberal leadership. That was more than evident to the councillor who had been made the 'convenor' of the rump Labour group, Keva Coombes:

> With so many candidates coming off through the disqualifications, the statistics were broadly in the Liberals' favour. They expected to take control. After the polls closed, I was going into the Municipal Building and I saw Trevor Jones from behind. I could tell he knew then that he hadn't won by the way his shoulders were down.

Jones and his fellow Liberals were not the only ones sent reeling. Gary Booth, one of Labour's two candidates in Melrose ward, recalls the moment at a local polling station when he realised that Labour had won and he himself would be part of the new administration:

> I'd been elected and, having won more votes than our other candidate, Frances Kidd, I got the four-year seat rather than twelve months. I stood there, thinking 'Christ, what am I going to do? I'm now on the council. What have I bitten off?'

As it was, Labour was returned to office with fifty-one seats, giving the party a majority of three. It was to be the beginning of a period of increasing numerical superiority on the council. Alas, it was also one that would later be overshadowed by another schism within the group.

My own recollections of the victory are unfortunately tainted with the memory of Hatton turning up at the count. At this point, he was no longer an elected councillor. He was nothing more than a bad smell, getting in every-where, but he stood around as if he owned the place, trying to take credit for things where no credit was due. The only time I was ever photographed with Hatton was on this night. It was staged to look as if we were in conversation about the results. In fact, I was lost in concentration on the returns, and he sat next to me with a photographer at the ready. He was always quick with a photo-opportunity. Nevertheless, the local press were not entirely gullible and they duly reported what I had said to him when I realised that he was hovering around me: 'Your days are over, Derek – you're gone. The politics of personalities have gone. The main policies are the same but the personality cult has gone.'[101]

As expected, many within the Labour group soon divided into caucuses. On the Sunday following the elections, non-Militant 'forty-seveners' Mike Black, Roy Gladden and Bob Lancaster helped to organise a meeting at the Pirrie Labour Club in Walton of those who would later become identified as the 'Progressive Left'. Time would eventually reveal this caucus to be a rather shaky alliance with no coherent perspective on the way forward for Liverpool. But at the start it was unified by a determination to marginalise Militant. The latter, meanwhile, were meeting with others in the notional 'Broad Left' caucus, a couple of miles away at Gillmoss Labour Club in West Derby. With the AGM arranged for the middle of the following week, these two gatherings were the key to who would take up the committee posts in the new council, and both sides were trying to pull in people who were not so readily aligned. Rather tellingly for what would occur later that year, Keva Coombes, a former leader of Merseyside County Council, attended both meetings. As he freely admits, the aim of this was to keep his hand in with all sides:

> I was hunting with the hare, chasing with the hounds, as the cliché goes. I thought the caucus system was unnecessarily bad. The real differences be-tween people were largely infinitesimal. I'd preferred several of the indi-viduals in the Progressive Left but I suppose my emotional sympathies were probably more with the Broad Left. I had always been and I still am anti-Militant but I believed that it was then possible to actually argue with Militant and win, and I preferred to do that rather than use conventional

bureaucratic and political methods. Most of my friends were non-Militant, and certainly some of the more able people were in the 'right' caucus, but I would have liked a mixture of the two.

One of his fellow councillors, Vicky Roberts, describes Keva's approach in more prosaic terms, however:

Keva couldn't quite decide where the numbers were so he offered himself to both.

As it turned out, the numbers were with the progressives. One of their key figures, Alan Dean, became deputy leader; and Harry Rimmer, who had not attended either caucus but who had long been a vociferous opponent of Militant, was elected leader, defeating the Broad Left's Tony Jennings by 31 votes to 20. Similar outcomes saw those within or aligned to the progressives take all of the committee chairs, as well as the positions of Chief Whip and Group Secretary. Nevertheless, as Alan Dean recalls, the balances were slight and they immediately put Liverpool's politics on edge:

It was the sharpest learning curve I've ever been through. It was unbelievably tense. We were all brand new. Every chair and deputy of the committees had been on the council a week. Most of them had never attended committee meetings. At the first group meeting, all fifty-one members were there, and it was a bear-pit. The atmosphere was unbelievable – you really could cut it with a knife.

One factor that allowed the progressives to move forward was an acknowledgement that they had to work with the remnants of the 'sensible/scabby six'. Asked to reflect on whether he recalls this being made clear to him at the time, one of the six, Paul Orr, is typically colourful:

A bridging period? Was there buggery. We didn't want nothing to do with them.

And Gary Booth also remembers the issue being problematic:

Clearly the Tendency would never have them but it was also difficult for us. One of the first discussions that we had was 'Should Paul Orr, Joe Morgan etc. be invited to our caucus?', and the initial response was 'Oh no, no, no'.

A rapprochement of sorts was, nevertheless, taking place, as Alan Dean affirms:

As far as I was concerned, they were members of the group. The history was long and complicated but, effectively, Paul Orr was always an integral part of the group. He had that much experience and knowledge that he had to be on board. It was like most things. When I was an activist outside, attending the DLP, I was led to see such people as Paul and Joe Morgan as bastards for going against the council, but as soon as I came on to the council and got to know them personally, I realised it was much more about their strongly-held beliefs.

The initial pleasure at retaining overall control of Liverpool's council, and seeing a suitable leadership put in place, was soon sidelined by a general election campaign, as Margaret Thatcher sought and received a third successive term of office for her government. Locally, one of the few real things of note was Neil Kinnock's visit to the Liverpool Mossley Hill constituency – a target marginal, held by David Alton for the Liberals – when our PPC, Joe Devaney, turned up late. Joe did not seem unduly bothered by the fact that he was late for an opportunity designed to promote him electorally. After this minor embarrassment, I travelled with Neil to Ellesmere Port on the Wirral, another of our target marginals. On the way we went through Wallasey, yet another marginal where our candidate Lol Duffy was believed to be a member of Socialist Organiser. Although there was no way that those running the national campaign would agree to Neil stopping for a photo-call, I actually found Duffy to be a model of rectitude in following the party's rulebook.

The one thing that I was most struck by during the general election was the way in which the party in Liverpool appeared to run its own campaign, quite distinct from that fought by Labour in the rest of the country and involving speakers with little or no hostility towards Militant. Typical of this was a rally held in the city's Philharmonic Hall, at which the platform included Arthur Scargill, Tony Benn, Terry Fields, Eric Heffer, Eddie Loyden and Tony Byrne. Up in the balcony, and afforded a special cheer, was the expelled 'martyr' Tony Mulhearn.

The day after the election, the local press featured a photograph of Mulhearn congratulating Loyden on retaking Garston. Also carried was a lengthy cliché-riddled excerpt from Fields' speech on retaining Broadgreen: 'a Militant is one who has got up off his knees. I wear the badge with honour. To be a moderate is to allow hospitals to close, patients to die; to allow homelessness while half a million construction workers stay unemployed. I will never be a moderate as long as I have breath in my body. I will always be a Militant.'[102] Hatton, of course, was not to be left out of this circus. Blaming

Neil Kinnock for Labour's defeat and Thatcher's third victory, he insisted that Militant would soon regain control of Liverpool. A few days later, speaking with ringmaster Peter Taaffe in Glasgow, Hatton claimed that he would be back in the party and back on the council. How wrong he was, yet again.

Another to misread the signs of the times was Keva Coombes, whose election to Liverpool City Council had come courtesy of a by-election in Clubmoor ward the previous August (following the death of Bill Lafferty). Turning his political attention towards securing the nomination for the parliamentary seat of Hyndburn, Coombes did so partly on the understanding that he would wash his hands of local government politics. However, having re-entered Liverpool's political atmosphere via Clubmoor, Coombes took on many of the group leader's duties when John Hamilton and the rest of 'the forty-seven' were disqualified (I insisted that he be referred to as 'group convenor' rather than leader). Neither of these moves endeared him to the Hyndburn Labour Party, and many within its local membership adopted an apathetic approach to his general election campaign, whereupon a flimsy Tory majority of twenty-two was turned into a more respectable one of over 2,000. As a result of this ignominious foray into national politics, Coombes earned himself the sobriquet 'gobsmacked of Hyndburn'.

Slowly but surely, Liverpool slipped into a familiar groove of political trench warfare. Small but significant changes began to occur. The number of further education sabbatical officers – recruiting sergeants for Militant – was reduced by three, and the council began to look into the alleged misuse of the Bryn Marl youth hostel in North Wales (on permanent loan to the Knibb-influenced Croxteth Community Trust) as a training school for young Militants. At another level, shortly after two ministers – David Trippier and George Young – had visited the city, raising the prospect of a new relationship between the city and the government, a proposed visit by Thatcher was cancelled. But then a few days later, Liverpool appeared on the list of councils to be 'rate-capped', further exacerbating the city's dire financial circumstances.

By recent standards, that summer was a relatively quiet one for Liverpool. This was perhaps not surprising given that many within the local Labour Party were coming to terms with another general election defeat. Even so, a hard-core of Militants and their associates began quietly bedding themselves into the structures of the council. They would be dealt with in time. More crucially, I was becoming increasingly concerned about the durability of the leader of the council group, Harry Rimmer. A reluctant figure at the helm, Harry, who had been deputy leader of Merseyside County Council from 1982 to 1986, was the only obvious candidate for the leadership at the AGM that followed the May elections. With most of the other councillors new and inexperienced, and older, more 'sensible' hands such as Orr and Roderick simply unacceptable to the vast majority of the group, the only other realistic option had been Coombes, but he was due to go off to Hyndburn. With Harry having to be persuaded to take on the job of leader, his tenure of the position always appeared fragile. I was not surprised, therefore, when attending Labour's 1987 conference, to hear that he had resigned.

What had transpired was that Harry had approached the Labour group with the idea that the council should seek a policy of 'redetermination', having gained assurances from David Trippier – the inner cities minister – that it would not be faced down. On paper, this would have seen considerable rent increases for the city's council tenants, increases which many could have covered through the housing benefit system, and Harry also made clear that the policy would come hand in hand with a 'claim it now' campaign. Even so, to a group that was, for the most part, brought up on the soundbites of the Hatton era, any rent increase was to be met with disbelief. The proposal was defeated forty-two to six, and, in Harry's eyes at least, there was only one way to respond:

> What I think it boiled down to was that they may have been prepared to trust me but they weren't prepared to trust a Tory secretary of state, and so they turned it down. Redetermination had to be debated entirely on its merits as a policy issue, and when they rejected it I decided to relinquish the leadership of the group.

Alan Dean, however, offers a rather different take, relating it to the 'hidings' he and Harry used to receive from Militant and its affiliates when giving reports to the Temporary Coordinating Committee:

> It got to the stage where, personally, Harry had had enough. He was getting abuse; we both were, but he probably got a little bit more than I did. He'd just had enough. The redetermination issue was the excuse he needed.

Essentially, Harry knew that he was offering the group an impossibilist position, and he was already making for the exit when they turned him down.

Alan Dean was also attending conference, and I took the opportunity to try to persuade him to push himself forward for the leadership. The only other names in the bag were Coombes and Tony Jennings, both of whom I thought unacceptable, and Gideon Ben-Tovim, whose supporters within the group could have met in a telephone-box. I realised that Alan did not have any depth of experience on the council, but he was well versed in most other areas of Liverpool politics, and sometimes you just have to grab an opportunity. As it turned out, he was indecisive. At the time I was not sure whether this was just him being his normal hesitant self or whether it was due to a deal he had reached with others. There was more to it than that, however, as Dean explains with a not-untypical tale of municipal life:

> At that stage, I didn't think I had the experience to lead the city, but the pressure was on and people wanted me to do it. Keva had been to see me and said, 'I want it and I'll do anything to get it, because whatever you and your colleagues want me to do I'll do it'. However, Keith Hackett and a load of others said 'Alan, you've got to do it'. I was extremely pleased but a little surprised. We were meeting on the Sunday to decide who from our caucus was going to be put forward. Keith was coming to pick me up, but about fifteen minutes before he came I received an anonymous phone call. At the time, I was living with my first wife, but I was also involved with another member of our group, Frances Kidd, and this person said, 'If you take the leadership, we will go to the press and tell them about your relationship with Councillor Kidd'. I was shell-shocked to say the least. When Keith arrived, I told him and he said 'You can't do it. You can't put your family through that.' So when we got to the meeting, we pulled about five or six people together, and I explained what had gone on. They all agreed that I couldn't go through with it. We met Keva and laid the condition down. We told him that we would back him against Tony Jennings but that we wanted a separate person to chair Finance and Policy.

Reluctantly, therefore, many within the progressive caucus threw their weight behind Coombes, allowing him to become leader; although emasculated by his absence from the chairmanship of the Finance and Policy Committee, he was able to satisfy his ambitions:

> I hadn't got into Parliament – which was what I'd wanted – and I had withdrawal symptoms and now wanted to be leader.

With hindsight, Coombes should never have been given the opportunity to lead the Labour group, let alone the city council. As events would show, he came across as everything that a leader should not be. On the one hand, he lacked bold and decisive leadership qualities, something made more than evident by his need to hold regular and exclusive meetings involving himself, the new chair of Finance and Policy, Keith Hackett, and the leader and deputy leader of the Broad Left caucus, Tony Jennings and George Knibb, but not his own deputy, Alan Dean (more suspicious minds may now care to reflect on the events which brought about Coombes's leadership). And on the other hand, he was a public relations nightmare.

Five months after taking on his role, Coombes was stopped by the police on a drink-driving offence, and it was discovered that he had a prostitute in his car. The woman in question actually told the police that she thought he was incapable of driving, so much so that she feared he would kill her. Of course, the whole incident did Coombes no good at all, damaging him both politically and personally in ways from which he was never to recover. It also revealed that he had this darker side to his personality, which led many to conclude that he was totally unfit for any kind of elected office. Coombes was to occupy the moral low ground between the Labour group's two factions for two and a half years.

In terms of the goals that I had set myself, there was much to be done during the back end of 1987. I had to ensure that we were well prepared for the DLP elections that were to take place following its reconstitution, as well as the constituency and ward elections which would immediately precede them. It was a period of one-on-one meetings with individuals in various wards, socialist societies and trade union branches, all of which would be influential in the rebuilding of the Liverpool party from the ground up. Naturally, Militant repeatedly tried to bait me. I recall debating the outcome of the general election with them in their Anfield lair, when all they wanted to do was attack myself, Neil Kinnock and the national party.

It was a regular routine of building up support, trying to recruit new members to help tip the balance against Militant's influence, and trying to forge networks between non-Militants. It was also a non-stop process of working with friendly, supportive people, like Mike Carr in the TGWU and Eddie Kirkpatrick of SOGAT, to build up support amongst local trade unionists. This was not easy, and it was made more difficult with the decision, taken by Ray Gill and me, to make the physical break away from the trade union centre and into a new office in Canning Street. We received a lot of criticism over this. It was widely known that I had never been happy in the trade union centre, and if it had been seen simply as a decision on my part, the comrades would have been up in arms. Ray and I discussed the matter at length, and he decided to take full responsibility for the move. But even now, those associated with the centre remain critical, as Jack Spriggs illustrates:

> We were happy that the Labour Party were functioning from here. We knew what they were doing anyway, and we as a trade union centre never really got involved – certainly the management and financial committees didn't. I don't think the move did them an awful lot of good because they had a resource here that could be used extensively for some of the various constituent members' needs.

That depends on your point of view. At the time of the move, the centre was a haven for activities that can be loosely described as anti- the national Labour Party, all of which served to undermine my attempts to turn around politics in Liverpool. My aims were geared to getting as many non-Militant trade unionists delegated to the DLP as possible. Given its almost talismanic standing within the local labour movement, capturing control of that body was vital if we were going to change the city's broader political hue. Remaining at the trade union centre would only have made that task more difficult than it already was. Interestingly, we also discovered that we and the Merseyside Welfare Rights organisation were paying the top rental rates in the trade union centre, much more than other preferred organisations, and three times per square foot what we were to pay for the new office. Once again, the Labour Party was seen as providing a blank cheque.

I also had to continue my normal monitoring of constituencies and branches Merseyside-wide. In October, I monitored a quite remarkable jam-packed AGM of the Halewood ward party, a branch of the Knowsley South CLP. Past midnight, we were still only half-way through the agenda when I decided to suspend the meeting. I was not prepared to put up any longer with the silly procedural games that were being played.

Overall, however, I appeared to be doing rather well, a view that was reinforced by the outcome of the meeting in December to reconstitute the Liverpool DLP, where Militant lost their influence quite dramatically. I chaired this, and I recall one of the Militant women shouting 'What about the tellers?' There were always suspicions about tellers and whether they were acting properly, so I said 'We've got tellers – Dawn and Gary Booth, Hannah Folan, Frances Kidd, John Winter and Chris Hemming'. On her shouting back 'Who elected them?', I swiftly replied 'I did; next business', and we moved on. Farce had to be met with force.

In the actual DLP elections, however, Militant attempted to play a clever game. One of their number was put forward for the position of vice-chair (Sylvia Sharpey-Shafer, who received seven of the 242 eligible votes), but in this case as in others, Militant had obviously instructed their members to throw their weight behind more acceptable figures of 'the left'. Loyden was supported for the post of chair, Paul Astbury and Tony Byrne for the two positions of vice-chair, Tony Hood for secretary, and Jimmy Parry for treasurer. As it happened, these five key posts were taken, respectively, by Eddie Sabino, Pat Harvey, Roy Gladden, Mike Carr and John Hamilton. With similar successes being picked up in the trade union section of the elections, the prospects for a much improved DLP appeared to have been put in place.

Telling for me personally at this time was the invitation to a small Christmas party at Mike Carr's home in Walton. That was to be the first time that I was able to relax socially with members of the Walton CLP, and influential ones at that. It was just nice to be able to chat and joke with people who had only previously seen me arguing with members of Militant. Although at that time there had been no talk of Eric Heffer's retirement, it perhaps sowed some thoughts in their minds about his eventual successor.

1988 started off at the usual frenetic pace. In the very first week of January, I attended a DLP executive on the Monday, Clubmoor ward AGM on the Tuesday, AGMs for Gillmoss, Grassendale and Old Swan wards on the Wednesday, and a full DLP on the Thursday. This pattern was to continue for the rest of the month, and all the way through to the spring. It became a total grind and there were many evenings when I was attending three, four and on at least one occasion five meetings. With great reluctance, my family was learning how to live with this. It was not that I was just dealing with the AGMs of wards and constituencies. Short-listing and the selection of candidates for that year's local elections was also afoot, and I was determined to make sure that we had as many non-Militant candidates in place as possible. Of necessity, I ensured that selection meetings were conducted late in the day, but it did not always go to plan and there were occasions when Militant extended their influence to the point that the vote of each member in a ward was vital to the outcome.

The most striking example came in Kensington ward. Here, a group of rabid young Militants were organised by Tommy Carrol. Along with some of his friends who lived in flats in the area, Carrol had helped Militant make major inroads into the ward that ultimately led to John Blackall, an absolutely horrendous councillor, being elected to the city council.

The Kensington party also included some real, old-fashioned, dyed-in-the-wool socialists such as Dave Shepperd and Frank Aldridge. Respectively a refuse collector and a gravedigger, this pair of GMB members were as tough as old rope, and their language was colourful, to say the least. There was also Frank Dunne. He had been quite a bright bloke until a motorcycle accident left him with some frontal-lobe damage. One consequence of this was that he used to stand up at meetings and embark on flights of fancy, rambling on about the strangest of things – for example, how the bus he had been travelling on that day had stopped outside 'a ladies' underwear shop'. This really wound up the Militant women, and then Frank would make it worse by telling one or more of them how attractive they were looking that evening. Although they usually allowed Frank's comments to go uncontested, because of his medical history, I often wondered whether he was deliberately testing their patience. Frank and the other stalwarts in Kensington could not bear the way in which Carrol and co. had come into the ward and tried to take it over, ramming their ideology down the throats of the established membership, and they were more than willing to square up to Militant. Wrongs were committed on both sides in the ways in which people conducted themselves, but I knew whose side I was on.

One humorous incident in Kensington followed the discovery of a Militant bank account titled 'The Sax Club'. In order to attract young recruits, Carrol had set up a 'music club' in the basement of his father's home. This not only became a source of membership for Militant but also allowed the organisation to replenish its coffers by the sale of alcohol at exorbitant prices. Frank Aldridge decided to check it out for himself but, being a mature man, failed to gain entry. An emollient Carrol tried to convince him that it was just what its name suggested – a club for those who appreciated saxophone music. Frank, not wanting to alert Carrol as to how much he actually knew, excused himself by saying he had been told it was a sex club, and that is why he had called.

Militant's successes in Kensington were brought to a sudden halt in February with the selection of the local election candidate. We ensured that their nomination, the sitting councillor Blackall, would not be reselected by maximising the anti-Militant turn-out. One vote swung it, and that partly resulted from my approving a legitimate transfer into the ward on the afternoon of the meeting. I actually collected the member in question, Barry Navarro, as he arrived home from work, persuaded him to attend, and then drove him to the meeting with only minutes to spare. On the way there, I drove to the opposite end of the ward to collect another solid member who was recovering from a heart bypass operation. The stakes really were that high. Sadly, time was to show that our successful candidate, Kevin Ratcliffe, was no more acceptable than his predecessor, albeit for very different reasons.

It was around this time that many of the ghosts of Liverpool's recent past appeared back in the limelight. Mulhearn, with Peter Taaffe, published his account of what had taken place in Liverpool during the previous decade, *Liverpool: The City That Dared to Fight*. A typically opaque Trotskyite tome, this obfuscated more than it illuminated. Shortly afterwards, Hatton had his own book, *Inside Left*, published, and on a lighter note, began his own radio programme, *Hatton and Co.,* on Radio City, Liverpool's independent station. He was showing an entrepreneurial ability which had matured during his spell as deputy leader but was coming into full bloom now that he was no longer a serious politician (if, indeed, he ever had been). It was also around this time that the Merseyside Police fraud squad began to look into Hatton's 'dealings', and I myself received a visit from the head of the inquiry, Chief Superintendent Geoff Rothwell, to see if I could be of any help in their investigation.

March saw the hearing to consider whether Tony Byrne should be disciplined, or indeed thrown out of the Labour Party, for continuing to give an address in Smithdown ward when everybody knew that he lived in Picton. The hearing took place at the TGWU offices in Salford, and Joyce Gould presented a very good case while Byrne, as ever, was totally arrogant. To our great surprise, however, the National Constitutional Committee decided that the case was not proven. That very same night, at a DLP meeting, Byrne embarked upon a tremendous attack on me personally. I had half-expected this, but what really surprised me was that he was allowed to walk away scot-free.

The same month, we successfully removed Josie Aitman and Elaine Bannister from the party, following another hearing in Salford, at the AEU offices. This had been a drawn-out case, and had taken on a comical dimension the previous summer when the accused sent a letter to David Hughes, the party's national agent, using a photocopy of their solicitor's headed notepaper (the solicitor being John Linden, one of 'the forty-seven'). Not only was the letter typed in an entirely different font to the previous legal correspondence that had been sent on their behalf, but they also used language that blew their cover, for example, 'Both our clients wish to state that, in order to get Broadgreen CLP reactivated ...'. It was akin to the type of letter a child would write in order to play truant from school – 'Dear Teacher, Please excuse Josie and Elaine from class, as we are ill'.

On arriving at the AEU offices, I was greeted by the usual mob shrieking like banshees, but it was all worthwhile. Having removed Hatton and Roger Bannister as chair and secretary of Liverpool Broadgreen CLP, we had now taken out their replacements. The protective layers around Militant MP Terry Fields were being peeled away. Ironically, it was he who gave the game away on the fake solicitor's letter, admitting to Phil Robinson 'You know how long solicitors take!'

At the same time, I began looking into the Broadgreen party's accounts. The former treasurer, Anne Hollinshead, had voiced some concerns with which I was greatly intrigued. There were large debits to 'cash' and to Fields' erstwhile 'political secretary', and there were numerous inter-account transactions which defied analysis on the information available. There was also one account, the 'Derek Hatton a/c' that had not been subject to approval by the constituency party. Moreover, the CLP had been loaned £1,000 by Woolton Labour Club, of which Hatton was a trustee. It appeared to be a very murky business. Unfortunately, the one continuous trustee in the constituency on whom we could have depended for an honest opinion died before we were able to make any real headway.

Fields, along with three of Liverpool's other MPs – Loyden, Parry and Heffer – continued to sully the name of Liverpool at national level, putting their names to any idiotic proposal that came forward. Musketeering for the mindless, the four of them threw their support behind the dreadful Ron Brown after he was suspended for three months from the Commons following his disgraceful behaviour in damaging the mace. In addition, Heffer announced, along with Tony Benn, a challenge to the leadership of Neil Kinnock and Roy Hattersley. If ever anyone missed the signs of the times, it was Heffer and Benn. It was hard to believe that they actually thought they could succeed, considering their overt support for all the many manifestations of 'the left' to be allowed to do whatever they liked within the party. Ultimately, their attempt was to be a resounding failure and served no more than to hammer the final nail in the Bennites' coffin.

Liverpool's other Labour MP, Bob Wareing, was at this time playing the passive observer as others sought to bring about his political demise. It was less than a year since the last general election but the long process of establishing parliamentary candidates for the next one had begun early because of complex new selection procedures. No longer were delegates to a constituency general committee to decide on who was to be the candidate. All party members, and members of affiliated organisations, were to have a say in an elaborate new voting process. West Derby was to be the first Liverpool constituency to go down this route, during which we had the first attempt to deselect Wareing. What depressed me about all of this was that he would just sit there at meetings and not defend himself. Unwilling to make the effort to look after his own interests, he looked to others to act for him. Much of the time, this role fell to me. Bob, of course, had finally come out against Militant, and I saw this as an opportunity to change the political climate of a constituency in which they had gained much ground.

The task was made more difficult by the lack of active support for Bob in West Derby. This in itself was not surprising. The local, non-Militant membership were probably the least organised of all on Merseyside, partly because the CLP was run by men of advanced years. The chair, Hugh Dalton, was seventy-four years old, and the secretary, Jack Hudson, was a victim of senile decay. The long-time treasurer, Ernie Brendon, was repeatedly committed to geriatric wards. More importantly, there was little obvious activity from Bob himself. Considering that his seat was riddled with chronic social and economic problems, it was amazing that he could not even be bothered to establish a full-time office, a long-term promise upon which he continued to renege.

During the run-up to the local elections, we printed *Liverpool Labour News*, offering an alternative view in the tradition of *Not the Liverpool Echo* (the publication put out in local elections during the early 1980s). It was an honest attempt to present the electorate with an official Labour version of what had been happening on the council, and indeed nationally. We were battling against great difficulties to ensure that we had a platform for Labour, and not Militant, and doing our damnedest to ensure that we had candidates in the election who were representative of the Labour Party. We had done our best to keep out overt Militants; the ratio of anti-Militant, Militant ally and Militant was approximately 2:1:1 amongst the thirty-three candidates. In time, it would become apparent that this was not enough to keep the local party on course and united; in marginalising members of Militant, we were sowing the seeds for yet another schism. In the short term, however, our efforts in the local election campaign paid off, with an increase in the number of Labour seats from 51 to 56. The number of Tory councillors halved to a derisory two, whilst the Alliance's 44 seats fell away to 37 of those who stood under the banner of the newly-formed Liberal Democrats. In addition, two 'SDP' candidates were elected and two 'Liberals'.

Following the elections, I came into contact with a young man called Steven Slater who was then a political officer for the EETPU and who was one of those who put their heads above the parapet for a short time before disappearing without trace. He had claimed to be prominent in the anti-Trotskyite Clause Four organisation, but I have never been able to clarify this. He subsequently worked for Eddie Haigh at the TGWU until he was caught releasing confidential information. After this, he spent a short while as a journalist on a national newspaper before fading from the scene. With hindsight, he might be viewed as a prototype of the bright young things who inhabit the periphery of the political scene, some of whom became such an embarrassment for Tony Blair's government during its first year in office. Certainly, as the red roses and smart suits became omnipresent in the party, so did an apparently rootless (in terms of the labour movement) and more individualistic type of person appear, on the political make. Many of these people helped to ensure the outcome of the 1997 general election, but I would like to think their significance within the Labour Party will wane sooner rather than later.

The summer of 1988 was not the best of times in relation to the party's ability to deal with its problems in the north west. We had had a year to get over the general election defeat and to start planning for the future, but the organisation in the region seemed to be going from bad to worse. The Regional Organiser, Ray Gill, was obviously having more and more personal problems and was rarely in work. When he did come in, he was most likely to be late and often only stayed a few hours before going off again. The disease seemed to be catching because the Assistant Regional Organiser, Phil Robinson, also seemed to spend a disproportionate amount of time out. Phil was never the most dedicated of party servants, but he was also in the process of adopting a young boy, and took a great deal of time off to be with him. All in all, Ray and Phil's absences did not lead to a happy working relationship at the regional office. One person who recognised the need for a general shake-up was Joyce Gould; I discovered that she had already decided that Ray was not up to his job and had to go. All of this had, worryingly, begun to occupy more of Joyce's thinking than matters on Merseyside, where her national role was vital in sorting matters out. However, she understood the problems through and through, discussed them with me, and then gave the practical backing required. She also understood the characters involved.

One of the more idiosyncratic Liverpool politicians was Harry Rimmer. I had a great deal of time for him as a person, but it was a recurring difficulty with Harry that he was forever on the verge of resigning. Having given up the leadership the previous autumn, he resigned in June 1988 as chair of the newly established Legal, Land and Transportation Committee after only two days in the post:

> Something happened in my personal life that made me decide 'Sod it. I'm not fit to be doing that.' So the day after the group meeting where they elected me, I told Keva not to put my name forward and to nip it in the bud before the list was given to the city solicitor. But for some reason or other, he thought he could talk me out of it and he put me in anyway. I said to him 'No, I'm not doing it'. Now Keva of all people on that group knew that if I said something like that I meant it, and that I wouldn't go back on it. The only way out of the impasse was for me to be chairman for a few days and then resign.

While this again highlighted the games that Keva Coombes was playing, Harry was developing a reputation for which he will long be remembered. He was one of the few politicians in Liverpool's recent past to come across as avuncular but still possessing appropriate gravitas. Sadly, he also lacked resilience in the face of adversity.

Meetings of the Labour group were becoming increasingly open to tedious and repetitive promulgations of the Militant line by members of the Broad Left caucus. Chief amongst the purveyors of such unrefined monologues was Lesley Mahmood (previously Holt), who had been appointed and then soon after removed as deputy chair of the Race Relations Committee. It was as if the Sam Bond affair had never happened. For me personally, Mahmood was to become a pain in the ear, whom I learned quickly to block out.

Another Militant figure on the council who was becoming vocal at this time was Frank O'Donoghue. He had been expelled from his trade union, SOGAT, in April for bringing it into disrepute. The union, mainly in the form of Eddie Kirkpatrick, now a national officer with the GPMU, had been particularly supportive of the national Labour Party's position throughout this period. Eddie understood intuitively how damaging Militant members were. It was not surprising; Jimmy Wilson, the Militant chair of Garston CLP, was another SOGAT member. Nevertheless, it was quite an event for O'Donoghue to be expelled. This was not done lightly by the union, nor supported with joy by its officers and members. It was simply a necessary evil to protect the union's wider interests. Once expelled, O'Donoghue began channelling his energies into disrupting the policies of the Labour group.

June also saw Neil Kinnock visit Liverpool. Having been pressed and pressed, he agreed to visit the trade union centre; and, although certain elements there showed no support for him as leader, he faced them down. I remain full of admiration for Neil. He had the wherewithal to face up to the need to change the Labour Party, and to do something about removing the malignancy of Militant. I believe that history will speak very highly of him for showing courage, imagination and, most of all, resolution, while others were trimming their sails and trying to avoid active involvement in a messy battle against a deeply entrenched enemy. I also believe that historians will point to him as the man who set the changes in place without which there would never have been a Labour government at the end of the twentieth century. For both these reasons, the party owes him a great deal. Personally, I had one or two minor difficulties with Neil as my ultimate boss, but he was always fair. A remarkably approachable and affable man, he was one of the warmest people imaginable and in social situations managed to put everyone at their ease – not that this mattered to the metropolitan chattering classes and their media friends. Subjected to sustained, vitriolic attack, Neil was ridiculed by Grub Street hacks and their mendacious editors rather than given the praise and support he deserved.

As the summer wore on, a number of colourful incidents involving Liverpool councillors served to illustrate how far we still had to travel in normalising politics in the city. For a start, Kevin Ratcliffe was charged with deception. This was particularly frustrating so soon after we had fought tooth and nail to have him elected (partly because he was the only person prepared to go forward) as an alternative to Militant in Kensington. Alleged to have claimed that he had not received a benefit cheque that had subsequently been cashed, Ratcliffe was in fact acquitted. It was not the last time, however, that he was to be up before the courts. A few years later, whilst serving on the Trading and Licensing Committee, Ratcliffe was charged with trying to extort money from, of all people, Steve Fitzsimmons, one of the city's two remaining Conservative councillors and the manager of Plummers, a popular city bar. Ratcliffe was said to have entered the bar and demanded not only free drinks but also cash to ensure that the licence would be extended. Once again, he was acquitted. In the Labour Party, however, more and more people began to see him as a rather unsavoury character, selected during unusual times but in no way representative of the values for which the party stood.

More ominous developments served to illuminate the activities of some of the seedier denizens of the city. An intriguing situation arose when Labour councillor Phil Hughes stepped down from a number of his committee positions, including the chair of Housing, citing health reasons. It was nothing to do with health, at least, as generally understood. One night, shortly after midnight, he telephoned asking to see me urgently. I went around to his house early the following morning to find that Phil had been up all night drinking whisky. Absolutely petrified, he had received a personal call from two well-known gangsters living in his neighbourhood who had made it clear to him that he should drop his opposition to certain proposals coming before the council. He actually wrote me a statement detailing how he had been intimidated for asking the wrong questions about matters in which these gangsters had an interest. Phil kept a copy for himself and I took the original into my office. Later that day, he came asking for it back. I was out at that time and my secretary, Maureen Byrne, gave it to him. He was so intimidated that he resigned his chairmanship, and a couple of years later dropped out of representative politics altogether.

A similar situation arose with another councillor, Kevin Feintuck. Kevin saw himself as a pure left-winger (he once referred to Liverpool's Albert Dock complex as 'a candyfloss development'). Yet while he was openly critical of Militant, anybody who did not share his particular views was seen as 'a right-winger'. Still, I am absolutely sure of one thing, that Kevin was as honest as the day is long and tried to conduct all his business by the book. At some point, however, he was faced with the nasty side of being a public figure. Even in his home, he was scared, nervously checking on callers, and acting like a man under threat. In time, he joined the long line of councillors who were intimidated and forced out by bully-boy tactics, and he quit both Liverpool – leaving for Sheffield – and politics altogether.

With Phil Hughes's resignation, the position of chair of Housing was

taken up by George Knibb, one of the leading figures in the Broad Left caucus. Bizarrely, or perhaps interestingly, his success in achieving this position
was aided by the support of what remained of the 'sensible/scabby six'. To
most people, George was George – a down-to-earth working-class bloke who
had lost his way (his style of oratory bears an uncanny resemblance to that
of Alexei Sayle's Bobby Chariot character). I, however, always believed him
to be a little more cunning. I also believe that his promotion was in fact engi-
neered by the would-be healer of political divides, Keva Coombes, aided and
abetted by the man Coombes anointed as his successor-designate, Tony
Jennings. The latter, at least, is central to George's own recollections:

> We had two or three people more than the progressives at the meeting. I
> didn't expect to be nominated because my role was personnel. I didn't
> have a clue about housing. I was on the housing committee and I knew
> what I wanted in terms of getting repairs and other commitments done,
> but I didn't have much knowledge about housing. Tony Jennings shouted
> my name out and I thought 'What the "f" is going on?' Next thing, I'm
> chair of Housing and it was a position I couldn't afford to lose or give up
> because it started to highlight the [Broad] Left again.

George's first move was to introduce himself to the city's then Director of
Housing, Jim Burns. In doing so, he made the terms of their relationship
clear:

> I said 'Look, you're on a thin line here. You do what I tell you to do, and
> what I tell you to do is the policy of the Labour Party who are in control of
> this city. Do that and, genuinely, you haven't got a problem. Don't do it
> and I'll make sure that you're gone.'

A not uncommon case of 'I'm wearing the trousers now', this still has a certain richness when we consider George's avowed lack of knowledge of 'housing'. Indeed, the whole issue of housing in Liverpool at this time was riddled
with contradictions. One startling example came when it was revealed that
several councillors owed in excess of a thousand pounds in rent. Legally, this
denied them any involvement in council decisions relating to such arrears,
and it also gave resonance to charges of sleaze.

Mulhearn and Hatton both reappeared on the scene at this time, albeit for
different reasons. In Mulhearn's case, he had set up a typesetting company,
Anteus Graphics, a year after being made redundant from the printing firm

Bemroses. Home of some of Merseyside's more argumentative printers – Jimmy Wilson was another one – Bemroses had relied on contracts from News International before the latter opened their own 'Wapping of the north' in neighbouring Knowsley, transferring the work there.

In Greek mythology, Anteus became strengthened every time he touched the earth, and the only way that he could be defeated was by holding him off the ground. Mulhearn no doubt took the title of Anteus to show himself as resolute, strong and willing to fight back, but I never really saw much prospect of him running a successful business. I was proved right on this when the company closed the following year. Hatton, meanwhile, was alleged to have bought a stolen horsebox. This was a bizarre tale, having much to do with the lifestyle Hatton embraced early in his public career. As well as having an expensive taste in clothes, a very nice home and what was for Liverpool a rather expensive car, he also had horses for his children, something that greatly impressed some of the local lumpen elements.

Hatton was cleared by the court of having bought the horsebox knowing it was stolen. More serious, however, and on a much greater scale, were the detailed reports that emerged about the Dovecot land deal. This concerned the sale and development of a former Merseyside Passenger Transport Executive site in Finch Lane. Hatton was central to this, and the deal allegedly involved unscrupulous characters from Liverpool's underworld. Keva Coombes was also to figure in the negotiations, and, peripherally, so was Cllr Frank Ruse, a trustee of the Merseyside Transport Sports and Social Club, which had an interest in the land. The offer price was somewhere in the region of £750,000; the development price was to be ten times that, with a Tesco supermarket as the key attraction. Later, councillors friendly to me were able to frustrate the project by delaying planning permission and granting it for a rival site a couple of miles away in Knotty Ash. Sainsbury's acquired the latter, and, naturally, this cut the value of the Dovecot land as a prime commercial site. It was subsequently used for new private housing – particularly amusing, considering the key social policy of Hatton's time on the council.

This was not the first occasion that questions had been raised about Hatton and planning permission. Early in 1985, there had been a major row at the DLP over a proposed Asda supermarket in the Hunts Cross area. The fact that Hatton had recently holidayed in Tangiers with Tony Beyga, a Knowsley councillor and public relations officer for Merseypride, the site's owners, caused great controversy. These concerns were exacerbated when it became public knowledge that Hatton had been negotiating on the issue for nine months, with Beyga present, without making any reference to the council leader, John Hamilton, or to colleagues in the Labour group. Despite the fact that the development was against the long-standing policy of the party, the Militant-dominated executive of the DLP tried to force through an omnibus resolution supporting the project. Six of the executive – Eddie Roderick, Mike Black, John Hamilton, Tony Hood, Ernie Taylor and Phil Gaffney – opposed this, but the resolution was carried through to the full DLP.[103] Here, however, it fell,[104] unusually for a Militant-backed motion and much to the fury of Hatton. Ironically, the Asda project eventually went ahead, thanks to the Tory government's policy on enterprise zones.

The reverberations of the Finch Lane deal were to carry on and on. A couple of years later, in a celebrated incident in broad daylight, one half of the Hughes twins, also known locally as 'the terrible twins', went to Hatton's office in Liverpool city centre and smashed in the bonnet of his BMW with a pickaxe. It was suggested that Hatton owed the twin in question twenty thousand pounds. What was particularly remarkable about the incident was that a local solicitor, Rex Makin, well-known in Liverpool circles and nicknamed 'Gollum' after a character in *Lord of the Rings*, rang me up as it was taking place to inform me that Hatton was under siege, but not to worry because (and I quote) 'Bobby McGorran, otherwise known as "Bob the Dog", is coming down to sort it out'. Hey presto, twenty-four hours later, Hatton and the Hughes twin appeared in the *Liverpool Echo* all smiles and pals together, leaning on the repaired bonnet of the BMW. It was quite an amazing illustration of what was happening in Liverpool at this time.

The original row over Finch Lane arose because Planning Committee records were quite rightly brought to the attention of the police by Alliance councillors. The appropriate files, which shed light on the property deals, subsequently – and mysteriously – disappeared, and council officers could not account for them in the consequent investigation. The disappearance of the files left a suspicion of corruption in the deal, but the difficulty, as always, was proving anything. Sadly, the phenomenon of *omerta* is not peculiar to Sicily.

Elsewhere on Merseyside, Peter Fisher, who had stood successfully as 'Labour against Militant' at the local elections, was readmitted into Knowsley Labour group. Also in the borough, the protracted attempt to eradicate the influence of Militant in the Knowsley North CLP led to expulsions. The danger here, however, was that people who were perhaps anti-council, anti-establishment or anti-George Howarth (the MP), were being caught up in what could genuinely be described as a witch-hunt. Such a situation was entirely different from dealing with entryists from another party, and it was necessary to develop mechanisms to adjust the disciplinary process to avoid the punishment of innocents. Further afield in St Helens, Cllr Allan Jackson was arrested on a fraud charge. At a full meeting of Wirral Borough Council, a group of protesters, deciding that a provocative demonstration was the best way in which to highlight their point, gave a collective 'mooney', exposing their buttocks to the meeting. The politics of the time were capable of throwing up almost anything imaginable, but this really was the bottom line.

Little did I know that this summer, with all its tribulations – which I thought were a passing phase – was merely to be a prologue to another explosion. In some ways, the future was to be even more tempestuous than it had been during the first purge of Militant. To remind me of how far we still had to travel, I had a tape recording presented to me of a meeting that had taken place between myself, Joyce Gould and a group of St Helens councillors. We now regularly faced the situation where people would secretly make such recordings to later use selectively as support for their arguments.

The battle that was approaching was hastened in September when into this *Alice in Wonderland* world of politics came the Mad Hatter of Tory policies, the poll tax. Across Britain, there was a broad spectrum of opposition to the tax involving not only ordinary members of the Labour Party and the trade union movement but also members of Trotskyite and anarchist groups, who were particularly apparent during the larger street protests. Militant, however, was an altogether more cynical organisation; their primary interest in the anti-poll tax movement was as a new source of membership and money. Under increasing pressure from the Labour Party, the poll tax gave Militant an opportunity to exploit a popular cause and build structures – the anti-poll tax unions – which could provide recruits, money and platforms. The anti-poll tax movement gave them an unlimited supply.

Eventually the poll tax, and the opposition to it, would lead to the downfall of Margaret Thatcher as Prime Minister. Yet it also caused tremendous problems for the Labour Party in Liverpool. As soon as the tax was announced, eighteen members of the council Labour group declared publicly that they intended to boycott it, and within a few days anti-poll tax unions had been established in the Netherley and Walton areas of the city. As time would reveal, these bodies were to become yet another source of supply of foot-soldiers for Militant in Liverpool.

The autumn of 1988 also saw the start of the selection process for the Merseyside East constituency in the European Parliament, involving the sitting MEP, Les Huckfield. Labour's youngest MP when he had represented Nuneaton, Huckfield had always been seen as a bright individual, but he was also hopelessly compromised in many different ways. Always in search of a seat, the phrase 'the chicken run' could easily have been created for him. In ending up as an MEP, he was able to indulge himself in his passion for making deals with the most incorrigible of people, the sole purpose of which was to protect his own immediate interests. Unfortunately for him, he was to come unstuck with a fraud inquiry into his affairs, centring particularly around his use of European money. This investigation was led by Detective John Pass of the Fraud Squad who, on raiding Huckfield's home in Goose Green, Wigan, found different copies of the same minutes with key parts amended. He also discovered variations on the same set of accounts governing Huckfield's constituency, and details of how money had gone through the books of Woolton Labour Club one day before being drawn out the next. Consequently, Huckfield received his just deserts, and, along with Jim O'Dowd and Trevor Ennis, two members of the party in St Helens who were also officers of his Euro constituency party, he was charged with deception.

Within Liverpool, the factional wound running through the Labour group reopened over the necessary reorganisation of primary schools in the city. Unable to gain the support needed to carry out his proposed programme of reform, Gideon Ben-Tovim resigned as chair of Education. Schools were not necessarily situated where the children were, and there were schools, particularly in parts of the inner city, that were well under-subscribed. The proposed reforms were not a repeat of the politics that the Liberals had played in the early 1980s, when they attempted to close down Croxteth Comprehensive, but a recognition that the demographics of Liverpool had changed drastically and that school-place planning had not reflected it. The problem had to be tackled because taking out surplus places in schools was vital to the council's finances; educational resources needed to be applied where there was most need instead of keeping schools open just for the sake of it. On occasion, such schools may have had a quality of teaching which benefited those children attending them, but this was less important than the overall provision and efficiency of education in Liverpool as a whole.

There was much more, however, to the resignation of Ben-Tovim, who had become a target for the Militants and their supporters within the Labour group. He was seen, firstly, as being a representative of the Black Caucus, sworn enemies of Militant, and, secondly, as being middle class and well-educated – a capital crime in itself as far as many workerists in the Broad Left were concerned.

Away from the council committee rooms, Militant continued to ride roughshod over the rules of the party, clogging up debates and stalling policies, particularly at the reconstituted DLP. Roy Gladden remembers one occasion when he was in the chair:

> I had to laugh because, as resolutions were coming up, the Tendency won the first two resolutions and then lost one and I said 'Okay, that's two–one to you isn't it? Now let's go for the draw.' It was so obvious what was happening.

Indeed, it was, and Militant continued to be a corrupting influence on everything they came into contact with. When Hatton's company was later raided by the police, they found one of the Militant councillors, Frank Vaudrey – who had earned himself the nickname 'Postman Pat' due to his reputed sending out of a mail-shot for Hatton using council facilities – sitting in Hatton's office, sorting out his mentor's mail.

Fractures, meanwhile, were beginning to emerge within the progressive caucus. Some of the younger councillors, including Dawn Booth, Keith Hackett, Juliet Herzog, Lyn O'Sullivan and Ian Scott, all of whom socialised together, started to be seen as an exclusive grouping with more than their fair share of access to the leader's, Keva Coombes's, ear. University-educated, mostly from out of town, and mostly based in the south end of Liverpool, they became known as the 'Sainsbury set' on account of their apparent tastes in food and wine. As Vicky Roberts observes, such labelling was steeped in a profound distrust of meddlesome outsiders:

> It was a way of playing on the 'Good Liverpool, working-class stock' against middle-class academics and incomers.

Still, the more the 'Sainsbury set' gave the impression of being a think-tank for Coombes, the more that cracks set in between themselves and others within their caucus; as Harry Rimmer recalls:

> It was felt that they ran things, and that the rest of the Progressive Left group had become voting fodder. Gradually, a resentment developed which I found quite astonishing when I realised how far it had gone. Of course, I wasn't part of it – the intrigue and the drinks in pubs.

As usual, this was underpinned by more than an element of personality politics. Interestingly tensions were most apparent between members of the 'Sainsbury set', such as Scott and Herzog, and Gideon Ben-Tovim, someone many would have thought was their natural ally. The reasons behind these disagreements still baffle Keva Coombes:

> I could never quite understand why. I still don't understand why, except that it was all personal. That was the sort of division, and I spent a lot of time trying to keep people's personal dislikes in some proportion.

Nevertheless, like Keva himself, the 'Sainsbury set' were seen as an arrogant grouping who thought that as incomers to the city they had particular insight into Liverpool's problems. Something that has struck me over the years is that so many people have wanted to tell the citizens of Liverpool how to conduct their own affairs, as if they were not capable of doing so themselves. This is partly the failure of the local labour movement to turn out people with the abilities necessary to conduct city-wide affairs, or to provide a political lead. Granted, there have been exceptions. Jack Jones, a man for whom I have tremendous respect, made his name in the movement well away from Liverpool, as did other, perhaps lesser, figures. The organisations for which they worked gained at Liverpool's expense. Sadly, there is something in the local culture of a 'tall poppy syndrome', as described in Horace's *Odes*, where those whose heads rise too high above the rest are swiftly chopped down. Taking such leadership out has only one result – everyone else is dragged down, too.

A second fracture within the progressive caucus was serious less for its political ramifications than for what it revealed about the role of outside influences. The councillors involved were Hannah Folan and Danny Bermingham – a partnership, and a strange pair, of whom Vicky Roberts offers a rather apt description:

> A couple of Vicar-of-Bray-type characters – they just changed according to the prevailing wind.

Folan, who ran a sandwich bar on Victoria Street in Liverpool city centre, was a councillor for Dingle ward and definitely not a Militant; in fact, she was quite outspoken against their line. Bermingham was a railway guard who represented Smithdown ward; initially a Militant supporter, he turned against them during the Sam Bond affair – so much so, in fact, that he was kept off the local government panel. In 1988, however, their political pendulum began to swing again. The local newspaper and various Liberal councillors alleged that they were meeting Derek Hatton. As Harry Rimmer explains:

> I began to hear whispers that she was being seen out having meals with Derek Hatton and others at around the time that Derek was running his Settleside business. I don't know what the strength of it was, but her attitude to the rest of us started to turn.

Naturally, their colleagues in the progressive caucus started to ask indirect questions about their new lifestyle, but it was of little consequence. Soon after this period, the pair joined the Broad Left.

On a lighter note, a tremendous insight into the mentality of one of Liverpool's councillors became available at the end of the year. Frank Ruse, a councillor in Valley ward and an odd character, had arrived on the political scene, as if out of the ether, in the early 1980s, and ended up on the council after the elections that followed the debarment of 'the forty-seven'. A member of the Confederation of Shipbuilding and Engineering Unions, Ruse took this very seriously and referred to 'the Confed' in rather reverential tones, as though it was a holy institution of some sort. Questionably, he made the claim that he had worked in Germany for eighteen years before returning to Liverpool. I may be wrong to flag a question mark up against this, but many other people had no idea who he was, and he was certainly something of a Walter Mitty character.

What was really amusing at this time, however, was a practical joke made at Frank's expense. He was on the council sub-committee that dealt with leisure and the arts, and had recently been to the BBC in London to appear on *Blue Peter* with the Chinese Youth Orchestra, an organisation he had taken under his wing. One of his fellow councillors acquired a piece of BBC-headed notepaper and sent him the following mock letter:

Dear Cllr Ruse,

We were delighted to receive you and the Chinese Youth Orchestra on Blue Peter recently. Any opportunity for our viewers to see prominent and hard-working Liverpool councillors is always appreciated by the nation. I now very much regret being instructed by the Board of Directors to write to you, following representations made by the Leader of Her Majesty's Opposition (the Rt Hon. Neil Kinnock, MP). The Board of Directors have considered the matter of your breach of the Group Whip and clear involvement with a proscribed organisation very carefully. They can, I am afraid, see no alternative under the circumstances but to insist on the return of your Blue Peter badge forthwith.

Yours sincerely, Biddy Baxter (Producer)

Not only was the letter such an obvious put-on, but also Biddy Baxter had for some time ceased to be the producer of the programme. Frank, however, took it rather seriously, and came to see me in my official capacity because he wanted to sue whoever had caused the BBC to request his badge back. He actually did send it back to them! Frank also wanted a personal apology from Neil, to whose office he sent a letter, detailing what had happened. God knows what Neil and his staff made of that. When I tried to explain to Frank that I thought it was in all probability a joke, and that somebody was merely having a laugh at his expense, he said 'Well, that's even worse'. I could not shake off his notion that there had been a deep insult to the Chinese Youth Orchestra by the suggestion that Frank – who, incidentally, is not of Chinese origin – should lose his *Blue Peter* badge. Worse was to come, though. In the early 1990s, he became a Liberal Democrat councillor, and now has one of the safest seats in Liverpool. Only last year, I was awoken from my morning slumber with a sudden jolt when I heard Ruse on BBC Radio Merseyside speaking about the local political situation. As I lay there, I wondered if *Blue Peter* had ever returned the badge to him.

The light relief of the Frank Ruse episode was welcome as the routine of meeting after meeting continued, trying to persuade key individuals and groups of the need to stay firm; helping them get organised; helping them win skirmish after skirmish, and battle after battle, against Militant, who were touting for fresh recruits amongst the anti-poll tax unions, bringing people into the party on a single issue, having already used their perfidious influence to corrupt them. We had to counter this by bringing in genuine members. The end of 1988 was also a time when I was consolidating the support of those influential people without whose help and advice I could not effectively operate, the most significant of whom were Mike Carr and Sean Hughes. Mike, who had become the secretary of the DLP, would subsequently become the MP for Bootle, while Sean was a classic case of 'a local lad who had made good', having succeeded Harold Wilson as the MP for Knowsley South. Liaising with the pair of them was essential in maintaining the struggle against Militant's attempted comeback. It was not just a case of me respecting and sharing Mike's and Sean's political positions. It was also that these two intrinsically decent people could be totally trusted. Tragically, they were both to die within the next eighteen months.

With hindsight, it is difficult to believe how much political activity was being packed into the limited time available. I seemed to spend every waking hour listening to arcane debates on the minutes of previous meetings. I doubt very much that I would put myself through it again if I had the time over. I never foresaw it being such a mind-blowing existence. It was abnormal, but it reflected the abnormal politics that prevailed in Liverpool and much of the rest of Merseyside at that time.

# 10 Tough choices

I did not realise it at the time but at the start of 1989 the pressure was beginning to tell on me personally. A fortnight into the New Year, I wrote a letter to Keva Coombes in which I referred to him as 'craven and cringing'. The letter was leaked to the local press (no need to be Poirot to know who leaked it) and it became front-page news locally. I already had a low opinion of Coombes, but it was plumbing new depths as I became more aware of the games he was playing as leader of the council. In the letter, I compared him to another lawyer, Khrustalev-Nosar, a shooting star of revolutionary Russia who had claimed credit for the 1905 Petrograd Soviet when the moving spirit was in fact Trotsky. I could not help but see parallels with the way in which Militant was still allowed to get away with things under Coombes's leadership. Like his Russian prototype, Keva was to end up outside politics, marked down as discredited; Khrustalev-Nosar, having tried to be all things to all factions, was eventually shot. But with hindsight, I was wrong to commit my thoughts to paper.

The main reason why I had written to Coombes concerned his failure to discipline those within the Labour group who had voted against moves to prepare for the poll tax. I had also been spurred on by the apparent ease with which Militant supporters were being allowed to rip off the local authority. Back in March 1985, Jimmy Hollinshead, deputy convenor of GMB Branch 5 and a leading Militant, ordered meals from the council for a lunch that followed a rally in the city, and he had still not paid the cost of these back. Even though the council had won a court order for him to do so, Hollinshead and others set about confusing the question of who was responsible for the bill, pointing the finger towards the National Local Authorities' Coordinating Committee. As this body no longer existed, the bill continued to remain unpaid until it was written off at the beginning of 1989. This was patently wrong. Not only should Hollinshead have been held responsible, but he should also have been disciplined. After all, he was a council employee. Rightly or wrongly, I suspected the hand of Coombes in the council's inaction.

## Left Behind: Lessons from Labour's heartland

February brought the sending of a letter to Mikhail Gorbachev by Liverpool's five Labour MPs, inviting him to the city during his forthcoming visit to Britain. This may have seemed ironic, coming a couple of years after the success of the Liverpool-based film *A Letter to Brezhnev*. For those like myself, however, who knew the five to be devoid of both irony and lateral thought, it was an attempt at little more than workerist symbolism. Indeed, what struck me most about their letter was the outdated language and references they used, in particular their celebration of 'socialist planning', at a time when Gorbachev was attempting to remodel the political economy of the Soviet Union. Given the opportunity, the famous five would no doubt have drawn parallels between the sailors of the battleship *Potemkin* and groups within the city council's workforce. This is not as far fetched as it might seem. Recalling the decline in the relationship between GMB Branch 5 and the Hattonistas, Ian Lowes remembers the occasion when he and other stewards were occupying the Municipal Building, and the police were called to remove them:

> We actually had Tendency councillors screaming at us, comparing us with the sailors at Kronstadt. I said 'Hang on, this is about six workers who are involved in an industrial dispute with their employer over work being given to private contractors that should have been given to us.'

Revolutionary, or indeed post-revolutionary, St Petersburg this was not, but Liverpool by the Mersey, at the mercy of the vivid imaginations of its more self-indulgent politicians.

As the furious five awaited Gorby's response, Margaret Thatcher visited Liverpool for the first time in almost five years (the previous occasion being the one when she literally sneaked in and sneaked back out again). In a truly spectacular display of gaucheness, the closure of the Bird's Eye factory in nearby Kirkby was announced the same day, putting more than a thousand people out of work. Thatcher, of course, would have been briefed about this in advance, and her visit, from a public relations point of view at least, was seen less as a disaster and more of a demonstration that she did not give a damn about Merseyside and its problems.

With concerns gathering strength about what Thatcher's poll tax would mean for Liverpool, March saw a number of public meetings on the issue. Some, such as the one at Alsop School in Walton, and another in Fazakerley, were hijacked by Militant, which was now operating at full pace behind the banner of the anti-poll tax unions. As a result, perfectly legitimate and worthy attempts to discuss the issues with the public were turned not only into a platform for rants against the Tory government – which was no bad thing – but also rants against anyone who disagreed with Militant on the tactics to be employed.

I was having some success in my fight to remove key Militants from the local Labour Party, particularly in Kensington ward, where I managed to have charges laid against Tommy Carrol and Richard Knights. Carrol was viewed by many members with the greatest distaste, while Knights was a full-time organiser for Militant, and a regular columnist for its newspaper, which presented him as some sort of industrial relations expert. My own information was that he had never worked in his life and that he came from a rather affluent background. To look at him, he struck me as the type of person who would have been equally at home as a preacher in a fundamentalist Christian sect.

Coincidentally, March 1989 also saw my promotion to the job of North West Regional Organiser. At the beginning of the year, I had been encouraged, indeed cajoled, into applying for this post, which Ray Gill had finally vacated. At first, I had very mixed feelings about taking on this role, mainly because I could only see it bringing more work and less quality time with my family. Nevertheless, I applied for the job and, following a successful if lacklustre performance at the interview, I took up the position. Bizarrely, Militant tried to make some capital out of my promotion. In comments to the local press, their Merseyside spokesman Richard Venton compared it to a promotion from the Commons to the Lords, adding 'Mr Kilfoyle has decided he can't stand the heat, so he is getting out of the kitchen'.[105] This was in spite of the fact that I had already made clear that I would continue to be responsible for Merseyside! It was typical of Militant to twist the truth.

In taking up the post, I tried to disturb the three existing Assistant Regional Organisers as little as possible. Phil Robinson continued to look after Lancashire, Peter Killeen had Cheshire and Chris Hemming had Greater Manchester. It was crazy, really, to have the Regional Organiser's responsibility plus responsibility for organising the most difficult area imaginable (I was also deeply involved in a campaign at a Liverpool school, St Francis Xavier's, of which I was a governor, to prevent it opting out of the local authority). But I had no faith in either Killeen or Robinson – both of whom I should have been able to look to for assistance – doing anything other than exacerbate the problems on Merseyside. To make things worse, relations between the staff within the regional office had become truly dreadful, with colleagues refusing to speak to one another. The real solution would have been a clear-out, but my superiors in the national party would not hear of such radical action. Things were near to total breakdown – filing was not being done, and the office resembled a bombsite. To set the right tone, Bernie, two of our daughters and I went into the office on the weekend I took over, and cleaned and tidied the place from top to bottom. We might as well not have bothered. Within a month, the office was back to how it had been before.

Despite my appointment, and my primary task of getting the north west section of the party in shape for the next election, I continued to attend a constant stream of meetings in Liverpool. People had to be convinced, either of the merits of Labour's cause or, more often than not, that it was worthwhile staying in the party and going through attritional warfare to get rid of Militant. As ever, most of the ordinary membership had things to do other than attend an eternal round of meetings, but I needed to convince them that we had to do this to prevent Militant consolidating what local influence it still had. They were still using procedural methods to stop people from having their legitimate way. They would deny access to people, saying that they had not paid their subscriptions when they had, and on a number of occasions they refused to accept subscriptions, most evidently in the treatment meted out to Stan Thorne, the former MP for Preston and long-standing member of Liverpool Garston CLP. They would interpret the rules as they saw fit, denying people the opportunity to vote on motions or to put motions forward. Alternatively, when they were outnumbered, they attempted to use the rulebook to scupper any progress that was not to their liking.

It was therefore vital for me to ensure that there was a healthy side to the party, knowing that when we were eventually rid of Militant we would need able people willing to take up the reins of office, both in the party and on the council. We also needed to ensure that meetings were held, as far as possible, according to the rules, constitution and standing orders of the Labour Party. I may have appeared overly officious at times, but it was a long-term strategy geared towards shifting the prevailing political culture. There was, of course, a strictly hegemonic dimension to all of this. We had to ensure that non-Militant people became officers and delegates to other bodies so that Labour's policies, as they were understood everywhere else, could be implemented in Liverpool and on the rest of Merseyside. It was a constant battle to achieve this, not only at all levels within the local party, but also in persuading trade unions to put the right people through as affiliated delegates to the CLPs, and authenticating the Youth and Women's sections.

Incidentally, it was about this time that I conducted a survey of the local women in the party, to discover what roles and responsibilities they held. Although they had a healthy share of council chairmanships, only a few were chairs of ward parties, and there were no female constituency chairs. Not surprisingly, the pervading culture within Liverpool Labour politics was one that relegated women to positions which included lots of work, such as treasurer or secretary, but little thanks.

At all times I aimed to minimise the influence of Militant, its acolytes and their gullible fellow-travellers. Of course, these people were not going to walk away lightly, as they made clear that spring. Cheryl Varley had been expelled from the Labour Party along with Hatton and co., but had since made her mark in student politics. Having been elected to the National Union of Students' Further Education National Committee in 1987, she was elected early in 1989 to the full executive of the NUS. From where I stood, seeing a Militant full-timer rise through the ranks of an organisation so closely aligned to Labour was frustrating; the NUS appeared to be shrugging its shoulders at Neil Kinnock. However, Varley's experience on the union executive was to be a salutary one, as she reveals:

> There was the National Organisation of Labour Students who were the right wing (oh, the good old days, that was the nearest you got to a right wing!), and independents, and then us, the SWP and Socialist Organiser on the left. On ninety-five per cent of resolutions, the left voted as a whole. But according to the Militant, I was supposed to get to conference, hate these people and attack them. I said 'I've been voting all year with these people, we might have our little differences but they're not my enemies'. I also started to listen to other people's perspectives and sometimes they were right. But you couldn't have that in the Militant. That would be tantamount to treason. Then I started to see the lack of democracy within the Militant. It's all right for one person to say 'Right, do this now', when you are fighting a big struggle, in which you have not got time for big discussions – you just have to do it. But our conferences just used to be one person after another getting up and saying what the people on the platform wanted to hear.

Varley soon started to become openly critical of Militant perspectives, and gradually dropped away from the organisation, which to her great surprise willingly let her go. Although she remains a resolutely political individual, Varley now works as a journalist on a Liverpool weekly freesheet – a far cry from *Militant* but a more riveting read.

Back in 1989, as Varley was raising her national profile, Militant again played a clever, if somewhat transparent, game at the elections for the executive of the Liverpool DLP. Rather than put their own people forward for key positions of influence, they instead nominated those whom they considered to be allies. This led to the sitting chair, Eddie Sabino, being beaten for the post by Eddie Loyden. As ever, this was the only position that Loyden had his eye on. He was still an MP and, even if he wished to, he could not put in the time and effort that was required to chair the DLP properly. But Loyden's election was an extremely valuable one for Militant, given that they dominated his constituency party. At the same time, 'forty-sevener' George Lloyd was elected unopposed for the position of secretary. Seen as a 'mister nice guy' figure in the middle, this was the same George Lloyd who would subsequently stand against Labour candidates in Old Swan ward, denying Labour victories at council elections. If that does not speak volumes for him, then what may is a comment relayed by Lyn Anderson from Lloyd's brother Peter (one of the original 'forty-nine' whose death prompted a by-election in January 1986, which Labour lost heavily amidst great media attention):

> Peter used to tell me that the problem with his brother George was that his brain and mouth didn't always connect together.

Of course, Militant were not beyond chancing their own hand. This was most apparent in the election of Sylvia Sharpey-Shafer as treasurer. In gaining office, she ousted 'old faithful' John Hamilton from a post that he had held, in the DLP's various forms, since the late 1960s and which he vacated in characteristic style by whinging about the ingratitude of Militant and their ilk. Considering his experience of Hatton, Byrne and others, it was more than a little puzzling to find John believing that some degree of courtesy pervaded Labour Party politics in Liverpool. I myself suffered no such delusions. A war was taking place, a point made even more apparent when Lesley Mahmood told the local press what she thought of the results: 'It shows that Peter Kilfoyle has not been very successful. These elections are the beginning of a return to the traditions of the hard left in the District Labour Party. It is a significant shift to the left.'[106] While this interpretation was as simplistic as I would have expected from a Militant mouth-piece,

Mahmood's argument at least revealed the extent to which the task in hand was unfinished.

I was, of course, facing greater demands on my time beyond the immediate requirements of Liverpool. Campaign launches were conducted in both Lancashire and Cheshire, and I was also involved in arrangements for the European elections. In addition, I attended my regularly monthly meeting at the Penguin Hotel, on the A1 near Wetherby. Here, the officers of the Northern, Yorkshire & Humberside and North West regions met to discuss regional government. It was our forum for keeping a cohesive and dynamic regional policy alive, something to which I remain committed.

On top of this, I had to oversee a visit to the region from Neil Kinnock. Phil Robinson was supposed to be doing this but asked to be excused because it was his wife's birthday. He really would look for any way of avoiding such responsibilities, and his commitment to the job appeared minimal. I pointed out to him that I tended to miss my wife's birthday most years, as it often coincided with conference, but that it was something that both Bernie and I could cope with. Alas, he would not be moved on the matter.

Another interesting vignette from this time was provided by my visit to Gerald Kaufman's home in Victoria Park, Manchester, to discuss the problems he was having in his own constituency. Gerald's was a lovely little house in a very private park, but what I was most taken with was his huge collection of books on Hollywood. In looking over his bookshelves, I cannot recall seeing publications on anything else – it was obviously a prize feature in his life. There were many biographies, as well as what must have amounted to every serious study that had ever been written on the studios or history of cinematography. What the workerists within Merseyside politics would have made of it, I do not know.

April 1989 was a cruel month in the history of Liverpool, and twisted with its own bitter ironies. On the morning of Saturday 15, the *Liverpool Daily Post* carried a front-page story announcing that verdicts would soon be given on the involvement of so-called fans of Liverpool Football Club in the stampede at the Heysel Stadium, in Brussels, in 1985 that left thirty-eight Italians dead. By late afternoon, however, the tragedy of Hillsborough had occurred and the city of Liverpool was mourning its own dead. I was not in Sheffield that day but I watched what was unfolding on television and, like many others, I was overwhelmed by the sheer horror of what I was witnessing.

## Left Behind: Lessons from Labour's heartland

The day after the disaster, Margaret Thatcher visited a number of hospitals in Sheffield and found herself spurned or ignored by the staff and injured alike. One would not have thought that what would normally have been seen as a humanitarian gesture could be construed as offensive. I spoke to Neil Kinnock's office about him coming up and told them to leave it for a couple of days until we could gauge exactly what was happening.

As it turned out, Neil came up on the Tuesday. It was a day I will never forget. I met him in Manchester and we drove over to Sheffield. Our first stops were at the various hospitals where the injured were being cared for. Neil was absolutely brilliant. His empathy was obvious, and he really did come across as the man of the people that he is. The one hesitation that I had was that the then leader of Sheffield City Council, Clive Betts (now MP for Sheffield Attercliffe), wanted us to go to the mortuary. Quite rightly, he referred to the tremendous job that had been done by the staff there, and how people tended to forget about them. I had worries of photographers taking rather morbid pictures of Neil going into a mortuary, and Neil agreed with me, but we went anyway. It really was one of the most moving experiences I have ever had. Four people were in the party – Neil, two of his staff, Sue Nye and Hilary Coffman, and myself. We had only been in the mortuary a few minutes when it became apparent that neither Sue nor I could hack it. To be honest, I was terrified of seeing the body of John Paul Gilhooley, who was only a little older than my own son Patrick. Neil's decision to carry on was further evidence of his resolution. Even so, he was as shaken by the experience as the rest of us. Afterwards, we returned to Manchester to our hotel and had a number of stiff drinks to recover from a very testing day. Incidentally, no photographs of the visit to the mortuary appeared in the press.

The events at Hillsborough continue to traumatise many of those concerned, in no way helped by the whispering campaign remaining in certain circles that Liverpool supporters only had themselves to blame. Biased from the start, this viewpoint draws its logic and 'inspiration' from stories first printed by the *Sun* a few days after the tragedy, which led to a widespread boycott of the newspaper across Merseyside (even now, its sales have not recovered). Wholly fallacious allegations were made about the behaviour of fans before, during and after the tragedy, which sadly fitted into some people's jaundiced view of Scousers. Why contemplate what really happened when your prejudices will explain it for you? Of course, this in turn gave strength to the belief of the people of Liverpool that they really were up against the tide of public opinion. Almost immediately, the city and its hinterland pulled together in a way that was most uncharacteristic of mainland Britain, at least in the 'no-such-thing-as-society' 1980s. Through the social services department, Liverpool City Council provided counselling for the injured, and the families of the dead and injured. The Hillsborough Families Support Group was established, a body that became the engine for the repeated attempts of the families to obtain what they considered to be justice. I was extremely supportive of this, and remain so, continuing to do all that I can to help within the bounds of the law.

With the fall-out from Hillsborough giving the national press good reason to keep Liverpool on their front pages, the city itself began to face up to the perennial problem of financing its municipal services. In a show of creative accounting that would have made Tony Byrne blush, chair of Finance Keith Hackett and council leader Keva Coombes hit upon the idea of selling assets as a way of raising more money. This included a number of 'attractive' business premises in the city centre and a host of public buildings that had once housed swimming baths or had been part of schools. Yet, as Harry Rimmer explains, the government was able to keep one step ahead:

> As Keva and Keith found these things to sell, the Tories were shifting the goalposts and eventually brought it in that any capital receipts had to go towards reducing debts. It became a battle of wits. But I thought the policy was fundamentally flawed. To sell these leaseholds that we had had around the city centre would substantially reduce annual income in subsequent years.

To me, this rather desperate move reflected little more than the continuing inability of the council to move away from the ever-mythical commitment to 'no cuts in jobs or services'. In a rather naive way, Hackett, Coombes and others were determined to remain loyal to this position – a position that masked an unwillingness to come to terms with the undeniable truth that you cannot pay people to sit around and do nothing.

The council's lunacy, however, began to plumb even greater depths as a vote was taken for a hand-out to the dockers should they stage a national walk-out in response to government plans to abolish the National Dock Labour Scheme. Naturally, this decision was swathed in the usual rhetoric, and some councillors gave renditions of the 'my father and his forty forefathers' speech upon which the nostalgia of Liverpool's industrial politics has been built. The inevitable walk-out, which led to a summer of strife at the port, was to have unfortunate consequences nearly ten years later during the 1995–98 dock strike. To many people, the stand taken by Liverpool's dockers was seen as highly principled. To me, it was just another example of the failure of sections of the labour movement on Merseyside to come to terms with reality.

Principles, however, came ten a penny in Liverpool at this time. In July, a large number of the Labour group signed up to the council's anti-poll tax pledge. Commenting on his own stance, George Knibb told the local press: 'I am prepared to go to jail. I will go rather than pay the poll tax. It is an issue I believe worth fighting for and I will go right down the line. I do not wish to be a martyr but if the final penalty is imprisonment then prison it will be.'[107] Predictably, he paid his tax and never did go to prison. Harry Rimmer, meanwhile, took a more considered view:

> I kept preaching to the group: 'This government can do what it likes, she can do what she likes, she can get things through on the payroll vote' (as in those with jobs in the government). The idea that one city or any local authority could attempt to defeat them was ludicrous. It could not happen. It would be futile, and I said 'What we have to do is to accept the fact reluctantly, do the bare minimum and stay within the law'. But I also said that 'this will be the rock that she'll eventually perish on'.

True to form, Coombes neither criticised the pledge nor signed it. Instead, he sat on the fence, offering 'support' to those who were prepared to engage in what he saw as legitimate civil disobedience. As usual, no consideration was given to the threat to city finances if such tactics succeeded. Moreover, the council gave free office space to the anti-poll tax federation and underwrote a £10,000 grant for an anti-poll tax gala at Walton Park on the August bank holiday. It was as if a collective nervous tension was taking over, where clear thinking gave way to all sorts of hare-brained schemes. Simultaneously, temperatures were rising in the council chamber, as Liberal Democrat leader Paul Clark alleged that Militant supporter Frank Vaudrey had threatened to head-butt him during a debate over plans for a new prison in Liverpool. 'The Liverpool kiss' may have amused television audiences when performed by Yosser Hughes in *The Boys from the Blackstuff*, but it was not an acceptable way to resolve political differences.

It was also around this time that Coombes's name was mentioned in connections with the Hatton-related Finch Lane land deal. He was not involved in this, but he did make a habit of appearing on the fringes of such things.

He really was an accident waiting to happen. With the allegations of Coombes's involvement surfacing as a former city architect, James Robb, was being tried for bribery charges (he was later acquitted), an unshakeable image of corruption was attaching itself to Liverpool's civic affairs. *Private Eye*'s lampoon of 'Murkyside' appeared to be taking on a life of its own.

None of this was helped by the actions of NALGO, which throughout the summer embarked on a series of national one-day strikes in their quest for a successful pay claim. Although supportive of the union's aims, the council opted to dock one-fifth rather than one-seventh of the strikers' weekly wages each time they supported a day of action (the fractions related to different definitions of the working week). This riled local NALGO officials, many of whom felt that they should have been able to go on strike with impunity, and culminated in the occupation of a full meeting of the council, a tactic they would come to employ with increasing frequency. A few weeks later, the council backed down, failing once again to assert its right to run Liverpool for the benefit of all of its citizens, not just an assortment of Trotskyite officials representing white-collar workers who were often middle-class Liberal and Tory voters living in surrounding boroughs.

The summer of 1989 also saw the return of Michael Heseltine to the local scene, as he once again became 'Minister for Merseyside'. For many politicians beyond Liverpool, taking on responsibility for the city would be deemed a poisoned chalice. One only had to recall what happened to one local government minister, Patrick Jenkin, when he attempted a settlement with the council over Labour's inheritance of the Liberals' artificially depressed rate. This had led to a massive shortfall in the city's finance, prompting the claim that the Tory government had stolen '£X million' (the precise figure varied according to the council spokesperson) from Liverpool. Jenkin, I believe in good faith, brokered a deal with the city council, understanding that Liverpool did have unique difficulties. However, the confidential talks were shattered by the public triumphalism of Hatton, which in turn enraged Margaret Thatcher; soon after, Jenkin was sacked.

Heseltine, however, seemed to relish the role of 'Minister for Merseyside', rising to it as if he were the governor of some far-off colony. I have only ever spoken to him across the floor of the Commons, but Heseltine has always struck me as a rather lofty individual – an old-style patrician. Still, after his experiences first time around, he dedicated a whole chapter of his autobiography to 'The Lessons of Merseyside', describing how the region had 'supplied me with one of those priceless formative experiences from which every politician takes strength; it tested many of my deepest political beliefs and instincts and intensified my convictions'.[108] In coming back for a second spell to an intensely anti-Tory Liverpool, he was either a sucker for punishment or losing his grip on political reality.

Despite the various problems we were experiencing in and around Merseyside, there was no real indication that these would erupt into something bigger, and for a time I began to concentrate more on regional matters. I tried to keep a watching brief on Liverpool. Indeed, I was already having regrets about taking on the position of Regional Organiser because of the huge range of places I was expected to attend. If there was a difficulty, it was assumed that I would be able to resolve it and bring the warring factions to a consensus. This was not always easy. For instance, I was brought in to try to negotiate between the Greater Manchester Labour Party (which, with the demise of the county in 1985, had no real reason to exist but insisted on carrying on) and the Association of Greater Manchester Authorities, a body that coordinated general matters such as Manchester Airport, of which all the councils that made up the association were part-owners. This was an unnecessary distraction from more urgent demands. Thankfully, an additional pair of hands was appointed on Merseyside, as Cllr Gary Booth took up post as local organiser.

Crucially, the parliamentary selection process had begun, and this was to become my major preoccupation over the next twelve months. I had already telephoned the forty or so Labour MPs in the north west to ask how I could be of assistance to them in arranging the timetable (the fact that I actually telephoned them to sort out their needs was to stand me in good stead later when I went into Parliament). I had also told my colleagues in the regional office that I would take on the more contentious selections. I had little choice – they were complaining of difficulties before we had actually started, and it was apparent that some of them were unable or unwilling to grasp how the process worked. Even so, two of the selections that I monitored were to be extremely controversial.

In October, Gerry Bermingham was deselected, at least temporarily, in St Helens South in a strange affair. The whole process had been protracted, and early on, after I had arranged the selection timetable, Bermingham contacted me to ask if it could be changed. Bearing in mind that I had set the timetable with his agreement as well as that of the constituency, I was more than a little miffed, particularly when he told me the reason – he wanted to go out on a legal case to the Caribbean! I put it to him straight that he had to decide between the trip and being reselected as an MP (St Lucia or St Helens South, as it were). He backed down and gave up his exotic trip, and we stayed with the timetable.

I went to great pains to make sure that everything was done by the book in this selection, and it initially seemed that Bermingham had been deselected. It was only later, after John Evans indicated that I ought to check the ballot papers more carefully, that I realised that something was horribly wrong. The process was important. Each affiliated organisation – for example, a trade union branch – received a ballot form and an authentication form. The ballot was filled in and sealed in a small envelope. The authentication, which had been cut or torn from the ballot, was then completed and placed in a second envelope. The first envelope containing the secret ballot also went into this.

Done this way, I could trace back which union or Labour club had actually cast the vote, while the vote inside – in its sealed envelope – still retained the privacy of the secret ballot. When the result was questioned, however, I was able to work out from the result which authentication form ought to have gone with which ballot paper. The reason was simple; although the two parts of the original form had been separated to protect the secrecy of the ballot cast, in most cases they had been roughly torn from one another. It was easy, therefore, to match up physically the appropriate ballot paper with the appropriate authentication. If the person(s) responsible had cut the forms in half rather than torn them, it would have been much more difficult to tell whether there had been any interference. Plainly, there had, as when I tried to piece them together they failed to match up.

Further investigations into Labour clubs and trade union branches showed a discrepancy between their decisions and the ballots cast. Alas, it was difficult to apportion blame. Some argued that the only way in which it could have been done was for the secretary of the CLP to have opened sealed ballots and replaced them with more favourable votes. Whatever happened, it had been done so amateurishly that it was possible to prove that something untoward had taken place, and it was on these grounds that the endorsement of the winning candidate was made void.

That candidate was Brian Green, a St Helens councillor linked to the local clique around Gerry Caughey and to the Militant chair of Liverpool Garston, Jimmy Wilson, with whom he had worked at Smurfitts. They were both active members of SOGAT, but where Wilson was seen as a nuisance by the union's national officers, Green was looked upon more favourably. Indeed, when I came to report on the St Helens South selection to the NEC, the SOGAT representative, Ted O'Brien, an old-fashioned right-winger, championed Green's cause alongside the likes of Benn and Skinner. It was quite odd that he should find himself so aligned, but the machinations within SOGAT were completely beyond me. As for the St Helens South candidature, Gerry Bermingham was eventually reselected. Green returned to the headlines the following year when he and others were arrested in connection with a number of land deals.

The second of the contentious selections came in Birkenhead. Here, the sitting Labour MP, Frank Field (known locally to many people as 'Flaky Frank') had long had difficulties with certain sections of the constituency party, but he was now becoming increasingly aggressive towards people who had once supported him. As a result, he was faced with two rival candidates.

One of these was a known Militant, Cathy Wilson. She had previously challenged Field for the selection in 1986, three years after she had earned the dubious distinction of gaining the lowest ever vote for Labour in a general election – 1,828 votes and 2.4 per cent of the 75,347 cast in the Isle of Wight seat. The people of Cowes and the rest of the island were obviously not politically mature enough to follow her revolutionary path. Although she tried very hard to come across as a more reasonable person at the Birkenhead selection, Wilson was a repugnant individual who abused her disability – she had a false leg – as a way of scoring political points. For example, she would invariably complain at conference about disabled access if there was even the slightest fraction of difference in levels between the inside and outside of a door. This never stopped her, however, from dancing quite vigorously at social events. She was also extremely confrontational in the way she conducted herself. There was always something quite reprehensible about the sheer bile that spilled out of her against those who were not with her politically.

Field's other challenger was a TGWU official, Paul Davies. A singular man, Davies was not a member of any of the factions within his union or, indeed, within the wider movement, and his status as a political loner allowed him to gather support from many sources. More importantly, however, he was able to relate to the Birkenhead party – a party which, despite the allegations of Field and his supporters, was not in the clutches of Militant or the 'hard left'.

The hustings for the selection took place at Birkenhead Town Hall. It was a very testing and tempestuous experience, extremely difficult to monitor and control, but I would go so far as to say that no selection at that time was conducted as rigorously. Before the start of the meeting, I was in the back room with the three candidates and, in line with normal procedure, I asked them all to produce their membership and trade union cards. Frank could not produce a union card, and being so fastidious about the rules, I was inclined to rule him out. Of course, with TV cameras outside, I did not relish the idea. Still, Frank knew that he had to produce such documents and I was left with the impression that he was deliberately trying to provoke me. In the end, Davies stepped in and said to me 'If I produce written evidence that Frank is a fully paid-up union member, will you accept it?' I asked him how he could do this and he replied 'Easily – I'm his official'. Much to my amazement, Frank was actually a member of a docks branch of the TGWU in Birkenhead. There and then, Davies certified Frank's membership in writing, and, on that basis, I agreed to go ahead.

When we came to the count, which took place at a separate meeting, Field was ahead on the first ballot. As he had won less than 50 per cent of the vote, however, the rules of the party meant that we had to carry out a second count, redistributing the votes of the third-placed Wilson according to their second preferences. Of course, few, if any, of those who voted for Wilson opted for Field as their second choice, and Davies duly benefited from the redistribution of her votes, coming through as the clear victor. Frank, of course, saw this rather simplistically as a 'Trot take-over'. The truth of the matter, which I stand by to this day, is that Paul Davies won fairly and squarely under the rules of the Labour Party as they were at the time.

That night, Frank infuriated me as he was to infuriate many others down the years. Part of my job was to verify and announce the result to the three candidates before announcing it to the constituency's general committee. After I had done this, Frank was determined to charge out to the cameras and tell them how he had been ousted by the forces of darkness, and goodness knows what else. Keen to prevent him from storming out, I told him that at the very least he ought to thank his supporters, who were waiting upstairs. He agreed grudgingly, but his thanks were perfunctory and implied the threat of a by-election unless the Labour Party overturned his deselection. Of course, afterwards he went outside into the street and briefed the waiting media.

I spoke to the NEC on this case on the same day that I reported on St Helens

South. At the time it was rare that an officer of the party addressed the NEC on two separate issues, and this partly contributed to one of the few strained experiences I have ever had with Neil Kinnock. Having earned the opprobrium of sections of the left and old right over Brian Green, I was faced with an exasperated Neil over the situation in Birkenhead. His irritation was initially directed at Eddie Haigh, the chairman and TGWU representative on the NEC, who had given me the opportunity to speak a second time. I made clear my feelings, that Davies had been elected fairly and squarely, and that Birkenhead was in no way overrun with Militants. I was not prepared to tell lies for Frank Field or anyone. But then I faced Neil's wrath.

When we came to leave the meeting, Neil stood at the exit for about twenty seconds with his hand across the door handle, then turned back and said 'I'm sorry, Peter, if I came across a bit hard on you, but this is a tough one and there's no offence meant'. I understood perfectly what he meant. The last thing Neil wanted was Field, with his middle-England acceptability, upsetting the apple cart, and the leadership of the party was afraid of the threat of a by-election, with Frank standing as an independent. After all, he would have received the support of the three surrounding Tory MPs, to whom, politically at least, he was closer than to his neighbouring Labour candidate, Lol Duffy, in Wallasey (during the 1987 general election, Frank said that if he had lived in the constituency, he would not have voted for Duffy). He has always seen himself as bigger than the party that has given him his political opportunities.

There was no by-election in Birkenhead, but Frank remained determined to use all of the weapons available to him. He does appear to induce tremendous loyalty in some people, at the same time as he alienates others. A number of his friends contacted me, effectively to ask if I would change my version of the events surrounding his deselection. Naturally I refused, and to this day we have no more than a working relationship. He also made some unfortunate and intemperate comments about individuals in the Birkenhead CLP, including the chair, Sue Williams, who, having previously supported Field, had become tired of his behaviour. Eventually this took Frank to the civil courts and left him considerably out of pocket. As for the outcome of the selection – well, that was to rumble on for a good while longer, as we shall see later.

As if all this was not enough, Eric Heffer then announced his intention to stand down as MP for Liverpool Walton before the next general election. In

October 1989, at a public meeting within the constituency, Eric referred to the direction that the Labour Party was taking as 'SDP mark II'. (Heaven knows what he would have made of Tony Blair's government, and the influence of people like Roy Jenkins and Roger Liddle within party circles. I dare say it would have moved him to apoplexy.) Eric had his own view of the direction he thought the party should be taking. It was a very traditional one, and generally very honourable.

Much of Eric's disenchantment was directed at the leadership, yet I have often wondered how he would have turned out had he been elevated to such lofty heights himself. Laura Kirton, who had been his agent for many years, once told me that when Heffer had a junior ministerial post, he repudiated Marxism, telling her that it was the market that was dominant and we had to be realistic and pragmatic. Although he soon resigned from this, his only governmental post, it is possible that this statement was Eric trying to adapt to the realities of elected office within an economy where it was no longer appropriate to take a purist view. By November 1989, however, he had travelled full circle, and now considered himself 'out of step with Labour'. This reminded me of the story – an urban myth, no doubt – of the proud mother who, on watching her soldier son at his passing-out parade, observed 'Oh look, he's the only one marching in time'. Eric had become like that, marching to a different tune from the rest of the party. Of course, his whole political history consisted of being at odds with the party leadership; maybe that was why he wanted so much to be part of it.

I had heard that he was thinking about stepping down, but I was still taken aback. Eric had never struck me as the retiring type; I thought that he would go on and on until he died in office (which, of course, he did, albeit rather sooner than anticipated). Once his thoughts became public knowledge, however, tongues started wagging over who would be his potential successor. As a member of another Liverpool constituency, I was not there to witness Eric announce his retirement, unlike Gary Booth:

> It was in the backroom of the Black Horse pub, and when he announced it, I passed a little note to Mike Carr, who was secretary, saying 'What the effing hell are we going to do now?' He wrote on the back 'We'll go for a pint – the way we always do'.

I heard about Heffer's announcement the following morning. It was a Saturday, and later that day, just before midnight, I was telephoned by Laura Kirton, who in her own inimitable way said: 'Peter, you know Heffer's standing down. Well, we [i.e. Laura and her old comrade, Winnie Hesford] have been thinking about this and we think that you ought to stand as his successor'. I was, to put it mildly, stunned. The last place where I ever thought I would be asked to stand for Parliament was Walton. I told her that I would think about it, said goodnight and put the telephone down. Then something clicked. Some months before, Laura and Winnie had turned up unannounced at my house. Along with Bernie and the kids, I entertained them, sitting and chatting for several hours. After they had left, we could not help but think that they had been running their eye over us for some reason. With Laura's phone call, I now realised that they had foreseen, well ahead of time, that Eric was going to stand down.

I still had a job to do for the party, of course. Across the north west, many more selection processes were at full throttle, and the six Liverpool seats still remained to be contested. I looked for advice to Mike Carr and Sean Hughes. Sean, in particular, was typically direct: 'Peter, if you get the opportunity, go for it. I'll give you my full encouragement and support.' Still unsure, I spoke to Neil Kinnock's right-hand man, Charles Clarke; both he and Neil showed little enthusiasm for me standing. They had a wider view of my role in the run up to the next general election, which was to return a load of north west marginals to the Labour Party (there was no expectation then of a by-election). I dwelt on the matter for some time before finally taking Sean's advice and 'going for it'. It was not best received in some quarters, and at least one person pointed out that should I fail, I would be a busted flush politically.

As Mike Carr was being pressed by his own union and other members of the Walton party to stand, we agreed early on in the process that we would have an informal joint ticket, to try and encourage our respective supporters to put the other as second preference, thwarting any candidate who, while perhaps not Militant as such, could be seen as a fellow-traveller from slipping through the middle. There was to be a curious parallel years later with Tony Blair when I challenged Derek Foster for the position of Chief Whip. Tony asked me if I thought I could win it and I said, 'Well I don't know but myself and Dick Caborn could take enough votes to render Foster's position untenable'. (That was the object of the exercise: to replace the Chief Whip and change the culture in the Whips' Office, which at that stage was ill-suited to the demands of the Labour Party going into office.)

December saw speculation within the local media about potential prospective parliamentary candidates. By this stage, both I and Mike had been linked with the Walton seat, but so were the Militants Lesley Mahmood and Cathy Wilson, council leader Keva Coombes, and one Reg Race, an associate of Heffer's who had previously been an MP but was now best known for being part of the trendy left set in London. Race's inclusion arose from Heffer's own arrogant thinking that he could decide who his successor should be. Perhaps he saw it as a way of repaying Race for his support in the 1983 leadership contest against Neil Kinnock, during which he had penned an article for *London Labour Briefing* entitled 'Heffer's the one!', he had presented Heffer as a tower of virtue, describing him as 'the only candidate who can command the trust and respect of the party'.[109] As it turned out, Heffer was not 'the one' to lead the Labour Party, but then neither was Race the one to represent Liverpool Walton. One other person tipped as a potential candidate for the seat was Frank Mills, a suggestion that struck me as most bizarre. Still, it probably inspired him to dust down the suits he had worn a few years earlier when accompanying Mulhearn and Hatton in front of the cameras.

At the end of year, Liverpool's civic and political life lost another bridge to saner times, with the death of Harry Livermore. The legal partner of Sydney Silverman MP, whose private member's bill in 1965 had led to the abolition of the death penalty, Livermore was not only a former Labour councillor in the city, but also one of the last of a generation of Jewish Labour representatives – a generation that included such luminaries as Ian Levin, Louis Caplin, Ben Shaw and Frank Gaier. Along with many others, they had provided a dimension to party circles in Liverpool that is sorely missed to this day. In one sense, their departure highlighted the final migration of many within the Jewish community away from Liverpool to more economically active areas. In another, it illustrated the drift away from Labour, individually and collectively, of a successful section of the local population.

1990 started, entirely consistently with previous years, with controversy surrounding two memoranda sent by Keith Hackett to Jim Burns, the city's Director of Housing. In the first, Hackett referred to the £23m rents debt as 'fucking appalling', adding 'Get the department's act together. The District Auditor is watching us – so now I'm watching you!'[110] When Burns complained, Hackett sent him a response that included the comment 'Fuck off, Jim!'[111] Unlike the Paul Orrs of this world, for whom expletives are part of their everyday language ('George Knibb's not a bad feller, but politically he's a fucking idiot'), swearing never struck me as being Keith's natural way of

expressing himself. It was certainly not the way to express oneself in a formal relationship with a senior officer of the council. The whole incident contributed heavily towards Burns taking early retirement. Upon choosing to
do so, he was not forgotten by the chair of Housing, George Knibb, who back
in the summer of 1988 had laid down the terms of their relationship:

> It's all right sacking people but you've got to remember that they have
> families. To cut a long story short, I got him a package where I said that
> he could be our contact on the National Institute of Housing at a time
> when he was taking over as president. I said 'Jim, we'll pay you x amount
> a year, but what you can't afford to do is go and criticise anybody in the
> Labour Party because they'll want the deal withdrawn'. He said 'Oh no,
> that's great. Thanks for all you've done for me', and we shook hands.

That George refers to Burns's 'sacking', and that the council was prepared to
sanction a pay-off suggests that there was more to this than met the eye.
The trouble with such 'arrangements' is that other than a very few who are
intimately involved, no-one ever gets to know what has really gone on. There
are many questions to be asked of councillor–officer relationships. Some are
made in heaven, others in hell. When the relationships break down, it is not
unusual for an 'accommodation' to be found between the two sides, even
when serious allegations have been made. Often, this is to maintain the integrity of the council concerned, or of a department within it. On other occasions the settlement is based on a need for mutual protection in what is, at
the very least, an embarrassing situation; the *quid pro quo* is a pay-off of
some kind in return for silence. What really happened with Jim Burns never
leaked outside the ranks of senior councillors and senior officers.

As for Hackett, he was fast becoming a caricature of himself, what he saw
as the rebellious, 'couldn't care less' type of councillor, and his rather choice
comments to Burns were not untypical of those he was making elsewhere at
this time. During one lengthy budget debate at the Town Hall, he was forced
to apologise to the Liberal Democrats for accusing them of being so bankrupt
of ideas that they were prepared 'to sell their bodies on Lime Street in order
to gain power'. On another occasion, he told them that they reminded him of
those who 'sniffed bicycle seats'. Then there was the infamous monitoring
meeting, at which leading councillors and council officers were discussing
spending targets, when Hackett replied to a request for more dusters with
'What's the matter with old shirts?', and to another for more toilet rolls with
'Why not use the *Daily Post*? I always do.'[112] All of this reflected his glib and

superficial side, but at other times, when he chose to be serious about his responsibilities, he would come across as neurotic. In doing so, he would draw parallels with Tony Byrne, as Alan Dean observed:

> Keith started to develop his own unique style. His was not the same as Tony Byrne but, in some ways, he was as single-minded and believed what he believed was the right thing. I think Keith was a little more open – things certainly weren't happening in the way they were with Byrne and Hatton. But Keith was determined to force through what he reckoned the group should be doing.

As able as he was, Hackett spent much of his time trotting out the tired old cliché of 'no cuts in jobs and services'. The truth of the matter, however, is that he did make cuts; and party to those cuts was his deputy at Finance and Policy, Tony Jennings. Hackett was one of those who was trying to effect what he saw as a rapprochement with Jennings and others within the Broad Left. With hindsight, I should perhaps have been more tolerant of that, and tried to help to bring them back on board, but suspicions were extremely high about the extent to which Militant was influencing that caucus. There was certainly no adherence on the part of many within the Broad Left to the rules and the spirit of the party, that once a decision has been made collectively it is supported by all. Instead, they were determined to press forward with their own agenda.

January also saw calls for the removal of the Labour group whip from Cllr John Livingstone. He was married to Bernie's aunt, so I knew him reasonably well. He was a very eccentric character; a staunch traditionalist Catholic, he was, and remains, true to an earlier age of Liverpool politics, and was wont to make many issues a matter of conscience. Having agonised over such matters, Livingstone would become genuinely shocked that others did not share his views. Whenever the opportunity arose, or more usually at his own behest, he would claim similarities between the Holocaust and the issue of abortion; the letter editors of the local papers appeared more than willing to oblige him on this topic. (He was, and remains, equally serious about his other hobby horse, Liverpool's naval history.) On this occasion, however, he was doing his best to be ecumenical, and had broken the group whip to oppose the closure of a Protestant Church School in his ward, Vauxhall.

In truth, this was the least of the group's worries. Towards the end of the month a great rumpus broke out regarding the appointment of two European

## Left Behind: Lessons from Labour's heartland

Liaison Officers, positions jointly funded by the Merseyside West MEP, Ken Stewart, and the council. It was not the nature of the appointments, as such, that caused the bother (although the actual job description was incredibly naive, referring only to one task – 'to maximise the funding potential for the city'), but the fact that the 'successful' applicants were Tony Mulhearn and Frank Mills. Something very strange must have transpired if this pair could even have been considered for these important posts, let alone offered them. The fact that Stewart had conducted the interviews alone apart from the company of Tony Jennings, the council's 'observer', did not make me feel any better about the matter. Mulhearn and Mills certainly had little if any experience of the European institutions, and even less knowledge of the economics of the relationship between a region like Merseyside and the European Community. Moreover, the languages that were required to adequately fulfil such roles were not those of Militant-variant Trot-speak or workerist gibberish, for which the two of them were renowned. Maybe they thought that their familiarity with 'Spanish practices' would stand them in good stead.

Naturally, questions were asked. David Alton, Liverpool's one non-Labour MP, saw it as a matter of sufficient concern that he put down an Early Day Motion in the House of Commons, and the national and local media had a field day over what they saw as 'jobs for the boys'. I myself went to see Ken Stewart at his home about the whole sorry mess. He tried to argue that he had been forced to accept them in the posts, but would not say by whom. Then he denied he wanted them anyway. As usual, I was not able to get a straightforward answer from Ken. I suspected that he had not thought things through, and had happily gone along with what was being put to him by others. Besides, 'jobs for the boys' was second nature to the only form of politics he had ever known or understood.

Many members of the Labour group also suspected that something untoward had gone on, and when the vote to sanction the appointments was placed before them, exactly half of those present expressed their disapproval. Thus the decision was left to the casting vote of Keva Coombes. Faced with this stark division of those in his charge, he voted in favour of Mulhearn and Mills, and booked his seat on the next train to political oblivion. Although this meant that the group effectively sanctioned the appointments, much disquiet remained amongst those who had voted against the decision. Breaches of council policy on advertising and interviewing for new posts had taken place, most notably in the lack of a trade union observer at the interviews, and pressure mounted for the decision to be voted down at the full council meeting, which was to take place a few days later. Not everyone was keen on breaching the rule that the discipline of the group should stand in the chamber. Twenty-three Labour councillors, however, did opt to vote with the opposition parties to scupper Mulhearn's and Mills's appointments, thereby ensuring that the posts were re-advertised in line with the council's practices and were filled by more suitable individuals.

This was not the end of the matter. Leaflets were put out by each side, detailing what they believed had occurred in fine, and in the case of the Broad Left inaccurate, detail. I myself was wrongly accused of having told Andy Pink, Public Relations Officer for the council and an associate of the Broad Left caucus, that I was attending the council meeting 'to see that they [i.e. the twenty-three] do a proper job'. One of the more bizarre outcomes of the whole affair was the letter sent to the *Liverpool Echo*, which not only defended the appointments of Mulhearn and Mills but also broached the subject of socialism and the Labour Party. This read:

> I would like to say to those twenty-four Labour councillors, including Peter Kilfoyle [sic], I am disgusted that members of a socialist working-class party would actually vote with Liberals and Tories just to keep Tony Mulhearn and Frank Mills from a job which they applied for along with twenty-eight other applicants. They were chosen for the short list with six in all, and finally succeeded, no objection was raised from these twenty-four councillors until it was known who were the successful candidates. If this is not a black list, or a witch-hunt, I don't know what it is. Maybe the twenty-four don't agree with Tony's good old fashioned socialist politics, what the Labour Party should be all about, 'True Socialism', but at least, since they were told they had the jobs, they should have been allowed a chance to show them, and the people of Merseyside, what they could have achieved if given half a chance.[113]

Who was the author of this clarion call for fairness? Why, of course, 'Mrs Mulhearn' (wife of Tony).

In the meantime, I had begun to conduct the selection procedures for the five Liverpool seats with sitting Labour MPs. As it was in many ways the most problematic, I timed the West Derby selection so that we could get it out of the way first. Here, Bob Wareing was up against Tony Jennings. Other candidates had been flagged up, but with Jennings so closely identified as an ally of Militant in the constituency, this contest was always destined to be a two-horse race. Roy Gladden, who had nominations from his ward party and trade union branch to stand against Wareing, explains:

> I went to see Bob and said 'Look, you know what's happening, and I'm going to decline these nominations because it will split the vote and Jennings will come through'.

Such support as there was for Wareing was less a reflection of a belief in his abilities than it was of people's opinions of Jennings, a bombastic man who believed he had a divine right to become MP for West Derby. Consequently, Bob won the nomination by a 60–40 percentage. Still, contrary to what he had said before and during the selection process, little was to change in his attitude towards his patch, as Roy Gladden observes:

> Bob went and made a number of promises and guarantees about setting up a constituency office but reneged on every one.

To casual or external observers, the selection process for Liverpool Garston would have appeared rather straightforward. Alas, it was not. Aside from the promises that had been made to MEP Les Huckfield, who by this stage was embroiled in a fraud inquiry, there was some contention over whether or not Loyden had indicated to key local Militants that he would stand down. That he did not, put a strain upon his relationship with the established hard core who ran the show in Garston, highlighting how Militant would turn on anyone who went against their wishes.

When I arrived to conduct the count at Woolton Labour Club, nobody else had turned up. The officers of the constituency had obviously not informed the membership, nor the rest of the executive, that the count was taking place that night. I immediately set about tracking down Loyden. When I found him – he was chairing a DLP meeting (I should have guessed!) – I discovered that they had not even bothered to let him know. It was one of the few times that he let his guard slip about his relationship with the Garston party, indicating that they had deliberately avoided telling him because they were not happy about him standing again. I also tracked down Bob Currey, the treasurer, a Militant sympathiser and Mulhearn's brother-in-law, and a powerful influence behind the scenes. Currey turned up at Woolton Labour Club and, in time, we located Steve Vose, the secretary. In the meantime, I had rung up Joyce Gould from the bar telephone and told her that I was determined to go ahead come what may. Even if nobody else turned up, I would announce the result to myself. As it was, I did it there and then before

Currey and Vose. The result was a foregone conclusion, of course, in that Loyden won, but more than anything the whole incident revealed how far things had deteriorated between him and Militant.

The first of the openly contentious selections was Broadgreen, where Militant MP Terry Fields was seeking to stay on as the candidate. The previous summer I had spoken to Mick Groves, of the Liverpool folk group The Spinners, to see if he fancied standing against Fields. In addition to Mick's profile as a show-business figure, his standing for selection would serve a number of other purposes. Most obviously, it would test the fair-mindedness of Fields and his supporters towards democratic challenge. They were quite shocked that he had been challenged and went overboard to ensure his reselection, which they managed. Even so, I considered the whole exercise a success, as it revealed publicly the extent of opposition to Fields within his own backyard.

In Riverside, Bob Parry was reselected as the candidate on the usual basis that there was no agreement on an alternative. With 55 per cent of the vote, he beat Coombes, who had more or less shot his chances by supporting Mulhearn and Mills in the Euro affair, and Martha Osamor, a councillor in the London borough of Haringey. Parry's post-selection comments to the local media revealed not only his relief at winning but also his lack of grace towards at least one of those who had challenged him: 'I was confident, but I didn't think it would be this decisive. Keva Coombes said it was now or never for him in Parliament. It will be seven years until his chance comes around again. That's it for him. Now he wants to sort out the city or resign.'[114] Naturally, there is no love lost the other way. Asked to comment on the quality of Liverpool's MPs at this time, Coombes responded caustically:

> They thought that they were hugely personally popular, and that the 28,000 people who had voted Labour all knew Bob Parry – 27,000 of whom were his brother ... Say you were trying to stop British Home Stores from closing, you ought to be able to get the Chief Executive of the council, the MP and the Chamber of Commerce people together for lunch in the Town Hall. You couldn't do that with Bob Parry.

Interestingly, reports were made that TGWU officials had threatened to discipline branches that wanted to support Coombes instead of Parry. I certainly had a phone call from Bobby Owens, the union's regional secretary, who sought my advice on how they could get their branches to ensure that they went with the national union's choice rather than their own. I pointed out that this was an internal matter for their organisation, and it was not for me to pass judgement. However, I did add that if a branch had arrived at a choice with which the union had not agreed then he must remember that it was the branch that was affiliated and not the union centrally, and that the vote was therefore legitimate. Throughout this telephone conversation, I could hear Parry screaming and shouting in the background, and generally creating mayhem.

Finally there was the big one – Walton. Here, more than fifty applications were received for the seat, including my own and one from Heffer's chosen successor, Reg Race. If ever evidence were needed that Eric had lost touch with the realities of his constituency, then this was it. What I remember most about Race is that he turned up to a nomination meeting wearing a reefer jacket, scruffy cords and an open-necked shirt and carrying his sandwiches in a butty-bag. This is not to say that you have to be a tailor's dummy, but there is an expression in Liverpool, 'fur coat and no knickers', which, while for some people it signifies a loose woman, has another meaning: that even if a person has nothing, they will at least try to show themselves at their best. Race was obviously unfamiliar with this side of Liverpool life, so I approached him on the subject. Gently, I tried to point out to him that people in Liverpool expected their representatives to look smart, and that Walton in particular was not some trendy part of London where being prolier-than-thou would wash with the membership. Race listened to what I was saying, but when I had finished gave me a look as if I were a piece of dirt and quickly moved away. As it turned out, he only received one nomination, ironically, from Jane Kennedy's old branch of NUPE:

> I'd moved to Oldham by then, as a full-time regional official, and I was no longer connected with the branch. Apart from my influence, the branch was not particularly politically aware. They were a lovely bunch of people, but there was a naivety. Reg Race was NUPE, and before anyone else they would have nominated a NUPE person.

Race failed to make the final short-list. As well as myself and Mike Carr, three other candidates were chosen to contest the selection – Lesley Mahmood, Militant's rising star at the council, Kevin Coyne, the head of the trade union centre, and Ray Williams, an NGA official and member of Warbreck ward.

Once the real contest was under way, I became even more aware of the double jeopardy in which I was placed. I had already been forewarned that if I failed to secure the selection then I was finished in politics. At the same time, I was unable to operate in the same way as the other candidates, lest I stood accused of being in breach of the rules governing the selection procedure. Indeed, I was even more circumspect because of Heffer's determination to stop me in my tracks, something that seemed to intensify after Race's failure. The constituency chairman, Jimmy Rutledge, actually came across a sheaf of photocopied documents raising questions over the selection procedure, with a sheet of Heffer's House of Commons notepaper on the front; the content made it more than apparent that he was doing all he could to scupper my selection. When Rutledge sent Eric a lengthy and articulate defence of what had so far taken place in Walton, he accused him of not being the true author of the piece, implying that I had written it for him.

I was constantly on my guard. On one occasion when I was out with two prominent members of the constituency and they raised questions about the selection, I refused to discuss it with them because the slightest foot I put out of bounds could be misinterpreted as canvassing for votes, something that was not allowed outside nomination meetings. On another occasion, I was in a street in Fazakerley with 'forty-sevener' Alec Gamble, when he casually spoke to a couple of elderly members. I did not initially realise they were members, and Alec called me over, saying 'I just want you to say hello to ...' I did so, but shortly after was charged with canvassing their votes.

If this was farcical, then some of the nomination meetings I attended were beyond belief. Fazakerley ward invited every person who had sent in a CV, and so many turned up that they only had five minutes each to speak. This was hardly fair for those such as Don Touhig (now MP for Islwyn, Neil Kinnock's old seat), who had to travel all the way up from South Wales.

As it turned out, I actually won that nomination, primarily through a straightforward numbers game. Of a different order, however, was the nomination meeting for the affiliated GMB Branch 5, the most notorious trade union branch in the country. They wanted to give the impression of being fair to all candidates, and I was duly invited for an interview. Presumably they never dreamt that I would turn up, but I was determined to go anywhere regardless of what had gone before. When I arrived, Ian Lowes and Steve Vose, as branch officers, both tried to persuade me not to go in – I think they thought it might get out of hand. They insisted that I had made my point; I insisted on being heard. It was not a pleasant meeting. I said my piece and, despite some rather nasty abuse, tried to respond to their charges from the floor. Needless to say, the nomination went to Mahmood, but I like to think that I won some respect from Branch 5, if only for turning up and facing them down.

In terms of overall nominations, it was apparent by now that a three-line whip had been put on Militant members not only to support Mahmood but also to maximise the support of others. The TGWU had thrown its weight behind Mike, and were less than pleased by the 'lone ranger' intervention of Coyne, a member of the TGWU national executive, who managed to dent Mike's campaign by picking up support from a handful of branches. Ray Williams, meanwhile, gave the impression that he was there to soak up any floating votes, both from union branches and individual members, but I saw his role as more clandestine (he was, after all, an associate of Mulhearn and Jimmy Wilson). Not to put too fine a point on it, he was a spoiler, acting in cahoots with Mahmood in order to deprive Mike and me of uncommitted votes. As for my support, I could do little more than appear formally at nomination and selection meetings, with my fortunes dependent on the hard work of Laura Kirton, aided and abetted by Winnie Hesford and other supportive friends. Laura revealed why she had been Heffer's agent for so long and was admired so much by her former colleagues in Militant. She was a brilliant organiser, pulling in votes which I did not know existed. But she was also very hard to please, and I remember her telling me how she did not trust Mike because he had once taken her flowers when she was ill at home!

Chris Roberts, the North Wales Regional Organiser, came over to oversee the process and the final hustings. This took place at the TGWU offices in Liverpool city centre, after which the votes were cast. All of the candidates spoke, except Williams, who pleaded an injured back for his absence, adding further to my suspicions. I only recollect two questions. One was an innocuous one from Mahmood's partner, whom I had never seen before and was never to see again. The other was from Harry Richie, a long-standing member of the constituency and an official of the GMB. (He was subsequently my agent in the 1992 general election; an enigmatic individual, he could be alternatively sarcastic and ingratiating.) He asked me about disarmament, and I answered evasively with references to the Lucas Shop Stewards' 'Alternative Economic Strategy' (to convert arms industries to peaceful purposes). Nevertheless, he seemed satisfied with the reply. Afterwards, Laura commented that my performance on the hustings had been good, before adding 'but so had Mahmood's'.

The count itself took place within Walton, at the SOGAT offices – the same offices where Hamilton had been ousted as leader in late 1986. Gary Booth recalls the atmosphere:

> It was the worst meeting that I have ever attended, a real battle royal. Everyone did the business in terms of getting their people there, something that was reflected in the closeness of the result. But the meeting was absolutely horrendous. People were shouting and bawling, and moving this and moving that. I had a blinding headache. Militant knew the writing was on the wall for them and they were convinced that they were getting stitched up. But at the end of the day there was no stitching up. That selection was won fairly and squarely by Peter through good organisation.

After the first round of voting, myself and Mahmood went through as the two candidates with the highest number of first preferences. Then after the redistribution of second preferences, I ended up just fractionally ahead in both the individual members' section and the trade union and affiliated societies' section. It was a very narrow win – 50.7 per cent to 46.5 per cent – but it was a win, and that was all that mattered. When the result was announced, the first person to congratulate me, warmly and well, was Mike. It was the sign of a true friend, and I like to think that I would have wished him equally well had he been the victor. All in all, it was a great night and I will always be extremely grateful to those who lent me their support. I dread to think what would have happened had Mahmood won. As I said at the time, it was a victory for common sense.

Of course, winning the selection was only the start of my problems. Initially, there was a flood of objections, saying that this or that had been done wrongly, all of which fell on stony ground. More serious, however, was the argument, originating from Heffer, that I should not have stood because as an officer of the party, I had gained an advantage within the CLP. In itself, this argument was debatable – the fact that my name was mud in some circles in Liverpool meant that the disadvantages far outweighed the advantages. Heffer was also a hypocrite. He himself had been instrumental in changing the rules of the party so that one of his great friends, Max Madden, who had been Labour's Director of Communications, could be selected to stand in Bradford. When I challenged Eric on this, he responded by saying that Madden was not active 'on the ground'. This was splitting hairs. As far as I was concerned, Madden, as Director of Communications, had had every opportunity to project himself for a whole host of seats. For the time being, however, Eric and I agreed to disagree (sad as it may seem, there really was no common ground), and I turned my attentions back to the tasks at hand, having had my selection for Walton endorsed by the NEC.

# 11  Divided they stand

In the aftermath of the selection drama at Walton, local attention turned to the poll tax. Liverpool City Council had yet to vote on the implementation of the tax, and everyone knew that when the decision was finally taken it would open up a whole new can of worms. The politics of the poll tax clearly reflected the polarised views held of Margaret Thatcher and her government, and convincing the more temperamental minds of the need to think of the long term was never going to be easy.

A couple of days before the vote, a meeting of the Labour group, which Joyce Gould and I attended, saw the Broad Left caucus defeated on non-implementation by 27 votes to 21, with two abstentions. When it came to the full council, I actually telephoned an instruction through to the group on behalf of the national party that all Labour councillors should vote in line with national policy. Nevertheless, eighteen of them ignored this instruction and voted against implementing the tax – sixteen of the twenty-one who had opposed it at the group meeting plus the two abstainees. The remaining five – Tony Jennings, John Brazier, Frank Ruse, James Doyle and George Allen – were not present in the chamber. It was no coincidence that they were all up for election in May.

It was also suggested that while Keva Coombes was speaking at length on the issue inside the chamber, the rebels had had their own meeting, at which they were addressed by Mulhearn. Whether this was true or not, I do not know; nor do I know what advice Mulhearn might have given. What I do know is that the vote itself set the course for another huge split within the Labour group. Eighteen years on from the rupture that followed the vote on implementation of the Housing Finance Act, little had changed. This time though, it was not Loyden or Mooney arguing that it was a matter of principle but Mahmood, who told the local media: 'Sometimes you have to accept that things are bigger than me or my position'.[115] Just like before, this was patently misleading. The split was not a matter of principle. It was a purely political move aimed at gaining control of the group and the council.

Having suspended sixteen of the 'rebels', Joyce Gould came back up to

## Left Behind: Lessons from Labour's heartland

Liverpool from London and together we met with the remaining members of the group. The meeting was geared towards fortifying them in what they needed to do to run the council as effectively as possible. There was, of course, some sadness about the suspensions, but this was outweighed by a growing understanding that the group, and indeed Liverpool, could not expect to exist in a legal and political vacuum. It was also made clear to the city's Labour leaders that they should expect the support of the 'rebels' in votes in the council chamber, as the latter had only been suspended from the group, not the party.

One direct consequence of the suspensions was the way in which it undermined Coombes. Since taking over as leader in the autumn of 1987, he had believed that he could straddle the divide between the progressives and the Broad Left by playing one off against the other. With sixteen of the Broad Left out of the equation, he was left with a rump, run by Jennings, and the 'Sainsbury set' as his principal supporters. The vast majority of the group, meanwhile, had begun to see him for what he really was – a weak man who had failed to impose himself authoritatively, and was far too devious in his concept of leadership. His position on the poll tax was a key issue, of course, but it was the last in a long line, including the drink-driving farce and the Euro jobs affair. The real reasons behind Coombes' involvement in each of these remained unknown, and left most councillors with deep suspicions of the man and his motives. His time was almost up.

Despite general misgivings, Labour actually made eleven gains at the May 1990 local elections. Amongst these eleven and the other new faces who appeared in safe seats, seven immediately aligned themselves with the Broad Left. The most vocal was Militant Cathy Wilson, twice challenger of Frank Field in Birkenhead, the holder of Labour's lowest ever vote in a general election, and one of the most vitriolic people I have ever had the displeasure to meet. There was also Susan Hogan in Picton, who reminded me of a painted kewpie doll with her big red cheeks, and the permanently angry Kevin Williams in Old Swan who, whilst never a Militant, saw himself as anti- the establishment, whoever and whatever that might be. Finally, there was Andy Duckworth in Arundel. He had gone directly from being an actual student politician to being a metaphorical one. Still, it surprised me that he joined the Broad Left as I had always presumed that he had a bit more sense. As a student union politician at Liverpool University, he had always seemed more sensible than to chance the problematical political path of illegality.

The elections also saw the arrival of a number of councillors who did not align themselves with the Broad Left and remained around for some time. One of these was a future leader of the council, Frank Prendergast. I had not been aware of Frank before, but he took over a safe seat in Breckfield ward, and within four years became leader of the Labour group. Tony Concepcion, meanwhile, took Broadgreen from the Liberal Democrats. A quiet, no-nonsense kind of guy, who worked at the Vauxhall car-plant in Ellesmere Port, Tony was to prove a very able councillor and eventually became chair of the Planning Committee.

The politics of the new intake was a fair reflection of those of the existing Labour councillors (the suspended included). Little changed immediately in the overall politics of the group and, by extension, the administration. But change was afoot. Personal problems had been mounting for Coombes. The local firm of solicitors where he worked had become disenchanted with the time that he was taking off to concentrate on council duties. After reducing his pay in April, they effectively sacked him in May, though they offered him a part-time post in their office in Stockport. This was ironic enough, given that it happened at a time when Coombes was expected to lose the leadership, but I myself thought that there was more to it; after all, it would have been surprising if the many unsavoury stories doing the rounds at that time in any way impressed his employers. Whatever, wheels had been put in motion, as Harry Rimmer recounts in fine detail:

Much to my surprise – and I was actually genuinely shocked – the front page of the *Echo* carried a headline, 'Challenge to Keva Coombes' leadership'. It was by Chris Walker who I knew quite well. It more or less said that there was a group within the Labour group who were going to challenge Keva, and the person they were going to put up against him was me … I walked into Alan Dean's office, where a number of people were sat around. Alan was sitting at his desk down the top end and Keva was also in there. There was a hubbub of conversation which diminished as I walked in. I went up to Alan, who was still the deputy leader, put the paper on his desk and said 'What the fucking hell is going on?' He said 'I don't know anything about it'. I said 'Nor do I but I'm going to find out'. I never said anything to Keva because, knowing how he worked, I half-suspected that it was him who'd done it in order to get people's tongues wagging, to make alliances. So I went down to the *Echo* to see Chris Walker. I said 'Chris, I know you won't tell me where you got this information from, but will you take it from me that I am not involved in any plot to unseat

> Keva. I don't know of one if it exists at all – no-one has consulted me. And
> I will not stand against him.

As it turned out, however, Harry did stand. Approaching the group AGM,
where leadership and committee positions would be voted upon, the wish to
replace Coombes became more urgent. At a caucus of the progressives, a couple of other names were thrown in the ring, but they either lacked support or
were unwilling to take on the post. By the end of the meeting, it became evident to Harry that he would have to eat his words:

> They were pressing me to stand. I kept on saying no, and I remember
> Dawn Booth getting quite ratty. I said 'If you're looking for someone to
> stand against Keva, then the logical one is Alan Dean'. Alan bluntly re-
> fused, and when asked why said that he didn't feel ready to do the job. He
> said that he had learnt in three and a half years as deputy that leading
> Liverpool was one of the highest profile political jobs that anyone could
> have anywhere in the country. At least he was being honest. However, the
> overwhelming feeling around the room was that I should. So I said 'All
> right then, you've had one go with me as leader, now you want me to have
> another, but bear in mind that I'm just exactly the same now as I was
> then. Any time that you don't agree with me in sufficient numbers, I'm off.
> That's the way it will be.' So, I reluctantly took it.

I was also surprised by Dean's reluctance to take on the leadership once
again. Whereas on the first occasion he alleged being scared off by an anonymous telephone caller, Alan's reasons for not doing so the second time
around appear to have been less troubled:

> Whether people liked Harry or not, the things he was doing and the sup-
> port that he got – his connections with people in the business community
> and the churches … I didn't think that he was a good leader, but he was a
> good front person. He was everyone's favourite uncle and that came
> across well.

Coombes's removal as leader occurred at a meeting of the Labour group that
was remarkable for a whole host of reasons. On entering the meeting in the
Municipal Annexe, I literally had to fight my way through a lobby by Militant and the Anti-Poll Tax Federation (the differences between them were
merely the banners they waved), as well as members of 'the forty-seven' and
those suspended from the group. Not only was I spat at, but at least two people aimed blows at me, one with a fist, the other with a knee.

Shortly after the start of the meeting, the remnants of the Broad Left (those who had not been expelled) and the new councillors who had aligned with that caucus decided that they were having nothing to do with the vote and staged a walk-out. This was obviously a pre-planned gesture on their part, geared mainly towards a show of solidarity with those massed outside the building. To be honest, they behaved like children at a birthday party, crying because they were not the centre of attention, and then leaving, taking home the presents they had brought with them – an embarrassing moment, but hardly the end of the party. Once they had departed, the thirty-seven councillors who remained voted thirty-two to five against keeping Coombes on as leader, and elected Rimmer in his place. It was a clear decision, and one that Keva had long expected:

> When the party chose to suspend a large number of the Labour group, my moment had gone and that was it – game, set and match.

Still, his response was not the most dignified on record. I was with him up on the top table, and he left his seat literally to cower and moan in the corner in a semi-foetal position, behaving as if he was about to have a breakdown. Afterwards, Keva referred to his removal as 'a blood-letting', called Harry 'a liar' and said that he had been 'politically mugged'. Even if the latter was true, his assailants would have found little on the man worth taking.

It was also at this meeting that Keith Hackett and others from the 'Sainsbury set' were removed from the chairs of key committees. Aside from his closeness to Coombes and his colourful, if somewhat contrived, language, Hackett had long been alienating those who believed him to be a competent chair of Finance and Policy. Much of this had to do with the policy of selling assets that had been thought up the previous summer, which by May 1990 was a cause for contention. Harry Rimmer, in particular, felt let down by Hackett:

> We had the last caucus before the finance committee before we went in to get approval on the proposed budget. There was a bit of an argument because, to balance that year, it relied on sixty million of capital receipts. Keith Hackett said that it was a budget we could be proud of, and I said to him 'I'm disgusted with you'. He asked why, and I said 'I can't see anything in it at all to be proud of'. He said 'Well, if it gets us through the year …', and I said 'But it's not just a case of getting us through the year. It's about starting to deal with the underlying financial situation. I doubt that you can get the money in one year anyway. So we're going to be faced

with a succession of financial crises throughout the year. So I'm not proud of you, mate.' He just shrugged his shoulders and walked away.

Hackett's removal as chair of Finance and Policy led to some extraordinary scenes. He screamed at me, accusing me of political corruption. He then insisted that the media be brought in so that he could repeat the accusation. What I was supposed to have done was unclear. I was applying the rules and constitution of the party, following the instructions of the NEC, which between annual conferences was the ultimate arbiter of how the party should conduct itself. Yet in his tirade, Hackett spoke of 'careerists'. With hindsight, this was an interesting label to pin on me; neither Hackett nor his wife, Teresa Griffin (who would herself become a Labour councillor in Liverpool), were to do too badly over the years in consultancy (including giving advice on Objective 1 funding). I have never objected to either of them making their living in that way, but it seems to me that the expertise gleaned on the council and elsewhere has subsequently come in very useful. It ill behoved Keith to abuse me for maintaining the integrity of the party that had given him his career opportunities.

Spring saw a Labour council in Liverpool revert to having a Lord Mayor for the first time since 1983, when the post was abolished and a chair of the Council appointed instead. It was felt that reinstating the title would show how Liverpool was being brought back to normality. I have little time for pomp and ceremony, and certainly none for antiquated practices. I did, however, recognise how such gestures have a powerful impact on the perceptions of outsiders, something that was necessary if the city was to move out of its semi-permanent rut. This took on an added urgency with the publication of a survey, conducted at Reading University, into the relative economic well-being of cities across the European Community. Of 117, Liverpool was rated 114th – down fourteen places from 1980 and slipping further behind Glasgow, Hull, Newcastle, Sheffield and Sunderland, all of which had suffered the high tides of the early 1980s recession but had managed to stay afloat. All three of the places worse off than Liverpool – Seville, Cordoba and Malaga – were in southern Spain.

Spring also brought the death of Alan Roberts, MP for Bootle. Elected in 1983, Alan had served his constituents well and was expected to carry on for some time. However, he had become ill the previous year, and failed to recover. It was said at the time that Alan led a dissolute gay lifestyle, during which he had contracted the illness that led to his death (his partner was to die a week later). Whatever the truth of that, the fact that Alan, who was a Protestant and Mancunian, had been selected in Bootle in the first place was an incredible feat. Bootle was not only an indelibly Scouse seat, it also had a very strong Catholic orientation, illustrated by the long domination of the Mahon family over the constituency's politics. Simon Mahon, in particular, was a very well regarded member of the Catholic church in Bootle and beyond, and had had a Papal knighthood bestowed upon him. As it was, Alan had been selected as a result, once again, of the conflicting claims of internal candidates, coming through the middle as a compromise.

By 1990, by-elections were no longer local beauty contests but barometers of the respective national standing of the main political parties. Although the final say over the candidate lay in the hands of the local membership, it had become essential for the national party to put forward a short-list of high-calibre individuals. Too often, the media circus had descended upon a highly localised contest to highlight the shortcomings of less adequate candidates in a way that reflected badly on Labour nationally – as was learned at the by-election selections of Bob Gillespie, a SOGAT official, in Glasgow Govan, and of Peter Tatchell in Bermondsey. Labour lost both by-elections. Gillespie had come through the system as the favoured local son, but was hopelessly inadequate in an era when presentational skills were essential. Consequently, Jim Sillars took the seat for the SNP. In Tatchell's case, it was single-issue politics; he was, and remains, consumed with gay issues to the exclusion of all else. The filter of the NEC short-listing panel was accordingly instituted.

Rumours abounded that Coombes, who was still licking his multiple wounds from the Riverside selection and his removal as leader of Liverpool council, would seek the Bootle nomination. These proved to be hollow. What I most recall about the short-listing panel was the way in which people folded under the relentless questioning. Partly aimed at ensuring that individuals did not have any skeletons in their cupboards, it also served to see if they could stand up to the rigours of a daily press conference. One trade union official was so terrified by his panel interview that he passed out within a minute of the interview beginning. Naturally, he was not thought capable of surviving a by-election campaign, and went no further in politics. Four candidates did make the short-list: Mike Hall, who later became the MP for Warrington South, Josephine Farrington, now a Baroness in the Lords, Joe Benton, leader of the Labour group on Sefton Borough Council and the present MP for Bootle, and Mike Carr. The national party would have been proud of any of them, but in the end it was Mike who took the nomination.

## Left Behind: Lessons from Labour's heartland

On the night of Mike's selection, I went with him and Bob Lancaster to their local pub, the Melrose, otherwise known as the 'Smelly Melly'. With Mike and I now both on the verge of becoming MPs, Bob asked us what we thought he would get, and I remember putting on a rather straight face and saying, 'Well, Bob, maybe one of these days you'll get a Euro seat'. While Bob, who was the secretary of the Walton CLP, had never expressed any ambitions to become an MP, it had become increasingly the belief of a number of Walton members that Bob had hoped to succeed Heffer. It was to prove to be beyond his reach. At one constituency meeting, when another member criticised something minor Bob had done as secretary, he packed up all of his papers and in a fit of pique stormed out of the room, leaving the general committee with no correspondence, resolutions, or anything else. If this was evidence of how he could react to criticism, he could not expect to be taken seriously as a potential parliamentary candidate.

The actual by-election contest in Bootle was an extremely enjoyable experience – one could not ask for more suitable conditions. Not only was it one of the safest Labour seats in the country, but the weather was beautiful for the duration of the campaign. What made it even more satisfying was being the agent for Mike, a true friend for whom I was happy to do whatever I could to ensure his election. I certainly had not forgotten our understanding in Walton, nor the way in which he reacted to my success.

Although we were assured a victory in Bootle, at no point did we drop our guard and become complacent. Nevertheless, there were some interesting interludes, and to while away the long hours of tedium we ended up playing practical jokes on one another. George Howarth, the Knowsley North MP, was Mike's 'minder' and they spent a fair bit of time out on the road. As the agent, I tended to spend most of my time in the office, often with the late Roger Stott, MP for Wigan, who was there as the representative of Jack Cunningham, the party's campaign manager. One day, George and Mike decided to play a trick on Roger, and rang the office up. I answered the phone, instantly recognising George, who pretended to be from Roger's Wigan constituency and wanted to speak to him to ask why he was wasting his time at a by-election in Bootle. I passed him over to Roger who, having justified his position, soon became very irate as George continued his very effective impersonation of the Wigan accent. Eventually I cracked, at which point I heard George start to laugh, giving the game away to a rather bemused Roger. Occasions such as this allowed us all to relax the tension that always goes with an election.

Although Mike walked the seat, with a majority of well over 23,000, perhaps the most memorable outcome of this by-election was the performance of the SDP. Even though its candidate could call upon Eric Ogden, the former MP for Liverpool West Derby, to address the hustings, they were well and truly beaten into fifth place – not just behind Mike, the Liberal Democrats and the Tories, but also behind the Monster Raving Loony Party, whose ever-present Screaming Lord Sutch took nearly three times the SDP vote. Some commentators took this as a reflection of the attitudes of Bootle's constituents towards electoral politics. It certainly heralded the death-knell of the SDP; within ten days, its national committee voted to suspend its constitution. Five weeks after that, realising that his latest charade was coming to a close, David Owen announced – to an audience in New York, of all places – that he would step down as an MP. He was, however, to loiter arrogantly around the fringes of Westminster politics for some time further, and openly cast his support for the Conservatives at the 1992 general election, which moved one pithy soul to remark that every other party had had to put up with him, so he didn't see why they shouldn't.

While I was busy helping Mike secure Bootle for Labour, one resident of the borough was giving the party hierarchy particular cause for concern, becoming increasingly vituperative in his comments about the national party's stance on the poll tax and airing this on platform after platform. This, of course, was Terry Fields, the Militant MP for Liverpool Broadgreen, monotony personified. Although reselected by his CLP, the decision had yet to be confirmed by the NEC. It was plain to me that Fields should not be allowed to stand on a Labour ticket ever again.

The previous year, I had driven across the Pennines to collect Roy Hattersley and his researcher David Hill (who later became the party's Head of Communications) from the Yorkshire Regional Organiser, who had driven them halfway. I was to take them to a meeting in the north west, but beforehand we had a meal, from which I remember two points of conversation. Firstly, I suggested to Roy that he should write an article on his trip because the service that myself and other Labour organisers were providing was a little like the Pony Express. He duly took this advice and the article appeared in the *Guardian* soon after. Secondly, I raised the issue about Militants in Parliament, and pointed out that it was unjust to expel people lower down the ranks for membership of the organisation whilst allowing Fields and Dave Nellist (MP for Coventry South East) to walk away scot-free. Roy responded with, 'Well, now is not the time' – an argument that could always be made while in the interim more and more damage would be caused.

Fields may have been a small aggravation to the party in the Commons, but outside he was a real liability. Yet Hattersley's attitude, which many others shared, was also short-sighted in parliamentary terms. Given what were then seen as the psephological possibilities, it was taken as read that a Labour government returned at the next general election would have, at best, a small majority. People who should have known better had obviously forgotten the lessons of the 1964–66 Wilson government and the behaviour of Woodrow Wyatt and Desmond Donnelly. They could not see the dangers of Fields, Nellist and their supporters having a disproportionate influence on a putative Labour government. The party could not afford to go into the next general election with such openly Militant candidates.

For me personally, the summer of 1990 was cruel. In June, Sean Hughes, the MP for Knowsley South, died of cancer aged forty-four. His family had a history of early cancerous deaths, and his own was a real blow. He left behind his wife, Tricia, and their young daughter Charlotte, and many others who thought of him as an outstanding person (even in his previous incarnation as a teacher, he had been incredibly popular). I owed Sean a particular debt of thanks because of his positive encouragement to accept Laura Kirton's challenge to go for the Walton seat. A rising star, Sean had been the young successor to Harold Wilson in Wilson's old seat (shortly after Sean's death, a mass was held for him in the House of Commons' crypt, at which I was shocked to see the condition Wilson was in). When Sean died, he was part of the shadow defence team, and it had been widely expected that he would attain high office in a future Labour government. His funeral was well attended and immensely moving, and I remember standing outside afterwards, saying to Mike Carr, 'What a loss'. Mike stood there agreeing with me, not knowing that a month later he would suffer a similar fate.

Mike's death, at the age of forty-three, came on the night of a Walton constituency party meeting, which I was attending as the PPC. It was a typically fraught gathering, held in a room behind the Black Bull pub, and Militant's local battalion was in hyper-confrontational mode. Mike was smiling at me from the back of the room, as if to say 'You're loving this, aren't you?', but then he indicated that he was going outside. It was a hot summer's evening and the atmosphere inside the room was getting nastier and nastier, so I assumed that he wanted some fresh air; anyone in their right mind would have wanted to get away. A few minutes later, somebody from outside came in and said that Mike had collapsed. With others, I quickly went outside and found Mike slumped by a bus-stop. From the way he was breathing, it appeared that he had had a heart attack, but as he remained conscious, we soon began to assume that he had just been overcome by the heat. By the time the medics arrived, we were so confident that he would be okay that we were joking with him. Jimmy Symes, a TGWU official at the docks and an old friend of Mike's, went with him in the ambulance, but there was not an awful lot that the rest of us could do.

With the meeting duly abandoned, I went for a pint with Bob Lancaster and Gary Booth, and then travelled home. Literally as I walked in the door, the telephone went; it was Barbara Hunter, the secretary of Bootle CLP, telling me that Mike was dead. I said to her: 'No, no. He's gone off to hospital in an ambulance, and he's all right.' She let me finish and then said, 'No, Peter. He was allowed home and, soon after he got back, he died.' Bernie and I immediately went over to Mike's house to see his wife Lynne and their kids. When we arrived, Ian McCartney, the MP for Ashton-in-Makerfield, and his wife Ann (who worked in the Bootle constituency office) were there, as was Bobby Owens, the TGWU Regional Secretary. We were all devastated.

The following day, I went to a local church to the ordination of Father David Gamble, whose dad Alec was a supporter of my candidature in Walton. It was a very emotional occasion; all I could think about was Mike and the events of the previous night. At Mike's funeral, I sat with Stan Orme, who was there on Neil Kinnock's behalf as chair of the PLP, and at the family's request I gave an oration. It was the hardest speech I have ever had to make and, although I managed to get through to the end, there were points where I almost broke down with emotion. Afterwards, there was a reception, to which some uninvited and unwanted guests turned up. I spoke to one in particular and made clear to him the family's view on his presence; what was a tense situation ultimately resolved itself. I have not spoken to the individual concerned since, although he is now a very senior trade union official, often found around Parliament.

Following Mike's death, an exchange of letters took place in a local freesheet, the *Liverpool Weekly Star*, between supporters of Militant and myself and other regular members of the party, highlighting how the whole situation on Merseyside was coming to a crunch. The exchange began with Joe Devaney observing how Militant 'were forcing votes when anti-Militants had left the meeting to tend to Mike Carr'.[116] Militant fired their first salvo back with a lengthy response from Richard Venton in which he disputed Devaney's claim, stating 'when it was announced that "a delegate" had collapsed, the socialist who was speaking immediately stopped and sat down. No attempt was made by Militant supporters to continue.'[117] I entered the fray by asking the editors of the newspaper why they continued to give over so much column space to Militant, while provoking the latter by labelling them 'an irrelevant group of bigots'.[118] This prompted further responses, the most notable being from John Williams, a GMB delegate to the Walton party who accused me of deliberately attempting 'to whip up and sustain hatred and hysteria against certain Labour Party members'.[119] The inevitable showdown was just around the corner.

August also brought the death of Pat Wall, the MP for Bradford North. A former Liverpool councillor who became a regular figure at conference and often stood for the NEC, Wall had risen up in the world. Before becoming an MP he was employed in a rather lowly job in the mail-order section of Littlewoods but was then promoted into a middle-income post as a hardware buyer. Subsequently, he began to lead what Michael Crick has described as 'the lifestyle of a man from a working-class background who has done well in life'.[120] Although he remained committed to Militant and its causes, Wall declined to serve on its central committee, preferring to indulge his various pastimes, the two most apparent of which were clay pigeon shooting and following Everton Football Club. He seemed so far removed from Militant that shortly before his death he was able to convince the NEC that he was no longer involved with the organisation. The eulogies at his funeral service suggested otherwise, and my own understanding of the event is that it was tantamount to a rally for Militant members, at which Wall was praised as an icon of the Revolutionary Socialist League.

Throughout this period, storm clouds were gathering over Liverpool City Council. Given the now legendary commitment to rent freezes, a major departure from the old orthodoxy arose when the Labour group voted to sanction a £3 rise. The obligatory demonstration took place, but it was the first increase in seven years, and it still left Liverpool with comparatively cheap rents. Many of those in council properties knew that they could not go on forever without an increase, and also knew that the worst-off would have the increase paid for through the benefits system. A week later, however, at the Town Hall, twenty-seven Labour councillors voted with the Liberal Democrats to defeat the rise. Rushing like Gadarene swine towards a political precipice, these so-called rebels seemed intent on putting themselves in the party dock for breaching its rules and constitution. Their number not only included those who had already been suspended from the group and the new intake of Broad Left councillors, but members of the 'Sainsbury set', and I found nothing more disreputable than Keith Hackett's opposition when he had previously backed the suggestion of an £11 rent rise.

Tony Jennings accused those who had voted for the rise of being guilty of cowardice of the highest order. It was strange how he had become the spokesman for the Broad Left. Coombes had always wanted him as his second-in-command, and he had been deputy to Hackett when the latter was effectively running the city treasury. Being deputy was the only way forward for Jennings. He knew he did not have the numbers to win positions outright, but he was lined up by others to realise his ambition to be 'the leader'. Perhaps he fitted the image which Coombes and Hackett shared of what a Scouse political leader should be like. They were wide of the mark. Jennings was a man who gave the impression of an authoritarian streak, the likes of which I could not attribute even to Hatton or Byrne; during his time on the county council, he had been thought of as being on the right. He was a complex character.

Some years before, I had been involved in an altercation with Hatton outside the Municipal Buildings when Jennings turned up and urged me to move back and let Hatton, who was with Mulhearn, shout his mouth off. This I did, and it prevented an escalation of the situation. It was good advice. But by 1990, Jennings had become carried away with the heady times and the high-pressure, introspective political milieu of the city. It was a pity, because he was able in many ways.

One of the newly elected councillors, Andy Duckworth, was amongst those who broke the whip on the rent rise. In doing so, he ignored the advice of a 'respected' third party – advice that Lyn Anderson had passed on to him:

> I rang Tony Byrne. By this time, he was involved in the Labour Party up in Scotland, and I asked him 'What's happening up your end over this rents issue?' He said 'We've put them up. You can't do anything else. Things have moved on. People have stayed in a rut in Liverpool when the situation has changed and there are different ways of focusing your campaign now.' I made that enquiry for Andy's benefit because he persuaded me 'to come out of retirement', if you like, to help organise his campaign in Arundel. I felt very motherly towards him. He'd been a student when he got involved in the ward, and I wanted to look after him. I didn't want him

to be confronted by the rent issue, so I said 'I've spoken to Tony Byrne and he's said it is crazy what is going on here. You shouldn't be doing this'.

But he did, along with the rest of the Broad Left. The peer-group pressure was too intense.

In August, the NEC decided what to do with those councillors who had broken the whip over the poll tax. The MPs Eddie Loyden and Bob Parry both sought to address the NEC before any decision was made, but they were refused, as were two councillors, Lyn O'Sullivan and Frank Vaudrey. Subsequently, fourteen of those involved were suspended from the party. At the same meeting, the DLP was also suspended, just over two and half years after it had been reconstituted. Sadly, the body had regressed to type. Not only was it subject to constant disruption from the floor, but its officers were failing to observe the rules and standing orders of the party, or to accept that they and the DLP ultimately had to comply with national policy.

The NEC also voted to suspend eight members of the Birkenhead party, a move that was to have a bearing on the second selection of its parliamentary candidate. In addition, Socialist Organiser, which had a significant presence in the Wirral seat of Wallasey, was added to the list of 'proscribed organisations', allegiance to which was considered incompatible with being a member of the Labour Party. As far as I know, none of those associated with Socialist Organiser on the Wirral were ever expelled. I always found their supporters to be very helpful, and saw no evidence of them operating outside the rules of the party. I was also of the view that Socialist Organiser were essentially what Militant had set out to be, a pressure group within the Labour Party rather than a truly separate organisation with its own rules and membership.

Back in Liverpool, Keva Coombes appeared from out of the shadows, offering to quit as a councillor after he made some rather odd comments about how the council, when faced with a private tender, had fiddled the figures to protect the jobs of its staff. A cynic might suggest that Coombes had made these remarks with a particular interest in mind. Sadly, he was dissuaded from resigning by the Clubmoor ward party. His replacement as leader of the council, Harry Rimmer, having failed to get the £3 rent rise through, turned down the Liberal Democrats' offer of an ad hoc coalition geared to ensuring the changes necessary for the overdue reform of council finances were passed. A £4 rent rise was voted through, courtesy of the Liberal Democrats' decision to abstain, whereupon the Broad Left, true to form, walked out of the chamber in protest. NALGO left many people in Liverpool sighing when the union once again occupied the Town Hall. This was quickly ended once a repossession order was gained from the county court, but things were reaching the point where NALGO were practising more take-overs than the Hanson conglomerate.

This was probably not the best time in the world to have a council by-election. There was one, however, when work commitments caused Liberal Democrat Richard Pine to resign his Tuebrook seat for being unable to attend council meetings. As it turned out, the Liberal Democrats faced down the burgeoning threat of the 'Meadowcroft Liberals'[121] who were becoming increasingly strong in the ward, while Labour came third. Our candidate was Alan White, the brother of professional Scouser and ardent Tory Cilla Black. Employed at the Ford plant in Halewood, 'our Alan' was himself a supporter of the Broad Left, and I saw him as having little to offer to the political life of the city – a view that was obviously shared by the electorate in Tuebrook.

The summer also saw the handing down of the judgement on the Hillsborough tragedy, the Taylor Report, which in its wisdom managed to find that nobody was culpable for what at that time was ninety-five (later to become ninety-six) deaths. Sheffield Wednesday Football Club was not deemed responsible; neither were the Football Association, the consulting engineers or Sheffield City Council, nor, indeed, the ambulance services or South Yorkshire Police. This was to cause additional trauma to the families and friends of those who died or were injured, as well as many others who had witnessed what happened. It was to have a souring effect in many ways, not upon relations between the cities of Liverpool and Sheffield – if anything that was strengthened – but between the people of Liverpool and the authorities concerned.

One person with comments to make on the judgement was Eric Heffer. Other than attempting to persuade the NEC not to endorse me as his successor, he had been extremely quiet since the start of the year. Consequently, speculation began to arise about his state of health. Like many other people, I was aware that Heffer was busy working on his autobiography, but I have never known whether at the time he was aware that he had a severely limited lifespan ahead of him. In September, I met him in the Strangers' Bar at Westminster, as I waited to address the north west group of Labour MPs. Not being a Member myself, I could not buy a drink, and Eric, true to form, bought himself two while not offering me one. Instead, he attempted to persuade me that his position on my candidacy was the only honourable one. The meeting with the north west group was being held on the Upper Committee Corridor, and in the lift on the way up, I made the mistake of enquiring about his health. Exploding with indignation, as only Eric could, he chastised me for my impertinence. However innocently, I had added further to his antipathy towards me.

This served to remind me of the time back in June 1986, at Pirrie Labour Club, when I attended my first meeting of Walton CLP as a full-time officer of the party. At the end of the evening, characterised by lengthy Militant diatribes against the NEC, Heffer began to accuse my colleague Phil Robinson of something or other. At this point, I started to walk out of the room, at which he shouted after me 'Hey you – I want a word with you'. I turned around and said 'Are you talking to me?', to which he shouted aggressively 'Yeah, you – I want a word with you'. So I told him: 'If you want a word with me, then address me properly'. He then came back at me with the rather pompous, 'Do you know who I am? I'm your boss; I'm on the NEC', to which I could only retort: 'I don't care who you are – I only work for the NEC!' That was it, of course, and he started bellowing. He followed me outside the club, haranguing me and threatening me with the sack. I bit my lip, got in my car and drove away.

By the autumn, there seemed to be no end to the controversy in Liverpool, as an argument broke out regarding a teaching pack sent to Liverpool schools by the council's Drugs Liaison Officer. Both Harry Rimmer, as leader of the council, and Gideon Ben-Tovim, as chair of Education, were genuinely puzzled by this. As it turned out, it was yet another crazy escapade involving people closely allied to the Broad Left. This was nothing new, of course. For a long time an area of Liverpool – Gillmoss and Croxteth – had been known as 'Smack City', and local figures associated with the Broad Left had been particularly antagonistic towards organisations that came on to their patch, especially those which they could not dominate. One such body was the Self-Help Against Drugs Organisation, known more usually by its acronym, Shado. Its patron was Kenneth Baker (now succeeded by Cherie Blair), who took a great deal of time in supporting their efforts, particularly when he was the local government minister. Shado was a highly respectable organisation, but Phil Knibb, Tony Jennings and others appeared set on destroying it. Happily, they never came remotely near to their objective.

Serious tensions were also emerging within the Broad Left over their relationship with the Labour group, and by extension the party. In line with their long-term tactic of using Labour platforms to win what they could, the Militants wanted to remain on board either to convert the existing members of the group to their cause or to manoeuvre their own people through the local government selection panel. Meanwhile, the less ideologically committed within the Broad Left were showing frustration at not having access to what they believed was their due – committee chairmanships – and began talking aloud about establishing their own party as a way of rectifying this. Some who argued this were relatively recent recruits to the Labour Party, but others, such as Jennings, were led by personal ambition.

Even so, what divided the Broad Left had yet to outweigh what united them, and at that month's full council meeting they combined with the Liberal Democrats to defeat the ruling Labour group on several issues. Having aided Harry Rimmer and the other progressives through the door of financial reform, with an understanding that they would be clipping at his heels, the Liberal Democrats had now started to tackle him from behind. More importantly, this revealed how clearly the Broad Left had become anti-Labour in all but name. These were not dissident voices on 'the left of the party', as some ordinary members still believed, but a relatively coherent group acting with their own interests at heart. This is certainly how Vicky Roberts saw them when in referring to the new make-up of the Hillsborough working party, she labelled Broad Left members 'outsiders'. There was also a clear physical division within the Municipal Building, with the Labour group based in the leader's and deputy leader's offices, and the Tendency and their fellow travellers holed up in the Labour Members' Room further down the corridor.

At the end of September, Keva Coombes finally got around to quitting his £4000-a-year part-time quango appointment on the Merseyside Development Corporation, a position he had acquired courtesy of his leadership of the council. He obviously had another iron in the fire, and this was soon revealed as a solicitor's post in Chester. Coombes had gone on the MDC at a time when it was anathema to most local people, who saw it as little more than a modern-day manifestation of the national Tory Raj. Intent on running a major slice of Liverpool on behalf of a hostile central government, many of the staff at the MDC indeed acted as if they were in a colonial outpost. This did not stop Keva, nor his successors – Harry Rimmer and, later on, Frank Prendergast – from taking up a post for as long as the organisation was to exist. In doing so, they gave a degree of credibility to some rather cynical people, who used their positions at the MDC to project themselves as benevolent towards Liverpool and the wider region. The only benevolence I saw in them was that of the benevolent despot.

The end of September also saw the Knowsley South by-election, to replace the almost irreplaceable Sean Hughes. For Labour, there had been two potential candidates, Derek Long and Eddie O'Hara, whose relative abilities could not have been separated by a cigarette paper. They were both pillars of the local establishment, and while they may have had differences in terms of who was friends with whom, politically there was absolutely nothing between them. In fact, the main battleground at the selection process was over who spoke the most languages – a mini-contest won handsomely by Eddie with eight to Derek's five. Eddie also won the nomination and duly took the seat at the by-election. A classically low turn-out, no-one really expected anything other than a Labour victory. As it was, the most memorable event of the campaign was a fight in the committee rooms between two local party members over the use of milk in tea. I split them up, and was twice called as a witness in the ensuing court action.

Neighbouring St Helens burst into the limelight with the arrest of Cllr Brian Green and others in connection with land deals in the area. There was always something murky about the ruling Labour group in the borough, and a small number of them certainly had 'relationships' with people in Liverpool politics, although they were politically poles apart. The one thing that they all had was a compulsion, to use a colloquialism, 'to get on', which often translated as 'making money by hook or by crook'. Of course, I was surprised by nothing by this stage. The St Helens Labour Party had started to serve as an indicator of the health of local parties in a handful of areas around Britain, some of which, like Doncaster and Paisley, were to haunt us for years as narrow bands of self-interested people claimed to speak for Labour and those loyal local electorates who continued to guarantee them one-party rule.

The political health of St Helens had also begun to suffer in other ways. Gerry Bermingham, one of the town's two MPs, alleged that the wheel-nuts on his car had been deliberately loosened, claiming this as evidence that someone was attempting to kill him. I treated this with a great deal of scepticism, given that such things rarely do happen; in any case, Gerry did not seem to spend enough time in the constituency for anyone to be able to follow through such a plot. Numerous councillors also approached me with tales of how others were out to do them physical harm. Such beliefs were built upon tensions that had arisen following the council's cancellation of funding for the local trade union centre. The latter did have some highly dubious characters linked to it, who would not be beyond threatening or committing personal injury to their enemies. Still, some of the accusations were quite over the top, and lacked the substance needed to warrant investigation. I understood the imagination running riot in the case of one or two of the more neurotic members, but a collective paranoia seemed to have taken hold, with many people convincing themselves that they were subject to tremendous threat.

October in Liverpool began in the time-honoured way with the establishment of a fund with a number upon it. This time it was for 'the twenty-nine', those councillors who, having defied the rules of the party, were now suspended from the Labour group. Two local branches of the GMB led the way by providing a thousand pounds' worth of support between them. This came as no surprise considering their vested interests, but it also indicated the extent to which battle lines were being drawn behind the scenes. Meanwhile, one of 'the twenty-nine', Frank Vaudrey, offered the local media the rationale of the fund: 'The sole aim of the fund is to keep us within the party, not out of it. The money in the fund is to help with expenses such as travel, it is not to fund election campaigns.'[122] On the face of it, this was a semi-legitimate point. The 'rebels' were no longer getting any financial support from the party, and nor were they able to draw the same council expenses as before, as they were not being given places on committees. The cheek of it, however, was that Vaudrey then went on to say that, should the councillors be expelled, some of them might indeed stand as independents. This was akin to eating your cake and having it. It highlighted the shoddiness of these people – in their politics, in their principles and in what passed for their ideology.

As the matter of 'the twenty-nine' unfolded, it seemed to me to be no different from what had occurred a few years earlier with 'the forty-seven', or indeed with 'the twenty-one' back in 1972. It was not just a refusal to toe the party line, but an inability to accept the discipline of the party and its rules, and it gave the impression of an anarchistic bent amongst those involved. In *Liverpool: Gateway of Empire*, Tony Lane has written of how the anarcho-syndicalist trends imported into Liverpool at the start of the twentieth century were perpetuated by the casual dimension of the labour market, and contributed to the highly reactive way of thinking that came to dominate the outlook of the local Labour Party. By 1990, this had transformed into a culture of contempt for national political processes.

It may be stating the obvious, but things were growing steadily worse in Liverpool at this time. The debt-ridden council was forever being hindered by strike action from NALGO, while seemingly irrecoverable rent arrears were becoming an increasingly hot potato. The Labour group was divided into two entrenched factions, which themselves appeared ready to split asunder. The official opposition, the Liberal Democrats, were in fact even more divided, but retained a façade of opposition behind their leader, Paul Clark, and the only ideology they knew, opportunism. This was not a happy time for the local authority to appoint a new Chief Executive. Liverpool council was crying out for someone with the necessary dynamism to begin the wholesale restructuring of both the workforce and services, but who in their right mind would want to step into this viper's nest of difficulties?

The filling of the post had been a long-drawn-out matter. Harry Rimmer had wanted to appoint Ray O'Brien, the former Chief Executive of Merseyside County Council, but alas, he was heavily involved with the Severn Trent water company and was quite happy to remain there. It was also rumoured that his doctor had warned him against taking on what was then considered to be one of the most stressful positions in local government (O'Brien did eventually come back to work in Liverpool, albeit in a lesser post). In August 1990, after a long period in which the post had remained vacant, two people made the first interview panel. With one of them seen as lacking the relevant experience, it left Tony Allen, the Chief Executive of Berkshire County Council. Yet the panel was split, and Rimmer, who held the casting vote, chose to veto Allen's appointment. This left Liverpool in limbo for a further two months, until October, when, following a second set of interviews Peter Bounds, the Chief Executive of Bolton borough council, was offered the post and accepted. It was certainly a brave move on his part. Whether it was the smartest move for the city, only time would tell.

It was also around about this time that the question of compulsory competitive tendering began to kick in in Liverpool. Thatcher's government had introduced this policy with the intent of making the 'cushioned' public sector face up to the same disciplines as the private sector, by bringing in a legal requirement that certain council services be put out to tender. Naturally, this would have deep consequences for existing municipal workforces, and where local authorities held on to the work, the 'competitive' aspect of tendering necessitated that many direct services be slimmed down. This was a reality that certain bodies in Liverpool refused to accept, as Alan Dean recalls:

> We spoke to the T&G and the G&M, and told them how to go about putting in their own bids. However, they wouldn't accept the realities of political life. We couldn't get the unions to accept the terms that we were prepared to work with, so that we could put the best case forward for them.

A particular cause for concern were the refuse workers, whose shop stewards' committee was invited to meet Harry Rimmer at his office:

> I remember saying to them: 'Look, lads, the game's up. What we're up against in your service is different from the others that we've faced, because they've been rather an unknown quantity to the private sector, whereas with waste collection and disposal there's been some big operations in this game for a while. They're bigger than you, bigger than the Liverpool DSO. They've got all the expertise and many of them own the tips. So unless you get your act together and cooperate, and get a reasonable tender in, you've had it, and there will be nothing this council can do about it.'

In other parts of Britain where municipal tasks had been taken over by private companies, they had been adamant that they would not take on every member of staff employed by the council. Moreover, where they had re-employed people, they had also made it clear that the relevant trade unions would no longer hold many of the restrictive practices and advantages they had previously enjoyed. This was something with which union representatives were having to come to terms. In Liverpool, those willing to cope with such changes and negotiate accordingly were the minority. The majority acted like cornered animals, attacking those closest to them. At one demonstration at the Pier Head, TGWU official John Farrell directed the attention of his members away from dealing with the changing realities of civic life and towards Labour councillors (such as Tony Concepcion, Alan Dean and Les Hughes) representing wards containing workplaces, such as Vauxhall and Ford, which were creating redundancies. Rather ominously, Farrell was reported as saying: 'If you see one of those councillors in the street, or in the pub or skulking around a back street, get hold of that councillor and ask him: "Are you prepared to put me on the dole?" If he says yes, tell him: "You have got the biggest fight you have had on your hands".'[123]

A few days later, when the council met to consider redundancies, the inevitable demonstration gave rise to a most bizarre sight, as a handful of grounds maintenance workers arrived at the steps of the Town Hall on grass-cutting machines. What such symbolism was intended to show, I do not know. Perhaps they were hoping to mow down those amongst the city's leadership they saw as 'tall poppies'. If only they had had the foresight to see how things were drawing in on them, they would have realised that circumstances were not in their favour.

Nor were circumstances in favour of 'the twenty-nine' who had been suspended from the Labour group, and eight others from the local party. At the inquiry into their conduct and behaviour, Joyce Gould and I were able to demonstrate clearly the existence of links between these self-styled renegades and Militant, and to make apparent how they had been working against the interests of the party both locally and nationally. Their general demeanour, portrayed at this time on *Panorama* and other television programmes, was to speak volumes to the great British public (a groundswell of sympathy arose after Harry Rimmer's tears on *Newsnight*). Of course, the openly Militant amongst the rebels once again droned on about how they had somehow been denied natural justice. Lesley Mahmood, for instance, informed the press, 'We don't particularly want to be taking the NEC to court, but they leave us with no choice'.[124] There really were times when I felt like telling Mahmood to stick another record on; she was one of the most tedious individuals I have ever met. I was not the only one who thought this way, as Gary Booth explains:

> I'll never forget the time that *Panorama* were doing a big exposé on Liverpool. Steve Bagshaw, who was behind it, said that they were coming to the council to do some filming, and asked if I could point out the key players. When it came to the day, we were sat in the Town Hall and he turned to me and said 'Okay, which one's Lesley Mahmood?' I said 'Oh Christ, you can't miss her. She's the one who, when she gets up, clears the auditorium'; and he said, 'Oh, come on, which one is she?' to which I pointed her out. Without a word of a lie, though, when the chair said 'Councillor Mahmood', there was an audible, collective groan followed by a mass exodus. Of the ninety-odd councillors who were there, only about twelve of them remained in their seats. Although those who walked out included those who were gasping for a smoke, the Lib Dems, who hated her with a vengeance, and our lot who couldn't stand her, the numbers also included many of the Broad Left's own non-Tendency people.

That autumn also saw the dealing of a real hammer blow to Derek Hatton and a whole host of people closely connected to him, as the Merseyside Fraud Squad's 'Operation Cheetah' culminated in twenty-two arrests. As well as Hatton himself, they included his friend and tailor John Monk, Knowsley councillor Tony Beyga, Liverpool councillors Hannah Folan and George Knibb, 'forty-sevener' John Nelson, Wimpey's regional manager Alan Worthington and two of his predecessors, and John Gidman, a former Everton and England footballer with whom Hatton had planned to open a golf driving range in Knowsley. Charges of fraud were laid down against Hatton (as well as Folan, Nelson and Monk), and the trial set for the following summer. But Hatton was to walk away unscathed from this; in time, he was to make as many escapes as Houdini in evading the attempts of the legal system to call him to account. With so many of his alleged misdemeanours openly discussed in Liverpool, it was only a matter of time before conspiracy theories blossomed. Hence Bob Lancaster's view of events:

> Laura Kirton once told me that she was convinced that Derek had been planted by the CIA. The more and more you think about it, the way that Derek's been protected ... I'll defend the man but he's led a charmed life, let's put it like that. I've been told that, apparently, the case in Mold which should have been directed by a criminal judge was directed by a family court judge, and something like only three of the nineteen charges were heard. The things he's been through and he's still not gone to jail. He's got something going for him somewhere. So I always remember what Laura said, and if you think what the political consequences are of Derek being in the party – he lost us an election.

It should be borne in mind that this is the same Bob Lancaster who insists that I was brought back from Australia 'to do a job' on Militant.

A few weeks after the 'Operation Cheetah' swoop, the *Liverpool Daily Post* quoted Hatton on the health of his company, Settleside: 'My business is fine. It will not go bust today and it will not go bust tomorrow.'[125] In literal terms, he was right. His business went bust a couple of days later, leaving poor old Derek to whinge on about how his arrest and the subsequent media coverage had led clients to pull their business out. While this was undoubtedly true, the heart of the matter was that people had become wary of his chameleon-like qualities. It was a particular irony, however, that the faltering of Hatton (Mark II: the businessman) came at the same time as the fall from grace of his old *bête noire*, Margaret Thatcher.

## Left Behind: Lessons from Labour's heartland

On the day that Thatcher stepped down as leader of the Conservative Party and the government, Harry Rimmer once again threatened to resign the leadership of Liverpool City Council and its Labour group. Following a meeting at the Municipal Annexe in which myself, Harry and others had met national union leaders, I returned with him and Vicky Roberts to his office, where the two of them set about having an almighty row. Vicky was keen to go with the idea of a deal with the Liberal Democrats as a way of finally resolving the council's financial problems. Having already discussed this with Paul Clark and others, she had gone behind Harry's back and attempted to ensure their support by altering the wording of a draft resolution. Extremely reluctant to go down this line, Harry became aggressively argumentative, to the point where Vicky ended up in tears.

It was a side of Harry that I had only seen once before, albeit a few weeks previously. This came during a meeting at the Campanile Hotel on Liverpool's waterfront to discuss the council's need to make redundancies. Harry and Bobby Owens, the TGWU regional secretary, were literally nose to nose, bawling at the tops of their voices. Neither was listening to the other, and they looked like two hugely overgrown children enjoying a collective monologue in full voice. None of the other people there – myself, Peter Horan of the GMB and Brian Devine of NALGO – could calm them down. Harry stormed off to his office, thereby ending the attempt at conciliation.

Despite this experience, I was quite taken aback by Harry's verbal aggression towards Vicky Roberts. The local media got wind of what had happened, and asked me to comment. Rather diplomatically, I stated that I could do no more than salve wounds between fellow party members, and that it was for councillors to run the council. Nevertheless, a second backroom deal was done, this time between Rimmer and Clark. It was a deal that neither leader could have taken to their respective groups and expect to be countenanced but, at the next full meeting of the council, the Liberal Democrats abstained on the crucial vote, allowing the Labour group to proceed with its programme of reform.

In the meantime, another row had broken out, after the Director of Environmental Services, Ken Robinson, sent a letter to Ian Lowes accusing him of being politically motivated in his threat to call a strike of his members. As it was, Lowes himself saw similar motivations on Robinson's part:

Rightly or wrongly, our branch was seen as the indicative, and if they were going to attack the wider workforce to make cuts, they had to first single us out. I'm sure that someone sat down and said, 'Okay, what problems have

we got, what would we like to achieve, and who would we like to get rid of?'
It was no coincidence that Ken Robinson was the most willing of the directors to get rid of jobs.

In all fairness, while I have some admiration for Lowes's ability as a union
official, it must have been extremely stressful to have to face up to him, his
fellow lay officials and his rather truculent members on a daily basis. I doubt
there was a worse job in Liverpool at this time. Ken's burden, however, was
shared with Vicky Roberts, who as chair of the Environmental Services
Committee also faced Lowes on a regular basis:

> On a personal basis, I liked Ian. I mean, I wouldn't have trusted him as
> far as I could throw him but you knew where he was coming from, and he
> knew where I was coming from. So on that level, we always had a reason-
> able relationship. He could be pretty nasty but I always knew it was
> tongue-in-cheek, and it was for an audience.

There was an upside to all of this – Vicky and Ken were eventually married.

With temperatures rising in Liverpool, it was quite a relief to be able to
spend some time up the road in Bootle, helping Joe Benton secure the seat
for Labour in the constituency's second by-election in six months (prompted,
of course, by the death of Mike Carr). It was always a foregone conclusion
that Joe would win, but more so because almost everyone in Bootle seemed
to know him personally. Still, his victory led to a rare event. When we arrived at the Star of the Sea Social Club for the post-count celebrations, instead of making a speech, Joe sang one of his favourite songs, 'The Pride of
the County Down', dedicating it to his wife Doris. It was the one and only
time that I have heard a successful candidate sing to his victory, although I
have heard Joe sing the same song many times since.

Over in Birkenhead, Frank Field was continuing to cause problems by
refusing to participate in a re-run of his selection contest, as ordered by the
NEC. Although this had come about as a direct result of his complaints
about the first selection, Field appeared to have changed his tactic to one of
attaining a 'guarantee' that he would win the nomination. Reflecting on this,
Larry Whitty has since commented:

> Had it been the same circumstances at a more neutral time, I think we
> could have found Frank a seat elsewhere. But there was a degree to which
> Frank really, to put it mildly, pulled out all the stops to ensure that he was
> reselected.

Of course, I remained adamant that Paul Davies had won the initial contest within the rules of the party. Partly because of my stance on this, but also because of my position as a prospective parliamentary candidate, Eileen Murfin was brought in from the East Midlands to oversee matters as Acting Regional Organiser (a post she would officially take up the following year). I was to have a slightly difficult working relationship with Eileen, in that I never understood where she was coming from, and I am sure she felt the same about me. Nevertheless, it was thought that she would look upon the situation in Birkenhead with a fresh pair of eyes.

This she did, and shortly before Christmas a full investigation was announced. In doing so, Larry Whitty asserted that whilst Militant were present, they were no great influence in the constituency. Frank, however, in responding to this accurate observation, revealed both his naivety of how Militant operated and his own tendency to state the absurd: 'Militant had forty-eight votes in the selection process, one in five. If the National Front had one fifth of the vote we would be up in arms.'[126] As it transpired, a dozen members of the Birkenhead party were expelled, including Geoff Barker, the deputy leader of Wirral Labour group. Frank was duly reselected as the candidate the following summer and carried on playing at being the maverick. Early in the new year, he helped launch the 'cross-party' Movement for Christian Democracy with David Alton and Ken Hargreaves, the Conservative MP for Hyndburn who had trounced Coombes at the 1987 general election. It was entirely consistent with Frank's political track record, being more in tune with the opposition than his own party. His streak of rebelliousness, allied with his obduracy, was to lead eventually to his early departure from Tony Blair's government.

With Eileen Murfin having taken on the problems of Birkenhead, I was concentrating on Militant in Liverpool, and having mixed fortunes. At the third attempt, I managed to remove Richard Knights from the party, but Tommy Carrol, who was due at the same hearing, failed to attend, claiming illness as his excuse. This came as no surprise, but if Carrol truly was ill, it was probably psychosomatic. He had a bit of a reputation as a hard case, but I always looked upon him as a bully who lacked the bravery to face up to situations which he could not control. His failure to make the hearing served only to prove this perception. He and Knights had been central to Militant's manoeuvres throughout the Broadgreen constituency, particularly in Kensington. It was perhaps ironic, therefore, that their hearing should have coincided with a court appearance of the ward's former councillor, John

Blackall (along with Broad Left Warbreck councillor Harry Chase) for non-payment of poll tax. What caught the national media's attention, however, was the court appearance of another Militant, also for non-payment of poll tax, before Sefton magistrates. Foot on spade, Terry Fields was starting to dig his own political grave.

1991 would see a dramatic climax to Militant's life within the Labour Party, and set me personally on a whole new course. Beyond Merseyside, the first two months saw John Major's attempts to settle in as leader of the Conservative government, the great cataclysm of the Gulf War, and the first stirrings of trouble in the Balkans. In Liverpool, however, the year began relatively quietly with little more than a twist of fate. Just as the latest District Auditor, Neil Edwards, was getting tough on the city's financial crisis, calling for the council to shed jobs and improve services, Tony Byrne appeared back in town, having been called in as part of the Merseyside Police Fraud Squad's continuing investigations into Hatton's business interests.

The city's council rents also rose again, this time by an average of £4.10 per week. Of course, the usual noises were made about ameliorating the lot of tenants, increasing their participation in running estates, improving the repairs service – and tackling racial discrimination in housing allocation, two years after the Commission for Racial Equality, in the form of Lord Gifford and others, had compiled a report on the extent to which racist attitudes affected municipal politics in Liverpool. These promises were little more than glib lines, trotted out to the supposedly gullible, and the failure to serve the citizens of the city continued much the same as before. I was to have one meeting with Liverpool's Chief Executive and Director of Housing, where they told me that a computerised system for housing repairs was to be piloted in the Speke area. Five years later, the same officials were to point out that this same system had not yet travelled beyond Speke, where it was still being piloted. *Plus ça change* …

Towards the end of February, two other issues started to reach a climax – the campaign against the poll tax and the acceptance that the city needed to shed jobs if it was serious about putting its finances in order. Although the two were indissolubly linked, they each, in their own separate ways, illustrated the depths of the malaise. With regards to the poll tax, it was estimated that 130,000 of the 327,000 poll taxpayers in Liverpool would be summonsed for non-payment, and that some 40–50,000 homes would receive a visit from the bailiffs. Although both sets of figures turned out to be gross exaggerations, one special session of the city's magistrates saw 9,000 people summonsed. It was an occasion that Militant, in the guise of the anti-poll tax unions, used for its own nefarious ends, as Bob Lancaster recalls:

> The Tendency were there with their buckets. These people couldn't pay their poll tax, but the Tendency were asking them for money and saying 'Oh, we'll sort you out'.

And, in their own symbolic way, they did. Having led a delegation to protest against the 9,000 being asked to queue in cold weather, Lesley Mahmood presented a petition to court officers requesting that the summonsed should be allowed to go home. She and her cohorts had some gall, given that they had encouraged these people not to pay, knowing perfectly well that the full weight of the law would eventually be brought to bear on them. It was hypocrisy of the highest order, and all geared towards raising the profile of Militant.

The thorny issue of redundancies, meanwhile, came into focus when it was announced that council officers had been given the go-ahead to shed up to 700 jobs, for the most part in four key areas: static security, maintenance and building, refuse collection and the city's engineering department. The fact that many individuals employed in these jobs had been kept on the books for so long when there was little or no work for them to do showed how hung up Labour councillors were with the ever-mythical cry of 'no cuts in jobs and services'. In confronting this head-on, they were finally coming to terms with the fact that the city had to trim back on these supernumeraries who contributed nothing to the value added by council services. Still, it was a decision taken after a considerable degree of soul-searching, as Alan Dean recalls:

> The vast majority of the group had a trade union background, and there was a strong commitment to retaining jobs and services. However, we recognised that some of our services were vastly overstaffed, and were being delivered way under what they should be. It was also a factor that if we said something was going to happen, people would react by going over the top and making it out to be more serious. So, it took us a long time to say, 'Look, we need to do this'.

Not that it impressed the government. At a meeting with 'colonial governor' Heseltine, it was made quite clear to Harry Rimmer that Liverpool was not going to receive any extra financial assistance. In a more positive light, the

meeting at least restored contact between Whitehall and Liverpool, something that Harry would have found particularly important. If there was one
thing of which he made a virtue, it was establishing personal contact with
senior figures: nationally, in the form of government ministers and the Labour Party hierarchy, and locally, in the form of the church and business
leaders. This was certainly true in his involvement with the self-styled 'first
eleven' – a group of business people including the Chief Executive of
Littlewoods and the chairmen of Everton and Liverpool football clubs – as
Harry himself acknowledges:

> They used to have a dinner. There was nothing official about it. It was
> just a group of people with influence who came together to see what
> could be done to help the regeneration of Merseyside, and Liverpool in
> particular. After I became leader again, I received an invitation to go
> and I went. The big query was 'What did the change of leadership
> mean?' I said to them that when I'd previously been the leader I'd tried
> to follow a certain direction, and that what I was intent on doing was fol-
> lowing on from there. I said that I felt the first priority was to try to get
> to grips with the underlying financial problem that the city had, to get
> away from the constant crisis culture, and at the same time to foster
> partnerships between the council and whoever could be persuaded to
> join us in trying to win extra resources from the government.

It was as if Harry felt that his personal authority would influence such people. I never saw a great deal of evidence to support this, but he was certainly
recognised by them as a force for moderation.

As the council rapidly approached the deadline for submitting a budget,
Harry's predecessor Keva Coombes resurfaced, reinventing himself as if
nothing untoward had happened. Attempting, for once, to appear decisive,
Coombes presented the Labour group with his own budget proposals, while
at the same time denying that this was part of a fresh leadership bid, telling
one journalist, 'I'm not Lazarus. Mr Rimmer is.'[127] As far as the group was
concerned, Coombes was politically dead and buried, and they rejected his
proposals almost out of hand. Instead, with rumours abounding that Harry
had again threatened to resign should he be defeated, the group voted for a
budget that included a £23m package of cuts and 1500 job losses. Reality
was being faced up to with a vengeance. But these proposals were not accepted at the full council, where Rimmer was voted down thirty-nine to
thirty-two by a motley alliance of councillors from the Broad Left and the

minority parties, swelled by a couple of 'dissidents' from the Labour group. The Liberal Democrats chose to abstain. They may have considered this clever politics, but to me it was just another in the long line of occasions when they badly let Liverpool down.

With illegality again looming on the horizon, a special council meeting was arranged for the following Sunday, 10 March, the date by which the city had to pass a budget. A nasty day by anyone's standards; Gary Booth recalls his arrival at the Town Hall:

> Me, Dawn, and Frances [Kidd] decided to come through around the back of the Town Hall. Those councillors who came down Dale Street were just getting abuse as they walked along. 'You're selling people's jobs, you bastard', and all this sort of thing. As we came through Exchange Flags, we could see the hundreds of people in front of the Town Hall, only kept back by the coppers. A big copper came over and was just about to say 'Show us your ID,' when I realised I'd left my pass at home. Fortunately, as we came into view, a gang of the stewards saw us and started shouting 'Yer bloody scab – scab, scab, scab'. So before he had even asked for my ID, the copper says 'Oh, so you're a scab, well, come this way then' and ferries us into the Town Hall.

Prior to the meeting, key figures from within the Labour group had met their opposites in the Liberal Democrats and reached the inevitable compromise. This guaranteed far fewer job losses than had previously been mooted – 386 to be exact, mainly in ground maintenance and security – plus a package of measures to bring down the total employment costs of the city. After rejecting all of the alternatives, the council voted 57–40 for these measures and the meeting was called to a close. This, of course, was not the end of the matter. Inside the chamber, Mahmood, Cathy Wilson and Sylvia Sharpey-Shafer assured their place in Militant history by performing a clenched-fisted rendition of the 'Internationale'. Outside, Harry Rimmer found himself caught up in a media mêlée, when a fellow councillor's partner came to collect him and Harry in her car; as Harry remembers:

> She drove right up to the Town Hall and there was murder. A police inspector escorted me to the car and the press were taking photographs, which meant it was all exaggerated as 'council leader gets police escort'. All he was doing was shepherding me across the pavement because some of the crowd looked particularly threatening.

Indeed they were. Following the meeting, Trevor Smith, the Deputy Lord Mayor and a councillor for Speke ward, was assaulted in a city centre pub, an attack that left him nursing a black eye. Ironically, he had actually defied the group whip and voted against the package.

As the budget crisis was unfolding, I was becoming increasingly preoccupied elsewhere in the north west, in Ribble Valley, where a by-election was taking place following the elevation of David Waddington, the former Home Office minister, to the House of Lords. Given the choice, I would rather not have been doing this, and I had actually written to Joyce Gould a few months earlier telling her as much. It was not merely the fact that I had overseen three by-elections in the previous nine months – Bootle, Knowsley South, and Bootle again. With Eileen Murfin now in place as Regional Organiser, and taking responsibility for local government selections, appeals and other key duties, I saw potential problems arising in having me as the agent. More than anything else, I was worried that Eileen might feel undermined in her role. Joyce went ballistic and raised the matter with Jack Cunningham, then the party's campaign coordinator. She could be very temperamental like that, reacting strongly to things intuitively – shooting from the lip, I called it. Perhaps she felt that I ought to be grateful for remaining in employment with the party, given that it had kept me on the books despite Eileen's appointment. It was a rare roasting from Joyce. She was overwhelmingly supportive during the really difficult times, and I still have nothing but admiration for her courage and her ability.

Of course, Joyce got her way, and I was duly dispatched to Ribble Valley. Our candidate was Josie Farrington (who had previously been nominated for selection in the first of the Bootle by-elections). She was great to work with and would have done her damnedest whatever the circumstances. The problem with Ribble Valley, however, was that the Labour Party had a mountain to climb. We started out with a very experienced press officer, Lesley Smith, but there was very little help on the ground. There was not much in the way of local membership, and it was difficult to draft people in from elsewhere. Our predicament was not helped by an early poll suggesting that we were way out in the lead, a wholly unrealistic position.

To be honest, a Labour victory was never on the cards. One of the blue-ribbon Tory seats in the north west, Ribble Valley would even survive the great wipe-out of 1997. On this occasion, though, the by-election ended with a win for the Liberal Democrats; and, irony of ironies, their candidate was named Mike Carr. More significantly, this defeat of the Tories in one of their heartlands signalled the death-knell of the poli tax – announced a few days later by John Major – and marked a milestone in the dissolution of the Conservative Party's lengthy political hegemony.

Towards the end of March, Eric Heffer was made a Freeman of the City of Liverpool. At this stage, he had weakened quite considerably, and the physical effects of his illness (cancer) were visible for all to see. Nevertheless, in an indication of his continuing resentment, Heffer refused to invite me, his putative successor, to the award ceremony, which was to take place at Westminster (although he did invite Mulhearn and others of that ilk). I was invited by the Lord Mayor, Dot Gavin, but I declined on the grounds that if Eric did not want me there, then I would not go.

The seriousness of Eric's illness and the nature of the occasion did not stop some of Liverpool's leading lights drawing inappropriate attention to themselves. Having travelled to London as part of the group presenting the award, Deputy Lord Mayor Trevor Smith – now free of the shiner he had received after the budget vote – snaffled up a fair selection of the reception buffet in a House of Commons carrier bag. Shortly afterwards, at Euston Station, he revealed this to Dot Gavin, at which point they had a stand-up argument in public (and in front of a number of journalists from Liverpool). Smith's excuse, that it was a long way back to Liverpool and that he wanted some food for the journey, illustrated just how small-minded some of the city's representatives were, and the uphill challenge that it was to teach such people to conduct themselves in a proper manner. It almost goes without saying that from that day on, Trevor became known as 'Doggy Bag' Smith.

Despite the apparent soundness of the council's agreed budget, the new financial year brought the same old problems into sharp focus. Following a re-evaluation, the first of many, of the redundancies necessary to balance the city's books, it was decided that around 900 jobs would be lost, more than twice the number that had been agreed. This really did fire things up. The day after this became public, local NALGO secretary Judy Cotter did her symbolic duty and burnt redundancy notices at a mid-day protest (at which Terry Fields also spoke), and this was followed in turn by an all-out three-day strike and selective action in all areas of council provision. In time, the council scrapped time-off pay for council union officials, who, it argued, were too busy organising strikes to fulfil their expected duties. The longer all this went on, the more tempers became heated.

This was certainly true of the more lumpen elements of the workforce, a handful of whom threw the city's deputy treasurer, Alan Chape, a long-time member of NALGO, down the steps of the Municipal Building. Pressures also began to build up on individual Labour councillors. Alan Dean, in particular, suffered almost constant threats of intimidation, with people gathering outside his house early in the morning:

> They would be standing there as I came out, greeting me with the usual abuse, following me down the street and on to the bus or train. People were spitting at me everywhere I went. I couldn't go anywhere without being vilified verbally, and on some occasions physically attacked.

Most appalling of all, however, was the arson attack on Harry Rimmer's home, a fourth-floor flat in a multi-storey block. Harry had already lost a couple of cars through fire-bomb attacks, and was used to being catcalled on Dale Street and receiving anonymous abuse down the telephone line, but this was something else:

> My wife's mother was seriously ill and we went to visit her at the nursing home in Norris Green. As my wife's brothers were there, we decided to go home at about nine o'clock and then come back at midnight. When we came home, there were fire engines and everything outside. It was a right kerfuffle and it turned out that someone had tried to set fire to my flat. The local police commander thought that it was sinister, but didn't think it was politically motivated – he thought it was vandals. However, when the Chief Constable got the Special Branch in, they were not so sure. They felt it was a determined attempt to cause me grief and aggro. It was certainly upsetting because an old lady with a pacemaker lived underneath, and all the smoke got into her place. Luckily, two sisters who lived on the same landing as me were alerted. They also got smoked out and the landing was burnt. Then we had to go back to the nursing home, and my mother-in-law died that night. I suppose you could call it a low period.

It was a new low in Liverpool politics – that someone could have deliberately gone out of their way to imperil the lives of so many people in a tower block. Yet, if this and other physical attacks (Dean was later head-butted by a council employee) signalled the depths to which individuals – or, indeed, organisations – would stoop, the verbal abuse was something that had come to be accepted as part of the job. This is certainly the view of Vicky Roberts:

> We've all stood on picket lines and called people 'scab' and stuff like that,

so you wouldn't really expect people to react any differently. And I have to say that I probably got off more lightly because they probably regarded me as middle class and with no trade union background – they probably didn't think that I was working class, so their attitude would have been, 'Oh well, you don't expect anything better from someone like that'.

An illustration of the polarisation came with the sacking of Cllr Frances Kidd. Employed as a book-keeper for the GMB, she was under increasing pressure at work due to her stance within the council, where she would not budge from supporting the Labour group position on the necessity of re-dundancies. As a result, the local GMB went out of their way to sack her, claiming that she had taken an unauthorised person into the union office – a police officer who had called on official business. At the subsequent industrial tribunal, Frances argued victimisation by her employers with regard to her council duties, and won the case. The GMB's General Secretary, John Edmonds, did nothing to assist in any of this, but that came as no surprise. Back in 1986, I had approached him at the TUC to seek his help with the situation in Liverpool, and he told me to go and see the regional secretary, John Whelan. Edmonds knew as well as I did that Whelan was wholly intimidated by some of the GMB's more bullying lay officials in the city and was incapable of helping me.

Even by the standards of the time, it was apparent that politics in Liverpool were building up to something spectacular. Crisis was succeeding crisis, and the renegades were becoming more and more reckless. At April's full council meeting, Frank Vaudrey expressed his view of the Labour group leadership by tossing his papers at them; he was ejected from the Town Hall by the police and was promptly followed out by the rest of the Broad Left. In such behaviour I saw an opportunity. With Eileen Murfin busy inquiring into the Militant connections of Mahmood, Sharpey-Shafer, Wilson and others, I was left to do virtually as I pleased on a Labour Party salary. So I chose to goad the Broad Left out of the party via the local media. On one radio debate, I repeatedly challenged Tony Jennings to have the guts to stand under his own banner and oppose Labour openly. At the time, he said it was an option to be considered – his first admission of such a possibility. As we were soon to see, he eventually took my advice.

The big issue in Liverpool had become the bin service. A reduction in the number of bin rounds in the city from sixty to forty-five, intended to make the service more efficient, led to a work-to-rule and the start of what was to be a prolonged refuse dispute. For a while at least, many people failed to notice a dispute was taking place – the service had been so atrocious that it was often difficult to tell whether or not your bins had been emptied. This was well documented; in statistics published by the Chartered Institute for Public Finance and Accountancy (CIPFA), the refuse service in Liverpool was shown to be not only the least efficient in Britain but the least efficient by a mile. There had been cases of members of the refuse service charging shopkeepers to remove rubbish, something that they had already paid for through their rates. Such incidents had led occasionally to refuse workers being fined. More crucially, there was a blindness about the refuse workers' refusal (no pun intended, but never have a group of employees been so appropriately named) to acknowledge that people had an expectation of and a right to a decent service. The political undertones to all of this were more than apparent to Alan Dean:

> It would have been different if they had been able to say: 'These people provide an excellent service, but the city council's saying that they want to give the contract to someone else'. Obviously, that wasn't the case, because putting services out to tender had become compulsory by law. Yet, they made it sound as if it was our decision. By then, *they* had done a very good job, over four or five years, of getting a Trot – or someone very close to a Trot – into each team or gang. They were constantly spouting the diktat to their fellow team members, hyping them up and telling lies about what we were doing.

In fact, the council had actually stuck their necks out for the refuse workers, above and beyond the call of duty, as Paul Orr reveals.

> We formulated a policy of refuse collection, and sent it to the GMB's work-study people to see what they thought. They responded by saying that they couldn't agree more, and promised to back us to the hilt. We were going to make a saving of £2 million by cutting down the number of depots. Then we sent it to the local unions, telling them 'Look, we're not going to put this money in our arse pocket. We're going to use it to engage more home-helps and people of that nature. You submit our plans as your tender to take over the refuse collection and we'll guarantee that you get it.' They called a general meeting, after which their leader Matty Cullen told us to fuck off.

Harry Rimmer tells a similar story:

> They were so ignorant – and they showed it, which made it worse. They

decided to have a showdown with their bosses, having agreed that they had to have smaller gangs and bigger rounds, because with some of the rounds they were at home by half-past eleven in the morning. They agreed that it would be the basis of new contracts. Then on the first day that the new rounds system was to start, they walked out of the depot! They came down to the Municipal [Buildings], hundreds of them in the corridor where my office was, catcalling and hissing me as I walked in. Matty Cullen had brought them out on strike but he didn't know what to do next. I had to run the gauntlet but when I got to my office I said to Matty 'If you want to see me, you and half a dozen others can come in but get rid of the rest'. Matty did, and he and a few others came in. I said 'So what's the problem? You negotiated those new rounds. All they were doing was starting to implement them.' It finished up with me taking him along to see the Chief Executive. We sorted it out and they started work the next day.

A continuing work-to-rule, however, had as much effect as any strike. As the chair of the Environmental Services Committee, Vicky Roberts, explains, this was due in part to a somewhat unorthodox tactic:

> They were sabotaging the lorries in the morning, kicking out lights and stuff like that, and then refusing to take the wagons out.

By early May, rubbish was piling up across Liverpool, and various places around the city, such as Walton Recreation Ground and Wavertree Playground, had been allocated as temporary dumps. Little did I realise that these were about to provide the backdrop for a much bigger battle.

The local elections in May 1991 saw the Labour group in Liverpool take in a new batch of non-Militant councillors including local women such as Eileen Devaney, Petrona Lashley, and Margaret Clarke and traditional trade unionists like Jack Spriggs. More significant, however, was the appearance in six of the city's wards of 'Ward Labour' candidates as challengers to the official Labour nomination. I worked in each of the wards during the elections and saw Militant and their allies within the Broad Left at their most vicious. In Everton, our candidate, Pauline Davies, and I were stoned in the vicinity of Holy Cross. Eggs and stones, along with abuse, were hurled at the Labour Party campaign bus in Gillmoss while Eddie Roderick and I addressed electors through its loudspeakers. I was abused and threatened on the streets of both Anfield and Valley by leading members of the Broad Left. And in

Netherley, car loads of Militants harassed myself and the then shadow Home Secretary, Tony Blair.

To my recollection, Tony was the only member of the shadow cabinet to come and campaign in Liverpool during those elections. We had a particularly disgraceful and intimidatory reception, as did the other supporters of the official Labour candidate, Barry Navarro, but I was impressed by Tony's dignity in what for him was a novel experience. He kept his cool and completed the visit, despite the tirade of abuse and other provocations. I was not to forget this when he decided to stand for the leadership of the party.

Five 'Ward Labour' candidates were elected to the council, something that angered me immensely. These people were denigrating the name of the Labour Party, and in years to come this was to have a great effect, not only on the morale of the Labour group but also on the perspective of the electorate. Who could blame them when they were faced with a 'Heinz 57' variety of different forms of Labour on a ballot form? Nevertheless, one positive thing that did come out of their arrival in the chamber was that the Broad Left finally crossed their political Rubicon. Within days, 'The Liverpool Labour Group of Councillors' was established, comprising the five 'Ward Labour' councillors and twenty of those who had been suspended from the official Labour group. George Knibb proffers his view on this development:

> The Labour Party left us in limbo. In suspending us, it meant that we couldn't go to the group, couldn't make decisions, couldn't have contacts or nothing like that, but they expected us to go to the council and vote with them. Now it was thought out – somebody up there thought it out, and the next thing I heard was that Tony Jennings had got together with some people and said 'We're going to form our own group – everybody sign the register'. They had a meeting which I couldn't attend. My argument was 'No, we don't leave the Labour Party. Don't let them force you down that road.'

Still, George did sign up. His nominal leader, Tony Jennings, attempted to deny that the body was built on confusion, telling the local media: 'We are Liverpool councillors elected by Liverpool people'.[128] This rather facile argument continues to be held by Knibb, who still sits on the council under the umbrella of 'Ward Labour':

> Our argument was that we belonged to the Labour Party – they're not taking that badge or title away from us – we are Liverpool Labour. There was nothing behind using 'Liverpool' – it was 'We're Liverpool councillors

and we're Labour', that's all. We didn't try to confuse people. Even when I put my leaflets out, it was 'Everton Ward Labour Party'. The people around me used to belong to the Labour Party, but walked out – none of them have been expelled. We're saying 'We are the Labour Party in Everton, not them'.

Incidentally, three councillors who had been suspended for breaking the group whip – Coombes, Hackett and O'Donoghue – did not register with either the Labour group or Jennings and co. If they had joined the latter, it would have led to the 'Liverpool Labour Group' replacing the Liberal Democrats as the official opposition.

This, then, was the situation in May 1991. The city council was in turmoil, facing ever more dire financial difficulties. Its management was inept and its workforce steeped in outdated and unacceptable practices. Its services were derisory and its costs exorbitant. The former Labour group was split down the middle, the Liberal Democrats could not see beyond short-term and cynical opportunism, and the local Tories had long ago been decimated. The city's relationship with the national government was virtually non-existent, save for the occasional 'advice' from Heseltine (who had recently revisited the city to talk to Rimmer about establishing Liverpool's first Housing Action Trust).

With jobs still flowing away, a pall of gloomy despondency hung overhead, suggesting that all the efforts made to turn Liverpool round since Neil Kinnock's 1985 Bournemouth speech had been in vain. Then two events occurred which would provide a turning point in the city's political history. Firstly, the Labour Party's NEC faced the inevitable, as the twenty Broad Left 'rebels' who had formed a group with the five 'Ward Labour' councillors were recognised as having left the party; in effect, they had expelled themselves, removing the need for the disciplinary process to be applied. Secondly, and more significantly, the ailing MP for Liverpool Walton, Eric Heffer, lost his long battle with cancer, thus prompting my candidature at the by-election. The final showdown was about to occur.

# 12  Come together

Upon his death, the appreciation of Eric Heffer in the *Liverpool Daily Post* ended with a quotation from the man himself: 'You should become an MP for your beliefs and do a job for the voters who elected you – to improve life for working people'.[129] This was a fine sentiment with which I agreed entirely, but perhaps it would have had more resonance had Eric offered more than the handful of grandstanding contributions that he made in Parliament during the 1980s. As it was, he had become a rather distant figure to the electors of Walton long before his illness set in – a local 'name' perhaps, but not one with which they associated their everyday lives. Any doubt about this was removed three weeks after his death, when a poll sponsored by the *Liverpool Echo* revealed that only 3 per cent of 312 people sampled in Walton were aware that Eric had died.[130]

Eric's last appearance in the House of Commons was in January 1991, when Parliament was recalled to debate the Iraqi invasion of Kuwait. One of the more depressing things about Westminster is that people take an intense interest in someone whose health does not appear to be in the most rude of conditions. It is as if they can almost smell death in a sitting Member. This was certainly the case with Eric, and I was later informed that many of the comments that followed his appearance reflected a macabre curiosity about him amongst his fellow MPs. This interest became increasingly evident to me throughout early 1991. In the five months following Eric's presence during the Kuwait debate, I was frequently asked about his health by MPs from all over Britain. At first, these were of a polite 'How is he doing?' type, but gradually they gave way to 'How long has he left?' It was as if they were looking upon me as the harbinger of the Grim Reaper, sitting by and taking an inordinate interest in the man's wellbeing, waiting for his last breath. This was not the case at all. At that time, I rarely saw him, and neither of us would have considered the other an associate in any shape or form, let alone a friend.

Eric did occasionally telephone me on a Sunday morning on some matter or other, but our conversation was always strained. Frankly, I disliked him almost as much as he disliked me. He was a terribly vain man, who projected himself as a working-class intellectual. He once swore blind to me over the telephone that Albert Nolan's book on liberation theology, *Jesus before Christianity: the gospel of liberation*, which I had in my possession, did not exist – he virtually called me a liar. I was so frustrated with telling him otherwise that I ended up buying him a copy!

I must confess, however, that, towards the very end he did speak to me in ways that indicated he was trying to repair the rupture in our relationship. In one telephone conversation, he actually said his position over the Walton selection had nothing to do with the way he felt about me personally. Unfortunately, his book, *Never a Yes Man*, published posthumously, contained a contradictory barb. Noting that I had given him advance notice of my intention to seek the nomination, Eric commented that he 'said little at the time'. This was not the case – he had made it abundantly clear that he was opposed to my standing. On the NEC rejecting his letter of complaint, he wrote: 'However, as no rules had been broken, they ruled that this time it [my selection] was permissible. Kilfoyle was selected, but only just. As someone remarked "He has received his sweets".' He then concluded: 'His selection is a recipe for future conflict'.[131]

Eric's illwill towards my selection was at marked variance with the letters of support that I received from various quarters. One in particular stuck in my mind. It read: 'Whatever the reservations of the establishment, everyone knows you will make a great MP and a fine representative of the people of Walton, and they are lucky to have you'. The author of these flattering lines? Peter Mandelson.

Five weeks before his death, Eric also attempted to reopen dialogue with Laura Kirton, herself ill in hospital. In a letter sent on behalf of himself and his wife Doris, Eric attempted to repair the breach caused by his failure to support Laura against Militant's take-over of Walton CLP:

Dear Laura,

We were terribly sorry to hear that you are in hospital but delighted to know that you got through the operation ... I've thought about you a great deal and realise how much you have played a part in my life. We may not always have seen everything eye to eye on all issues but that has been the exception, not the rule. I would like to say thank you for all that you have done for and with us over the years. I look back on those days with real affection. I think we can say between us that we built Walton into one of the best seats in the country. It is just regrettable that we get old but that's how it is and there's nothing we can do about it. I certainly have no regrets and would do it all over again ...

Doris and Eric

Laura's response was typically hard-nosed:

Dear Doris and Eric,

Thank you for your letter of good wishes. I read in it all I can get and then some. You reckon you would not have changed everything that you have done in your life. My way of expressing that is that you don't change in life, you only become more so. So far as I'm concerned, nothing has changed capitalism. I can see no reason why my attitude should change towards it. I stand where I stood forty years ago and can see no reason to deviate one iota – the same goes for Winnie. I'm not in a fit state to argue in any shape or form. Perhaps that may come later, but for now I would like you to know why, having looked at all the parliamentary candidates, I plumped for Peter Kilfoyle. He, among them all, had the closest industrial record to your own. Indeed, I saw many similarities in your hard-tackling attitudes. No-one like you two, who have done battle where it counts at the point of industrial contact, and not been afraid to pitch in and be counted, could do other than understand what it is all about. I get tired of carpet-baggers, the chancers and the ravers. A little bit of hard application is what we now need. God knows where it is to come from. On the lighter side, if you pop over to the other side before me, weigh up the position. We could do with a spot of angel reorganisation. It's time they all got their fingers out and perhaps we're the pair who can motivate them.

Laura[132]

It was right that some form of rapprochement was effected. After all, Laura had been Eric's agent from 1964 until 1979. She was an excellent organiser and motivator within the Walton constituency, turning it from a Tory-held seat into one of Labour's safest. Eric owed her a great deal – which he acknowledged – and it would have been a relief to them both that the ice on their long-standing comradeship was broken before their respective ends.

Eric's funeral took place on 3 June at St Mary's church in a part of Walton known locally as Walton Village. Referred to in the Domesday Book, this area in fact predates central Liverpool, which developed more than a century later after receiving its charter from King John (he required a base in the north west from which to exploit Ireland). In marking Eric's passing, St Mary's was to witness one of the more extraordinary events in its long history. It was quite remarkable to see at the funeral the massed ranks of Militant; they turned up to hiss, jeer, spit at and generally abuse me as I walked into the service. It was all part of a pantomime they conducted to authenticate Eric as a hero of 'the left'. Personally, I think he would have been appalled by the way in which they behaved, at what was supposed to be a time of solemnity. The noise and the banners were one thing, their aggression was something else. One would have imagined that I was personally responsible for Eric's death. The atmosphere inside the church was no less bizarre. I sat in a section reserved for MPs, in which I was surrounded by friendly faces, including Stan Orme, George Howarth, Eddie O'Hara and Roger Stott. Other seats were reserved for Hatton, Mulhearn and the like, who, having been amongst the throng outside, entered the church like boxers parading before a championship fight, arrogantly flashing the cut of their cloth and jutting their chins out as if to say 'Come on then – give us your best shot'.

In his funeral oration, Tony Benn extolled Eric as a skilled craftsman, and referred to his devout Christianity. A few days later, I related this to a bed-ridden Laura Kirton. Bemused, she responded by telling me the story about the shelves Eric had put up for her that had collapsed within a couple of days, and, more caustically, that he had found religion on the Via Dolorosa at the same time that he found the ambition to be Prime Minister.

I have never been a great devotee of funerals, and given the hostility exhibited beforehand by Militant and their allies, I was glad to get away from St Mary's as soon as possible. I had always thought that a funeral was an occasion to mourn a passing and to celebrate a life. Eric's had little relevance to him as a person, and was instead used by those who wished to set a ritual challenge to the Labour Party. Led by Terry Fields, a noisy, ramshackle political march made its way from the church to the crematorium, celebrating not Eric, but Militant. That procession, however, was to be a premature wake for the latter – a precursor of the organisation's expiry. In doing Eric's memory such a great disservice, Militant merely convinced even more people of the bankruptcy of its ideas. More immediately, the gloves were off. I was to champion the Labour Party, and the arena was to be the by-election.

In the week after Heffer's funeral, politics in Liverpool shifted into a higher gear. Keen to get the by-election under way, the national leadership of the Labour Party acted swiftly to get the writ moved through the Commons, and, in doing so, prompted the local party machine into campaign mode. Meanwhile, Militant were about to make what was to be their most tactically erroneous decision ever. Perhaps they thought that they had nothing to lose – they had been excised from Liverpool City Council Labour group, and many of their more active organisers had been expelled from local parties across Britain. Nevertheless, deciding, with the support of their Broad Left acolytes, to stand their own candidate against the Labour Party really was a case of cutting off your nose to spite your face.

Of course Militant were not entirely open about it. Their nominee, Lesley Mahmood, entered the contest like a political Salome behind the veil of 'Walton Real Labour'. I was not surprised by any of this, least of all the reluctance of Militant's hierarchy to admit finally to the public and politicians alike that they were an organisation distinct from the body from which they had been feeding for so long. Still, as their supporters would be expected to flood into Walton from all over Britain, it was to be a ready-made opportunity for the real Labour Party to identify these people individually with a view to removing them from their local parties. Rapidly modernising, we were about to shed ourselves of a most debilitating parasite.

By sheer luck or misfortune, depending on one's viewpoint, the backdrop to the by-election was to be a Channel 4 television series called *GBH*. Complex in its plot, the programme possessed a context and characters that were uncannily similar to Liverpool at the time of Hatton and co. The fact that the author was Alan Bleasdale, one of Liverpool's foremost writing talents, and someone whose work had long used the city and its people for inspiration, served only to add fuel to a furious debate, raising questions about the wisdom of running the programme during the by-election. Bleasdale himself vigorously denied that Liverpool circa the mid 1980s was the model for the drama. Alas, as the series unfolded, there was endless media speculation that the major character, 'Michael Murray', was a less than subtle caricature of Hatton.

With an eye on his forthcoming trial for fraud, but perhaps also sensing an opportunity for some publicity, Hatton attempted to link *GBH* to Liverpool, appearing on a handful of national television programmes, such as *Wogan* and *Right to Reply,* and spoon-feeding prose to some of the newspaper journalists who had set up camp in Liverpool's hotels. Naturally, there was also an attempt to portray my own role against the backdrop of *GBH*.

## Left Behind: Lessons from Labour's heartland

Michael Murray's antagonist in the series was a 'soft left' schoolteacher called Jim Nelson, who obsessively washed his feet each night. At the initial press conference of the campaign, the very first question put to me was whether I did likewise. I responded quickly, with 'Of course – doesn't everybody?' It broke the ice, and in terms of the media's own agenda gave them something with which to draw parallels.

If the truth be told, I did not pay too much attention to the national media's coverage of Liverpool during the by-election. Indeed, I was advised to avoid newspapers for the duration. Having been a by-election agent, I knew that my role was as 'a legal necessity'. The less I knew of the publicity, the better a candidate I would be. As it turned out, nearly 500 articles appeared between the dates of Heffer's funeral and the by-election post mortem. Trawling through them, it is evident that the media were sending out mixed messages about what was going on. They were in some senses party political, but were also a reflection of deep-set prejudices against Liverpool and its people. The city was shown as being in 'chaos', with various factions 'at war' with each other, and having lost its 'purpose' as a place on the map. Stereotypical 'qualities' of Scousers were conjured up, ranging from humour and music on the one hand, to violence, intimidation and petty gangsterism on the other. And more than a passing reference was made to the time when the city's dead went unburied during the 'winter of discontent'.

More accurately, the media fastened on to the breakdown of the refuse service, and the threat of industrial action to other public services. This struck a chord with the electorate, which was sick and tired of lousy municipal services, and even more sick of the mountains of rubbish that had arisen from the work-to-rule. Journalistic licence was abused, however, when a number of articles on Liverpool's 'rat-infested rubbish dumps' followed an incident near a canal in neighbouring Bootle, when a small child was bitten by a rat. From the beginning, I made my position on the dispute quite clear. Without hesitation, I condemned the unwarranted actions of that section of the local GMB whose intransigence had brought about the dumps in the first place. When Onyx UK, the company who took over the tender, came in and cleared up the mess, there was widespread relief. It was obvious to all that the public simply wanted the basic service for which they had paid and to which they were entitled.

In terms of the by-election, it seemed that the media were 'on side' with the Labour Party from day one. I was never convinced that Heffer had been the darling of the lobby that he had always claimed to be. Indeed, I had never taken for granted anything that Eric had to say about himself – how many 'poor' in the 1930s had four cooked meals a day, holidays in Margate, and not one, but two, apprenticeships? (All this information is volunteered in his biography.) In fact, the lobby correspondents I spoke to during the by-election were more than conscious of Eric's real 'contribution' to the background events that had long preceded this showdown with Militant. They were also smart enough to perceive that the mass of people in Walton, and in Liverpool at large, wanted nothing whatsoever to do with Militant. The latter's claim to local legitimacy was seen as wholly spurious. Moreover, those within the lobby who understood Liverpool's history immediately recognised that Militant's way of operating had more in common with the Tammany Hall way of politics that had characterised the city's past than with any notion of 'permanent revolution'.

Seeing and hearing Mahmood for the first time, with her sour expression and grating voice, could only have put paid to any residual doubts the lobby correspondents may have had. The other candidates were none too splendid either. The Liberal Democrats brought in Paul Clark, who had recently conceded his leadership of the local party to Mike Storey, as a replacement for their official PPC, Richard Roberts, a worthy but charmless local councillor. This was presumably because Clark was more experienced, having stood against Heffer at the 1987 general election, and in the belief that he more than anyone would be able to take advantage of voter dissatisfaction with 'the split in the Labour Party'. The Tory, Berkeley Greenwood, was a decent cove, but he was finished once it was revealed that his only previous election contest, at Liverpool University's Student Union, had seen him gain less support than a dog named Muttley. Support for his party, meanwhile, fell so desperately that rumours started to emerge that its chairman, Chris Patten, had approached the Liberal Democrats with a view to forging an alliance in Walton. There was also Screaming Lord Sutch, whose stated policy to put a 'Scouse tax' on Cilla Black and Paul McCartney, and make Ken Dodd the city treasurer, caused the *Independent* to remark: 'This beguiling manifesto may be no madder than some of the antics that brought a once-great city to its knees'.[133]

The Labour Party needed to make apparent the stark difference between itself and the Militant supporters and stooges who were masquerading as 'Walton Real Labour'. Even though Walton was one of our safest seats in the country, we still had to dispel any confusion that might have arisen amongst the electorate, and this led to quite a heavy schedule. Each day began with a briefing from two very capable Walworth Road professionals, Nick Sigler and Jo Moore. This was then followed by a press conference, chaired by Bruce Grocott MP, involving myself and a visiting front-bench spokesperson. We would try and establish a daily theme – education, health, unemployment – after which came the daily photo-opportunities, themselves often consonant with the day's theme. These were much of a muchness – standard by-election fare with the candidate and a 'name' photographed in an everyday situation, typified by the one with myself and Harriet Harman talking to children outside a school, or those with me and Robin Cook at a hospital.[134] Other photographs, however, were downright embarrassing, in particular those of Roy Hattersley and me playing football in the street outside Goodison Park.[135] It would have been worse if we had donned our respective club's colours – Everton and Sheffield Wednesday. Two middle-aged men of ample girth should have known better!

Behind the scenes, the campaign team, chaired by John Evans MP, met every day to plan our strategy and devise tactics. Having been an agent, I knew the form – the candidate should be seen and not heard, at least, not by the campaign team. Therefore, I made no effort to discover what was going on, nor did I question their game plan. I knew exactly what our respective roles were and had the utmost faith in the team's ability to think things through. The master stroke was to make my fellow regional organiser and good friend Fraser Kemp (himself now an Honourable Member) my driver and minder. He, too, knew intimately how by-elections operated, but more than that, he had a keen sense of humour and a very cool head. He certainly needed the latter. On more than one occasion, I was out of the car and challenging Militant canvassers. It made my blood boil to see them on the streets of Walton, despite having worked to bring them out into the light of day. Fraser, however, would get me back into the car and on to my next scheduled visit without turning a hair.

The only other aspect of the campaign that annoyed me were the telephoned death threats made against me and my family. Thanks to the advice of Joyce Gould, I had had a recording device attached to the telephone, enabling me to present the police with a recording of any threatening messages. From then on, all telephone calls to my home were intercepted. The threats stopped, but the police were unable to apprehend those responsible.

Occasionally, the organisation of the daily schedule was interrupted; but that is part and parcel of campaigning, and it will never be possible to cover for every contingency. One such interruption occurred prior to the daily 'event' on the first of Neil Kinnock's two trips to Liverpool during the by-election. Word had got out that Neil and I were paying a visit to a sheltered housing project and, as we arrived, it became apparent that a large crowd had gathered. Sadly, their number included a dozen or so Militants and their associates, who began to hurl abuse at us. Riled by this, the rest of the crowd, few of whom were Labour Party activists, sent them packing down the street before returning to give Neil and myself a rapturous welcome. It was at this point that I was left in no doubt that the electors of Walton recognised Militant for what it really was – a separate group, far removed from the Labour Party to which they gave their support.

For much of the campaign, Mahmood and her 'Walton Real Labour' supporters came across as a rather parochial force, constantly playing on their 'local' credentials and referring to the legacy of Heffer. At times when they were making noises about Neil Kinnock's 'attacks on the people of Liverpool',[136] it was difficult not to see them as a separatist group, ready to claim UDI on behalf of 'the historic people' of the Mersey basin – a sort of Scouse version of Herri Batasuna or the Lega Nord.[137]

The true spirit of socialism, meanwhile, was being shown by two other MPs, Denis Turner and Dave Clelland. Leaving one of our committee rooms, they saw a very disconsolate group of children outside an adjacent school. On enquiring why the kids were looking so glum, they were told that the coach that had been hired to take them on their summer day out had broken down and the trip had been cancelled. Denis and Dave, however, would not hear of this. The children were quickly organised into a sing-song on the pavement, while the candidate rooms hired a fresh coach, paid for by the two MPs. Within an hour, the children and their teachers were off on their day out, all thanks to two generous and caring comrades.

They were not the only ones. I was taken by the enthusiasm with which the real party came to Walton to campaign. I was truly delighted to see former colleagues like Larry Whitty and Peter Mandelson willingly go canvassing on the streets. In fact, over one hundred members of the Parliamentary Labour Party came to Liverpool to assist.

On one occasion, members of the PLP took me to dinner in a local hotel. There must have been about twenty-five of them altogether, and it was their opportunity to greet and size up someone who was about to join their ranks. To my surprise, I was expected to say a few words. Trying ineffectively to be humorous, I used a quote from Bagehot that 'Parliament is a large gathering of more or less idle men'. I was mortified when Clare Short corrected my pronunciation of 'Bagehot'. Being an autodidact in these (and most other) matters, I had never confirmed the correct way in which it should be pronounced. I learnt my lesson well. Such occasions as this were opportunities to see MPs from many parts of the country at their best. It was gratifying to see so many of them commit themselves to the campaign. I had seen similar numbers in other high-profile by-elections, but I had never been so aware of the shared sense of purpose that bound us all together into the Labour Party. That common ideology gave a strength to our campaigning that would overwhelm the most sophisticated of marketing techniques. The latter undoubtedly complements such zeal, but can never replace it.

In stark contrast to all this, the Labour MPs for some of Liverpool's other constituencies were increasingly notable by their continuing absence from the campaign. Terry Fields let it be known that he was 'too busy' to involve himself. This came as no surprise. Most observers were well aware whose side he was on; and following his defence of Militant during a parliamentary debate on the government of Liverpool (on June 24), his political fate was sealed. Eddie Loyden, meanwhile, remained wholly silent on his activities. Considering the number of times that Loyden had put meetings in Liverpool ahead of parliamentary business, it was perhaps ironic that he should have spent so much of the by-election attending the House of Commons – but then again, perhaps not. Bob Parry turned up once, and was sent leafleting for a short while in the furthest extremity of the constituency. Later, however, Parry considered suing Robert Kilroy-Silk and the *Daily Express* over an article suggesting that his absence from the campaign was a result of him being a closet Militant.[138] When his lawyers approached me, I confirmed his short presence in Walton, but pointed out that, if it went to court and I was called as a witness, my testimony would be far more damaging than the named article. I heard nothing more of the libel action.

Although being a candidate was a less taxing experience than those I had endured as an agent, the campaign soon became a grinding routine of visits and photo-opportunities. The one aspect of the by-election that I did enjoy immensely was the press conferences. Two in particular still make me smile. At the first, someone from one of the more obscure papers referred to a protest march against war due to take place with the words, 'If Eric Heffer were alive, he would have been leading this march. What do you say to it?' I have always been a great fan of the war poets, and the first thing that came into my head was a line from one of them. So I replied: 'I'm mindful of Wilfred Owen's famous lines, "The old lie: dulce et decorum est, pro patria mori [it is sweet and proper to die on behalf of the fatherland]".' The individual who had asked the question was taken aback, as were a number of the other journalists present. I was later told that Bill Deedes, a columnist at the *Daily Telegraph* and a staunch Conservative, had apparently said 'We haven't got much chance against a Labour Party, if they can provide candidates like this'. Presumably, he believed that a Labour candidate in somewhere such as Liverpool would more than likely be illiterate. I was quite happy to put him right on that score, even with a lucky quote!

Shortly after this, I was at another press conference with the Shadow Chancellor, John Smith, when a journalist asked me to comment on each of the various political parties. In desperation, I offered: 'I think about Lesley Mahmood, and Medusa comes to mind. I think of Paddy Ashdown, and he reminds me of Janus, facing both ways. John Major – well, he is Cyclops, because in the party of the politically blind, the one-eyed man is king; and this man [turning to John Smith] evokes Hercules, because he has the Herculean task of turning around the economy after the next general election'. I just launched into this, and much to my amazement, the assembled journalists stood up and applauded. It was all very flattering, but – I fear – only because it challenged their preconceptions of Liverpool people. On any other occasion, my rant would have fallen apart.

This was not to deny that Walton, like the rest of Britain, had – and has – its underbelly of individuals seemingly beyond the reach of reasoned argument. This was evident when two visiting Labour MPs to the city, Ron Davies and Tony Lloyd, knocked on a door in some flats they were canvassing, and a Liverpool version of Rab C. Nesbitt answered with 'What the fuck do you want?' When told that they had come to canvass for his vote – they actually put it in those terms – he said, 'If you're for that Paki bitch Mahmood, you can sod off'. Now the man was obviously both a racist bigot and a misogynist, but they pressed on: 'So obviously then, you'll be voting for the Labour Party candidate, Peter Kilfoyle'; to which 'Rab' quickly replied: 'What, that left-footer bog-trotting bastard? He's one of fourteen kids – I'd sooner vote for the Pope than vote for him', thereby revealing a sectarian edge to his outlook (the phrase 'left-footer' being a Protestant term of abuse for Catholics). Even so, as Ron and Tony walked away, they decided to mark the man down as a 'doubtful'.

I never doubted for one minute that Labour would win in Walton. As I had said early on in the campaign, Mahmood and her ilk stood more chance of victory in Tirana North, Enver Hoxha notwithstanding. Granted, Paul Clark and the Liberal Democrats did make more ground than I would have liked, but they were never considered a threat at any time (their national leadership later accused the BBC of being biased in its coverage of the by-election). As for the Tories, well, to borrow Kenneth Clarke's overall view of the by-election, they were 'irrelevant'.[139] Like Lord Sutch, they were there to make up the numbers, a fact highlighted by Berkeley Greenwood's 2.9 per cent share of the vote – the lowest recorded by a Tory in a by-election since 1945, and a lost deposit to boot.

On the day of the count, I went for a quiet lunch with my family, Mo Mowlam, George Howarth, and Fraser, who was still there 'minding' me to the finish. In the evening, I spent some time preparing an acceptance speech, alternating this with attempts at playing my guitar, while waiting to hear that an announcement of the result was imminent. Just before 10.30 P.M., I received the call, and with Fraser, Bernie and my press officer, Jo Moore, I made the fifteen-minute journey from home to the counting rooms at Liverpool University. The count was in the student union room, where, during the campaign, a debate between the candidates had been televised. On our way there, there was no display of nerves – both Fraser and Bernie were terrific in keeping me occupied with small talk. As I walked into the hall, I saw that Charles Lasham, the acting returning officer, was just about to inform some of the other candidates about spoilt papers and other details. He looked up, caught my eye and winked, and I knew then that we had triumphed.[140]

The night was spent in celebration at the Trader's Club. An ex-working men's club in the Walton constituency, when I arrived it was literally heaving with party members, MPs, well-wishers, friends and family. I even received a telephone call from Rio de Janeiro, from my brother Billy, who said that his business associates in West Africa had seen the occasion on television and telephoned him in Brazil to alert him. Miraculously (indeed, mysteriously), he had managed to obtain the restricted number of Fraser's mobile phone.

It truly was such a memorable night that I celebrated by dancing on the stage. But late into the morning, the implications of the result began to sink in. No longer could Militant infect the Labour Party in any numbers. No longer could they claim electoral legitimacy beneath the banners and colours of the Labour Party. No longer could Neil Kinnock be accused of failing to take out those who were using the Labour Party on behalf of another organisation.

A few years earlier, Taaffe and Mulhearn had written: 'Merseyside was to be a laboratory in which the ideas of both Militant and its opponents would be tested'.[141] The outcome in Walton signalled the end of their organisation's grotesque political experiment. Frankenstein's monster was dead.

Soon after, many of those who had worked for Mahmood's campaign in Walton were removed from the Labour Party, as was Terry Fields. His intransigence towards the national party had deepened, and coincided with an almost inevitable prison sentence for his refusal to pay the poll tax, where it was alleged that he set about writing his own 'Prison Notebook' – no doubt entitled 'A worker's MP on a worker's wage'. By the end of 1991, however, the game was up for Fields and Militant's other representative at Westminster, Dave Nellist. Militant itself – i.e. the Revolutionary Socialist League – embarked on a lengthy post-mortem of its own, wherein divisions became evident amongst its executive committee over strategy and other matters (Ted Grant took others in the hierarchy to task for the vociferousness with which they had condemned me, arguing that I was not as bad as I had been portrayed). In time, and with the reality sinking in that they could no longer exist within the Labour Party, Militant finally came out of the political closet and announced that it was, indeed, a separate organisation. From that day on, its support fell into rapid decline.

As for Liverpool, the legacy of Liberal Democrat and Militant incompetence during the 1970s and 1980s, and Thatcher's cold heart, was to be visited on a new generation of local politicians. They were to be subject not only to the financial straitjacket bequeathed to them, but also the even more formidable psychological impediment of the maxim 'no cuts in jobs and services'. Yet at the turn of the millennium, there is strong evidence to suggest that Liverpool is at last emerging from its quarter of a century of political and economic purdah. New investments, a new sense of optimism, and a new ruling party (the Liberal Democrats – something I am naturally cautious about), all point towards Liverpool having turned a corner. If so, it is not before time. It has been little short of tragic that such a creative city – in Britain, second only, perhaps, to the capital – should have been unable for so long to reinvent itself.

Maybe, in years to come, it will be seen that the most important effect of the Walton by-election was to break a mould in Liverpool politics – a mould which certainly predated Labour's ascendancy in the city. If that is the case, then my own contribution towards putting to rest the battles which had begun at the time of the Housing Finance Act back in 1972 was worthwhile. The motto of Everton Football Club reads: *nil satis, nisi optimum*, which loosely translates as 'nothing but the best is good enough'. As I said in my maiden speech to the House of Commons, two weeks after the by-election, it is a dictum that ought to apply to both the city and the people of Liverpool.

# Epilogue: Full circle

Nine years have now elapsed since my by-election. Sometimes it seems like a lifetime ago; on other occasions, reminders of the battles of the past rush into focus. Only Hatton and Wareing of the old guard remain in the public eye, the former as a radio presenter, the latter fighting to hang on to his seat. The rest have retreated into obscurity. Sometimes people remark on my own role in facing down Militant as if it was still a live threat. It is not, of course, but the dangers posed by passivity in the face of unrepresentative entryist elements remain.

I had recognised that it would take some years to mop up the remains of that period, but I truly believed that we would win the following general election in 1992. Given his Stakhanovite labours in turning around the Labour Party, in both organisation and policy, it seemed only right that Neil Kinnock should be given the opportunity to demonstrate his ability to lead the government and the nation. The electorate denied him that opportunity, preferring instead to extend the tenure of office of a dull, if decent, man on a soapbox.

It was a sobering experience to have suffered our fourth election defeat in a row. Neil Kinnock was so dignified in the post-election period. Once he had announced his retirement as party leader, I received a telephone call from Anji Hunter, asking whether I would join Tony Blair for dinner. I agreed, but she did not know where we might go. I suggested Vitello D'Oro, an Italian restaurant near the House of Commons. As we ate, Neil arrived with his office staff for a farewell dinner. There was a brief exchange of greetings, but other than that, no conversation. Tony seemed constrained in his chat with me, and I wondered why he had asked me to join him. Only much later did I figure out that he had been planning to run for deputy to John Smith before the latter struck a deal with Margaret Beckett.

There were two other occasions when I observed Neil closely before the election of John Smith as his successor. On one occasion, myself, George Howarth and Jane Kennedy took him and Glenys out for dinner. It was the least we could do to show our regard for him; after all, we each owed him a great deal. Not once did he allow an unkind word to spill from his lips. I was taken with his dignity, his refusal to be cowed by those who had worked to undermine him or had simply abused him. On the second occasion, we ate some takeaway food in his office and had a drink. He was less sanguine on that occasion about the rough hand dealt with him by Fate.

Nevertheless, business had to proceed, and we were faced with a straight choice between John Smith and Brian Gould. Robin Cook rang me from his home in the New Forest on behalf of Smith. I told him that I would indeed support John, but not Margaret Beckett, his running mate, since she had signed the minority report on the Liverpool District Labour Party in February 1986. Instead, I publicly advocated John Prescott as deputy leader in my first attempt at a 'head and heart' combination for the leadership.

John Smith and Margaret Beckett, of course, won the leadership and deputy leadership respectively. John quickly set to to win over the hearts as well as the minds of his party. Unlike either his predecessor or his successor, his family home was in his beloved Scotland, not in London. That meant he was a 'House of Commons' man, one of those who have a regular drink in the smoking room and eat in the dining room. This, in turn, made him a familiar and friendly figure to the majority of Labour Members of that time who had their homes in Scotland, Wales or the English regions.

He also struck an immediately independent tone in his leadership. Significantly, he had no truck with Peter Mandelson, who had been close to Neil Kinnock's leadership and was to be even closer to Tony Blair's. I can only speculate as to why he kept the Member for Hartlepool at such a distance, but he did. John could be extremely acerbic – he said of one member from the Welsh valleys that he would not only not have him in his government, he would not, if he had his way, have him in the Labour Party.

John also dabbled, in what seemed to me a half-hearted way, in membership and selection reform. I wrote him a note urging caution – I had seen the results of loose rules in these critical areas. Even then, I was concerned at the danger of slipping into the Americanisation of British politics, with even less active participation by rank-and-file members. This was perhaps not so much a concern for John, being a member of the traditional right of the party; yet it was – and continues to be – a concern for anyone worried by non-participatory 'democracy'.

Shortly after a hugely successful visit to the north west, John collapsed and died, on the morning of 12 May 1994. It was a tremendous blow to all of us in the labour movement. He was respected by all and loved by most. His funeral resembled a state occasion, and it was very moving. Yet the business of politics grinds on. It was alleged in the tea-room that even in the hours following John's death, the spin-doctors were at their contemptible worst, promoting, or denigrating, potential candidates for the now-vacant leadership.

At the NEC, John Evans pointed out that, according to the rules, Margaret Beckett became party leader until the normal annual conference. Margaret strenuously opposed waiting until conference to elect a new leader and deputy, and supported the idea of a special conference to elect the new leadership. Presumably she believed that this would be more advantageous to her longer term interests. If that was so, it was to prove so very wrong.

Wisely, a decision was made by the party that there should be a moratorium on campaigning for the leadership until after the Euro elections, on 9 June. Naturally, the media continued to speculate on the likely candidates, fed scraps, no doubt, by the spin-doctors. This carried on throughout the period of mourning between John's death and his burial. The potential candidates were in a no-win situation. Their names were being bandied about, yet they were unable to comment publicly. What they were able to do was to take soundings among the electorate, the first element of which was the Parliamentary Labour Party.

On the evening of Saturday 21 May 1994, I received a telephone call at home from Tony Blair. It was a short call, as we had visitors at home, and I agreed to ring him back on Sunday morning. The second call led to my agreement to help Tony with the leadership nomination. I discovered that Mo Mowlam was on board, and we agreed to meet Tony in his office the following morning.

With Anji Hunter also in attendance, we quickly compiled a list of those who would be helpful in canvassing the PLP for support, and by Monday evening we already had half a dozen regional contacts. Soon, we had a link in every region and every group in the PLP, and people to cross-check soundings, to be absolutely sure of the level and detail of support.

It was a fascinating period. It became my job to deliver the result in the wider PLP, and we considered it inconceivable that the party would disagree with the PLP's choice (the Bennite period was well over!). I kept a list of those who came on board Tony's bandwagon. Mo apart, the first member of the Shadow Cabinet was Chris Smith, the last, an indecisive Harriet Harman. Halfway through the first week, Tony said he wanted Jack Straw as his campaign chairman (I had suggested Mo). Jack appeared at one meeting of the acting campaign committee, saw who was there, spoke for two minutes and then disappeared. Subsequently, he agreed to chair Tony's campaign.

Once again, I went for the 'head and heart' line, Tony Blair and John Prescott. To this end, I met regularly in the smoking room with Ian McCartney, who was on John Prescott's team, to see how we could bring our respective candidates together. It was always quiet in there in the mornings, after the two campaign teams had had their daily meetings. The pairing was to be a successful approach. Within three years, they were to lead the Labour Party into government for the first time in eighteen years.

Yet there was something not quite right from those early days. The first sign was the alacrity with which the campaign committee began to rewrite recent policy documents. I had not signed up to the campaign for that – it was, I felt, a matter for wider consideration than for our self-selecting little group. The second was the nature of the emerging 'project', ill-defined though it was. The campaign quickly became much wider than simply promoting the Blair ticket. That had been established by Saturday 11 June, the second day of official campaigning, when the *Guardian* published the names of a clear majority of members of the PLP intending to nominate Tony Blair.

The third major signpost was the 'Bobby' remark at the celebration in Church House of Tony's election as leader. 'Bobby', as we all now know, referred to Peter Mandelson. He had never figured in the Blair campaign team. Who knew of his involvement, I will never know. What was known was that he was a negative factor with potential supporters of Tony Blair. One must presume that that was the reason for keeping him hidden, while using his well-trained poodles in the media to devastating effect.

It all added up to a strategy aimed at more than winning the leadership and, subsequently, the next election. It increasingly appeared to be designed to change the party and the country in ways which many would never have agreed to if they had known what was to come. All of this was packaged under the sobriquet 'New Labour', with its young, charismatically-sketched leader.

The iconic Clause IV was to go; we were to perform contortions over grant-maintained schools; trade unions were to remain circumscribed compared to the period before the draconian Tory employment laws; and much else. To me, it all appeared distinctly ad hoc – at least until the ex-communist Peter Mandelson and the ex-SDP member Roger Liddle – typical examples of the 'New Labour' rainbow coalition – published *The Blair Revolution*. In its preface, the authors wrote that the book 'bears nobody's imprimatur but our own'. As I wrote in a review of it in *Tribune* at the time, I breathed a sigh of relief reading that. The book was a disturbing mish-mash of notions alien to me as a committed member of the Labour Party. I wanted to believe that if this was being pressed on our new leader, people like me were duty-bound to provide a counterbalance.

This was to prove a naive delusion, as I watched the 'New Labour' project unfold. It became less and less possible to make any meaningful amendment to the programme being advanced. As the Tory government fell apart, the proponents of the new creed were ever more determined to reshape the Labour Party in their own image and likeness. Shadow Ministers generally fell into line; most of those who did not were dispensed with. Those considered beneath the standards of New Labour were weeded out both before and after the 1997 general election.

The election campaign itself became a showcase for a small number of New Labour luminaries, with a few 'old' Labour types thrown in as insurance. Behind the scenes, the web was being woven in ever more intricate patterns, designed to entrap some and provide a platform for others. I became more and more alarmed as the detail of the promotion of New Labour figures became apparent. I knew, for example, over a week before election day that I was to be ousted from the education team in the government. Many others did not have that privilege, nor the chance to serve elsewhere in government.

The first of May, 1997, was a great victory, but much has been wrongly read into it. It is true that we won seats in areas where we never anticipated success. However, despite the added boost of Tony Blair's appeal to middle England, I am convinced that we would have won a handsome majority anyway, on the back of the very real loathing of a sleazy Tory party together with excellent targeting of marginal seats throughout the land. These target seats were delivered by hard-working, loyal activists on the ground, and their thousands and thousands of personal contacts.

Such party members and supporters are the bedrock of success. It is they who knock on doors and deliver leaflets; it is they who argue our case at work, and in pubs and clubs throughout the land. The *post facto* wisdom that it was the tabloids, or Millbank Tower, or a small exclusive group, which ensured victory is palpable nonsense. Of course, each element is important, but, as the blue-rinsed ladies quietly did the work for the Tories for years, the critical factor for Labour was a highly motivated army of volunteers across the land, determined to get the Tories out.

So where does that leave Labour as it races towards its first test in office since the debacle of 1979? What lessons can be drawn from our years of opposition? Indeed, what lessons can be drawn from the example of Liverpool over nearly twenty years of fratricidal political warfare?

For me, the first lesson is that a party needs ideological glue to hold it together. That does not mean a nebulous notion of better managerialism in government. If that is the object, we might as well leave government to professional managers – they would probably make a better fist of it than politicians. By ideology, I mean a coherent combination of ideas and principles, behind which members and supporters of the Labour Party can rally, and go out and seek the support of others. That is not a threatening proposition to anyone who believes there is widespread sympathy with their ideas. It is only dangerous to those who wish to impose their views on others. Within Militant, that meant democratic centralism. Within 'New Labour', it is seen as control freakery.

It follows on, therefore, that there is a need to project further a sense of ownership of the party's platform by the wider membership. In the past, large sections of the party were regularly alienated by the haughty use of the trade union block vote, and demanded for years the principle of 'one member, one vote'. But I believe this requires more than simple mechanistic adjustments to voting procedures. In a modern and mature democratic organisation, there is a need for internal pluralism in the process of debate. No-one should be vilified for arguing a case outside whatever is the current prevailing orthodoxy. One man's subversive is another man's prophet, pointing the way to new solutions to old problems.

Clever structures designed to keep the membership in check frankly will not work. They will only lend a sense of disenchantment amongst those who are needed to do the donkey work of campaigning. Of course, if one does wish to follow the American model, a distancing of the membership would be ideal. Amassing funds for media campaigns, and courting media moguls, is a proven way of achieving power in the United States, particularly if the media campaign is primarily about trashing opponents. Unfortunately, such a political style dumbs down debate on the issues, and leaves many voters contemptuous of electoral politics. Too many in the ghettos and trailer parks of America have, and seek, no political voice.

We should also beware of personality politics. The lesson of Derek Hatton is not to place too much trust in a sharp-suited personality trading in soundbites. Remember that Hatton took in both Militant and the Labour Party before he was rumbled. In fact, a number of the Militant full-timers presented themselves in exactly the same fashion, hiding the true nature of their message under a visually media-friendly image. They only showed their teeth when their credentials and transitional programme were put under scrutiny.

Of course, their room for manoeuvre was limited by the orders received from their central committee – a strongly disciplined *modus operandi* known as democratic centralism. This was based on the fallacy that the leadership had a monopoly of wisdom. The fact that it did not, and that we might laugh at the suggestion, does not detract from the effectiveness that it had, or might have, in an organisation without the checks and balances traditional in the Labour Party. These checks and balances are very important to the health of the party, providing conduits for the expression of legitimate dissent and concerns. This was one of the principal roles of annual conference – jealously guarded by the National Executive Committee – affording all members the hope, at least, of their voice being heard. It is true that, at times, conference provided the worst possible advertisement for a party seeking government – but this was a consequence either of a leadership out of tune with its membership, or of a conspiracy to subvert the party by extremists. It was never a result of too much party democracy.

Another lesson to be drawn is the importance of political organisation throughout the country. The Labour Party cannot be run centrally, by Millbank Tower or anything else. It relies upon a national network of highly trained, highly motivated and highly experienced regional party officials. There is still massive diversity within our country, in politics as in other areas of life. A flexible, responsive and responsible regional network can help lay party officers through the myriad tasks undertaken by volunteer helpers; they can adapt national strategies to regional exigencies; they can mould campaigns in the light of local priorities and conditions. In short, they can be a powerful local resource in completing the national political jigsaw.

Party officials cannot be seen as simply message carriers for the London centre. Of course, on occasion the job in the regions can be testing and requires immense support from outside – the battle against Militant confirmed that. Yet proactive and knowledgeable regional officers are essential catalysts in helping members feel involved and integral to the national party. That role cannot be filled by remote national officials appearing to send irrelevant, or even insulting, diktats to the members who pay their wages.

A shared ideology; open policy debate; a sense of ownership; fair voting; professional support and organisation – these are not revolutionary matters, merely the requirements of a modern and mature political party. Without them, at best we will end up as a rump party without an identity, standing for nothing. With them, we can, as Tony Blair says, dominate British politics this century, to the advantage of all the nation.

The first great test of our brave new political world will come, of course, at the next general election. We will see if the trend towards lower turnouts has been checked or not. We will also see if Labour voters – of whom some have said they have nowhere else to go but Labour – turn out to vote at all or stay at home. We will see whether or not middle England has kept faith with Tony Blair's 'project'.

Then we will also discover whether the realignment of British politics, so dear to the heart of New Labour, will move forward. Will Europhile Tories drift to New Labour? Will Liberal Democrats be lured by the prospect of ministerial office and proportional representation? What compacts will be made in Scotland and Wales, or even London? Or will it simply be the case that the clichéd 'New' Labour title is seen as passé, and a new brand name takes its place?

The only thing of which I am certain is that there will still be many people actively involved whose commitment will remain to social justice, to wealth redistribution *and* creation, to equality of opportunity, and to the many other things which bind the present Labour Party together. But they will be far wiser as a result of this period of government, and perhaps far less ready to buy a pig in a poke.

# Notes

1   Cited in P. J. Waller, *Democracy and Sectarianism – a political and social history of Liverpool 1868–1939* (Liverpool: Liverpool University Press, 1981) p. 349.

2   A. Howard, 'Cook County, UK', *New Statesman*, 31 July 1964.

3   Final Report of the Liverpool Trades' Council and Labour Party, 25 April 1969.

4   R. T. Mackenzie, *British Political Parties – The Distribution of Power within the Conservative and Labour Parties* (London: Mercury Books, 1963 (second edition)), pp. 543–6.

5   Cmnd 4728.

6   Ibid., p. 1.

7   Peter Walker, cited in *Observer*, 30 April 1972.

8   'Housing Act, 1972 – a guide', *New Society*, 28 December 1972, pp. 734–7.

9   J. Hillman and M. White, 'The rent payers' uncertain future', *Guardian* (Extra), 7 January 1972.

10  'Defying the bill', *The Economist*, 29 April 1972.

11  *Guardian*, 8 July 1972.

12  26,500 tenants faced a rise of £1, 48,660 of 85p, 15,800 of 49p, and 7,000 no rise at all. Figures reprinted in B. Morris, 'Militant Tenants', *New Society*, 9 November 1972.

13  See M. Parkinson, *Liverpool on the Brink* (Hermitage: Policy Journals, 1985), pp. 85–90; and P. Carmichael, *Centre-Local Government Relations in the 1980s* (London: Avebury, 1995), p. 145.

14  See, for example, C. Price, 'Rebellion in Camden', *New Statesman*, 11 August 1972.

15  The rates portion of their rent was then paid on to Knowsley. During the 1973–74 reorganisation, these properties were transferred to Knowsley.

16  Morris (1972), op. cit.

17  On a 29.9% turn-out of the 10,501 electorate, the result was Labour 1760, Tenants' Association 1184, and Conservative 202.

18  Howard (1964), op. cit.

19  Ibid.

20  This cannot be overstated. Richard Crossman, writing in his Cabinet diaries, noted the events leading to and during his visit to Liverpool in 1964 as Housing Minister: 'I had been asked by the Labour council to come and I had told them I would postpone my visit until Bessie Braddock told me she wanted me there. When I got the double invitation I accepted, whereupon Bessie thought *she* had invited me and could run the visit. And Alderman Sefton, the leader of the Labour group, thought

he was running the visit, which he actually was. Three days had been spent in the most furious altercation: Bessie wanted me to be photographed for the press and on television seeing the scandals of Canning Street, a slum street in her constituency; Sefton wanted me at all costs not to give Bessie her regular publicity in Canning Street, since it is absurd that each minister should be photographed in this particular street. Of course he was right. But on the other hand MPs, Bessie or any other MP, have the right to ask a visiting minister to go and see something in the constituency. So I had to try and make peace between them. When I arrived in Liverpool at ten o'clock on Friday evening I found the battle still in full swing. Bessie was on my doorstep threatening to cause a demonstration and block the street and stop the charabanc in which I and the councillors were going to make our visit. I had to think up a compromise which was that she should enter the bus when we entered her constituency and leave the bus when I left it on the other side. This satisfied her pride. She agreed, and to my proposal Sefton also agreed.'
R. Crossman, *The Diaries of a Cabinet Minister, Vol. I: Minister of Housing 1964–1966* (London: Hamish Hamilton and Jonathan Cape, 1975), p. 56.

21  Sefton, however, began to apply his style elsewhere. As one of his fellow county councillors has written: 'In those days the leader of the party dispensed office in Chicago-boss style; I was told years later that I was appointed to keep me out of trouble.' M. Simey (1988), *Democracy Rediscovered – a study in police accountability* (London: Pluto Press, 1988), p. 30.

22  T. Lane, *Marxism Today,* November 1978.

23  S. Mole, 'The Liberal Party and Community Politics' in V. Bogdanor (ed.), *Liberal Party Politics* (Oxford: Clarendon Press, 1983), p. 261.

24  Cited in Mole (1983), op. cit., p. 266.

25  G. Weightman, 'Liberalpool in trouble', *New Society,* 12 September 1974.

26  *Liverpool Echo,* 15 April 1978.

27  C. Cook, *A Short History of the Liberal Party 1900–1984* (London & Basingstoke: Macmillan, 1984).

28  Parkinson (1985), op. cit., p. 20.

29  Carmichael (1995), op. cit., p. 143.

30  County-wide, the Conservative Party took 67 of the 99 seats.

31  Aigburth, Allerton, Childwall, Church, Croxteth and Woolton West.

32  In 1978, the turn-out in the eleven wards captured or held by the Conservatives averaged 35.5%. In thirteen wards captured or held by Labour, the turn-out averaged 27.5%.

33  For a fuller history of Militant, see M. Crick, *Militant* (London: Faber and Faber, 1984), and its updated and expanded version, M. Crick, *The March of Militant* (London: Faber and Faber, 1986).

34  Liverpool District Labour Party, minutes of meeting 5 August 1976.

35  Liverpool District Labour Party, minutes of meeting 31 March 1977.

36  Liverpool District Labour Party, minutes of meeting 3 February 1977.

37  Liverpool District Labour Party, minutes of meeting 3 February 1977.

38  Liverpool District Labour Party, minutes of meeting 1 December 1977.

39  Crick, op. cit., p. 152.

40  D. Hatton, *Inside Left – the story so far...* (London: Bloomsbury, 1988), p. 27.

41  Ibid., p. 28.

42  Minutes and records of Sheffield Trades Union and Labour Council (1961–79), LD 2318–2327, Archives section, Sheffield City Libraries.

43  Liverpool District Labour Party, minutes of meeting 1 March 1979.

44  Liverpool District Labour Party, minutes of meeting 5 April 1979.

45  Liverpool District Labour Party, minutes of meeting 6 May 1979.

46  The full result was, Conservative 49,646 (45.2%), Labour 42,419 (38.7%) and Liberal 17,650 (16.1%).

47  Liverpool District Labour Party, minutes of meeting 10 June 1979.

48  Liverpool District Labour Party, minutes of meeting 5 July 1979.

49  Liverpool District Labour Party, minutes of meeting 2 August 1979.

50  *International Guardian,* 7 January 1984.

51  See M. Williams, 'White Liverpool loses patience', *New Society*, 26 August 1982, pp. 333–36.

52  F. F. Ridley, 'The government of divide and rule', *Guardian*, 22 November 1985. See also F. F. Ridley, 'Liverpool is different: political style in context', *Political Quarterly*, Vol. 57, No. 2, 1986, pp. 126–27.

53  Roy Jenkins, one of the SDP's founding Gang of Four, was well known for his taste in wine; 'claret and chips [for lunch]' became a catch-phrase of the party's 1981 by-election campaign in Crosby, and, later, the title of a book on the early years of the SDP (Hugh Stephenson, *Claret and Chips: The rise of the SDP* (London: Michael Joseph, 1982)).

54  P. F. Carspecken, *Community Schooling and the Nature of Power: the Battle for Croxteth Comprehensive* (London: Routledge, 1991).

55  *Liverpool Echo*, 18 May 1983.

56  Liverpool District Labour Party, minutes of meeting 24 February 1983.

57  M. Crick (1984), op. cit., p. 148.

58  Liverpool District Labour Party, minutes of meeting 3 September 1981.

59  Hatton, op. cit., Ch. 1, passim.

60  Crick (1986), op. cit., p. 226.

61  T. Lane, *Liverpool: Gateway of Empire* (London: Lawrence & Wishart, 1987), p. 161.

62  Ridley, op. cit., p. 133.

63  Respectively the Spanish socialist leader and prime minister (1982–96); the Greek socialist party; its leader and prime minister (1981–89); and the former German social democrat leader and chancellor (1969–74).

64  The dates and subjects of the fifteen debates were as follows: 4/7/1983 – Liverpool (Unemployment); 9/1/1984 – Merseyside Area Health Authority (Budget); 8/2/1984 – Education (Liverpool); 22/2/1984 – British American Tobacco (Liverpool); 15/3/1984 –

Liverpool (Council Budget); 1/5/1984 – Liverpool (Finance); 3/12/1984 – Liverpool (Housing); 15/2/1985 – Port of Liverpool; 21/2/1985 – Liverpool; 11/6/1985 – Soccer Violence [The Heysel Stadium disaster]; 18/11/1985 – Liverpool; 20/12/1985 – Housing Co-operatives (Liverpool); 16/1/1986 – Urban Deprivation (Liverpool); 27/3/1986 – Government Policies and Liverpool; 18/3/1987 – Liverpool (Financial Situation).

65   Hansard, 18 November 1985, col. 114–15.

66   For further evidence of this, see Eric Heffer, *Never a Yes-Man: The Life and Politics of an Adopted Liverpudlian* (London: Verso, 1991), p. 191.

67   *Sunday Times*, 20 January 1980, cited in Crick (1984), op. cit., p. 165.

68   Hansard, 21 February 1985, col. 1323.

69   Crick (1984), op. cit., p. 155.

70   Secretary's Report to Liverpool District Labour Party, 16 July 1984.

71   Parkinson, op. cit., pp. 63–67.

72   J. Straw, 'How Liverpool undermined the real anti-Tory struggle', *Tribune,* 29 November 1985.

73   Philip M. Williams (ed.), *The diary of Hugh Gaitskell, 1945–1956* (London: Cape, 1983), p. 441.

74   From Ian Williams's personal statement to the NEC.

75   Liverpool District Labour Party, minutes of meeting 12 June 1985.

76   D. Selbourne, 'On the Mersey waterfront', *New Society*, 29 November 1985, p. 366.

77   P. Taaffe, *The Rise of Militant – Militant's Thirty Years* (London: Militant Publications, 1995), p. 346.

78   *Liverpool Daily Post*, 15 November 1984.

79   See P. Taaffe and T. Mulhearn, *Liverpool: The City That Dared to Fight* (London: Fortress, 1988), passim.

80   Taaffe & Mulhearn, op. cit., p. 278.

81   Heffer, op. cit., p. 214.

82   *Liverpool Echo*, 22 October 1985.

83   *Liverpool Daily Post*, 30 November 1985.

84   *Guardian*, 9 December 1985.

85   Labour Party National Executive Committee, 'Investigation into the Liverpool District Labour Party', Majority Report.

86   Labour Party National Executive Committee, 'Investigation into the Liverpool District Labour Party', Minority Report, 3.14.

87   *Guardian*, 4 December 1985.

88   *Guardian*, 9 December 1985.

89   *Observer*, 2 March 1986.

90   *Guardian*, 27 March 1986.

91   *Guardian*, 27 March 1986; and letter to, 2 April 1986.

92   Letter to *Guardian*, 4 April 1986.

93   *Liverpool Echo*, 9 July 1986.

94   Taaffe and Mulhearn, op. cit., p. 390.

95   *Guardian*, 24 May 1986.

96   Taaffe and Mulhearn , op. cit., p. 391.

97   *Guardian*, 13 June 1986.

98   *Sydney Morning Herald*, 4, 16 and 17 December 1997.

99   Taaffe and Mulhearn, op. cit., p. 404.

100   *Guardian*, 8 March 1986.

101   *Liverpool Daily Post*, 8 May 1987.

102   *Liverpool Daily Post*, 12 June 1987

103   Liverpool District Labour Party, minutes of meeting 31 January 1985.

104   Liverpool District Labour Party, minutes of meeting 14 March 1985.

105   *Liverpool Echo*, 7 March 1989.

106   *Liverpool Daily Post*, 25 March 1989.

107   *Liverpool Daily Post*, 6 July 1989.

108   M. Heseltine, *Where There's a Will* (London: Century Hutchinson, 1987), p. 139.

109   R. Race, 'Heffer's the one!', *London Labour Briefing*, No. 32, August 1983, p. 3.

110   *Liverpool Daily Post*, 3 January 1990.

111   Ibid.

112   *Liverpool Daily Post*, 11 January 1990.

113   *Liverpool Echo*, 8 February 1990.

114   *Liverpool Daily Post*, 20 February 1990.

115   *Liverpool Daily Post*, 29 March 1990.

116   *Liverpool Weekly Star*, 9 August 1990.

117   *Liverpool Weekly Star*, 16 August 1990.

118   *Liverpool Weekly Star*, 30 August 1990.

119   *Liverpool Weekly Star*, 6 September 1990.

120   Crick (1984), op. cit., p. 170.

121   Those who had opposed the merger of the Liberal Party and the SDP to form the Liberal Democrats, and left the party to fight as 'Liberals' under, amongst others, the former Liberal MP for Leeds West, Michael Meadowcroft.

122   *Liverpool Daily Post*, 9 October 1990.

123   *Liverpool Daily Post*, 1 November 1990.

124   *Liverpool Daily Post*, 24 November 1990.

125   *Liverpool Daily Post*, 21 November 1990.

126   *Liverpool Daily Post*, 7 December 1990.

127   *Liverpool Daily Post*, 4 March 1991.

128   *Liverpool Daily Post*, 3 May 1991.

129   *Liverpool Daily Post*, 28 May 1991.

130   *Liverpool Echo*, 18 June 1991.

131   Heffer, op.cit, p. 226.

132   A special thanks to Winnie Hesford for allowing us access to these two letters.

133   *Independent*, 4 July 1991.

134   *The Times*, 28 June 1991; *Daily Telegraph* and *Independent*, 3 July 1991.

135   *Liverpool Echo*, 14 June 1991; *Guardian*, 15 June 1991.

136   *The Times*, 25 June 1991.

137   Respectively Basque and northern Italian nationalist/separatist parties.

138   *Daily Express*, 24 June 1991.

139   *Daily Mail*, 6 July 1991.

140   The result was: Labour 21,317 (53.1%); Liberal Democrat 14,457 (36.0%); 'Walton Real Labour' 2,613 (6.5%); Conservative 1,155 (2.9%); Monster Raving Loony Party 546 (1.4%); Independent 63 (0.2%). A year later, at the 1992 general election, the Labour Party vote increased to 34,214, 72.4% of the turn-out.

141   Taaffe and Mulhearn, op. cit., p. 68.

# Index